Instructional Strateg... ... ... and High School Social Studies

Instructional Strategies for Middle and High School Social Studies: Methods, Assessment, and Classroom Management is an exciting methods-based text that integrates appropriate management and assessment techniques with seven distinct teaching strategies. Writing explicitly for pre-service social studies teachers, veteran teacher educator Bruce E. Larson offers detailed descriptions of a range of instructional strategies, along with guidelines for deciding how and when to use each.

Part I offers the foundations for teaching and learning in a social studies classroom, and explores contextual, theoretical, and policy factors that all teachers need to consider before entering the classroom. Part II delivers a range of comprehensive strategies for providing instruction that is appropriate for particular lessons, student abilities, and classroom environments. The practical strategies in Part II build upon the learning theories described in Part I, positioning *Instructional Strategies for Middle and High School Social Studies* to be the go-to, all-inclusive teacher's guide to the social studies classroom.

New to this Edition

- A list of goals before each chapter presents an overview of the chapter's content focus, and provides an outline for the chapter review.
- Extensively revised Part I (chapters 1–4) provides an updated review of national standards developed for teaching history, geography, civics, and economics. In-depth applications of the Common Core State Standards for the social studies are also explored.
- New "Reality Check" feature provides directions for integrating field-based experiences into the chapters, and contextualizes the ideas in the book for a classroom setting.
- Each chapter in Part II (chapters 5–11) has been expanded to include a section labeled "Enhancing Student Learning with Technology," offering websites, links, and other resources for integrating recent technologies into the classroom.
- Chapters 5–11 include a new "Making Your Lesson More Meaningful for ELLs" feature, which provides ideas—based on current research and theories about learning language—for engaging ELLs, specific for each instructional strategy.
- Expanded discussion of the "Understanding by Design" model equips teachers to design learning experiences that promote student understanding by intentionally designing what happens in the classroom, and developing authentic formative assessments of student learning.

Bruce E. Larson is Professor of Secondary Education and Social Studies at Western Washington University.

Instructional Strategies for Middle and High School Social Studies

Methods, Assessment, and Classroom Management

SECOND EDITION

Bruce E. Larson

Routledge
Taylor & Francis Group

NEW YORK AND LONDON

Second edition published 2017
by Routledge
711 Third Avenue, New York, NY 10017

and by Routledge
2 Park Square, Milton Park, Abingdon, Oxon, OX14 4RN

Routledge is an imprint of the Taylor & Francis Group, an informa business

First edition published by Routledge 2011

Library of Congress Cataloging-in-Publication Data
A catalog record for this book has been requested

ISBN: 978-1-138-84677-7 (hbk)
ISBN: 978-1-138-84678-4 (pbk)
ISBN: 978-1-315-72727-1 (ebk)

Typeset in Bembo and Helvetica Neue
by Apex CoVantage, LLC

Contents

Introduction

Teaching is a wonderful and exciting profession, and the pages of *Instructional Strategies for Middle and High School Social Studies: Methods, Assessment, and Classroom Management* are written to excite and empower the next generation of classroom teachers. This is the second edition of the book, and it is designed for pre-service teachers who are planning to teach social studies in grades 6 through 12. Social studies in these grades include subject areas such as ancient civilizations and cultures, world geography, U.S. history, world history, government, contemporary world issues, and civics.

WHY THIS BOOK?

This book is designed to be the primary text for pre-service middle school or high school teachers enrolled in a social studies methods course. That term, a "methods" course, simply describes a course designed to help social studies teachers learn the methods of teaching and learning. You, the student in that course, are the audience I kept in mind as I wrote the chapters. It is helpful to think of yourself as an aspiring teacher, because you aspire to become an effective teacher who will help your students learn. I frequently notice, however, that aspiring teachers struggle with selecting instructional strategies, and often the strategies they select do not line up with the curriculum. For example, a teacher will decide to lecture because it is efficient, and not because it is deemed as the best strategy for helping students learn a set of key concepts; or a teacher will use a simulation or group project to "add some variety" to the day, and not because these approaches will promote student learning more effectively than others. Similarly, decisions about the assessment of student learning, differentiating instruction so lessons are understood by all the students in a classroom, classroom management, use of digital technology, and many other common areas of the classroom, are difficult for aspiring teachers to make because each decision is modified based on the content being learned and the instructional activities planned for the class session. Aspiring teachers need guidance as they make decisions, and this is why I revised *Instructional Strategies for Middle and High School Social Studies*.

LINKING INSTRUCTION, ASSESSMENT, AND MANAGEMENT

In this book, you will explore assessment and management with a different approach than other textbooks. I introduce assessment of student learning and ideas for managing the classroom in Chapter 3, and then build on that introduction in each of the chapters that explore specific instructional strategies. In this way, assessment and classroom management are contextualized within the framework of specific instructional strategies. This also helps to ensure that the manner in which you check students' understanding (another way of saying that you assess their learning) is accurate, valid, and authentic. The overview of assessment in Chapter 3 sets the stage for an assessment section in each of the strategies chapters. For example, valid assessments of what students learned from a role-play activity will be different from assessments following a classroom discussion. As much as possible, I attempted to provide contextualized examples from actual social studies classrooms to provide tangible ideas for the reader. Examples of unit plans, lesson plans, and rubrics from the many teachers who provided input to the contents of this book exist throughout the pages.

Another common worry for aspiring teachers is how to manage a classroom with 30 students and how to discipline students who are disruptive. Many student teachers will not try student-centered activities for fear of "losing control" of their students. As with assessment, this book addresses concerns such as these by introducing guiding principles for establishing an effective classroom learning environment in Chapter 2, and then providing specific classroom management ideas for each of the instructional strategies described in chapters 5 through 11. It is very difficult to use a strategy effectively without considering unique management concerns and assessments for each strategy.

Over the course of the text you will explore seven instructional strategies. Decisions for including these strategies were informed by conversations with many middle school and high school social studies teachers, teacher educators, and principals. All agree that the seven strategies included in this text are commonly used by teachers, are effective for helping students learn, and are necessary for all teachers to understand. By listing step-by-step procedures for using these instructional strategies, this text gives aspiring teachers a deep understanding of each strategy and the tools to determine how to best use each with a classroom of adolescents. Aspiring teachers reading this text are encouraged to observe these strategies in an actual classroom.

All of the ideas presented in this book are theory based, and the practical suggestions are built on extensive examinations of current and longstanding research. In writing this text, I made great efforts to focus on the day-to-day teaching and learning that needs to occur in classrooms, because we all aspire for future teachers to have and use the tools to proactively manage their classrooms and ensure that all students are learning. The following ideas directed the development of the book's contents:

- Effective teaching promotes student learning of the course content; teachers matter!
- Students bring diverse abilities, interests, and needs to the classroom, which the teacher must accommodate.
- Teachers need skill with a large and diverse set of instructional strategies to help their students learn.
- The social studies content that students will learn will help determine the instructional strategies selected by the teacher.
- Each instructional strategy has unique assessments, and teachers must closely match the assessment to the strategy if they are to accurately and validly know what their students learned.
- Aspiring teachers need tools for developing effective classroom management skills and student discipline strategies. Teachers often forget that each instructional strategy presents unique classroom management considerations, so part of a teacher education program needs to apply management theories to each instructional strategy.

- Teaching is largely a relationship that is developed with students. Fostering that relationship is intentional and necessary.
- Teaching requires constant decision making. As such, decisions about class activities, student discipline, classroom management, and student assessment will be better if the teacher engages in a thoughtful decision-making process.
- Teachers need to account for the needs of a diverse group of students, and are likely to encounter English language learners (ELLs). It is imperative that teachers are mindful of ELLs when they are planning and implementing their lessons.
- Teachers need to know when and how to make effective and appropriate use of technology in the classroom.

THE STRUCTURE OF THE BOOK

Instructional Strategies for Middle and High School Social Studies is divided into two parts. Part I is titled "Foundations for Teaching and Learning Social Studies," and Part II is titled "Instructional Strategies for Social Studies." Allow me to briefly describe each part.

Foundations for Teaching and Learning Social Studies

The four chapters of Part I explore the content of what is taught in middle school and high school social studies classrooms, the national and state standards that guide social studies curriculum, theories and research about learning and adolescent development, and specific strategies and outlines for planning lessons and units of study. Part I provides the foundation for the content of the book. Teaching extends beyond pure methods and strategies, and includes areas such as tone of voice, subtexts of curriculum, classroom environments, and classroom management. The first section describes contextual factors that all teachers need to consider when planning, teaching, assessing learning, and reflecting on their teaching. These factors include:

- motivating students to learn
- diverse characteristics and needs of students
- differentiated instruction, with a focus on English language learners
- the use of digital technology
- guiding principles for classroom management and discipline
- national, state, and local standards and the Common Core State Standards
- determining classroom curriculum
- domains of learning
- assessing student learning.

Additionally, the first section presents reasons for learning targets, differentiating instruction and assessments for lessons and unit plans, and ideas for appropriate sequencing of content.

Instructional Strategies for Social Studies

The seven chapters in Part II provide ideas for teaching effectively, and will help a teacher provide instruction that is engaging, varied, and most appropriate for the content being learned. Each chapter guides you through the process of selecting classroom activities that are appropriate and are based on current ideas from educational researchers and theorists. Each chapter is devoted to a specific category of instructional strategy to allow an in-depth examination and provide step-by-step procedures for implementing the strategy in the class-room. To accomplish this, chapters are written to purposefully explore the following areas for each strategy:

- an overview of the strategy
- a description of what research has found about the strategy
- step-by-step procedures for planning and implementing the strategy
- a realistic exploration of the logistical concerns related to each strategy, including benefits and obstacles when using the strategy
- classroom management and student motivation unique to the strategy
- appropriate assessment techniques to use with the strategy
- ideas for integrating technology to enhance student learning
- specific suggestions for making lessons more meaningful for English language learners (ELLs)
- guidelines for deciding if a strategy is appropriate for the content of a lesson
- opportunities for you to consider how to use the strategy with content you will teach, called "making it work in your classroom."

The instructional strategies are described, beginning with those that are teacher centered, and moving to strategies that are increasingly student centered. These seven chapters integrate and contextualize the management, assessment, and learning theories developed in the first section of the book by examining many examples from a wide range of middle school and high school classrooms.

PUTTING IT ALL TOGETHER

Hopefully, all teachers will establish classrooms that have a positive impact on all their students' learning. Consider this example: If students need to learn the history and context around the development and writing of the U.S. Constitution, why might a teacher use a simulation, as opposed to a class discussion, classroom lecture, or an inquiry-based research project? Might these other strategies be more effective? How will the teacher and the students determine what was learned? These questions are not easy to answer, and are a continual part of the teaching process. To maximize student learning, the strategies that a teacher selects for engaging students requires a complex series of decisions that include the learning preferences of the students, the content being learned, the setting of the classroom, assessment procedures, and a teacher's comfort level with a particular approach to leading the class. When a teacher selects an instructional strategy without considering the content or student, all sorts of problems abound. This text provides clear guidelines for helping aspiring teachers engage in a thoughtful and effective decision-making process.

Classrooms are composed of diverse learners, and future teachers must consider how each strategy might allow for differentiating learning for students, integrating appropriate digital and computer technology into the lessons, and assisting English language learners interact with classmates and course content. Additionally, each chapter has at least one section titled: "Making It Work in Your Classroom." In these sections, the reader is asked to apply the ideas presented in the chapter to a specific social studies subject or class setting. This is a tool for encouraging aspiring teachers to explore what is taught in middle school and high school, and to note the differences and similarities with how subjects are taught at the university level.

NEW IN THE SECOND EDITION

The first edition was co-authored with Dr. Timothy Keiper. Tim has moved on to an exciting opportunity preparing teachers and establishing a rural school in Tanzania. His ideas are still present in this second edition, along with pertinent revisions, updates, and completely new features.

 For this edition, goals have been added for each chapter. This will provide the reader with a quick overview of a chapter's content focus, and provide an outline for the chapter review. Part I received extensive revisions and restructuring. It provides an updated review of national standards that apply to the social studies. Standards have been developed from the specific areas of history, geography, civics, and economics. The Common Core State Standards apply to the social studies as well, and are examined closely to help clarify their role in shaping the curriculum. The National Council for the Social Studies has developed ten themes to guide learning, and a powerful framework that intends to prepare students for college, careers, and civic life (known as the C3 Framework). Each of these standards, themes, and framework are explored in depth.

 New to this edition is an expansion on the well-known work of Grant Wiggins and Jay McTighe for organizing lessons and units of study, called "understanding by design." I build on their ideas of determining essential questions and key learning assessments, and then designing lessons and units back from that point. By establishing what students need to understand and learn, and then engaging in a "backward design" approach to planning, teachers are better able to design learning experiences that help students develop the needed knowledge and skills.

 I added a new feature called "Reality Check," which provides directions for integrating field-based experiences into the chapters. Ideally, the reader will have access to middle school or high school social studies classrooms as they read the text. These check points provide concise tasks for contextualizing the ideas in the book. If the reader is not in a classroom setting, then s/he can easily return to these highlighted reality checks when they have access to a middle school or high school classroom.

 In Part II, each of the seven instructional strategies chapters has a newly updated and enhanced section labeled "Enhancing Student Learning with Technology." Websites, links, and many other ideas for appropriately integrating recent technologies into the classroom for the purpose of enhancing student learning abound in these sections.

 A very important addition to each instructional strategy chapter (5–11) is the feature "Making Your Lesson More Meaningful for ELLs." Chapter 2 has an extensive overview of English language learners and effective strategies for promoting learning amongst this important and growing group of students. The "Making Your Lesson More Meaningful for ELLs" feature builds on Chapter 2 and provides ideas for engaging ELLs, specific for each instructional strategy. The ideas are based on current research and theories about learning language, as well as suggestions from a network of middle school and high school teachers.

The number of students who do not speak English as their primary language is increasing, and teachers must be able to help all students learn. Additionally, many students who do speak English as their first language do not understand the language of the classroom; this is often referred to as "academic language." This feature will prepare you to help all students learn.

Each instructional strategy chapter begins with an opening vignette to help describe how it might look in the classroom. As in the first edition, the strategies are ordered from "most" teacher centered to "most" student centered. Therefore, the first instructional strategy chapter—Chapter 5—lecture is a teacher-centered approach; Chapter 11—student-directed investigations—is a very student-centered approach. To help you think about these ideas, each chapter has a chart to illustrate where the instructional strategy falls within a student-centered and instructor-centered continuum.

Many other revisions and updates exist, and are the result of feedback from social studies professionals. I wish you well as you embark to develop your own ideas about helping your future students learn!

PART I

Foundations for Teaching and Learning Social Studies

CHAPTER 1

The Social Studies

CHAPTER GOALS

In this chapter, you will learn about:

- The definition and overview of the social studies
- The Common Core State Standards
- The National Council for the Social Studies Thematic Curriculum Standards, the College, Career, and Civic Life Framework, and other national standards
- Curriculum influences on teachers, and practical ideas for determining what students learn in your future classroom.

There is no more exciting field of study than that of individuals and society, both women and men, in different settings and cultures, in different time periods, engaging in the ordinary and extraordinary events of daily life. We should make social studies irresistible for students. What drama is more exciting than studying about people who make a difference in our lives past and present?[1]

INTRODUCTION

The reason the above quotation starts this book is because it is a powerful call to action for all social studies teachers. When you think about your future as a teacher, it is exciting to realize that you will be helping students understand the wide range of social studies topics. You will help your future students in middle school and high school examine themes and ideas, and develop skills and dispositions that will help them make sense of the world around them. The social studies provide many opportunities to explore the world here and now, and to understand the world historically. The content is ready to explore and examine, and you will be able to engage with your future students as they learn.

This probably seems exciting and daunting at the same time. Exciting because of the content, but daunting because you have not had much experience teaching and helping students learn and understand. You are not alone in your effort to be an effective social studies teacher. The National Council for the Social Studies (NCSS) is the largest organization in the U.S. that promotes social studies education. The mission of the NCSS is to "provide leadership, service, and support for all social studies educators" and for promoting student learning of socials studies knowledge, skills, and democratic attitudes. According to the NCSS, social studies is:

> the integrated study of the social sciences and humanities to promote civic competence. Within the school program, social studies provides coordinated, systematic study drawing upon such disciplines as anthropology, archaeology, economics, geography, history, law, philosophy, political science, psychology, religion, and sociology, as well as appropriate content from the humanities, mathematics, and natural sciences. The primary purpose of social studies is to help young people develop the ability to make informed and reasoned decisions for the public good as citizens of a culturally diverse, democratic society in an interdependent world.
>
> (From the National Council for the Social Studies,
> http://www.socialstudies.org/about)

This is a very complex description of social studies in the schools. What this definition highlights is the importance of social studies content and skills, and the use of them for the purpose of being an engaged citizen. Have you considered this before as the purpose of the social studies? The disciplinary knowledge of history or geography or political science provides background and insight for us as we participate with others in our society. Without this knowledge we are unable to make "informed and reasoned decisions for the public good." However, *without* the focus of promoting civic competence, knowledge becomes inert rather than active and dynamic.

When we think about civic competence, it is useful to start thinking about what makes an effective citizen in America. The National Council for the Social Studies defines an effective citizen as "one who has the knowledge, skills, and attitudes required to assume the office of citizen in our democratic republic" (NCSS, 2015).[2] We do not often think about citizenship as a political office that we all hold. This is a useful idea, however, because by doing so, you start to think about the duties and responsibilities needed to be a citizen (in the same manner that a mayor or senator would need to be aware of the duties and responsibilities of those offices). John Dewey, one of the leading thinkers in American education, suggested the value of schools as a location for learning the skills, social dispositions, and perspectives needed to engage with other citizens about public issues. In Dewey's estimation, schools, and as a result your future classroom, could become laboratories of democracy, where you and your students engage in activities aimed at developing civic competence in a democratic society, much the same way that science lab activities are aimed at developing scientific competence.[3]

Paul Carr (2008) states that "thin" and "thick" democracy are helpful metaphors when thinking about civic participation and civic competence. Participation in a democracy could be characterized in terms of a representative democracy (where the focus of democratic participation is voting for appropriate representatives) versus participatory democracy (where the focus of democratic participation is critical engagement and social justice). In a representative democracy, a citizen does not engage in the political system, and has little invested in engaging with others about the betterment of society. This is what Carr calls "thin" democracy, because engagement is very basic. In participatory democracy the citizen in engaged in and challenges the current state of affairs to work at improving the status quo: a much "thicker" type of democratic action. James Banks encourages teachers to enable their students to become what he calls "active" and "transformative" citizens, or citizens who take action beyond voting and begin to support, maintain, and challenge laws, conventions, and political structures (2008, p. 136); this is thick democratic work. To this end, Banks proposes a typology of citizens that differentiates the level of participation in society, and it is helpful to look at these types of citizens when thinking about civic engagement and your future students:

Legal Citizen:
A citizen who has rights and obligations in the nation-state but does not participate in the political system

Minimal Citizen: A citizen who votes in local and national elections on conventional candidates and conventional issues

Active Citizen: A citizen who takes action beyond voting to actualize existing laws and conventions. The actions of active citizens are designed to support and maintain—but not challenge—existing social and political structures.

Transformative Citizen: A citizen who takes action to actualize values and moral principles beyond those of conventional authority. An interest in taking action to promote social justice even when their actions violate, challenge, or dismantle existing laws, conventions, or structures

(Banks, 2008, pp. 136, 137)

The legal and minimal citizen practices thin democracy, and the active and transformative citizen engages in a thicker form of democracy. Engagement as an active or transformative citizen will lend itself to promoting the common good in the broader community.

The quotation at the start of this chapter is more than a motivational statement about the purpose of the social studies in schools. The two social studies educators who made this statement (you may want to flip to it and read it again) remind us that social studies content is compelling and exciting. It carries a reputation with many students, however, of being the opposite. Instead of being "irresistible," as the quotation states, it is tedious. You may have read that opening quotation and questioned whether it was possible to make the social studies so appealing. To make social studies irresistible, history needs to be much more than you, the teacher, telling stories, or students answering questions at the end of the chapter. Geography needs to be much more than reading maps. Civics and government needs to be much more than reading about the structure of governments. And on and on. In this book, you will explore various instructional strategies that will allow the social studies to come alive with your students, because they will be compelled to think, understand, and participate.

The social studies integrate each of the different social science disciplines, because each provides important insights about our world. To help you understand each of these disciplines, the following section provides statements from the national organizations for history, geography, economics, and civics; four of the disciplines that fit under the heading of the social studies.

History

Setting standards for history in the schools requires a clear vision of the place and importance of history in the general education of all students. The widespread and growing support for more and better history in the schools, beginning in the early grades of elementary education, is one of the more encouraging signs of the decade. The reasons are many, but none are more important to a democratic society than this: Knowledge of history is the precondition of political intelligence. Without history, a society shares no common memory of where it has been, what its core values are, or what decisions of the past account for present circumstances. Without history, we cannot undertake any sensible inquiry into the political, social, or moral issues in society. And without historical knowledge and inquiry, we cannot achieve the informed, discriminating citizenship essential to effective participation in the democratic processes of governance and the fulfillment for all our citizens of the nation's democratic ideals.

(From the National Standards for History,
http://nchs.ucla.edu/standards/dev-5-12a.html)

Geography

Every member of society must be geo-literate. Geo-literacy is the ability to rationally consider and make reasoned decisions about the interconnections between human and physical systems. As environmental systems go through global transitions and more rapid local changes in land cover and land use it is necessary that people make personal, civic, and workplace choices that result in sustainability of both the natural and human systems.

(From the National Council for Geographic Education,
http://www.ncge.org/i4a/pages/index.cfm?pageid=3299)

Economics

The inclusion of economics . . . recognizes the value of economic understanding in helping people comprehend the modern world, make decisions that shape their futures, and strengthen major institutions. The principles of economics bear directly on the ordinary business of life, affecting people in their roles as consumers and producers. Economics also plays an important role in local, state, national, and international public policy. Economic issues frequently influence voters in national, state, and local elections. A better understanding of economies enables people to understand the forces that affect them every day, and helps them identify and evaluate the consequences of private decision and public policies. Many institutions of a democratic market economy function more effectively when its citizens are articulate and well informed about economics.

(From the Council for Economics Education, http://www. councilforeconed.org/ea/program.php?pid=19)

Civics

The goal of education in civics and government is informed, responsible participation in political life by competent citizens committed to the fundamental values and principles of American constitutional democracy. Their effective and responsible participation requires the acquisition of a body of knowledge and of intellectual and participatory skills. Effective and responsible participation also is furthered by development of certain dispositions or traits of character that enhance the individual's capacity to participate in the political process and contribute to the healthy functioning of the political system and improvement of society.

(From the Center for Civic Education, http://www.civiced.org/index. php?page=stds_toc_intro)

Each of these statements describes the importance of learning specific content. However, when you read these statements it is also apparent that the reason content knowledge is important is so we are all better able to participate with others as members of a society, and be informed as we participate as citizens. Later in this chapter we will explore the specific national standards for each social studies field.

KNOWLEDGE/SKILLS/DISPOSITIONS

Teachers need to know course content to effectively help their students learn social studies information. This *knowledge* centers on key facts, concepts, and understandings that are part of a given social studies course. For example, consider the knowledge needed for teaching a United States history course that focuses on the 20th century. It is also important for you to have *skills* that will help them learn. Skills such as facilitating group discussion, using assessment strategies validly, and developing a lesson plan are three of the many skills needed to be an effective teacher. *Dispositions* are also important for you to develop. Dispositions are attitudes or mindsets that will help you and will help your students. The expectation that you can help all of your students learn is a disposition that will help you be an effective teacher. We will explore these more in Chapter 3, when we look at learning targets. Your future students also need to learn knowledge, skills, and dispositions in your social studies classroom. Consider the following definitions for these three terms:

- *Knowledge* refers to the content of a course. The knowledge base for a course such as United States history will include facts (such as dates, names, timelines) and concepts (such as democracy, civil rights, revolution).
- *Skills* are the abilities and tasks needed for a course. The skill of researching a topic online, or supporting an opinion with facts, or reading a chapter in a geography textbook could all be important for students to learn in a course.

- *Dispositions* are the attitudes or mindsets that students need to learn. The disposition to be a life-long learner, or that an opinion can change with new information, or that participation in the community is an important role for democratic citizens are three attitudes or dispositions that might be learned by students in your future social studies classroom.

When reading the descriptions of social studies, history, geography, economics, and civics you can see that knowledge, skills, and dispositions are interwoven in each. However, you will need to be intentional about helping students learn skills and dispositions along with social studies content knowledge. We will explore this more in chapters 3 and 4.

THE SOCIAL STUDIES IN MIDDLE AND HIGH SCHOOL

The "Four Ps of the Social Studies" is a simple but powerful idea for thinking about the importance each of the fields of study in the social studies brings to the classes you will teach:

- people
- places
- problems
- perspectives.

Consider the interplay of these four areas. People, throughout time, have interacted with the places in which they live (the environment) in a variety of ways. All of us—all people—face problems and opportunities, which are greatly a result of the places in which we find ourselves, and the perspectives we hold. Anthropology, economics, geography, history, political science, and sociology all allow for a more in-depth exploration of people, places, problems, and perspectives. To teach a history course, for example, without the perspectives of geography and anthropology (not to mention all of the social sciences) will prevent a full exploration of the content. A surface understanding of history will not allow students to fully understand the content, and thus limit their ability to engage as informed citizens. The social studies, therefore, demand an interdisciplinary approach to promote citizenship and to promote a more in-depth and richer understanding of course content and skills.

If you were to look at the report card of most middle school and high school students you will rarely see them enrolled in a course titled "Social Studies." They will, however, be in courses with titles such as "World History," "United States History," "Geography," "Current World Issues," or "Economics." In the past decade many high schools have included more advanced placement courses (AP). For example, schools now offer United States History as well as Advanced Placement United States History (often referred to as APUSH). Depending on the needs of students, and the academic background of the teachers, schools will offer any number of AP courses. Middle schools will at times title a course as "Social Studies," but again, the content addressed is more aptly labeled along the lines of "Ancient Cultures," or "State History." Therefore, the courses you will teach will focus on specific fields within the social studies (for example, history or geography). You and your students will understand these fields, however, when you bring ideas from all of the social studies into your classroom. In fact, it is difficult to learn the content of any course if you do not include the other areas.

Imagine teaching about the Mayan civilization without bringing in geographic insights about the place where they lived, anthropological ideas about their culture, economic principles about trade, and civic insights about their system of governance *along with* historical findings. It would be a rather dry exploration for both you and for your students.

The NCSS uses the metaphor of an orchestra to further explain its vision of using social studies knowledge and skill from all of the fields or subject areas:

> Consider a musical ensemble such as an orchestra (the social studies program) as it performs a specific musical composition (a grade level or specific course within the curriculum). At certain times, one instrument (a discipline such as history) takes the lead while others (such as geography and economics) play supporting roles. At other times, several instruments (history, geography, economics) play together on an equal basis to explore the composer's thematic aims. The quality of the performance is the result of the composer's writing of the music (design of the social studies curriculum), the unique qualities of individual instruments (the contribution of individual disciplines), the acoustics of the setting (expertise of curriculum planners and teachers, school site facilities, and instructional resources), and the skills of musicians and the conductor (the abilities of students, teachers, and program planners).
>
> (From the National Council for the Social Studies,
> http://www.socialstudies.org/standards/execsummary)

DEFINING THE CURRICULUM

When teachers think about what they will teach, they are thinking about the curriculum. The term *curriculum* is used in many different ways, and has many different definitions. Consider the following examples: A teacher's daily plan that provides detailed information about how he will help students read and understand the works of Langston Hughes during a series of lessons about the Harlem Renaissance is a form of curriculum; a history textbook is a type of curriculum; when a teacher instructs her students to raise their hands before speaking, she is making a decision related to the curriculum; if half of an afternoon class is excused to attend a cross-country meet, that is part of the curriculum as well. Keep in mind that in this text the term *curriculum* will answer questions related to *what to teach* and *how to teach it*. This includes the expected learning outcomes of the classroom, the content students will learn, and the lesson plans that provide detailed description for each class period.

The school curriculum includes much more than deciding what should be included in courses. Before we get to the practical aspects of constructing classroom curriculum, it is important to offer some background on the idea of curriculum for you to consider so you can have added insight when you begin making decisions for your students. It is often helpful to think of the curriculum as having five parts, though some suggest there may be more (Cuban, 1996; Eisner, 1985). While these may have different labels and subheadings, the five basic parts to the school curriculum are: the formal curriculum, the delivered curriculum, the learned curriculum, the hidden curriculum, and the null curriculum. The basic premise behind this partitioning of the curriculum is that to plan curricula you need to be aware that your students will not always learn what you intend. Sometimes they will, and other times they will learn more or less than you planned. Consideration of this will help with planning for your class. Here is an overview of these five parts.

The Formal Curriculum

The *formal curriculum* consists of all that educators purposefully intend to teach students. This is also referred to by some as the *intended, planned, explicit,* or *official curriculum.* This is the part of the curriculum that you might think of first. The formal curriculum takes many forms. It includes documents such as course outlines or syllabi, unit plans, lesson plans, national and state standards, and textbooks. It might be a document that a school district distributes to parents, describing the content of a seventh grade ancient cultures course. It might be a calendar used by a government teacher that identifies what his students will learn during each week of the course. It might even be the textbook that a world history teacher will use in her tenth grade world history class. The formal curriculum has been authorized, or formalized, as being the acceptable curriculum. If a school board decides to ban a particular video or book depicting World War II, then the board is deciding about changes to the formal curriculum. Decisions at this level often result in debates and deliberations, because the changes will become official policy for a school. If you were to ask a teacher, "What are your students supposed to learn in your class this year?" he would reply with the formal curriculum for that particular social studies course.

The Delivered Curriculum

The *delivered curriculum* is also known as the *taught curriculum,* and can be thought of as the instructional processes or methods used to communicate the formal curriculum. This includes the organization of the course, the instructional strategies you will use, and the sequence of learning activities designed for a lesson. An effective teacher does not always follow the formalized written plan, but may decide to change course and follow up on a "teachable moment" for deeper reflection. This may be a spur-of-the-moment decision. Of course, a teacher will need to balance spontaneity with purpose, and will want to be sure to not omit the formal curriculum. For example, imagine that you plan a simulation to explore the idea of scarcity, and that one of your students asks how the price of oil is set. You did not plan anything about oil or other similar commodities in your simulation, and you must make a quick decision about leaving your planned activity to consider this student's question. For the sake of example, let's say that you spend the rest of the class period talking about this question with the students, and as a result you are able to explain oil pricing from a different perspective that actually enhances your students' understanding of scarcity. The delivered curriculum may have actually been better than what you planned from the formal curriculum. However, if the student in the above example proceeds to ask whether "oil refineries pollute the air too much," then your discussion will swerve way off the subject, and the delivered curriculum no longer is supporting the intent of the formal curriculum; the question is certainly interesting and one to which you may want to return, but it does not fit in with the overarching curricular plan for the day, namely understanding scarcity. The delivered curriculum is heavily influenced by learning theories that we will explore in Chapter 2. These theories help determine the activities used during class. The teacher and the students also influence the curriculum that is delivered or taught.

The Learned Curriculum

The *learned curriculum* is a representation of all that a student learns in school. Some refer to this as the *realized curriculum*, and it comes into play when assessing the students and the overall curriculum itself. We cannot assume that the formal and planned curriculum, or the delivered curriculum, will be the same as the learned curriculum. This is one reason that most educators refer to what they intend for their students to *learn*, and not what they intend to *teach*. Learning targets are provided to students, and not "teaching targets." The difference is subtle but important. If you focus on what you will teach, you may be less aware of your students' understanding. If you think in terms of what your students will learn, then you will be focused on how closely what you planned was learned by your students. When we explore formative assessment later in this book, we will consider the learned curriculum directly. The learned curriculum has been of major concern to educators in recent years as the accountability movement has given rise to standardized tests used to measure student learning. Test scores are not the only way observers judge the educational system and student performances. A good example of this can be explored with the civil rights movements in the 1960s. At that time, the social studies curriculum came to the forefront as the country began to push for comparing values and exploring controversial issues. And, of course, you will play the most important role related to the learned curriculum, because as the teacher you will always be assessing students enrolled in your classroom. Teachers use this information to assess both their students' learning as well as their own teaching.

The Hidden Curriculum

The *hidden curriculum* can be thought of as part of the delivered and the learned curricula, but is worth mentioning separately. The hidden curriculum consists of student learning that is not part of the formal curriculum. It is "hidden" because teachers and other curriculum writers are often not aware of what students may be actually learning. For example, attitudes, values, or beliefs are learned through observation or participation in the normal routine of the school day. This is the curriculum that people "pick up" through immersion in school culture. Philip Jackson has been credited as one of the first to make educators aware of the hidden curriculum, in his book *Life in Classrooms* (1968). However, John Dewey also has noted that, in addition to course content, students learn values, socialization cues, and other important content simply by being in school together (1938). Dewey thought this "untaught" content might even be learned more than the planned curriculum. Given its hidden status, however, you will want to think about how you can reveal some of the hidden curriculum in your future classroom. Often the hidden curriculum is criticized as a tool for maintaining the status quo in the classroom and in society. Education theorist Michael Apple (1986) suggests that the hidden curriculum is a misnomer and that it purposefully enables some students (typically those in the dominant culture) and disables others (typically those students who are marginalized by socioeconomic status, ethnicity, and ability). Thus, the hidden curriculum is not perceived by all as learning "by accident," but is thought of as a way to perpetuate the current social and power structure of a school. The hidden curriculum might be a teacher calling on boys more frequently than girls in a civics class to answer difficult questions (thereby students "learn" that boys may be better skilled at solving public issues than girls), or a school canceling classes during the state basketball playoffs so that all students can attend the games (thereby students may "learn" that athletics has greater importance than academics at the school). Both of these examples portray the hidden curriculum as a negative influence. This portion of the curriculum can be a positive learning element, such as when a student learns that hard work pays off or that there are rewards for determination. However, this curriculum is most often referred to when pointing out learning that reinforces misperceptions, such as the notion that studying hard to get good grades is when students of color are "acting white," or that girls are not spatially/geographically inclined. Negative elements range from oppressing students (based on gender, ethnicity, ability, etc.) to "sending the wrong message" that one aspect of school is more important than it should be. Cornbleth (1991) suggests the following examples of the hidden curriculum in schools:

- grading policies and systems
- the separation of schools into subject areas
- elevating textbooks as the most accurate and important sources of information
- the arrangement of the daily school schedule
- the distribution of materials and resources
- school rituals and traditions.

Consider Cornbleth's attempt to "unhide" the curriculum with these categories, and identify examples for each. If you think about it, you will probably be able to come up with several things you have learned along the way through "courses" in the hidden curriculum.

The Null Curriculum

The *null curriculum* is simply the content that students do not learn. Consider Eisner's (1994) detailed and long-standing comment on the null curriculum:

> There is something of a paradox involved in writing about a curriculum that does not exist. Yet, if we are concerned with the consequences of school programs and the role of curriculum in shaping those consequences, then it seems to me that we are well advised to consider not only the explicit and implicit curricula of schools but also what schools do not teach. It is my thesis that what schools do not teach may be as important as what they do teach. I argue this position because ignorance is not simply a neutral void; it has important effects on the kinds of options one is able to consider, the alternatives that one can examine, and the perspectives from which one can view a situation or problem.
>
> (p. 97)

This component of the curriculum may send implicit messages to students about the importance of some information over others. As a teacher you cannot teach everything. In my work with future history teachers we often think about the obvious point that three and one-half decades of history occur during a 35-year teaching career, yet the number of days in a school year will be the same, and teachers need to determine what to include and what to leave out of those 35 years of history. It is a difficult task to consider what you leave out when most of your energy is spent trying to determine what you want students to learn. However, it is important to reflect on the range of possible topics that you *could* teach, to ensure that you are planning for students to learn the most important content, skills, and abilities.

MAKING IT WORK IN YOUR CLASSROOM

We will revisit these components of the curriculum later in this chapter. It is interesting to ask teachers how much control they have in developing their course curriculum. Talk with social studies teachers (but remember they may not be called that, but instead are world history teachers, or government teachers, or world geography teachers, etc.), and ask them who develops the following parts of their course curriculum:

- the units for their course
- the textbooks and/or other supplemental texts they use in class
- the videos they show in class
- the service learning activities they engage in with their students
- the tests/exams students take
- the daily lesson plans and learning targets.

Do teachers feel a good deal of autonomy, or do they feel constrained by outside sources? Compare your findings with others.

WHAT SHOULD YOU TEACH?

Decisions about both curriculum and curriculum plans reflect philosophical assumptions about the way adolescents learn and what they should know. So, for example, in the *Republic*, Plato argues that the purpose of education is to support a just Athenian state. Justice would flow naturally from a well-educated citizenry that is ordered and well balanced. A just society, then, would display a harmonious balance between different social groups acting in the interests of the society as a whole. Individuals would be educated for service to the state according to the nature of the individual. In Plato's just society, the most intelligent would be taught to become wise leaders, the athletic would be taught to be soldiers for the defense of the state, and so on.

Educational theorists have used ideas like those of Plato to help them decide what should be included in the curriculum. Of course, this can lead to a variety of perspectives. For example, the ideas of E. D. Hirsch (1987) and James Banks (2003) provide two different approaches to making curricular decisions, though both are influenced by Plato. Cultural literacy is an idea advocated by Hirsch to respond to concerns that American youth are not learning a shared knowledge. According to proponents of this view, the lack of common knowledge adversely affects our ability to communicate with one another, and it weakens the commonalities that hold the country together. Hirsch's core knowledge curriculum attempts to address this concern by detailing a sequential approach to acquiring the knowledge that is essential for becoming a fully functioning citizen. Critics might contend that the knowledge necessary to be culturally literate is determined by the dominant group. They would ask, "Literate of *whose* culture?"

Another curricular perspective is multicultural education, advocated by Banks, who responds to the concern that there has been little respect in the school curricula for the contributions made by the many diverse cultures that make up our country. Banks advocates creating a curriculum that moves classrooms beyond merely mentioning the names or celebrating holidays of ethnically diverse heroes and heroines. Proponents of this view intend to transform the curriculum into one that represents a wide variety of perspectives and encourages students to become socially active. Critics of this perspective might contend that this approach contributes to the balkanization of America by focusing students on our differences rather than our commonalities. History courses are often scrutinzed by critics from both perspectives. Questions about history being "revisionist" and changing because of current societal values are often raised by a Hirsch perspective, and concerns that history merely solidifies the status quo would be raised by Banks. Both of these provide examples of how the ideas above influence the curriculum.

You should be aware that making these decisions can be politically charged. In general, while new teachers are attentive to the curriculum (what to teach), they are most concerned with the curriculum plan (how to teach). This is interesting because, at the same time, the public eye is focused on the content and skills being learned, and most controversy surrounds this issue. For example, you will make critical decisions about what to teach. As we mentioned in the previous section of this chapter, selecting one topic causes others to be omitted because of the limited amount of time in the school year (this "limit" enforces the hidden curriculum that schools must promote efficient learning). This decision may prove to be highly controversial, such as ignoring a certain perspective in history, for instance the impact of Chinese migration, or choosing one novel over another.

School curriculum should be purposeful and have an aim. The illustration below (Figure 1.1) may help explain the links between three elements: *schooling*, *education*, and *life*.

The *life* box represents all the time and experiences that people have. A significant part of our life is when we learn, or are educated. This is represented in the *education* box. We learn information, skills, and attitudes in both formal and informal settings. One formal educational setting is school. The *school* box stands for the time and place in which people receive their formal education. Of course, learning occurs both inside and outside of school. Our

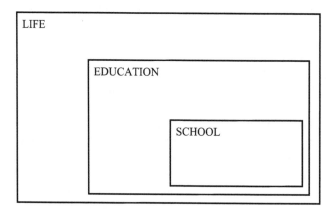

Figure 1.1 Linking Life, Education, and School.

focus in this illustration is the link between *school* and *life*. Here, school is separated from life because it provides a time in the day when students focus on learning. Some of the things students learn at school have little or no connection to life but are part of their education. For example, students learn strategies for taking tests. A curriculum problem arises when school and life are separated. Most curriculum theorists argue that school should enable a student to live a good, fulfilling life. The curriculum questions that follow this are simply, "What kind of social studies content, skills, attitude, and thought processes enable a person to live a good, fulfilling life?" and "How can your course curriculum improve your students' lives?" Schubert (1986) contends that this should be the question behind all curriculum decisions.

Understanding assumptions and purposes behind curriculum theory is not merely an academic exercise. Decisions based upon these theories have deep significance, because they will impact your future students.

A HIERARCHY OF CURRICULUM INFLUENCE

Standards and guidelines for curricula exist at the national, state, and local levels. These standards will impact the curriculum that your students learn. Figure 1.2 shows the different levels, or the hierarchy, of the curriculum relative to different stakeholders. National standards are the broadest and farthest removed from the classroom, and lesson plans are the most specific and developed with your students in mind. *Stakeholders* are groups who exercise some influences on the classroom curriculum. Given the level of the curriculum, stakeholders hold different amounts of influence:

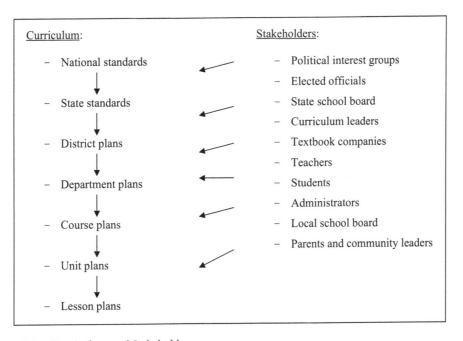

Figure 1.2   Curriculum and Stakeholders.

Think about the levels of curriculum each stakeholder will most likely influence, and why they are considered stakeholders in the curriculum. For example, what level will parents influence? How about elected officials? Also, consider what stakeholders might contribute to the curriculum, and potential problems that could arise from their involvement.

NATIONAL STANDARDS AND THE COLLEGE, CAREER, AND CIVIC LIFE FRAMEWORK

The history of national education standards is a great social studies lesson in itself. It is a great example of the tension between states' rights over education and federal control. It can be viewed as a small example of the debates that Federalists and Anti-Federalists would have had. This development of national standards is helpful for understanding the social studies standards you will be working with in the schools. In 1983 the U.S. Department of Education's National Commission on Excellence in Education published the report *A Nation at Risk* (National Commission on Excellence in Education, 1983). As the title states, the report proclaimed that our nation was and is at risk because of problems in education. This report was heralded by some as pinpointing the key problem with public education: Students are not learning. Others criticized the report as unfairly blaming schools for societal problems. Many other publications followed that both refuted and praised the report (Boyer, 1983; Sizer, 1984; United States Department of Education, 1991) and were instrumental in sparking the national movement toward content-area standards. In the decades that followed, professional organizations from each area and discipline developed what they considered the essential elements that every student should learn, and these documents have become the national standards for these content areas. These standards were not developed by the federal government, but rather from professional organizations. The national organizations for history (National Center for History in the Schools), geography (National Council for Geographic Education), civics and government (Center for Civic Education), and economics (Council for Economic Education) gathered teachers and other content experts to develop standards specific to their fields. Each developed robust standards that teachers can explore, and can access easily at the websites for each organization.

National Standards from Social Studies Organizations

- Civics: National Standards for Civics and Government; www.civiced.org
- Economics: National Council on Economic Education; www.councilforeconed.org
- Geography: National Council for Geographic Education; www.ncge.org
- History: National Center for History in the Schools; www.nchs.ucla.edu

At the same time, the National Council for the Social Studies (NCSS) put together its panel of experts and developed a set of ten standards. They do not specify content in the manner that the above standards do, but are more along the lines of ten themes of social studies that can help teachers and curriculum developers to identify specific content and concepts to be learned. The following provides a great suggestion for how to integrate these standards (which are also referred to as themes) with other standards:

> The standards are expressed in statements that begin "Social studies programs should include experiences that provide for the study of" – for instance, Culture . . . Teachers and curriculum

designers are encouraged [to use] the social studies standards as a guide, and then to use the standards from history, geography, civics, economics, and others to guide the development of grade level strands and courses. Using all of these standards in concert with one another allows educators to give adequate attention to both integrated and single discipline configurations.

(National Council for the Social Studies, www.socialstudies.org/standards/execsummary)

The ten NCSS themes are as follows:

1. Culture: the study of culture and cultural diversity
2. Time, Continuity, and Change: the study of the past and its legacy
3. People, Places, and Environments: the study of people, places, and environments
4. Individual Development and Identity: the study of individual development and identity
5. Individuals, Groups, and Institutions: the study of interactions among individuals, groups, and institutions
6. Power, Authority, and Governance: the study of how people create, interact with, and change structures of power, authority, and governance
7. Production, Distribution, and Consumption: the study of how people organize for the production, distribution, and consumption of goods and services
8. Science, Technology, and Society: the study of relationships among science, technology, and society
9. Global Connections: the study of global connections and interdependence
10. Civic Ideals and Practices: the study of the ideals, principles, and practices of citizenship in a democratic republic.

(http://www.socialstudies.org/standards/strands/)

At this point, a social studies teacher has a set of standards from many of the social sciences (e.g., history, geography, civics, economics, etc.), and a set of thematic standards to help explore ten important areas. Recently, the National Council for the Social Studies produced an additional framework for further helping teachers determine the social studies content that should be learned in the schools. Called the College, Career, and Civic Life (C3) Framework, this builds on the standards listed above. Michelle Herczog (2013) provides a clear description of how the C3 Framework might be of assistance to teachers, and describes the idea of an inquiry arc:

The C3 Framework centers on an inquiry arc—a set of interlocking and mutually supportive ideas that frame the ways students learn social studies content. It calls upon students to use the disciplines of civics, economics, geography, and history as they (1) develop questions and plan investigations; (2) apply disciplinary concepts and tools; (3) gather, evaluate, and use evidence; and (4) work collaboratively to communicate conclusions and take informed action. Unlike standards, the [C3 Framework] focuses primarily on an inquiry-based approach to acquiring important conceptual understandings. It is not intended to prescribe the content necessary for a rigorous social studies program but is designed to guide states in their efforts to upgrade their social studies standards and to inform the pedagogical approaches of social studies educators across the nation.

(Herczog, Social Education, 2013, p. 331)

At the heart of this framework is developing knowledge and skills needed to engage in inquiries about social issues. This is a powerful statement about inquiry, because it centralizes inquiry as the skill/tool for citizenship in a democracy.

These national efforts will impact your future teaching, because they influence the standards that states have created. State standards influence the local school district standards for your content area and, ultimately, your classroom curriculum. You can imagine the process this was by reviewing the "Stakeholder and Curriculum" diagram on page 15 (Figure 1.2).

Before going further, think about this series of events since 1983. Some believe that the "standards movement" provides an excellent guide for states, districts, and teachers in helping develop the formal curriculum. Some worry that these standards take away from the professional judgment of teachers in determining what their students need to know. As you likely know, the standards movement has led to an "assessment movement" in which most states have developed standardized competency tests for many content areas. These tests assess how well students learn the content identified in the standards; these assessments are praised for holding schools accountable, and criticized for reducing teaching to "test preparation." What do you think about the standards movement? How does a set of national and state standards impact the social studies positively? What negative impact might it have?

An important question for anyone teaching in the social studies is "How do the national standards interface with each other?" Take some time to follow the links on page 16 to specific national standards of the social studies fields that have been developed for educators. Some fields, for example anthropology and sociology, have not created their own set of standards for educators. You can also join any of these organizations and then receive information about research and teaching in the content area, whether the organization has developed standards or not. Usually, membership dues include a subscription to a journal or magazine that provides ideas for helping students learn content/knowledge and skills in that area. Try to find some time to "play around" on these websites and locate the standards, as well as to identify how the national organizations affiliated with the social studies might help you as you prepare to teach. The standards are an excellent starting point for focusing your lesson plans. They are a planning resource. Near the end of this chapter you can read how an experienced teacher develops curriculum. This teacher suggests that the first step is to read the standards.

THE COMMON CORE STATE STANDARDS

National organizations may direct the content taught in your future classroom, but they have no legal authority to determine curriculum. In the same way, the classroom teacher has no legal authority to decide what is taught, as such authority has been granted to the state. Traditionally this authority has been passed along to the local level—to the district, school, department, and on to the classroom teacher. In the last 30 years, along with the national standards movement has come an emphasis by the federal government on assessment and accountability, the rationale being that for federal funds to be expended, evidence must be shown of student progress.

In addition to the 10 NCSS Themes, the C3 Framework, and the content-specific standards listed in the previous section, the **Common Core State Standards (CCSS)** has been directing most states' curriculum. The Common Core State Standards is an initiative that intends to create a consistent expecation of what students learn across the country. It is a state-developed plan to have a common set of agreed-upon standards that spans state borders and reaches across the country. The Common Core State Standards Initiative describes this as follows:

> The standards are informed by the highest, most effective models from states across the country and countries around the world, and provide teachers and parents with a common understanding of what students are expected to learn. Consistent standards will provide appropriate benchmarks for all students, regardless of where they live.
>
> These standards define the knowledge and skills students should have within their K–12 education careers so that they will graduate high school able to succeed in entry-level, credit-bearing academic college courses and in workforce training programs. The standards:
>
> - Are aligned with college and work expectations;
> - Are clear, understandable and consistent;
> - Include rigorous content and application of knowledge through high-order skills;
> - Build upon strengths and lessons of current state standards;
> - Are informed by other top performing countries, so that all students are prepared to succeed in our global economy and society; and
> - Are evidence-based.
>
> (http://www.corestandards.org)

Currently Common Core State Standards have been developed for two content areas:

- English/language arts (addressing areas such as reading, writing, speaking/listening, language, media technology)
- mathematics.

Social studies standards are currently situated within English/language arts. With 45 states and the District of Columbia adapting these two standards areas (a 46th state has only adapted the CCSS for English/language arts), the projection is that these states, and most likely many of the remaining four states, will replace their current state learning standards with the Common Core standards as they are developed.

The social studies are listed under the CCSS for English/language arts. They are referred to as the "Grades 6–12 Literacy in History and Social Studies." Because they focus on literacy (mainly reading, writing, speaking, and listening), they do not provide many suggestions for discipline-specific content. For example, the Common Core provides an excellent list of "text exemplars" that includes fiction, poetry, and informational texts that can be used at each grade level.[4] However, specific content, or citizenship skills that are specific to the social studies, are not delineated by the Common Core documents.

The NCSS's College, Career, and Civic Life (C3) Framework views the Common Core State Standards as establishing a foundation for inquiry in social studies. They are not intending to replace the Common Core, but they are intending to help identify how the literacy standards improve state social studies standards, and inquiry skills. "The C3 Framework emphasizes and elaborates on those skills in the Common Core Standards that explicitly connect to inquiry, and recognizes the shared responsibility social studies plays in honing key literacy skills . . . [for example] the Common Core Anchor Standard for Reading 1 asks students to read texts closely to both determine 'explicit' information lodged within the body of the text as well as draw 'logical inferences' based on the text." Students are also expected to "cite specific textual evidence when writing or speaking to support conclusions drawn from the text."

The Common Core places states in an interesting situation, because they do not specify particular content/concepts/information related to social studies. They do specify skills, however, and those skills fit well with the C3 Framework and other standards. Content standards, however, are a bit more tenuous, and the states are left trying to determine the social studies content students should learn. As of the writing of this book, for example, Washington state specifies content to be learned in the social studies as fitting under four general social science fields of history, geography, civics, and economics. Washington has content standards that were developed from national standards before the development of the Common Core, and that state still uses them to specify social studies content. These standards are called the Washington State Essential Academic Learning Requirements (the EALRs). Check to see what standards your state uses to specify social studies content for middle school and high school students. Also, check to see if your state has adopted the Common Core, and how that decision has affected the social studies.

States continue to have the flexibility and authority to choose the assessment they believe is best to measure all statewide academic standards, including the CCSS. Many states are working together to develop common assessments that will provide meaningful feedback to parents, teachers, and policymakers about student achievement. Two state-led consortia for developing CCSS assessments exist today: (1) Partnership for Assessment of Readiness for College and Careers (PARCC); and (2) Smarter Balanced Assessment Consortium (Smarter Balanced). What assessment group is working with your state? You can find out by visiting your state's education website.

So, what does all of this mean for you the classroom teacher? Obviously, with these types of pressures, as teachers you will need to tailor your classroom curricula and include time for preparing students in the taking of state tests. You can see then how state influence on the local classroom curriculum has increased dramatically in recent years. However, there still is a great deal of local control and influence over the curriculum.

DISTRICT PLANS

Each school district has at least one administrator in charge of coordinating the social studies curriculum. Usually, these coordinators oversee the curriculum of many subjects in addition to social studies. They are often former classroom teachers who are sympathetic to the balancing act a teacher must perform among the various influences on the curriculum. Their role is to help ensure that state initiatives are being implemented by working with department chairs. A curriculum coordinator oversees how the state social studies standards are being addressed in the classroom. Curriculum coordinators also ensure that the social studies departments offer courses that are aligned and presented in a logical order for students. For example, school districts will often articulate the grade levels at which students will learn American history. Traditionally, eighth grade is when students learn about European contact with the Americas up through U.S. Reconstruction after the Civil War. In eleventh grade, American history reviews the Revolution and the formation of the Constitution, and then picks up in the mid-1880s and continues to the present day. By identifying the content (in this case, the chronology of American history), districts help ensure that the content students learn, and the order in which students learn it, is the same across the schools.

DEPARTMENTAL PLANS

At most schools, the social studies department chair works with district administrators, department chairs at other schools, and social studies teachers to outline content and skills for both individual courses and all departmental course offerings. The schools' social studies departments use district plans to help facilitate this. In the case of the American history example, the social studies departments at the middle schools and high schools work to ensure that the teachers organize their course curricula around the district plan. Teachers are then in a position to design their course, the units in their course, and their daily lessons to fit within this plan. This type of alignment allows for the district to better utilize resources when purchasing textbooks and materials for the classroom. Therefore, daily lessons, units, course outlines, and department or district outlines are all curriculum plans.

Many departments prefer to entrust the classroom teacher with these decisions. Even with the influences that affect the curriculum, most teachers have considerable freedom to develop plans for the classroom because they are supported and trusted at the local level. The curriculum will be a fluid document pushed and pulled by those with keen interests. As with any truly democratic pursuit, parents, students, and the local community have the right to be involved with decisions related to the classroom, and their involvement should be embraced. However, in the final analysis, the teacher is almost always the final gatekeeper of the curriculum and instruction that occurs in her classroom. Thornton (2005) has expanded on the idea that teachers are the curricular gatekeepers who have the final say about how local, state, and federal standards are learned by students. This means that you, as the teacher, will determine what your students will learn regarding social studies topics. This is a sobering yet exciting aspect of teaching: sobering in that the expectation for student learning is great, and exciting because it should make you feel as though you can make professional decisions about the needs and interests of your students. Many beginning teachers report that state standards provide excellent direction about which content and skills to teach. Many teachers, however, worry whether the assessment tests will accurately determine what their students have learned. Teachers as gatekeepers cannot escape the fact that their teaching is being assessed when their students are tested. In Chapter 3 we will discuss classroom-level lesson plans in detail.

PRACTICAL SUGGESTIONS FOR DETERMINING CLASSROOM CURRICULUM

As a new teacher, sometimes you simply need practical ideas for getting started thinking about social studies curriculum. With all the talk of educational philosophy, curriculum theory, and influences it can be somewhat overwhelming. Consider these four practical ways to begin thinking about curriculum:

1. ask the important questions
2. seek advice from experienced teachers
3. write out course goals, and yearlong scope and sequence
4. determine the role of available materials.

Ask the Important Questions

The most well-known curriculum writing prompts are commonly referred to as the Tyler rationale (Tyler, 1949). Often times, you will see these prompts used to help with school-wide curriculum decisions, but they are helpful at the classroom level as well. The Tyler rationale is organized around four important questions that we will modify for the classroom level:

1. *What educational purposes should the class seek to attain?* Tyler suggests that these purposes should be determined by considering studies of the student as a learner, the practices of society, and recommendations from subject matter experts. These purposes should then be translated into stated course goals.
2. *What educational experiences can be provided that are likely to attain these purposes?* Tyler suggests that once goals have been formulated, the teacher should begin collecting ideas, activities, and materials that can be used to meet the goals. This collection can show alignment with the goals.
3. *How can these educational experiences be effectively organized?* Tyler recommends that each class would have organizing elements upon which to build. This might be related to a value (e.g., respect) in a history class or certain skills in a geography course. Considering these elements is useful in the building of lessons, or in integrating several topics or content areas.
4. *How can we determine whether these purposes are attained?* Assessing student learning and evaluating if they have attained the desired aims is a key component of Tyler's rationale. Assessment techniques should go hand in hand with the stated goals of the course.

It is interesting to many that this approach is still dominant in schools today—over 65 years later. It provides a rational and systematic approach for developing curriculum. It is this sequential, four-step process that has made the approach so popular, and provides a starting point for curriculum development (Ornstein & Hunkins, 2004). Tyler's approach is certainly flawed. It is built on behaviorism (which assumes that the taught curriculum will be close to the learned curriculum), and it may oversimplify curriculum development as being a series of small performances. Nonetheless, it a proven and long-standing approach for developing course curriculum.

Seek Advice from Experienced Teachers

Another suggested step in making decisions about your future social studies classroom curriculum is to seek the advice of experienced social studies teachers. Some schools assign first-year teachers with a mentor, but even if you have no one teacher at your school to lean on, you will find that there are many teachers who will be able to offer you insight from their experience. Obviously, each teacher's experience will be unique to some degree. However, it may be helpful for you to read about one high school social studies teacher's process for deciding what to teach in her government course. Jen Reidel's district did not have an outline for her course, and her department had only generally agreed upon classroom-based assessment; one suggested by the state. She had the opportunity to create her own curriculum, and describes this process as follows:

> I typically use both state standards (grade level expectations) and the national strands in determining the essential concepts, terms, and ideas to be taught. Often I will also consult

education organizations (Center for Civic Education, Foundation for Teaching Economics, Street Law) for their view on what they believe is most essential to teach in that specific discipline. Once I have determined what the essential concepts/terms are to be taught I start investigating what sources of curriculum exist to help me amass materials to teach the course (textbooks, simulations, Internet resources, videos, primary documents, etc.). I shy away from running a textbook driven classroom which tends to discourage students' passion regarding the subject. I try to use the textbook as the starting point—not ending point for the teaching of specific concepts and for the kids that need information in black and white to best comprehend it. I do use pocket Constitutions though to teach students about the guarantees and structure of the Constitution and I'll use other textbook material as a supplement.

Consequently, I have created all my own materials to teach about our governmental system, structure, and current issues related to it. This does give me the ability to modify my curriculum as the times change and when a current event is in the news that effectively illustrates what I am teaching. The downside to creating all my own materials is that often I as the teacher become the sole source for knowledge (versus a textbook). This fact alone can cause teachers to become incredibly worn down creating their own curriculum on a daily basis. I have drawn my materials from the Internet, from conferences I have attended, from materials purchased from Civic Education organizations, and from materials that I have purchased/located on my own.

For a new or a pre-service teacher, I would definitely encourage them to seek some sort of guidance from their district's plan. If the district does not offer one, they can't go wrong consulting the state and national standards for their discipline to narrow down what should be taught. They also might look at both the state and national standards in terms of any potential building or district goals (i.e. increasing reading, writing, math skills or emphasizing diversity). Once the essential concepts that must be taught have been identified, I think then the teacher can choose to teach what they are passionate about concerning the subject. Students more times than not will become most interested in a subject that they see their teacher excited about. My government class is proof of this. I love the subject . . . and yes I am geeky about it—particularly the court system. So as a result, I have a huge amount of knowledge to draw from when teaching the students. That translates to the ability to give in depth responses to a student's question as well as the fact that I can develop much more meaningful assignments and assessments when I am excited and knowledgeable about my subject.

Jen's approach is helpful. She suggests that the district curriculum plan, state standards, and national standards will provide you with a starting point for knowing what to teach. Her message is that these standards are not to be feared, but used as a tool for determining critical skills and concepts. When this is determined, the teacher is "freed up" to decide how to best promote student learning. She is the gatekeeper (Thornton, 2005), but she leans on others to help her determine what will be let in to her classroom.

Write Out Course Goals

A third step is to write out goals and consider a yearlong scope and sequence; this is described in more detail in Chapter 4. As Tyler suggests, the creation of written goals is a natural outcome of determining the purposes of the course. Goals, not to be confused with targets, are broad general statements that allow a teacher to focus. Goals are usually written for the entire course as well as for segmented sections of the course called *units of instruction*. Course goals will be made more explicit by the unit goals and unit targets. It might be helpful to think of it as creating an outline for an essay. It might look like this:

A. Course Goal
    1. Unit Goal
        i. Target

The idea is to help you focus on your overarching aim while not becoming overly burdened by prescriptive paperwork. Unit targets will be discussed in detail in Chapter 3.

    Goals should be written so that they convey broad expectations. For example:

- This unit will help students expand their awareness of human impacts on the environment.
- Students will familiarize themselves with the cultural influences of Chinese dynasties.
- While studying the western movement in North America by Europeans and Euro-Americans, the role of women during this time will be better appreciated.

State and national standards are filled with broad expectations that could be helpful in determining goals. In fact, sometimes these expectations are thought of as encompassing too much—of being too vague—when teachers are looking for a more specific learning target rather than a broad goal. When writing a goal, keep in mind two things: First, a goal is something you want students to accomplish over an extended period of time; and, second, a goal is something you hope for your students to learn. Because of this, it is helpful to consider for a moment the verbs you might use when writing a goal statement. Some of the verbs teachers find helpful for goals include:

Apply	Appreciate	Believe	Comprehend
Demonstrate	Enjoy	Expand	Familiarize
Grasp	Imagine	Know	Like
Recognize	Think	Understand	Value

If a yearlong curriculum plan is not provided to teachers by the school district or department, then writing this plan naturally follows the development of course goals. Usually a teacher will sketch out the year into units of instruction to begin getting an idea of the amount of time he can spend on certain topics. These topics become the foundation for writing unit plans.

Determine the Role of Available Materials

Determining the role of materials that are available is often undertaken at the same time that plans are being made for the year. For example, U.S. History or American Government courses will often have a textbook that the district selected as the formal curriculum guide. Textbooks are becoming less prevalent in schools, because of cost and the availability of online resources. The Internet is filled with materials that could be used in the classroom: You will find lesson plans, primary source documents, pictures, audio, and much more. As you sift through this material you will get ideas that will help your curriculum planning. The five national organizations related to the social studies mentioned earlier in this chapter have links on their websites with many lesson plan ideas. These sites are rich with resources for you to use in your future classrooms. These are not the only websites with lesson and content information, but they might serve as a useful starting point for thinking about lesson planning. We will examine lesson plans in both chapters 3 and 4, and the entire Part 2 of this book.

MAKING IT WORK IN YOUR CLASSROOM

Consider for a moment some of the predominant metaphors of schooling. This is important as you develop curriculum because if the "student is the worker" (Sizer, 1984), then what is the role of the teacher? How would this affect the curriculum? Kliebard (1987) has devised three predominant metaphors of schooling for curriculum literature. These are, in other words, three ways to think about education in order to develop curriculum in an educational setting:

1. The Production-Industrial Model

Teacher = overseer of production

Student = raw material

Curriculum = skilled worker who shapes and forms the raw material into a product.

A rough diamond becomes expensive jewelry. The teacher is able to form students to meet a predetermined goal. In this model, the student is passive, and viewed more as a commodity that brings little to the educational setting except potential. The teacher is the primary determinant for what a student will learn.

2. The Growth Model

Teacher = insightful gardener who nurtures, feeds, prunes, and nourishes the plants

Student = the potential-filled plant that relies on the gardener if it is to survive

Curriculum = the gardener cares for plants and helps them reach their potential

Unlike in the first metaphor, students in the growth model will develop and learn without the teacher, but they will not reach their full potential unless the teacher interacts and assists the process. The teacher knows what is best, and the students depend on the teacher's insights.

3. The Journey Model

Teacher = the tour guide

Student = traveler

Curriculum = student and teacher are touring knowledge, information, skills, and learning experiences

The student is a traveler who focuses on many different things depending on their interest, and much of what should be seen is pointed out by the teacher/guide.

Your metaphor for teaching will likely be better than these. Choose a metaphor that seems to fit your perspective, how you envision your class. Share your ideas with a group or the class. After you have written some of your first curricular materials, come back to this idea. How does what you have planned reflect your stated metaphor? What do you suppose students would use as a metaphor for schooling? What might students suggest?

CHAPTER REVIEW

Five parts to the school curriculum:

- formal
- delivered
- learned
- hidden
- null.

Hierarchy of curriculum influence involves a variety of external and internal influences.

National Standards are developed by national organizations in each of the social sciences:

- History (National Center for History in the Schools)
- Geography (National Council for Geographic Education)
- Civics (Center for Civic Education)
- Economics (National Council for Economic Education)
- Social studies (National Council for the Social Studies).

The National Council for the Social Studies has also developed the College, Career, and Civic Life Framework (C3 Framework) to guide curriculum development.

The Common Core standards are the result of an initiative to have all state standards align. District and department standards build on national and state standards, and provide additional levels of specificity in regard to the knowledge and skills that students are expected to learn in a given district or school.

Four ways to construct your classroom curriculum:

- prompts found in the Tyler rationale
- seek the advice of an experienced teacher
- write course goals and a yearlong outline
- determine the role of available materials.

NOTES

1. Hartoonian and Laughlin (1997).
2. National Council for the Social Studies (2006). Creating effective citizens. Retrieved August 6, 2015, from http://www.socialstudies.org/system/files/publications/se/6505/650511.html.
3. Dewey, J. (1938/1965). *Experience and Education.* New York: Collier Books.
4. Visit this site to access a PDF with a list of social studies text exemplars: http://www.corestandards.org/assets/Appendix_B.pdf.

REFERENCES

Apple, M. (1986). *Teachers and Texts.* New York: Routledge and Kegan Paul.

Banks, J. A. (2008). Diversity, group identity, and citizenship education in a global age. *Educational Researcher, 37*(3), 129–139.

Banks, J. A. (2003). *Teaching Strategies for Ethnic Studies,* 7th ed. Boston, MA: Allyn & Bacon.

Boyer, E. L. (1983). *High School.* New York: Harper & Row.

Carr, S. (2008). Educators and education for democracy: Moving beyond "thin" democracy. *Interamerican Journal of Education for Democracy, 1*(2), 147–165. Document available in: www.ried-ijed.org.

Cornbleth, C. (1991). *Curriculum in Context,* London: Falmer Press.

Cuban, L. (1996). Curriculum stability and change. In P. W. Jackson (Ed.), *Handbook of Research on Curriculum* (pp. 216–247). New York: Macmillan.

Dewey, J. (1938/1965). *Experience and Education.* New York: Collier Books.

Eisner, E. W. (1996). Curriculum ideologues. In P.W. Jackson (Ed.), *Handbook of Research on Curriculum* (pp. 302–326). New York: Macmillan.

Eisner, E. W. (1994). *The Educational Imagination: On Design and Evaluation of School Programs,* 3rd. ed. New York: Macmillan.

Eisner, E. W. (1985). *The Educational Imagination: On the Design and Evaluation of School Programs* 2nd ed. New York: Macmillan.

Hartoonian, H. M., & Laughlin, M. A. (1997). Social studies standards: A pathway to professional development. In M. E. Haas & M. A. Laughlin (Eds.), *Meeting the Standards: Social Studies Readings for K–6 Educators* (pp. 8–9). Washington, DC: National Council for the Social Studies.

Herczog, M. (2013). The links between the C3 Framework and the NCSS National Curriculum Standards for Social Studies. *Social Education, 77*(6), 331–333.

Hirsch, E. D. (1987). *Cultural Literacy.* Boston, MA: Houghton Mifflin.

Jackson, P. W. (1968). *Life in Classrooms.* New York: Holt, Rinehart, and Winston.

Kliebard, H. (1987). *The Struggle for the American Curriculum 1893–1958.* London: Routledge and Kegan Paul.

National Commission on Excellence in Education (1983). *A Nation At Risk: The Imperative for Educational Reform.* Washington, DC: U.S. Government Printing Office.

Ornstein, A. & Hunkins, F. P. (2004). *Curriculum: Foundations, Principles, and Issues,* 4th ed. Boston, MA: Allyn & Bacon.

Schubert, W. H. (1986). *Curriculum: Perspective, Paradigm and Possibility.* New York: Macmillan.

Sizer, T. R. (1984). *Horace's Compromise: The Dilemma of the American High School.* Boston, MA: Houghton Mifflin.

Thornton, S. J. (2005). *Teaching Social Studies that Matters: Curriculum for Active Learning.* New York: Teachers College Press.

Tyler, R. W. (1949). *Basic Principles of Curriculum and Instruction.* Chicago, IL: University of Chicago Press.

United States Department of Education (1991). *America 2000: An Education Strategy.* Washington, DC: Author.

CHAPTER 2

The Learner, and the Classroom Learning Community

CHAPTER GOALS

In this chapter, you will learn about:

- Adolescent development and its implications on learning and teaching
- General theories and ideas about learning
- Motivating students
- Diverse characteristics and needs of adolescents
- The role of appropriate technology for helping students learn
- Importance of classroom management.

As a future social studies teacher you will face many challenges that will be similar to those faced by every teacher in your school. You will find that knowing your students is a key ingredient to being successful. Compounding this issue, your students are wrestling with their own identity and roles in the world, while trying to understand their growing and developing bodies as they leave childhood and become young adults. The purpose of this chapter is for you, the future teacher of adolescents, to consider many issues that surround student learning. By understanding how adolescents develop and how they perceive the world, you will be able to more effectively help them learn social studies content, intellectual thinking skills, and interactive social skills. In addition to thinking about your students, the learners, you will also consider ideas for motivating them, and managing the classroom. Many books have been written about the topics in this chapter, so do not expect this chapter to present every idea. Instead, it should make you start to think and marvel at adolescents, and the complexities of teaching and learning. I encourage you to make notes in the columns about questions you have, or areas you want more information. Then pursue those personal curiosities to start understanding your future students, and how to make your future classroom a learning community.

Many studies show that classroom management is a significant worry for beginning teachers. That term, classroom management, implies a teacher-directed notion of controlling student behavior. It might be better to think how you and your students might work together to create the most effective learning environment or community. Rather then managing the classroom, you are working to create a type of eco-system where students are safe to question, think, and learn. Several ideas for developing this are addressed in this chapter. Throughout this book you will return to many of the ideas introduced in this chapter that pertain to the student as a learner, and the classroom as a community. Think of this chapter as providing a foundation for thinking about your future students, and for helping you to develop an increasingly complex understanding of how to effectively promote your students' learning.

ADOLESCENT DEVELOPMENT AND INSTRUCTION IN THE SECONDARY SCHOOL

When you walk down the halls of any middle school you will be amazed at the vast physical differences of the students. Some sixth grade boys and girls look as though they are still in elementary school, and some eighth grade boys and girls would appear to be high school students. Even students who are the same age develop very differently. All adolescents' bodies are going through dramatic physical changes, but they are not necessarily experiencing them at the same time. Your students will differ greatly in their biological, psychological/cognitive, and sociocultural development. The exciting news about this is that opportunities abound when teaching adolescents, because of their newly developing cognitive skills, social interactions, and awareness of the world. One fruitful approach for thinking about middle school and high school students is to consider three areas of human development:

- biological and physical
- psychological and cognitive
- sociological and cultural.

Biological and Physical Development

This considers the influence of the body's changes on the adolescent. It applies to learning and teaching, because physical changes impact adolescent body size and shape, nutritional needs, mood swings, and the many other changes that are occurring in the body. In many cases your future students will be observers of their own bodies, wondering how changes will affect them. Girls and boys develop at different rates within their same sex, but they are also developing noticeably differently between the two sexes. In sixth grade, girls are often the tallest in the class, and this slowly changes as boys experience growth spurts around the tenth grade. Puberty—with all of the hormonal influences that accompany it—occurs for all students eventually. Mood swings are a huge aspect of hormonal secretion. Not only do moods change, they also are magnified to extremes (high highs and low lows). The fact that students develop at different rates means you will have some students who are much more physically mature than others. The challenge is to realize that physical development is not linked to social maturity, emotional stability, or cognitive ability. For example, a 15-year-old student may look like an adult, but still have the maturity of a child. Physical changes will affect girls differently from boys (a topic we will explore later in this chapter), and physical changes will affect social, emotional, and academic domains of an adolescent. These physical changes will influence the instructional strategies you choose, the ways you manage the learning environment, your relationships with students, and many other elements of teaching.

Psychological and Cognitive Development

Psychological and cognitive development considers how the mind impacts the adolescent. As children grow physically they also increase their cognitive abilities. Thinking skills improve as they develop, and adolescents begin to have cognitive abilities that were only starting to emerge in the fourth and fifth grades. For example, students in middle and high school will become increasingly able to think about possibilities, hypotheses, and abstract concepts. Adolescents gain the exciting ability of introspection, or the abilities to analyze and evaluate themselves and others. Specific theories about how adolescents develop cognitively are examined later in this chapter. The important idea to think about is that your future students have very capable cognitive/thinking abilities. You will help your students enhance these abilities by providing opportunities through which to practice using them. At times this presents a paradox for adolescents and teachers alike. Beamon (2001) suggests several of these contradictions that may be resolved simply with practice in your classroom:

- Adolescents may be technologically "savvy," yet lack skills to organize, evaluate, and synthesize data.
- Adolescents may be used to fast access of information, yet lack motivation to see a task to completion.
- Adolescents may be socially active, yet lack the skills for purposeful social interactions.
- Adolescents may be independent minded, yet be vulnerable to peer and societal lures.
- Adolescents may be intellectually capable, yet be unpracticed in higher cognitive thinking.

Your classroom becomes an ideal place for developing and refining these cognitive abilities.

Social and Cultural Development

These forms of development receive a tremendous amount of attention when thinking about teaching adolescents, because they are closely linked to physical, psychological, and cognitive development. As adolescents struggle with their own identity, they experience a series of identity crises (Erikson, 1959, 1968). These crises are closely tied to self-concept—our ideas and thoughts about who we are. As we make decisions about our identity, we question how we love, with whom we have intimacy, whether we have autonomy and initiative, and the effectiveness of our work ethic. Our culture, ethnicity, economic level, social status, athletic ability, academic prowess, and self-esteem are a few of the many aspects that are part of our identity. They each have a role in shaping our sociological development.

In *All Grown Up and No Place to Go*, David Elkind (1998) suggests that the cognitive and physical development of adolescents puts them sociologically in a time of extreme egocentrism. Children demonstrate this "crisis" as they deal with an "imaginary audience" and a "personal fable." These two phenomena are initiated in early adolescence, and although we learn to manage them, they may never leave us completely. Imaginary audience "accounts for the teenager's extreme self-consciousness. Teenagers feel that they are always on stage and that everyone around them is as aware of, and concerned about their appearance and behavior as they are themselves" (Elkind, 1998, p. 40). The idea of a personal fable stems from their thinking that they are "special, different from other people . . . [it gives them] courage to participate in many necessary but frightening activities" (pp. 43–44). In addition to creating a sense of invulnerability ("I won't be in a car accident"), the personal fable helps convince adolescents that no one has ever loved so deeply, been so excited, or experienced such emotions as they have. As Elkind summarizes, bringing the fable "in line with reality is part of maturing . . . only in finding out how much we are like other people, paradoxically, can we really discover our true specialty and uniqueness" (p. 45). The impact of sociological and cultural influences on adolescents, and implications for teachers, will be expanded upon in the coming pages of this book.

LEARNING

Our adult memories of adolescence can be detailed and specific. However, an adult's thinking about her adolescence is very different from the thinking we did when we were actually adolescents. Adult memories of overcoming an obstacle, confronting a peer, interacting with a teacher, or studying for an exam are influenced by the fact that we know how the situation ends. Adolescents are in the process of living out these scenarios without this perspective; they therefore may look at them differently from how adults would. When teachers consider how to best help students learn in school, their own memories of school should serve as a guide but not the driving force behind decisions. Certainly, teachers have all been apprenticed by the teachers who taught them. In fact, teachers tend to teach in the manner they were taught (Lortie, 1975). So our memories are useful, but not as reliable as we may think.

It is important for you to think about learning, since that is what teachers help students do in school. Many different theories attempt to understand how people learn. One definition of learning that teachers find helpful is provided by Ormrod (2006), who posits that learning is a "relatively permanent change, due to experience, either in behavior or in mental representations or associations" (p. 184). Teachers, then, work with their students to help bring about this change. For example, some suggest that memorizing is not "learning," because it is usually not permanent; it takes rehearsal, and memorized information usually fades over time. Others suggest that memorization is one form of learning, because the process has brought about change. More important for you, however, is the realization that your opinion about this will impact the type of instructional strategies you select. If a sixth grade social studies teacher wants her students to learn about Mexican culture, she will choose classroom activities that are based on her belief about learning.

Behaviorism is a long-established approach for thinking about learning. According to behaviorists, learning occurs when the overt behavior changes. Over 100 years ago the famous behaviorist experiment by Ivan Pavlov involved a person ringing a bell and feeding a dog. After repeating the stimulus of ringing and feeding, the person rang the bell only. The dog had learned to associate the bell with food, and began to lick its lips in anticipation of food. This idea that behavior (salivating) could be influenced by a particular stimulus (the bell) ushered in the notion of behaviorism. B. F. Skinner (1953) believed that an organism's interactions with the world (or the environment) conditions behaviors. In other words, people are continually coming into contact with stimuli. At times these stimuli encourage us (e.g., praise when doing a good job), and at times they discourage us (e.g., punishment). Skinner has suggested that these stimuli shape who we are and what we learn.

The idea that behavior indicates learning is unsatisfying for cognitive approaches to learning. *Cognitivism*, or cognitive approaches, attempts to address what is happening inside our brains when we are learning. Jean Piaget (1970), Lev Vygotsky (1978), and other cognitive psychologists investigated how our brains functioned, and not just our behaviors. For example, Piaget believed that the brain becomes increasingly able to learn complex and abstract information as we grow. Adolescence begins in the final years of Piaget's "Concrete Operations Stage." During this stage children organize their thoughts logically and sequentially. Piaget suggests that, near the age of 12, children engage in "formal operations," in which their thought becomes more abstract. They are able to generate abstract propositions, multiple hypotheses, and possible outcomes. Thinking becomes less tied to concrete reality. Vygotsky theorized about a "zone of proximal development" that exists between our current level of understanding something and the next level. To arrive at this next level, we need help. Tutoring, modeling, and guiding all provide examples of how to expand on our current levels of understanding. Current thinking about ideas tied to Vygotsky's initial theory have led to such terms as *scaffolding*, *constructivism*, and *hands-on learning*. These all imply that learning occurs when some additional source provides a support network to promote learning (e.g., in the same way that a scaffold provides support for a building).

The main goal of learning is to promote student achievement. In *How People Learn: Brain, Mind, Experience, and School*, Bransford, Brown, and Cocking (2000) suggest that three findings consistently emerge from "research on learners learning and teachers teaching" (p. 14) to promote student achievement: prior experiences/knowledge, deep understanding, and metacognition. Below is a brief explanation description from *How People Learn*, followed by a concise expansion of each idea:

> Students come to the classroom with preconceptions about how the world works. If their initial understanding is not engaged, they may fail to grasp the new concepts and information that are taught, or they may learn them for purpose of a test but revert to their preconceptions outside the classroom.
>
> (p. 14)

Students come to classes with a wide range of experiences and prior knowledge. If this knowledge is accurate, then teachers have the opportunity to tap into a wealth of knowledge that comes from these students. (Imagine how a unit on Japanese culture could be enhanced if one of your students had lived in Japan.) Conversely, misconceptions need to be "unlearned" so that students can relearn proper information. (Middle school and high school history students often have a misconception that the U.S. government has always acted altruistically.)

> To develop competence in an area of inquiry, students must: (a) have a deep foundation of factual knowledge, (b) understand facts and ideas in the context of a conceptual framework, and (c) organize knowledge in ways that facilitate retrieval and application.
>
> (p. 16)

Researchers have examined the performances and learning of experts and novices in several subject areas. An expert understanding of key concepts facilitates understanding of new knowledge. This allows experts to identify patterns, and note similarities or differences in a manner that novices cannot. Therefore, teachers should be able to teach key concepts and/or facts in depth. These "defining concepts" are important if students are to learn additional ideas and information, and they are important for helping students learn content on their own.

> A metacognitive approach to instruction can help students learn to take control of their own learning by defining learning goals and monitoring their progress in achieving them.
>
> (p. 18)

Metacognition, or "thinking about one's thinking," frequently takes the form of an internal conversation. Adolescents can be taught effective internal dialogues that will promote learning. For example, predicting outcomes, explaining an idea to yourself to improve understanding, noting when you do not understand, referring to background knowledge, and using strategies for studying are all elements of learning to be metacognitive. These are not used by all students, and should be taught by the teacher through modeling and other explicit ways of bringing out the hidden/internal voice for the students to observe (p. 21).

LEARNING STYLE PREFERENCES

Litzinger and Osif describe learning styles as "the different ways in which children and adults think and learn" (1993, p. 73). Often teachers engage students in a wide range of learning activities in order to provide a variety of learning opportunities. Given the earlier definition of learning, the idea of *learning preferences* does not imply that students will learn material differently; it means that students may prefer one type of instruction over another. For example, some students will prefer to work on inquiry or research tasks, others will prefer to listen to a lecture, and still others may prefer to see examples as they hear new information. If you believe that all students have different learning preferences, then you will quickly realize that you have preferred styles, too. The challenge is to teach with a variety of styles, and not solely using the style you most prefer.

MULTIPLE INTELLIGENCES

Howard Gardner, whose *multiple intelligence* theory suggests that long-standing ideas about intelligence such as the intelligence quotient, or IQ, are limited, developed the idea of more than one form of intelligence. Gardner notes that our society tends to value linguistic skills (speaking, reading, and writing) and logical-mathematical skills (number sense and reasoning). People who are "well spoken," "logical," and "calculated" are highly esteemed. This value might overlook students who have intellectual capabilities in non-language or non-mathematical areas. Some in our society may not value actors, designers, musicians, dancers, counselors, and naturalists, because their capabilities are different. Gardner's multiple intelligence theory (1983, 1999) suggests that there are at least eight different intelligences, and that these account for a broader conception of what we think about human potential. Gardner stated that he is concerned about educators confusing multiple intelligences with learning styles (2003). Whereas learning styles are preferences that a learner has in how he is taught, intelligences are learning aptitudes, or ways of thinking about the world around him.

We do not learn differently, but rather have different preferences and strengths when we do learn. The eight intelligences proposed are:

- *Linguistic/verbal intelligence:* This involves abilities with spoken and written language, the ability to learn languages, and the capacity to use language to accomplish certain goals. Writers, poets, lawyers, and public speakers are among those who usually have a high linguistic intelligence.
- *Logical-mathematical intelligence:* This consists of the capacity to think logically, carry out mathematical operations, and investigate issues with a systematic/scientific approach. This intelligence includes the ability to detect patterns, reason deductively, and think logically.
- *Musical intelligence:* This involves skill in the performance, composition, and appreciation of musical patterns. It encompasses the capacity to recognize and compose musical pitches, tones, and rhythms.
- *Bodily kinesthetic intelligence:* This gives rise to the potential of using one's whole body or parts of the body to solve problems. It is the ability to coordinate bodily movements. Gardner sees mental and physical activity as related, since the brain tells the body what to do.
- *Spatial intelligence:* This involves the potential to recognize and use the patterns of wide space and more confined areas. The world around one makes sense because of patterns and organizations that others without this intelligence may overlook.
- *Interpersonal intelligence:* This is the capacity to understand the intentions, motivations, and desires of other people. With this intelligence a person works effectively with others. Educators, salespeople, religious and political leaders, and counselors utilize this intelligence.
- *Intrapersonal intelligence:* This entails the capacity to understand one's own feelings and emotions. With this intelligence a person has a useful understanding of herself and is able to use this information to regulate her life.
- *Naturalist intelligence:* This involves abilities to sense patterns in and make connections to elements in nature. People with a naturalist intelligence may have a strong affinity to the outside world or to animals, and may show unusual interest in such subjects as biology, zoology, botany, geology, meteorology, paleontology, or astronomy.

Gardner does not suggest that teachers teach to all eight intelligences. He does, however, suggest that teachers will have students who look at the world and understand it in terms of one or more intelligences. The principal implication of this is that teachers should provide a variety of activities that focus on different intelligences. Consider how this might impact you in the classroom. If you were to teach eighth graders in a world geography class, you might have your students read about a particular region in the world (linguistic/verbal), look at a map of that area (spatial), and examine demographic information about that region (logical–mathematical). They could then record their impressions of that region in a journal (intrapersonal) and discuss them in groups of four (interpersonal). What Gardner's theory provides is a challenge for the teacher to help students learn content by thinking about it in ways that benefit the students' strengths.

GROWTH MINDSET

The brain has been examined in the last decade in unprecedented ways, yet much about its function remains unknown. Many researchers refer to the brain as having a certain amount of "plasticity," or ability to change and develop on its own and affect its structure and functioning as a result of changes to the body or environment. This leads many cognitive scientists to suggest that our brains are not fixed with a certain amount of ability or even potential. Brains seem to change and grow, and we can have an effect on that as well. The "fixed" notion of IQ or ability is being challenged, and it will be interesting to see the outcome of this in the coming years. Carol Dweck (2007) identified the term "growth mindset" to describe the thought that intelligence can be developed and increased over time. A growth mindset, according to Dweck, embraces challenges, because they allow for improvement. The opposite of growth is a "fixed mindset," where challenges provide occasions where you might fail or you might succeed, but it is all based on a certain amount of inherent (fixed) ability. With a growth mindset, your self-image is not tied to your success and how you will look to others. Effort is seen not as something to be avoided but as necessary to grow and master useful skills. Criticism and feedback are sources of information about a current ability level, and will spur improvement. The intriguing part of this is twofold: (1) Dweck and her colleagues found that students with a growth mindset were more successful and wanted to learn more than students with a fixed mindset about growth and ability; (2) your students (and you) can learn how to develop a growth mindset. The following teaching techniques are helpful for you to consider as you work with students, because they are research-supported ideas for developing a mindset that looks to improve and learn.

- Set up lessons as learning tasks and not judgments of ability. Characterize the activity as a learning process and present skills and material as being learnable.
- Praise the effort not the ability. For example say, "I see that you've been working really hard on using evidence to support your argument" and not "You are a natural when it comes to making strong arguments."
- Encourage students to cultivate their knowledge in an individual topic or develop a specific skill. Knowledge and skill development imply that ability is not fixed.
- Ask students to reflect upon which of their friends have changed the most over time. Students realize their thinking and brains can change and improve.
- Recount proverbs that highlight the capacity for individuals to change. "It's never too late to learn."
- Study geniuses or those who have made significant contributions to their field, emphasizing how hard they work to develop their abilities.[1]

If this idea is intriguing to you, consider reading more about mindset. Much is being written about its place in schools, and it will impact the way in which you praise students and offer rewards to them.

MAKING IT WORK IN YOUR CLASSROOM

Along with all of the cognitive developments that occur as adolescents develop is the ability to analyze and evaluate others and themselves. Think of at least one way that you can make use of these emerging thinking skills when teaching your class. For example, how might a history teacher use students' introspection, analysis, or evaluation abilities when reading a biography of John Adams? How might a geography teacher use them during a mapping activity?

DIVERSE CHARACTERISTICS AND NEEDS OF MIDDLE SCHOOL AND HIGH SCHOOL STUDENTS

The learners in your social studies classrooms will be very diverse. When considering some of the ways in which students might be different from one another, the following provides an adequate but incomplete list: students will have different cultures, ethnicities, primary languages, economic backgrounds, religions, family structures, physical abilities, and learning abilities. These differences are not exclusive, either. For example, some students who are English language learners (ELLs) are also gifted, and some will have physical disabilities. In this section we will examine several aspects of diversity in your future students so that we can establish several key ideas. Before we move on, pause and consider what a wise teacher will remember: We *don't* teach social studies—we teach people.

Before addressing the specifics of diversity, consider an important concept related to the diverse needs of students in your classroom: *differentiated instruction*. Your students will learn best when you are informed about their interests, ability and readiness levels, learning preferences, and other areas of their lives that allow you to maximize their specific learning potential (Tomlinson, 2004). As with any examination of adolescents, a caveat needs to be in place about exploring student diversity: Generalizations about any group are not intended to create stereotypes. Since there are not universally applicable generalizations about teaching adolescents, it will be up to you to get to know your students as individuals. Diversity is a characteristic of your future students that should be enjoyed and considered for the range of ideas, viewpoints, and experiences that it will provide. Differentiated instruction is a learning methodology based upon the premise that instructional approaches should vary depending upon the diverse students in the classroom. The practice of differentiating instruction requires flexibility on the part of the teacher to adjust lesson planning to the students rather than requiring students to adjust to the curriculum.

According to Hall, Strangman, and Meyer (2003), to differentiate instruction is to:

> recognize students' varying background knowledge, readiness, language, preferences in learning and interests; and to react responsively. Differentiated Instruction is a process to teaching and learning for students of differing abilities in the same class. The intent of differentiating instruction is to maximize each student's growth and individual success by meeting each student where he or she is and assisting in the learning process.
>
> (pp. 2–3)

In Figure 2.1, these authors help us visualize the learning cycle used in differentiated instruction. Note the three primary elements of curriculum that can be differentiated are content, process, and product (Tomlinson, 2004). You will find as you continue learning about this topic that student-centered instructional strategies, such as student-directed inquiries or cooperative learning, are highly conducive to the principles of differentiated instruction. As a result, you will revisit these ideas when the instructional strategies are examined in Part II of this book.

Tomlinson (2004) suggests three aspects of differentiation that will help us focus on planning appropriately for our diverse classrooms. Student *interest* can be addressed by allowing students to pursue questions tied together by the topic and learning targets. For example,

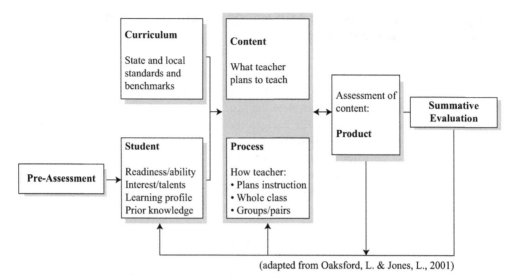

(adapted from Oaksford, L. & Jones, L., 2001)

Figure 2.1 The Learning Cycle in Differentiated Instruction.
Adapted from Hall, Strangman, and Meyer, 2003.

students could create questions they would like to pursue on the topic of ancient Rome such as: How did the Roman arch successfully improve architecture? What were the lives of gladiators like? What medical treatments were available for illnesses? Second, student *readiness* can be differentiated by allowing for writing and research tasks that reflect criteria for success agreed upon by student and teacher. For example, an agreed-upon writing project and rubric is supported by a wide range of print and media resources, a variety of support from peers, teacher, or access to experts. Third, *learner-profile* differentiation is reflected by the variety of ways a student prefers to learn or present their learning. For example, the student might be given an option to express their findings through journal writing, an oral presentation, or through a video they have created. Keeping these three aspects of differentiation in mind while planning for learning will help create an environment that assists all students.

MAKING IT WORK IN YOUR CLASSROOM

Turn to a lesson you have written for one of the social studies courses you are likely to teach during your first year (for example, a commonly taught course for new teachers would be world history or U.S. history as opposed to Advanced Placement government). Explain how you think this lesson might address differentiation in terms of:

*   interest
*   readiness
*   learner profile.

Is the lesson you selected conducive to adjusting for all three of the above? Two, one, or maybe none? If you were to adjust this lesson, what information would help you plan more effectively?

ETHNIC AND CULTURAL DIVERSITY

A common term closely tied to diversity is *multicultural education*, which Banks and Banks define as follows:

> Multicultural education is a field of study and an emerging discipline whose major aim is to create equal educational opportunities for students from diverse racial, ethnic, social-class, and cultural groups. One of its important goals is to help all students to acquire the knowledge, attitudes, and skills needed to function effectively in a pluralistic democratic society and to interact, negotiate, and communicate with peoples from diverse groups in order to create a civic and moral community that works for the common good . . . consequently, we may define multicultural education as a field of study designed to increase educational equity for all students that incorporates, for this purpose, content, concepts, principles, theories, and paradigms from history, the social and behavioral sciences, and particularly from ethnic studies and women studies.
>
> (Banks & Banks, 1995, pp. xi–xii)

One implication of this definition is that multicultural education moves students' stories and experiences into the school curriculum. Instead of feeling as though they are not a part of the school and curriculum (often referred to as being "marginalized"), students from ethnic minority groups see their culture, history, and perspectives incorporated into the standard curriculum. In addition, students in the "dominant culture," or the culture of the social or political group that holds the most power in a school and community, need to learn about and embrace stories, cultures, and experiences that are not the same as their own. Gloria Ladson-Billings (1995) has called teaching with students' culture and background in mind "culturally relevant teaching." An excellent place to read a summary of culturally relevant teaching is at the website of the Education Alliance at Brown University (http://www.brown.edu/academics/education-alliance/teaching-diverse-learners/strategies-0/culturally-responsive-teaching-0). For example, the Education Alliance suggests seven principles for meeting the needs of ethnically and culturally diverse learners. A summary of these principles follows.

Principles for Meeting the Needs of Ethnically and Culturally Diverse Learners

1. Positive Perspectives on Parents and Families

Parent involvement should not be limited to participation in school functions. Often, religious and cultural differences preclude active participation in school activities. However, parental involvement also includes how parents communicate high expectations, pride, and interest in their child's academic life (Nieto, 1996). Teachers should try to understand the parents of their students, because that will often provide insight into the student at school. This requires communication with parents through such avenues as phone calls and email, school visits from the parent, home visits from the teacher, and even informal conversations at community events. Additionally, teachers can help inform parents of the various social and academic services offered by the school and by organizations associated with the school. If you have not had experience with the culture of a parent, you should learn about cultural activities and beliefs. This will provide a beginning level of knowledge that will help you begin to communicate with parents.

2. Communication of High Expectations

All of your students should hear that you expect them to attain high standards in their schoolwork. This message must be delivered by teachers, counselors, coaches, administrators, and other school personnel. Teachers should understand students' behavior in light of the norms of the communities in which they live, which is why the first point describes the importance of talking with parents.

3. Learning within the Context of Culture

Schools have a dominant language. Typically this is the standard American English that is common in middle and upper socioeconomic groups. Your students who do not live in a home and/or culture that is close to that of the school may be inhibited from learning because of "language barriers." Other barriers also exist, including preferences for learning. Some cultures emphasize speaking whereas others value silence. Some cultural groups put value on cooperation and others do not, preferring individual work. By gaining knowledge of the language and culture of your students you will be able to create lessons that promote learning because they will use contexts with which your students are familiar.

4. Student-Centered Instruction

During student-centered instruction, learning is a cooperative venture; students are more engaged in learning the content than when the teacher is the center of attention. This may entail everything from brainstorming topics, to study, to student-led discussion groups, to cooperative learning projects, to service learning activities in the local community. These types of activities provide opportunities for students to develop their own ideas, and receive feedback on these ideas. Students from diverse backgrounds are able to bring their ideas and cultural perspectives to the classroom, and to work on projects that are culturally and socially relevant to them.

5. Culturally Mediated Instruction

Culturally mediated instruction and learning occur in an environment that encourages multiple viewpoints and allows for inclusion of knowledge that is relevant to the students and to their diverse cultures and backgrounds. Your goal should be to create an environment that encourages and embraces culture by using management and learning strategies familiar to students' culture, provides students with opportunities to share their cultural knowledge, and even questions and challenges students' beliefs and actions. Students should learn that there are often multiple ways to interpret a statement, event, or action. By being allowed to learn in different ways or to share viewpoints and perspectives in a given situation based on their own cultural and social experiences, students become active participants in their learning (Nieto, 1996).

6. Reshaping the Curriculum

The curriculum should use resources other than textbooks for study. For example, students could research a topic within their community, interview members of their community, or provide information to other students on alternative viewpoints or beliefs on a topic. Students' strengths in one subject area will support new learning in another. If your students use their personal experiences to develop new skills and knowledge, a more meaningful connection between school and real-life situations is established (Padron, Waxman, & Rivera, 2002).

7. The Teacher as Facilitator

As teachers, you should develop a learning environment that is relevant to and reflective of your students' social, cultural, and linguistic experiences. You will act as guides, mediators, consultants, instructors, and advocates for your students, helping to effectively connect their culturally based and community-based knowledge to the classroom learning experiences. Teachers should use the students' home cultural experiences as a foundation upon which to develop knowledge and skills. Encourage students to share artifacts from home that reflect their culture, write about traditions shared by their families, or research different aspects of their culture. Teachers should also work to accommodate learning preferences of their students that are linked to cultural background and take into account varying levels of English-language proficiency. This might also occur by using a community speaker, or inviting parents who can demonstrate alternative ways of approaching a subject or a problem to class (Ladson-Billings, 1995; Padron, Waxman, & Rivera, 2002).

TEACHING ENGLISH TO STUDENTS OF OTHER LANGUAGES

You might relate to the following reflection from a recent student teacher:

> My university supervisor came to my World History class one day to observe. After class he was encouraging me to consider ways I could include all the students and not only the ones that volunteered to speak-up. He asked if I noticed the three students sitting in the back corner that didn't say a word the entire class. I did notice them. They speak Ukrainian and I had no idea what to do.

The demographics of the United States, including the number of those who speak languages other than English, are changing rapidly. Teaching students who are learning English as their second or third language is not new but it has become increasingly common. In addition to immigration from the traditional European regions, a new and profound wave of immigration from Asia, Africa, and Latin America occurs today. As seen in Figure 2.2, the percentage of those self-identifying as foreign born has approached the 1900 highs and the total number of recently immigrated is double that of any time in the history of the nation.

As immigration nears record numbers, it follows that the number of students with limited English proficiency is growing rapidly. Statistics that reflect school population change have been used to support what has been referred to as the *demographic imperative*. It is imperative for us to prepare ourselves to teach all of our students.

Year	Number of foreign born	Foreign born as percentage of U.S. population
1850	2,244,602	9.7%
1880	6,679,943	13.3%
1900	10,341,276	13.6%
1930	14,204,149	11.6%
1950	10,347,395	6.9%
1980	14,079,906	6.2%
2007	38,059,694	12.6%

Figure 2.2 Immigration and Your Students

Source: www.census.gov.

Note: For more information on the topic of immigration and the social studies, see the special issue on immigration and citizenship education in the November, 2009 issue of *Social Studies and the Young Learner* (a journal of the National Council of the Social Studies).

Obviously, not every new teacher will choose to become a certified expert in teaching English as a second language; however, there are several ways for every teacher to be better at helping all students learn. An important start is learning about the four basic elements for engaging students who are not proficient in English. First, it is important to be able to understand some basic terms used so that when are placed in your internship or begin your first teaching position you can ask informed questions. The terminology is specific and tailored to language learning. A person could walk into the teacher's lounge and hear talk of ESLs, TESOLs, ELLs, ESOLs, bilinguals, emergent bilinguals, and LEPs. The glossary of terms below will prepare you with some key words and phrases, as will the brief glossary of terms that relate specifically to ELLs.

A BRIEF GLOSSARY FOR TEACHING STUDENTS WITH ENGLISH AS A SECOND LANGUAGE

Academic Language: The language used to describe complex ideas, higher-order thinking processes, and abstract concepts, especially within a specific discipline. This term is used for native speakers of English as well as ELLs. See CALP.

Bilingual: An ability to speak two languages.

Bilingual Education: An approach to instruction that includes the continued development of the student's native language, the learning of a second language, and the use of both languages to teach academic content.

Biliteracy: An ability to read and write in two languages. See Freire (1978) for information about the implications of biliteracy or literacy on issues of social justice.

BICS: Basic interpersonal communicative skills. This might be thought of as conversational language. A distinction between BICS and CALP was introduced by Cummins (1979). See CALP.

CALP: Cognitive academic language proficiency. Immigrant children typically take two years to acquire a conversational fluency (BICS) in a new language. It may take the same child at least five years to reach an academic proficiency (CALP) in the new language.

ELL: English language learners or students who are not proficient in English

ESL: English as a second language. A program or system of instruction designed to teach English to those who speak other languages. This system typically will use academic content and is usually thought of as a component of bilingual education.

ESOL: English to speakers of other languages. Some prefer this to ESL because it recognizes that English could be the third or fourth language of the student and that this should be acknowledged. For example, a student from Mexico may speak Mixteco (a Native language) as their first language and Spanish as their second language.

Immersion: Technically this is a bilingual immersion program developed in Canada, where 90% of the early-elementary-aged student's day is in the minority language (the non-mainstream language). Many times, however, this term is used in school to refer to placing a student in a mainstream classroom (not necessarily as part of a well-thought-out program).

LEP: Limited English proficient. This is usually used as an adjective to describe students, as in *the LEP student*. Some prefer not to use this term for the same reason some prefer not to use the word "disability"—it focuses on what a student *can not* do instead of what they *can* do.

TESOL: Teaching English to speakers of other languages, or the professional organization Teachers of English to Speakers of Other Languages.

Second, it is important to know that you are not alone. There usually will be a teacher in your school who specializes in teaching ESL. Her program could look like one of the many possible varieties of teaching English but most likely will reflect current trends of teaching ESL. This means that students of all levels of English proficiency come to her class to either learn the academic subject (ESL content class) or have class time to support them with their assignments from your social studies classes; support may be in English or in their first language, depending upon obvious variables. Of course, some students will attend introductory-level English classes as well. This is important to keep in mind, but—without question—conscientious teachers will not shift all of the responsibility for the learning of an ELL onto the ESL teacher.

A third element to consider is the way people acquire new languages. Having a basic understanding of language acquisition theory will help as you try to design or modify lessons. While taking a course on second language acquisition theory would undoubtedly benefit any teacher, here we will focus on two of the components that influence language acquisition in a school context (Cummins, 1979; Thomas & Collier, 1997). Students learning English will tend to begin by learning social language. They learn what they use in everyday conversations. Immigrant children typically take two years to acquire a conversational fluency (BICS) in a new language. Students take much longer to negotiate their way into the more formal academic language. It may take the same child at least five years to reach an academic proficiency (CALP) in the new language. The catch is this: An unknowing teacher may assume that because he hears a student speak English during class that the student is equally proficient in academic language, the language of teaching and learning. This will most likely not be the case. In addition, because history or geography textbooks are written in academic language, the student's actual proficiency could easily be overestimated and they might not be provided with adequate assistance for understanding what they read for class.

The teaching of academic language is not something unique to those with limited proficiency, however. Some of your students will certainly have advantages if they come from homes that speak dominant dialects, with access to computers, books, conversations, and other mainstream English language resources. By contrast, other students have recently immigrated, come from homes with non-mainstream English language resources, no computers, few educational resources, or come from homes where dominant English is not common in their homes. While this group clearly has unique needs, both groups are academic language learners.

Another consideration for teachers is that some students may not have a literacy base at all. In other words, they may not read or write in their first language. This obviously would have an impact on their ability to read or write English even if they are verbally performing well. All of our students need to be taught academic language, and many of the techniques used to assist with teaching academic language are beneficial for both groups (Zwiers, 2008).

The final element for you to consider is inclusive methods of teaching. TESOL specialists tell us that many of the techniques used to support ELLs are also helpful for every student. You will see in Part II of this text that techniques of teaching are unique to the instructional strategy chosen by the teacher. Techniques for implementation, assessment, and classroom management used during a discussion will be different from those in a lecture. When working in mainstream social studies classes with varying English ability levels a teacher will choose common instructional strategies but purposefully modify or add techniques that aid language development. For example, in a world history class you may have decided to have a discussion about the similarities and differences between South African apartheid and Jim Crow laws in the U.S. South. Providing discussion time in class between native and English language learners is an outstanding aid to language and content learning. Student peers can often speak in a way that is more comprehensible to the ELL, and a good mix of small group and large group discussion helps the ELL feel more comfortable participating. In this apartheid discussion, the teacher then might begin by spending time building background before jumping into the discussion, she might be sure to use plenty of visuals to help students understand concepts, and finally, she might choose to ask small groups of students to review and discuss background materials she provides prior to starting a large group discussion. As with most every aspect to teaching, there is no one-size-fits-all approach to teaching ELLs.

In Part II of this text you will find ESL strategies and ideas that could be beneficial for each of the instructional strategies we will explore. In addition, you can easily find lists of ideas on the Internet that will be helpful as you consider a variety of approaches, based upon your instructional strategy choice. A good place to continue your learning is Dave's ESL Café (www.eslcafe.com).

MAKING IT WORK IN YOUR CLASSROOM

Imagine you are planning a lesson on William Wilberforce and his attempts to end the slave trade in Britain. You have determined that this lesson will rely on lecture and discussion. Next to each of the ideas below used by TESOL instructors to help support ELLs, either leave blank or write down the name of one of these two instructional strategies that you think might be a good match. After you have read Part II, come back to this section to see how you have done.

- Activate prior schemata by making connections to students' background knowledge, or providing contextual information to help provide that background.
- Hand out a paragraph with blank words for students to fill in.
- Provide a graphic organizer.
- Stop speaking every ten minutes and ask a question.
- Explain your learning target.
- Use exit slips.
- Be aware of your speech patterns.
- Let them know straight out what you want them to be able to do or produce at the end of the day.
- Break the class into pairs before a large group debriefing.
- Show common language patterns on a poster in the room: for example, "I see what you mean, but I think . . ."
- Place students in mixed-ability groups.
- Provide participation roles such as timekeeper or note taker.
- Ask for written notes on a poster in a different color for each student.

EXCEPTIONALITIES

In your future classrooms you will teach students with unique needs, talents, and interests. One challenge you will face will be to differentiate the curriculum so that every child has opportunities to learn in an environment that is safe and least restrictive. What this means for you is to consider how you might make your daily instruction individualized for each of your students. You can manage this task for many of them, but you will also have students who will need to receive special services—or special education. These students are frequently referred to as "exceptional students," and teachers have a legal, and ethical, obligation to provide lessons to them that will promote maximum learning. Culatta and Tompkins (1999) developed this list of exceptionalities your future students may have: mental retardation; learning disabilities; behavioral or emotional disorders; communication disorders; physical and/or health impairments; hearing and/or vision impairments; severe or multiple disabilities; and giftedness.

Exceptional students may receive special services from an instructional assistant who attends classes with them, or from courses and programs that pull a student out of the general education classroom. When possible, however, exceptional students are kept in the general education classroom. This is known as the "inclusive model" because the general education classroom is a place that includes all students. It is easy to understand that many educators disagree about how to educate children with exceptionalities. Proponents of a fully inclusive model speak to the benefits that all students have when in a room with diverse learners. Students of all capabilities work together to help one another learn. The challenge for teachers is to provide opportunities for learning that account for the wide range of students. Opponents of inclusion suggest that placing students in programs separate from the general education classroom allows for more individualized instruction and learning; they argue that the burden on the classroom teacher will be too great if all students are placed together. The challenge for these "pullout" programs is to ensure that academic expectations remain high. Additionally, boys are identified as needing special services more than girls, as are students of color and students from homes that are disadvantaged economically. Whether these students should be taught separately, included in the general classroom, or taught with some combination of these two is a raging debate in the schools. In any case, you will need to consider how you will help students who have exceptionalities learn when they are in your classroom.

One of the most powerful tools that you will have as a teacher in an inclusive classroom will be your exceptional students' individualized educational plan, or IEP. When a public school child needs special services, an IEP must be designed. These are developed by the special education teachers/specialists in your school, with the help of parents, other teachers, school personnel, and, at times, the student. An IEP gives details about the educational supports and services that will help the child with a disability receive appropriate instruction. An IEP may specify instructional strategies, strategies for managing behavior, motivational techniques, and other insights about how to best help the student learn. Test scores, physician reports, and psychological, cognitive, and/or other medical reports might also be included. By contacting your special education expert(s) in the school you will have powerful strategies for meeting the needs of your exceptional students. New regulations emphasize that the IEP team must consider a student's strengths as well as areas of weakness when formulating an educational plan. An IEP is required by federal law whenever a student has a recognized disability. In 1997 the Individuals with Disabilities Act was passed into law, specifying disabilities and strengthening the expectations of learning for all students. Each state, or in some cases each county or each school, designs its own IEPs for its students with disabilities. Some students do not have disabilities that require special education services. They might not receive an IEP, but they could receive a 504 Plan, which is a program of instructional services for assisting special-needs students who are in a regular education setting. A student who has a physical or emotional disability, who has an impairment that restricts one or more major life activities (e.g., caring for oneself, performing manual tasks, walking, seeing, hearing, speaking, breathing, working, or learning), or who is recovering from a chemical dependency should receive a 504 Plan.

The instructional strategies that we will examine in Part II of this book can be adapted to meet the individual needs of students. They allow for all students to learn, whether they are considered general education students, students with learning disabilities, or gifted students.

GENDER CONSIDERATIONS

Teachers often communicate different expectations for male and for female students. Teachers often give male students more attention and provide them with more opportunities to share during class activities. Some studies conclude that teachers tend to praise boys for the intellectual contributions to class, and praise girls for their proper behavior in class (McCormick, 1994; Sadker & Sadker, 1982, 1994). As a result, teachers may reinforce societal norms about gender-biased behaviors that actually limit girls' academic performance and enhance boys' achievements. In recent years a series of programs have encouraged girls' participation in mathematics and science classes, and improvements in girls' performances in these areas are starting to be realized. Concern is now beginning to rise about the low number of male students who attend colleges, with some estimates suggesting that in the near future two female students will graduate from college for every male student. Suffice to say that gender differences exist, and you need to reflect on your interactions with students to ensure that gender bias is not affecting your students' opportunities to learn.

For years, reports have concluded that in early adolescence, girls' IQ scores drop and "their math and sciences scores plummet. They lose their resiliency and optimism and become less curious and inclined to take risks" (Pipher, 1994, p. 19). This could partly be on account of changes from the transition from elementary school to middle school, changes brought about by puberty, and/or increased awareness of peer and societal influences on their behavior. More recently, gaps between girls and boys are narrowing. Achievement in mathematics and the sciences are not as wide as they were even a decade ago. The emphasis on closing the gender gap seems to be having a positive effect, especially on girls. Boys are changing as well, repressing emotions and feelings and even using aggressive behavior in order to fit in with societal expectations (Sadker & Sadker, 1994; Sadker & Zittleman, 2012; Thorne, 1993). Boys in middle school and high school engage in more "at risk" behaviors (gang membership, drug use, physical daring, etc.) than girls. Boys tend to receive lower grades, and make up the majority of students referred for special education services. For example, 71% of students identified as learning disabled and 80% of those identified as emotionally disturbed were boys (Sadker & Sadker, 1994).

For these reasons and more it will be important for you to consider the role gender plays in your content area. Poetry is perceived by many high school students as being feminine even though famous poets throughout history have been men; mathematics is often perceived as being masculine even though women have made significant contributions to that discipline. Women's roles are often omitted from historical accounts; men's conquests dominate the conventional stories. Check your curriculum to identify if you are missing important opportunities for clarifying misrepresentations of women and men, or if you are under-representing the roles of women or men in the content your students are studying. When teaching, reflect on the nature of your interactions with students. If you teach in accord with the sample that McCormick examined in 1994, you will probably give boys five times more attention than girls. Work to provide gender equity in your classroom.

POVERTY IN SCHOOLS

According the United States Bureau of the Census, 37 million Americans are living in poverty. Of these, 13 million are under 18 years of age (http://www.census.gov/ hhes/www/ poverty/poverty.html). The socioeconomic status of your students is likely to impact their learning and the educational resources available to you. The National Commission on Teaching and America's Future has issued a report that supports over 20 years of research on poverty and schooling. The commission concludes that:

> children at risk, who come from families with poorer economic backgrounds, are not being given an opportunity to learn that is equal to that offered to children from the most privileged

families. The obvious cause of this inequality lies in the finding that the most disadvantaged children attend schools that do not have basic facilities and conditions conducive to providing them with a quality education.

(Carroll, Fulton, Abercrombie, & Yoon, 2004, p. 7)

Gorski (2005) follows up on this report, noting that:

schools with large percentages of low-income students are more likely than schools with large percentages of wealthy students to have an abundance of teachers unlicensed in the subjects they teach, serious teacher turnover problems, teacher vacancies and large numbers of substitute teachers, limited access to computers and the Internet, inadequate facilities (such as science labs), dirty or inoperative student bathrooms, evidence of vermin such as cockroaches and rats, and insufficient classroom materials.

(p. 3)

Many implications can be derived from these accounts. It is important to recognize the impact of poverty on schooling, in terms of both educational opportunities for your students and the support systems available to them outside school. You will want to consider whether your assignments and activities unfairly allow students with more resources to have an advantage over those with fewer. Teachers used to be discouraged from finding out the socioeconomic status of their students lest it bias them. Today, the thinking is that teachers must be aware of student differences so they can help each child uniquely. When you know students are living in poverty, you then check if you are assuming that all students come to school from the same background. Poverty is systemic, and it is difficult for schools and teachers to devise a list of strategies for overcoming it. The following list of topics related to poverty and wealth will help you think more broadly when you are planning your classroom activities. This is not an inclusive list, but a starting point for considering economic diversity in your classroom.

- Some students work for pleasure, some to help pay bills, and some will not work at all.
- The value of education varies dramatically in the homes of your students.
- Opportunities to travel, have access to materials and resources, and use the Internet outside school are correlated with higher economic status.
- Parent/guardian availability to help with students' schoolwork is widely varied.
- Some students have nutritious breakfasts and lunches, whereas others will eat little or eat poorly.
- Crime rates and other safety issues could impact students' opportunities to complete schoolwork.

Many ideas in the previous pages attempt to point out diversity in your future classrooms. As a social studies teacher, you will find that diversity is a wonderful attribute of a learning community that allows you to explore the richness of a democratic society. Students who are different from others in your classroom—maybe even different from you—bring assets and strengths with them. It is flawed for teachers to look at a student who is an ELL and focus only on the student's lack of English. This is "deficit thinking." Instead of focusing on the deficits, consider the assets, or strengths, that the student brings. Imagine the resiliency, the focus, the courage, and/or the motivation needed to go to a school that is taught in a language different from your primary language. This doesn't stop at language, but applies to any category where students may be different from the majority of the students in the class. A deficit-based way of thinking about your students could result in missed opportunities for differentiating learning, or building on the experiences and strengths the student brings besides language.[2]

MAKING IT WORK IN YOUR CLASSROOM

Think of three specific strategies that you might use in your future classroom, that will raise the status of students who are typically marginalized because of ethnicity, exceptionality, or gender. Consider the following examples to get you started thinking about this: If you will teach civics, then you could ask a female judge to be a guest speaker to talk about stereotypes about women. If you plan to teach U.S. history, you might select a story about the Buffalo Soldiers because African Americans are often underrepresented. If you plan to run a mock congress in your civics course, you might consider having students who are not in leadership roles at your school hold offices of class president or ambassador during the simulation.

CONTEXTS OF TEACHING IN A CHANGING AND TECHNOLOGICAL SOCIETY

You will find that in educational circles technology is defined in many different ways. Some, such as the Association for Educational Communications and Technology (AECT, 1994), define educational technology very broadly so that it includes procedures and resources for learning. This could involve the process one uses while including a tool for learning as itself a type of "technology." Others might define it almost exclusively as the use of resources as tools for learning. Tools might include many resources, from common pencils to sophisticated systems for interactive communication (e.g., laptop computers or cell phones). For the purposes of this text, the term *technology* will refer specifically to modern electronic resources found in classrooms that can be used for teaching and learning. Most often I will be referring to digitally oriented resources used by and found on computers.

The technology available has changed dramatically over the last 20 years. This is obvious to many of us, but to others who have grown up with the changes, it may have gone under-noticed. The frantic pace of technological change is an unremarkable way of life to many middle and high school students of today; these students have spent their entire lives learning new software, playing video games, updating their computer operating systems, and looking forward to the latest programs with state-of-the-art audio and graphics. Some have described these students as native speakers of the digital environment, or "digital natives." That, by extension, would make those not born into the digital world "digital immigrants"—those trying to grasp the myriad technological changes, those who tire of repeatedly learning new versions of software, those who speak with digital "accents," and those who, according to some, think differently (Owston, 1997; Prensky, 2001).

As long as we are considering this metaphor, it is important to note that some have purposefully decided to stay in the "old country" and not (or try not to) "immigrate" at all. These note how technology does not always have a positive impact on our society and, in fact, takes more than it gives (Oppenheimer, 1997; Postman, 1995). Just as it is important to consider ways to include ESL students while planning lessons, it is also important to consider ways to include the digital language of our students, as well as to take into account our own fluency in that language. Some teachers are naturally apprehensive about using the new language (a computer), whereas others do not realize that they are speaking with a "heavy accent" and that their students are the "native" speakers (i.e., highly skilled with computers). In addition, it is important to remember that asking your students to use technology implies that students will need access to computers and other electronic devices. Much has been written about the "digital divide," the socioeconomic gap between communities and people who have access to computer technology and those who do not. For example, if you assign students to access the Internet as part of a homework assignment, you are assuming that all students can do this outside school. If some can, and some cannot, then you are placing students who do not have access at a disadvantage. This is not equitable. Care needs to be taken when implementing student activities tied to technology.

Through the years, teachers and aspiring teachers share a common sentiment: Most teachers do not want to be "technologists." Teachers are less interested in learning about the gadgets than in learning how they can be used in a lesson. One of the most important things a person can discover about using technology for teaching and learning is that the focus in the classroom should be not on the technology, but on how it can be used to promote student learning. "Digital immigrants" can be a skeptical group because most of us have seen the well-meaning use technology in a manner that adds little value to a lesson or, worse, becomes a distraction. Adding technology has become the easy part of teaching, but not necessarily the best part. The question we ask ourselves should not be "How can I infuse technology into this lesson?" but instead "Can value be added to the lesson by using technology and, if it can, then how?"

As a student, you have likely seen technology used in well-thought-out, valuable ways. Some have argued that technology helps increase student motivation. Of course, any teacher would be interested in something that is motivating. Unfortunately, motivation due to the use of a new gadget is somewhat shallow and often expensive. On the other hand, motivation due to increased control of one's own learning is empowering, and technology can help facilitate this. However, this takes a rethinking of the way we teach, not simply the addition of more technology to our classes. Technology can also be used to promote, establish, and support dynamic instructional strategies that are designed to meet learning objectives. In fact, in a review of cases studies, the CEO Forum on Education and Technology (2001) concluded that technology has the greatest impact when it is integrated into the curriculum for the purpose of achieving clear, measurable educational objectives. In the chapters describing instructional strategies that follow in this book, you will read how technology could play an important role when using specific instructional strategies to help students learn.

MAKING IT WORK IN YOUR CLASSROOM

Think critically about the use of technology in a high school or middle school classroom you have visited recently, or taught in recently. What technology is to be used? Do you think the technology will help students learn the content more effectively? If so, why? If not, why did the teacher use technology and what could the teacher have done differently?

MOTIVATING STUDENTS TO LEARN
AND ITS RELATION TO PLANNING

Motivation might best be thought of as a force, or energizer, that helps us accomplish a task. Many things motivate us, and when we lack motivation we usually accomplish very little. Theories and research about motivation are expansive, so the purpose in this section is to focus on the most salient aspects so that you the teacher can consider how to best motivate your students. When you consider motivation while you are planning, and while you reflect "on," "in," and "for" action, you will have all the more insight into student learning.

Students will arrive in your classroom with different motivations. Some will have little interest or motivation to attend class, whereas others will have a high interest in learning social studies content. On more than one occasion I taught high school students who received money from their parents for the grades earned at school (e.g., $50 for an A, $40 for a B, etc.). At the same time, many students will be motivated to complete an assignment simply because they want it to be their best work. As we begin thinking about motivation, it would be interesting for you to consider what motivates you to do various tasks; even to read this book at this time. These are often called *motivating factors*. What factors in your life motivate you? A few might be personal satisfaction, a sense of accomplishment, financial rewards, increased status among peers, or pleasing an instructor/supervisor. The question of motivating factors leads us to consider two different forms of motivation: extrinsic motivation and intrinsic motivation.

Extrinsic motivation is motivation brought on by external factors we believe will provide desirable outcomes, such as praise, a reward, or even avoidance of negative consequences (Pintrich & Schunk, 2002). Extrinsic motivation is a means to an end; we are motivated to do something because the end result will be better. Teachers extrinsically motivate their students in a variety of ways: points for assignments, letter grades, praise for good behavior, assigning after-school detention for misbehavior, allowing free time if students all read silently for 30 minutes, or allowing students to revise their assignment for a higher score.

Intrinsic motivation refers to motivation to engage in an activity because of the satisfaction derived from the activity itself. Students who are intrinsically motivated view the learning process as valuable and genuinely want to understand the content. Teachers are able to encourage intrinsic motivation, though it is more challenging. Researchers suggest that the following types of activities tend to intrinsically motivate learners: challenging tasks that question existing understanding and create a sense of curiosity, tasks in which learners have some control over their own understanding, and tasks that evoke some aspect of our emotions (Lepper & Hoddell, 1989; Ryan & Deci, 2000).

Extrinsic and intrinsic motivation can both be used effectively in the classroom. Although it is important to realize that motivating one's students solely with extrinsic factors may promote learning for the sake of a reward (or for the sake of avoiding punishment), extrinsic motivation is not necessarily bad. For example, most people gain some motivation to go to work for the extrinsic reward of a paycheck. However, teachers need to consider how they might also provide opportunities to promote intrinsic motivation, whereby students want to learn because they genuinely enjoy the process. Researchers in this area are quick to remind us that motivation is neither intrinsic nor extrinsic exclusively (Pintrich & Schunk, 2002). A student might study so she can receive a good grade and be eligible to play on the basketball team (extrinsic) and at the same time study because the course content is genuinely interesting to her (intrinsic).

Although it is important to think about intrinsic and extrinsic factors, as a teacher it is equally important to consider what Brophy calls "motivation to learn" (1998). Brophy describes this as the "students' tendency to find academic activities meaningful and worthwhile and to try and get the intended learning benefits from them" (p. 162). Students who are motivated to learn may not have intrinsic motivation for all tasks, but they see the purpose and value of school. As a result, they are motivated to attend class, think about content, complete assignments, and engage in the activities because they believe that learning will be worthwhile. When you help your students understand how the content and activities are useful and beneficial you promote their motivation to learn. This might be accomplished by modeling to your students your interest in the content, and sharing how you motivate yourself to learn. Creating a classroom environment that exudes your enthusiasm for learning your subject, as well as your interest, care, and concern for your students' learning, will both help develop your students' motivation to learn.

"FLOW" EXPERIENCES AND MOTIVATION

An interesting approach for thinking about motivating students comes from a theory of intrinsic motivation called "flow" (Csikszentmihalyi, 1990, 1997). When someone is highly motivated from within, he is in a flow experience. This stems from a general belief that our abilities match the challenge of a task so well that we can simply enjoy the experience. During a flow experience we are unaware of time, because we are so involved and concentrated on a task that we are only aware of the present. Additionally, we have confidence in knowing what needs to be done and how to accomplish it. This engagement creates a sense of calm and reward of its own. Most of the people who theorize about flow suggest that people can learn how to create a flow experience. Figure 2.3 operates on two axes: one is the perceived challenge of a task; the other is a person's perception of their skill or ability to accomplish the task.

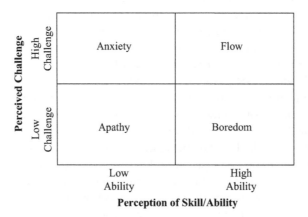

Figure 2.3   Intrinsic Motivation and "Flow."

Consider how this graph might help you understand motivation and, more important, help you provide appropriate motivating factors for your students. When we perceive that a task presents a low challenge, we will respond with either apathy or boredom, depending on our perception of our skill or ability. If we see ourselves as highly capable, an unchallenging task will bore us. If we see ourselves as having low ability, it will lead us to not care. In contrast, a task that is perceived as highly challenging will promote anxiety (if we do not perceive our abilities or skills as being capable of completing the task), or it will promote a flow experience if we perceive a match between our ability and the challenge (Csikszentmihalyi, 1990, 1997).

This can be directly applied to the middle school or high school classroom in several ways. Low-challenging tasks rarely serve to motivate students. Figure 2.3 outlines that students will feel varying degrees of apathy and boredom; therefore, one needs to consider how to challenge them. If the task is so challenging that the students believe it is beyond their ability level, then they may be so distressed that they cannot complete the task. Students also need help in their perceptions. Tasks may appear too difficult when focus is only on the final product. However, when the task is broken into smaller, sequential activities, it becomes more manageable. Likewise, students may at first perceive themselves as lacking sufficient skill for a task. Often with proper modeling or "scaffolding" the students learn that they do have the skills after all. Consider the following examples, and possible ideas for moving students closer to a flow experience.

- *Boredom:* A student who is an advanced reader may show little interest in reading a biography that is far below her reading level. She appears bored because the challenge is far below her ability. If the reading task is made more challenging, boredom will be less of a problem.
- *Anxiety:* A shy student may decide to skip class on the day he is scheduled to make a ten-minute presentation to the class, because the stress of standing in front and talking is too great. If the student is coached on how to present, given opportunities to practice, or even allowed to present privately on video, he may perceive his ability as more aligned with the task.
- *Apathy:* A student who speaks English as a second language may simply give up trying in an ancient civilization class if he cannot understand the first chapter of the textbook. He thinks that he will never be able to do well in the class, because he has such difficulty with the very first reading assignment. If the teacher expresses her own strategies for reading expository text (i.e., history textbooks), and some of the strategies that are suggested by those who study second-language acquisition, then she provides a model of how to work through problems. If the student is provided with opportunities to practice on specific areas and master those areas, he may see his skills improving.
- *Flow:* A low-achieving student who loves to work on the computer is able to provide technical support to her classmates as they develop their personal websites for a current event. Classmates' challenges become her opportunities to see how well she can solve problems, and it makes her happy when others begin to rely on her to help with the assignment.

You will not be able to motivate all of your students for every task, but if you think of their motivation in these terms it will help you focus your effort to help them.

SELF-EFFICACY AND LOCUS OF CONTROL

Self-efficacy is our expectation or belief about what we can accomplish as a result of our efforts. This in turn influences our willingness to attempt tasks, and what our expectations are (Dacey, Kenny, & Margolis, 2004, p. 173). Bandura has researched efficacy extensively, and his ideas can be directly applied to the expectations you might have for your future students:

> Self-efficacy beliefs determine how people feel, think, motivate themselves and behave . . . A strong sense of efficacy enhances human accomplishment and personal well-being in many ways. People with high assurance in their capabilities approach difficult tasks as challenges to be mastered rather than as threats to be avoided . . . In contrast, people who doubt their capabilities shy away from difficult tasks which they view as personal threats. They have low aspirations and weak commitment to the goals they choose to pursue. When faced with difficult tasks, they dwell on their personal deficiencies, on the obstacles they will encounter, and all kinds of adverse outcomes rather than concentrate on how to perform successfully.
>
> (Bandura, 1994, p. 71)

Self-efficacy is developed through a wide range of factors, including family, peers, cognitive ability, and previous experiences. As a teacher you can work to increase a sense of self-efficacy by planning to model successful strategies for students, providing opportunities for success, and helping your students develop strategies for overcoming obstacles. Similar to self-efficacy is the idea of *locus of control*. This is a concept that examines how much control people believe they have over events in their life. If you attribute success or failure to forces beyond your control (for example, you believe you were "just lucky" or you are "not sure why you failed"), you express an *external* locus (location) of control. If you attribute your behavior to forces you can control (for example, you "studied hard for the test" or "won because of practicing"), you have an *internal* locus of control. As a teacher, opportunities to help your students develop internal attributions will be beneficial, since control over their achievements/behavior will be from themselves and not from unpredictable outside forces.

MAKING IT WORK IN YOUR CLASSROOM

Partner with a classmate and generate examples of how students might behave in your classroom for each of the four student behaviors proposed on the intrinsic motivation and flow diagram (Figure 2.3). For example, how might a student be apathetic in a geography class, and how would he then behave? How might a student be anxious, bored, or in flow? For the three behaviors other than flow (apathy, anxiety, and boredom), come up with at least one approach through which you could modify either the student's perception of his skill, or the perception of the difficulty level of the task.

GUIDING PRINCIPLES FOR DEVELOPING A CLASSROOM LEARNING COMMUNITY

After many interviews with teachers (both pre-service and in-service), I have concluded that developing the class eco-system and student behavior are closely linked to the instructional strategy one is using, and therefore closely linked to planning and learning. Each instructional strategy has its own management concerns/issues; the chapters in Part II on instructional strategies specify how to best address the classroom while using a particular strategy, and how you might effectively discipline students during each strategy. Therefore, the chapters in Part II build on the management and discipline principles that will be examined in this section of Chapter 2. As I mentioned at the start of the chapter, management implies something the teacher does to his students; he manages them much the way a baseball manager does with players and coaches. While that is a term you will find often in the schools, push yourself to think about co-creating a learning environment where the students are not controlled or managed by you, but where they are part of a learning community alongside of you. This section provides some general terminology and overviews of key components for managing an effective learning environment.

One of the greatest worries in the minds of many student teachers has to do with management and discipline problems. Pre-service teachers often wonder if they will be able to maintain order, earn student respect, oversee group activities, or effectively handle all of the logistic and organizational tasks of the classroom. Also, specific questions arise from working with teachers, such as "Am I really not supposed to smile until December?" or "What should I do if a student says 'no' when I ask him to do something?" These are very real concerns. Many worries fade when you meet your students, but new concerns often arise. Effective teachers are able to manage the classroom and discipline students so that optimal learning can occur. In addition, teaching will be much more enjoyable for you when the classroom is a community of learners in which you and your students are comfortable.

DIFFERENCES BETWEEN MANAGEMENT AND DISCIPLINE

When preparing to help students learn, you will use a series of instructional strategies. While these strategies will help you determine appropriate ways to assess your students' learning, they will also provide guidance as you identify the activities students will engage in, select materials and resources that you and the students need, and consider the logistics of having the day's events work together to promote student learning. The best-planned lessons can be unsuccessful, however, if you do not think through how you will manage the learning environment, and if you are unable to effectively discipline students who are behaving inappropriately.

It is helpful to differentiate between classroom management and discipline as follows: *classroom management* is a proactive approach to helping students learn, and *discipline* is a reaction to student misbehavior. Classroom management addresses all of the aspects of the classroom that will promote student learning. You are overseeing all that happens in your classroom. Many educators refer to the classroom as a "community of learners" in which you and your students are committed to making the classroom environment a safe place where knowledge, skills, and dispositions are developed over the school year. As the adult leading that community, you need to ensure that students are supported, cared for, challenged, and meeting the learning outcomes for your course. Classroom management involves overseeing the classroom so this happens. *Discipline* specifically refers to how you can effectively direct students so their behaviors maintain the sense of community in your classroom. Part of discipline enables students to self-monitor their behaviors (so they literally become self-disciplined), but part of discipline involves the specific action that teachers take when a student disobeys a rule or fails to meet an expectation. Although teachers need to discipline students, many problems arise simply because the classroom is poorly managed.

Consider the following very real dilemma that a teacher might face: Students are seated in groups of four around the room. One group of students needs the teacher to help in understanding the assignment. A second group of students, on the opposite side of the classroom, is being disruptive and not working on the assignment. The teacher knows that her proximity has a significant impact on disruptive behavior; that is, when she is in close proximity to the disruptive group they quiet down and work. However, this keeps her away from the group of students needing her help. What could the teacher do to manage this situation? How could she address this proactively? What discipline issues are at work?

RELATIONAL TEACHING

Many conflicts and problems can be avoided if teachers try to build appropriate relationships with their students. The term I use for this is *relational teaching*. As the term implies, relational teaching places high value on the relationship the teacher has with the whole class as well as with each student. Rather than thinking of your students as a group of adolescents who come to your classroom, you think of them individually, with each possessing their own unique experiences, struggles, strengths, and weaknesses. During the school year you look for opportunities to build a teacher/student relationship with each member of your class. This takes time and effort, but it is surprising how quickly you can get to know your students. Benefits from a relational teaching approach include knowing how to assign students to groups because you know each student's strengths and weaknesses; understanding pressures and influences on a student that may affect their behavior in class; developing a sense of mutual respect; reducing "acting out" or misbehavior by students because they do not want to harm the relationship you have developed; and increasing interest in the development and learning of your students as you become more invested in their lives.

A wonderful example of relational teaching is seen in the work of Wolpow and his colleagues in their book *The Heart of Learning and Teaching: Compassion, Resiliency, and Academic Success* (2011).[3] Their book informs us of the enormous difficulties faced by youth exposed to traumatic events such as abuse, neglect, homelessness, and domestic violence. Students who have experienced traumatic conditions often have difficulties with learning, forming relationships, and being appropriate in school settings. This book provides guidance and background information about trauma and learning, self-care, classroom strategies, and building supportive partnerships. It contains vignettes and case studies to consider that will enhance your ability to help all students learn.

Relational teaching also has to do with developing what is often called "with-it-ness." When teachers are "with it" they are described as being keenly aware of all that is happening in the classroom. Sometimes it seems as though a "with it" teacher has eyes in the back of his head, or has an extraordinary sense of hearing and can hear comments whispered on the far side of the room, or is able to pre-empt a potential problem before it starts. A significant part of being so tuned in to your students that you are "with it" requires developing a positive rapport with them.

With a partner, consider how you might develop positive relationships with students in your future social studies classroom. What are some ideas for getting to know the interests of your students? As you talk about these ideas, check if you understand the idea of "with-it-ness." Have you observed teachers or coaches who are "with it?" What did they do?

APPROACHES TO CLASSROOM MANAGEMENT

Every teacher develops his own approach for developing a learning community in the classroom. A successful teacher will often claim that he does not have management or discipline problems, but when you watch him teach he is continually monitoring and interacting with students to ensure that they are acting pro-socially and adhering to classroom expectations. If a student begins to fall asleep, the successful teacher casually walks by and taps her on the shoulder. If two students are passing notes, the teacher does not draw attention to the behavior but simply continues talking while standing next to the two students. His proximity makes them put the notes away. If a challenging assignment is beginning on Monday, the successful teacher has anticipated student questions and is able to address most of them when the assignment is described. In this way students feel as though their ideas and worries are considered. In each of these situations the teacher manages the learning environment with an approach that works. In this section you will read about seven effective and long-standing approaches to classroom management. What you end up using will undoubtedly be a hybrid of these, but an initial examination of these seven will allow you to start thinking about effective management approaches.

Behaviorism

Remember that you read about this term earlier in the chapter when thinking about learning. Skinner did not describe an approach to classroom management, but the principles of behaviorism that he established provide some general ideas. The most useful principle for classroom management is *behavior modification*. Behavior modification operates on positive and negative behavior. True to the stimulus–response of behaviorism, a teacher notices a student behaving properly and acknowledges, praises, or in some way reinforces that behavior. The reinforced student, along with his classmates who witnessed the reinforcement, is likely to repeat this behavior and perceive it as beneficial. Students who are misbehaving are not acknowledged, and in an effort to earn praise also behave appropriately. Students receive external rewards for behaving appropriately; these often take the form of tokens or other tangible items. For example, a teacher might put a pencil in a mug whenever all of the students are sitting down before the bell rings to start the period. When the mug is full (about 15 pencils), the class receives a "free day" to learn about a topic of its choice, or even to have a pizza party. Rules are established and rewards are provided for following them.

Canter's Assertive Discipline Model

This model (Canter & Canter, 1976, 1992) provides a set of clear-cut expectations for the classroom. Students can expect teachers to provide a safe learning environment, and teachers can expect students to pay attention and not disrupt the class. The teacher establishes clear expectations, justifies why these expectations are needed, and lists the consequences for mis-behavior (not meeting expectations). Once established, the teacher expects adherence to the classroom rules. Students have the choice to behave in accord with the rules or to misbehave. Misbehavior is considered to be a poor choice, and the teacher must be assertive and follow through with the stated consequences. This will teach students to behave responsibly in the classroom. When helping students remember the expected behavior, the teacher should state the expectations to the student ("Chris, remember to bring your book to class"), or to praise a student in front of the class for behaving properly ("Chris remembered to raise his hand. Nice job!"). If a student perpetually misbehaves, then the teacher "moves in" close to the student, establishes eye contact, restates the expectations, and indicates the next consequences of continuing to misbehave.

The Dreikurs/Albert Model

Dreikurs (Dreikurs & Cassel, 1972) suggests that the classroom needs to be democratic, but his ideas became more applicable after Albert, Roy, and LePage (1989) refocused them spe-cifically to classroom management. This has implications for how the rules are decided and for the instructional strategies that are employed. Students impose limitations on themselves for the purpose of directing behavior so that it promotes learning. The teacher and students cooperate to determine classroom procedures, rules, and even the discipline for misbehavior. Democratic teaching is very different from "autocratic teaching" (in which the teacher is always in charge of the classroom policies and disciplining students, and students have no need to develop self-discipline), and it is different from "permissive teaching" (in which the teacher does not help enforce the classroom policies and students do not learn about responsibility, accountability, and self-discipline). The democratic teacher engages students in the process, and fosters a sense of self-discipline among the students. Students have goals that they strive to attain, one of which is a sense of belonging to the classroom community. If a student does not follow the class-developed rules, then authentic consequences result. Dreikurs suggests that misbehavior is the result of a student's seeking after one of four wrong goals: (1) getting attention; (2) seeking power; (3) getting revenge; or (4) withdrawing and not participating. As the teacher manages the classroom, she looks for students who are pursuing these wrong goals and then redirects them by enforcing the natural consequences of breaking rules.

Ginott's Model

This model is built around the key term of *congruent communication*, or communication that is about situations rather than student character or personality. In other words, instead of telling students that they are being rude by interrupting during a classroom discussion, the teacher might say, "This is a whole class discussion. We need to allow everyone a chance to express their ideas." Students' behavior, thus, is managed by addressing the situations that students are in and inviting students to cooperate. In the teacher's comment, the first sentence addresses the situation (a class discussion), and the second sentence asks for coop-eration (letting everyone speak). When the teacher does not attack a student's character or personality, the student may be more willing to discuss his feelings about a situation in the classroom. This open line of communication, along with the teacher modeling appropriate behavior, enables the teacher to change the attitudes and beliefs of students and not merely their behavior. This takes time, and depends on repeated opportunities to communicate with students. Ginott feels strongly about the powerful role that teachers play in students' lives, writing:

> I am the decisive element in the classroom. It is my personal approach that creates the climate . . . As a teacher I possess tremendous power to make a child's life miserable or joyous. I can be a tool of torture or an instrument of inspiration . . . in all situations it is my response that decides whether a crisis will be escalated or de-escalated, and a child humanized or de-humanized.
>
> (1972, p. 13)

As a result, Ginott suggests that communication without attacking the student's character will lead to a well-managed classroom.

Glasser's Model

According to this model (Glasser, 1992), the teacher expects all students to produce good-quality work. Teachers must lead students in learning activities that students and teachers agree are worthwhile and useful. This model suggests that students want basic needs met: survival, belonging, power, fun, and freedom. Survival is not always tied to the school (though it can be if the student feels unsafe), but the other four needs can be met at school. When these basic needs are not met, students are frustrated. When they are met, students are satisfied. If students' needs are not being met, the frustration leads to apathy, and the learning is seen as irrelevant. Teachers must manage the classroom to create an environment that has some fun, allows students a certain amount of power, has some degree of freedom, and helps students feel part of the classroom learning community. This can be partly accomplished when the teacher has high expectations for the quality of work, and provides opportunities to learn course content in depth. Students then need encouragement to determine their own paths for attaining this level of quality. The teacher's role is to encourage quality work by challenging students to solve problems, building relationships with students, and continually being available to help. This can be done individually or during class meetings where expectations for quality work are further refined.

Jones's Model

This model (Jones, 1987) differs from the others in its emphasis on nonverbal communication. The teacher's "body language, facial expressions, gestures, eye contact, and physical proximity" (Charles, 1996, p. 128) each send important messages to the students and help manage the learning environment. The messages from teachers to students about their behavior can be very powerfully sent without saying anything. Some teachers allude to this when they proclaim that when they simply give their students "the look," everyone knows it is time to behave. The importance of proximity is also highlighted by Jones. By simply standing near students who are misbehaving in some fashion, a teacher is able to quickly end the behavior without drawing a lot of attention to the situation. This model also suggests that teachers provide incentives for students that are genuine and will motivate all students in the class. Incentives such as extra credit will motivate select students, whereas an ice cream party will likely motivate all students. Tied to this is Jones's suggestion to follow "Grandma's Rule": First eat your vegetables, and then you can have your dessert. Translated to the classroom, teachers should remember that students should behave properly before receiving any rewards for their behavior. Teachers must not reward students based on students' promises to behave well.

Aside from nonverbal communication, Jones suggests that teachers should not spend too much time with any one student. Part of managing the classroom is to move around to all students. If a teacher spends too much time/attention on one student, the other students in the class are not monitored—for behavior or for understanding. Also, students need opportunities to work through academic problems without building dependency on the teacher to answer every question. Jones suggests that teachers should provide efficient help to students, and limit interaction to 20-second intervals. He suggests three steps: (1) acknowledge what the student has done correctly; (2) suggest what needs to be done next; and (3) leave the student to work on the details.

Kounin's Model

Kounin's (1977) ideas about classroom management center on teacher behaviors that engage students in the lessons. He suggests that misbehavior rarely occurs when students are actively learning. Kounin's principal concepts are succinctly described by C. M. Charles (1996, pp. 45–46):

- *The ripple effect:* This is a phenomenon in which the teacher's words or actions are directed at one student, but spread out and affect the behavior of other students. Similarly, if misbehavior is ignored by the teacher, the ripple effect could spread a belief that the teacher will not enforce certain rules.
- *With-it-ness:* As described earlier, this term refers to a teacher's knowing what is going on in the classroom at all times. Students do not think they can "get away" with anything if their teacher is "with it."
- *Momentum and smoothness:* Lessons need to keep moving by not spending too much time on details ("overdwelling"), having smooth transitions from one lesson to another, and varying class activities to keep students engaged.
- *Student accountability:* This term refers to the teacher's efforts to keep students alert and involved in the lessons. This may involve calling on students to answer questions, or other requests that require students to be attentive.
- *Overlapping:* This is Kounin's term for multitasking—the ability to attend to two or three tasks at the same time. For example, the teacher is able to write on the board while answering a question and redirecting a group of students working on a group project.
- *Satiation:* This means that students are done thinking about a topic, and that the teacher needs to change his approach. Satiation can be brought about by boredom, repetition, or frustration.

- *Valence and challenge arousal:* This is Kounin's term for how teachers might make activities more enjoyable/challenging. Variety of activities, teacher enthusiasm, and multimedia presentation are ways to keep students engaged (and not satiated).

CREATING THE LEARNING ENVIRONMENT

As mentioned earlier, exuding a sense of being "with it" and using your proximity to students for making your presence known will help a classroom environment. Establishing classroom rules and routines will also help you manage the learning environment. Rules might be established by students, the teacher, or both in concert together, but they need to be consistently adhered to by everyone in class. It is more effective to state your expectation in terms of what should be done, rather than what you do not want. For example, the rule "Do not be late to class" is not as effective as "Be ready to start class when the bell rings." Or the rule "Do not interrupt" is more clearly stated as "Let a classmate finish her thought before you talk." In work that I have done with teachers, it appears that fewer, more general rules and expectations are more effective than many specific rules. "Respect other's opinions" is vague, but it may be a better rule than ten specific rules about respect. If you are going to ensure that all students follow the rules, then you do not want to provide so many rules that they get in the way of your planning and instruction. In many ways the teacher who is effectively managing the classroom is like a good baseball umpire: Everyone knows he is there and is not afraid to enforce a rule, but he does not allow the rules to overshadow the game. In the case of the teacher, the rules do not overshadow the activities of the day. Similarly, the placement of tables, chairs, and students can help the management of the classroom. The classroom setup needs to vary depending on the instructional strategies you use. For example, you might have students in neat rows during a lecture, but they will need to be sitting in circles during a group project. More specific examples for each instructional strategy are examined later in this book.

Effective teachers also establish classroom routines that help address questions such as when to turn in homework, when to raise hands, what is expected when the bell rings at the start or end of the period, what the procedure is if someone needs to leave class, where class announcements will be posted, or what materials are needed for class (e.g., textbook, binder, pencil). When clear routines are established, students are able to focus more on the learning and less on the logistics.

MAKING IT WORK IN YOUR CLASSROOM

To put some of these theories into practice, try completing three tasks.

First, consider how "daily life" in your classroom might operate; examine what you will do regarding classroom management. What routines will you use (e.g., beginning/ending class, homework collection/return, bathroom passes)? What will your policy be about late work? How will you determine seating assignments and desk arrangements?

Second, create an introductory assignment or student-interest survey that you might use to get to know more about your students. Be creative in what you ask of students; try to find out information that will assist your management of the classroom and give insight into their lives that will help you be a more effective teacher. Contextualize this by identifying a specific social studies course (e.g., world history, U.S. history, ancient civilizations).

Third, and with the specific social studies course in mind, generate a one-page hand-out that you might give to your students that articulates your classroom guidelines and/or expectations. These can be developed by taking "bits and pieces" from the management theories presented on the previous pages. Keep in mind the following:

- Strive for a suitable level of generality.
- State your guidelines positively (say what you expect them to do) and clearly.
- Specify your expectations about students' behavior, respect for property, respect for others, academic achievement, safety, and other elements you think are important.
- List the positive and negative consequences of not adhering to your guidelines.

CHAPTER REVIEW

- Adolescent development and its implications on learning and teaching
    - Adolescents' bodies are changing rapidly
    - Cognitive development advances: thinking skills develop
    - Social development advances: Adolescents learn how to interact with the world around them
- General theories and ideas about learning
    - Learning defined: "relatively permanent change, due to experience, either in behavior or in mental representations or associations" (Ormrod, 2006, p. 184)
    - There are many theories about learning (e.g., Gardner, Piaget, Vygotsky, etc.)
- Motivating students
    - Motivation: a force, or energizer, that helps us accomplish a task
    - Intrinsic motivation: motivation to engage in an activity because of the satisfaction derived from the activity itself ("flow" theory)
    - Extrinsic motivation: motivation to do something by outside, or external, factors that we believe will provide desirable results
    - Self-efficacy: self-expectations or beliefs about what we can accomplish as a result of our efforts (concept of "locus of control")
- Diverse characteristics and needs of adolescents
    - Classrooms will have students with different cultures, ethnicities, primary languages, economic backgrounds, religions, family structures, physical abilities, and learning abilities
    - Multicultural education: emerging discipline whose major aim is to create equal educational opportunities for students from diverse groups
    - "Exceptional students": those who have disabilities, impairments, giftedness or disorders
        - "Exceptional students" are required to have an Individualized Educational Program (IEP) or a 504 Plan
        - When possible, they are kept in general education classrooms
    - Number of ESL students has increased dramatically
        - Learning of social language in the classroom
    - Reinforcement of gender bias in the classroom: Males tend to receive more attention than females

- The role of appropriate technology for helping students learn
  - Focus in the classroom should not be on the technology but on how it can be used to achieve something meaningful; to promote student learning
  - Be mindful of finding ways to include ESL students
- Classroom management, and creating a learning environment/eco-system
  - Management: proactive approach to helping students learn, and discipline is a reaction to student misbehavior
  - Discipline: how you effectively control students so their behaviors maintain the sense of community in your classroom.
  - Establishing classroom rules and routines helps you manage the learning environment
  - Theorists each have a different perspective that will help in the classroom

NOTES

1. Dweck, C. (2007) and S. Warren, personal communication, June 11, 2014.
2. In 2011, Laura Roy and Kevin Roxas contextualized these ideas in an excellent article: Whose deficit is this anyhow? Exploring counter-stories of Somali Bantu refugees' experiences in "doing school," *Harvard Educational Review*.
3. This book is available as a free download through the State of Washington's Superintendent of Public Instruction at the following site: http://www.k12.wa.us/compassionateschools/pubdocs/TheHeartof LearningandTeaching.pdf.

REFERENCES

Albert, L., Roy, W., & LePage, A. (1989). *A Teacher's Guide to Cooperative Discipline: How to Manage your Classroom and Promote Self-esteem.* Circle Pines, MN: American Guidance Service.

Association for Educational Communications and Technology (AECT) (1994). *Instructional Technology: The Definition and Domains of the Field.* Bloomington, IN: AECT.

Bandura, A. (1994). Self-efficacy. In V. S. Ramachaudran (Ed.), *Encyclopedia of Human Behavior* (Vol. 4, pp. 71–81). New York: Academic Press. (Reprinted in H. Friedman [Ed.], *Encyclopedia of Mental Health.* San Diego, CA: Academic Press, 1998.)

Banks, J. A. & Banks, C. M. (Eds.) (1995). *Handbook of Research on Multicultural Education.* New York: Macmillan.

Beamon, G. W. (2001). *Teaching with Adolescent Learning in Mind.* Glenview, IL: Skylight Professional Development.

Bransford, J. D., Brown, A. L., & Cocking, R. R. (Eds.) (2000). *How People Learn: Brain, Mind, Experience and School.* Washington, DC: National Academy Press.

Brophy, J. (1998). *Motivating Students to Learn.* Boston, MA: McGraw Hill.

Canter, L. & Canter, M. (1992). *Assertive Discipline: Positive Behavior Management for Today's Classroom.* Santa Monica, CA: Canter and Associates.

Canter, L. & Canter, M. (1976). *Assertive Discipline: A Takecharge Approach for Today's Educator.* Seal Beach, CA: Canter and Associates.

Carroll, T. G., Fulton, K., Abercrombie, K., & Yoon, I. (2004). *Fifty Years after Brown v. Board of Education: A Two-tiered Education System.* Washington, DC: National Commission on Teaching and America's Future.

CEO Forum on Education and Technology (2001, June). *The CEO Forum school technology and readiness report: Key building blocks for student achievement in the 21st century.* Retrieved October 21, 2009, from http://www.ceoforum.org/.

Charles, C. M. (1996). *Building Classroom Discipline* (5th ed.). New York: Longman.

Csikszentmihalyi, M. (1997). *Finding Flow: The Psychology of Engagement with Everyday Life.* New York: Basic Books.

Csikszentmihalyi, M. (1990). *Flow: The Psychology of Optimal Experience.* New York: Harper & Row.

Culatta, R. & Tompkins, J. (1999). *Fundamentals of Special Education: What Every Teacher Needs to Know.* Upper Saddle River, NJ: Prentice-Hall.

Cummins, J. (1979). Cognitive/academic language proficiency, linguistic interdependence, the optimum age question and some other matters. *Working Papers on Bilingualism, 19,* 121–129.

Dacey, J., Kenny, M., & Margolis, D. (2004). *Adolescent Development,* 3rd ed. Carrollton, TX: Alliance Press.

Doda, G. and McEwin, K. (1987). 10 current truths about effective schools. *Middle School Journal, 18*(3), 3–5.

Dreikurs, R. & Cassel, P. (1972). *Discipline Without Tears.* New York: Hawthorn Books.

Dweck, C. S. (2007). *Mindset: The New Psychology of Success.* New York: Random House.

Elkind, D. (1998). *All Grown Up and No Place to Go: Teenagers in Crisis.* Reading, MA: Perseus Books.

Erikson, E. (1968). *Identity: Youth and Crisis.* New York: Norton.

Erikson, E. (1959). Identity and the life cycle. *Psychological Issues,* 1, 1–171.

Freire, P. (1978) *Pedagogy of the Oppressed.* New York: Continuum.

Gardner, H. (2003). 20 years of multiple intelligences: Reflections and a blueprint for the future. Keynote address made to the general membership of the American Educational Research Association, April, 2003, Chicago, IL.

Gardner, H. (1999). *Intelligence Reframed. Multiple Intelligences for the 21st Century.* New York: Basic Books.

Gardner, H. (1983; 1993). *Frames of Mind: The Theory of Multiple Intelligences.* New York: Basic Books.

Glasser, W. (1992). *The Quality School: Managing Students Without Coercion,* 2nd ed. New York: Harper and Row.

Gorski, P. (2005). Savage unrealities: Uncovering classism in Ruby Payne's framework. Retrieved April 4, 2006 from http://www.edchange.org/publications/Savage_Unrealities.pdf.

Hall, T., Strangman, N., & Meyer, A. (2003). *Differentiated Instruction and Implications for UDL Implementation.* Wakefield, MA: National Center on Accessing the General Curriculum. Retrieved June, 2010, from http://www.cast.org/publications/ncac/ncac_diffinstructudl.html.

Jones, F. H. (1987). *Positive Classroom Instruction.* New York: McGraw Hill.

Kounin, J. (1977). *Discipline and Group Management in Classrooms.* New York: Holt, Rinehart, and Winston.

Ladson-Billings, G. (1995). But that's just good teaching! The case for culturally relevant pedagogy. *Theory into Practice, 34*(3), 159–165.

Lepper, M. R. & Hoddell, M. (1989). Intrinsic motivation in the classroom. In C. Ames & R. Ames (Eds.), *Research on Motivation in Education: Vol. 3. Goals and Cognitions* (pp. 73–105). San Diego, CA: Academic Press.

Litzinger, M. E. & Osif, B. (1993). Accommodating diverse learning styles: Designing instruction for electronic information sources. In L. Shirato (Ed.), *What is Good Instruction Now? Library Instruction for the 90s* (pp. 73–82). Ann Arbor, MI: Pierian Press.

Lortie, D. (1975). *Schoolteacher: A Sociological Study.* Chicago, IL: University of Chicago Press.

McCormick, T. M. (1994). *Creating the Nonsexist Classroom: A Multicultural Approach.* New York: Teachers College Press.

Nieto, S. (1996). *Affirming Diversity: The Sociopolitical Context of Multicultural Education,* 2nd ed. White Plains, NY: Longman.

Oppenheimer, T. (1997). The computer delusion. *Atlantic Monthly, 280*(1), 45–48,50–56,61–62.

Ormrod, J. E. (2006). *Essentials of Educational Psychology*. Upper Saddle River, NJ: Prentice-Hall.

Owston, R. D. (1997) The World Wide Web: A technology to enhance teaching and learning. *Educational Researcher, 26*(2), 27–33.

Padron, Y. N., Waxman, H. C., & Rivera, H. H. (2002). *Educating Hispanic Students: Effective Instructional Practices* (Practitioner Brief #5). Available at: http://www.cal.org/crede/Pubs/PracBrief5.htm.

Piaget J. (1970). Piaget's theory. In P. H. Mussen (Ed.), *Carmichael's Manual of Psychology* (pp. 703–732). New York: Wiley.

Pintrich, P. R. & Schunk, D. H. (2002). *Motivation in Education: Theory, Research, and Applications,* 2nd ed. Upper Saddle River, NJ: Prentice-Hall.

Pipher, M. (1994). *Reviving Ophelia*. New York: Ballantine Books.

Postman, N. (1995). *The End of Education: Redefining the Value of School*. Westminster, MD: Random House.

Prensky, M. (2001). Digital natives, digital immigrants. *On the Horizon, 9*(5), 1–6.

Roy, L. & Roxas, K. (2011). Whose deficit is this anyhow? Exploring counter-stories of Somali Bantu refugees' experience in doing school. *Harvard Educational Review, 81(3),* 521–541.

Ryan, R. M. & Deci, E. L. (2000). Self-determination theory and the facilitation of intrinsic motivation, social development and well-being. *American Psychologist, 55,* 68–78.

Sadker, D. & Zittleman, K. R. (2012). *Teachers, Schools, and Society: A Brief Introduction to Education* (3rd ed.). New York: McGraw Hill.

Sadker, M. & Sadker, D. (1994). *Failing at Fairness: How America's Schools Shortchange Girls*. New York: Charles Scribner's Sons.

Sadker, M. & Sadker, D. (1982). *Sex Equity Handbook for Schools*. New York: Longman, Inc.

Skinner, B. F. (1953). *The Possibility of a Science of Human Behavior*. New York: The Free House.

Thomas, W. P. & Collier, V. P. (1997). *School Effectiveness for Language Minority Students*. Washington, DC: National Clearinghouse for Bilingual Education.

Thorne, B. (1993). *Gender Play: Girls and Boys in School*. New Brunswick, NJ: Rutgers University Press.

Tomlinson, C. A. (2004). *How to Differentiate Instruction in Mixed-ability Classrooms* (2nd ed.). Upper Saddle River, NJ: Prentice-Hall.

Vygotsky, L.S. (1978). *Mind and Society: The Development of Higher Mental Processes*. Cambridge, MA: Harvard University Press.

Wolpow R., Johnson, M. M., Hertel R., & Kincaid S. (2011). *The Heart of Learning and Teaching: Compassion, Resilience, and Academic Success*. Available at: http://www.k12.wa.us/CompassionateSchools/pubdocs/TheHeartofLearningandTeaching.pdf.

Zwiers, J. (2008). *Building Academic Language: Essential Practices for Content Classrooms*. San Francisco, CA: Jossey-Bass.

CHAPTER 3

Preparing Learning Targets and Assessing Student Learning

CHAPTER GOALS

In this chapter, you will learn about:

- Long- and short-term learning targets
- Different domains of learning
- Assessing student learning, and the specific importance of formative assessment.

Learning targets and assessments provide specific details for meeting the goals of a lesson or unit. When you write targets, you provide a focus for the lesson and unit, and you determine how you will assess students' learning. But that is only part of the purpose. Your students must know how they will be assessed in your social studies classroom before a lesson or unit even begins. This idea is often referred to as a "backward design model," because the teacher designs lessons with the end goal or assessments in mind. Wiggins and McTighe (2000) describe backward design as follows: "One starts with the end—the desired results—and then derives the curriculum from the evidence of learning called for by the standard (learning target) and the teaching needed to equip students to perform" (p. 8). Thus, targets and assessment are closely connected, and this is why we will examine them together in the chapter. This chapter establishes background information for Part II of this book, where seven instructional strategies are examined. Suggestions for learning targets and appropriate assessments for each strategy are provided so the ideas presented in Chapter 3 can be richly contextualized. You may want to revisit this chapter as you read chapters in Part II.

THE PURPOSE OF LEARNING TARGETS

Before teaching a lesson, you will want to write out learning targets; these help teachers answer three basic questions related to teaching and student learning:

1. What social studies content do students need to learn?
2. How will student learning be assessed?
3. What activities will students engage in to promote learning?

A concise examination of these three areas helps clarify the content and purpose of learning targets.[1]

What Social Studies Content Do Students Need to Learn?

As you read in Chapter 1, you will likely have a social studies textbook for your future classroom, your state will have social studies curriculum guides, and your future district/school curriculum plans for social studies will provide direction about what to teach. But you will still be left with the freedom to decide how to best help students learn social studies knowledge and skills in your classroom on a day-to-day basis. Consider the following example: If you are going to be teaching world history in a high school, you will likely have district goals that are based on local, state, and national standards for history along with Common Core State Standards for English and history, and the college, career, and civic life frameworks (we explored these in Chapter 1). In addition, you will usually have a district-adopted world history textbook and curriculum suggestions. Before the school year starts, you need to consider each of these content recommendations, and then determine the most effective way to help your students learn. That is a lot of input about social studies content. You will have help and guidance from the middle school or high school, however. You will not likely be determining this on your own, but with your fellow social studies teachers at the school. You will want to agree with the decisions, however, and believe that students will learn important content. Learning targets help you narrow down the content so you can promote student learning. The number of targets you have for each day is determined by the complexity of the content your students are learning.

How Will Student Learning Be Assessed?

The second component of a target helps you determine whether students have learned the content during the activity. It is this area that serves as an assessment of student learning, and helps you know if your students have met the target. By connecting assessments with targets, you ensure that they coincide with the content to be learned and the activities planned for the class session. Assessments need to be observable, but they do not always need to be graded or quantified into points. Learning is assessed using a variety of approaches. For example, you might have a student present her results from an Internet search about the civil rights activist Rosa Parks, take a quiz about keys events of the "civil rights era," or write a book report on Malcolm X. As the teacher, you determine how well students need to perform on the assessment in order for you to feel confident that they have learned. A score of 100% on a review quiz might be your minimum achievement expectation, because the students have already used the words before. A book report on Susan B. Anthony that identifies a central theme of her activism might be what students produce to show they have learned about this historical figure. Therefore, the target and the assessment have two components related to

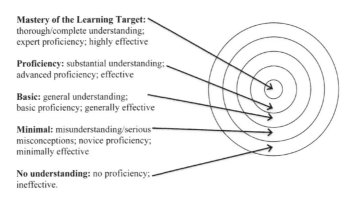

Figure 3.1 Learning Target Metaphor.

Source: Moss and Brookhart, 2012, p. 47

learning: (1) a statement of the content to be learned (e.g., civil rights activists in the 1960s took great personal risks) and (2) the criteria for what they need to do, and how well, for you to determine they have learned (e.g., describe an example of an activist being willing to take a risk that could have been physically traumatizing. Many have called this a "performance expectation," or "student success criteria" (Moss & Brookhart, 2012).

The metaphor of a target is helpful when thinking about learning and when planning how to assess students' learning. Consider the following from Moss and Brookhart:

Daily learning targets are lesson-sized observable and measurable statements of students' learning. The performance expectation, or success criteria, is a concise statement that students and teachers can refer to in order to assess learning. Typically, we don't tell students much about our expectations for their learning. Said another way, teachers need to tell students the criteria for being a successful learner. Learning targets and student success criteria provide both. Since teachers share this with their students, many find using the sentence starter of "I can . . ." helpful. Consider the following learning target and success criteria: "I can describe two examples of revolutions that were started by a small number of activists" or, "I can give examples of socialism in the world today, and non-examples of socialism." Consider a lesson you just watched or taught. What was a learning target for that lesson? Try to write it using the "I can" model describe above.

What Activities Will Students Engage in to Promote Learning?

Once the content and assessments have been determined, you will need to select learning activities for your students. These activities may last 15 minutes (for example, a brief introduction to the day's topic, or a review of previous content), or they may last several days (for example, a research project on the North American Free Trade Agreement (NAFTA) using online resources). Sequentially, the activities derive from the content you want students to learn, and the activities prepare students to demonstrate their understanding when they are assessed. An old adage among teachers is to change the activity every 20 minutes so that students stay engaged. Although changing an activity every 20 minutes is not required, it is important that you observe students to be sure they are engaged during any activity. Generally speaking, when students learn more difficult content and engage in more cognitively demanding tasks, the activity requires more time. For example, a ten-item quiz about the Bill of Rights likely requires less time than a research activity on freedom of speech (from the First Amendment). Often you may find that an activity lasts more or less time than you planned. By reflecting on this you will become more skilled at determining how long an activity will need to last so that all of your students may learn the material. Targets specify the content that the students will learn during a particular activity.

It is important at this point to introduce the idea of "student-centered" learning. Student-centered learning and teaching implies that the best starting point for school is a student's genuine interest areas. For student-centered social studies this means investigating students' questions as you work with them to learn the social studies content. Student-centered learning and teaching also means that learning is active and hands-on, and authentic in terms of how they might use social studies content and skills outside of the classroom. Textbooks and memorization activities water down complex ideas in the social studies. Complex ideas are ones that are public issues that citizens struggle with understanding and responding. These types of issues are challenging but also engaging, and set the stage for student-centered learning (Zemelman, Daniels, & Hyde, 2012).[2] Imagine you are teaching a ninth grade world geography course (if you prefer to imagine teaching another social studies course, be sure to specify grade level and course title). What would you anticipate will be students' genuine interests? For example, would ideas around sustainability be of interest? Would they be interested in the impact of physical features (mountains, rivers, canyons, etc.) on culture and society? Would they be interested in how borders are drawn between countries and states? Then, as a reality check, interview several ninth graders to hear what they hope they will learn in a world geography course and see how close you came. A student-centered geography course would incorporate these interests into the curriculum.

LONG-TERM AND SHORT-TERM TARGETS AND GOALS

You may recall from Chapter 1 that goals provide the general direction for a course. Simply said, they are what you hope your students will learn and accomplish over time. Targets specify how and when you can help students meet those goals. A social studies teacher might have as a goal: *Students will appreciate the personal sacrifices of civil rights leaders.* This does not specify how they will learn about the sacrifices, how they will develop an appreciation for the sacrifices, or how to determine if students meet this goal. These specifics come from the targets. Targets can be long-term or short-term. *Long-term targets* will be accomplished during a longer unit, a semester, or even an entire course. Targets that are met during an activity or after a few class sessions are *short-term targets*. These labels are not critical, except to help you understand that long-term and short-term targets provide a sequential approach to meeting your goals. The inverted triangle diagram (Figure 3.2) shows the relationship and level of specificity regarding goals and targets.

Consider again the goal stated earlier: *Students will appreciate the personal sacrifices of civil rights leaders.* Long-term targets could be:

- After learning U.S. history from 1950 to 1980, students will be able to list two sacrifices that a leader made for the cause of civil rights.
- Students will show how they have benefited from the sacrifices of civil rights leaders by stating at least one area in which their life is better now than it would have been in 1960.

Short-term targets could be:

- I can write a three-page biography on Rosa Parks that describes three sacrifices she made during her involvement in civil rights movements.
- I can share with my group at least one hardship that faced Martin Luther King, Jr. and his family as a result of his involvement in civil rights protests during the 1960s.

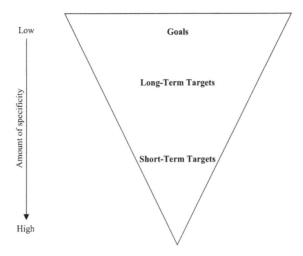

Figure 3.2 Inverted Triangle of the Relationships of Goals and Targets.

Long-term and short-term targets will need to be restated or revised if students need repeated assistance learning a skill or understanding a concept. For example, adolescents have difficulty criticizing ideas, and not people, during discussions about controversial issues. A target for developing this skill could be: *I will respect classmates' human dignity during the discussion by critiquing ideas, not the person bringing forth the ideas.*

This is certainly attainable as a short-term target, but it is a skill that students will need to practice continually. Therefore, you could restate this target whenever you plan to have classroom discussions.

MAKING IT WORK IN YOUR CLASSROOM

Think of a goal that would be appropriate for a course on ancient cultures (usually, grade 6 or 7). In Chapter 1 we described the use of social studies standards at the national and state levels, so it may be helpful to refer to those again to help you determine an appropriate ancient cultures goal. Next, devise at least one long-term and one short-term target for this goal. Refer to the examples on page 70 on civil rights as a guide for the level of specificity for these two types of targets. Be sure that the targets have a student success criteria so that you can be sure to help your students meet the target during the lesson and/or unit.

DOMAINS OF LEARNING

Bloom (1956) and Krathwohl, Bloom, and Masia (1964) have suggested that educators should categorize learning targets to help focus instruction on specific areas, or *domains*, of learning. This type of focus helps teachers select the content students should learn, and activities that will promote student learning. Two domains are generally considered by social studies teachers when writing learning targets:

• the cognitive domain
• the affective domain.

These two domains provide hierarchies for learning. They move from the less complex (targets typically easier to attain by your students) to the very complex (targets more difficult to attain at first). As a teacher, you will write less complex targets, but you should continually consider how you might progress to a higher level on each of these domain hierarchies. Bloom and his colleagues developed in-depth taxonomies for the cognitive and affective domains. Consider the following descriptions for each of these domains.

Cognitive Domain

The *cognitive domain* addresses the thinking skills and academic content to be learned in the classroom. Of the two domains, this is the one that is most common, most easily assessed, and the focus of most educational reforms. When you hear about "getting back to basics," "academic learning," or "concepts and skills," it is usually referring to the cognitive domain. Cognitive targets are synonymous with research done by Benjamin Bloom in 1956. His six-level taxonomy classified the types of questions that teachers pose to their students, and the type of thinking that is required when answering these questions. Today, Bloom is used for more than categorizing questions. His taxonomy helps evaluate the cognitive tasks in which students engage. Commonly used terms such as "higher-level thinking," or "higher-order thinking skills" (HOTS) have their roots in Bloom's Taxonomy. The base level of the taxonomy is called "knowledge," and the pinnacle of the taxonomy is the level called "evaluation." As students move in the taxonomy from knowledge to evaluation, the types of questions, activities, and cognitive tasks they engage with are more difficult and require different understandings of course content. The following outline provides a sample question and brief description for each of the six levels of Bloom's Taxonomy (Biehler, 1971; Bloom, 1956):[3]

1. Knowledge

Can students recall information?
The issue is recall of information. At this level, it is important that students remember what they have read, were told, or saw.

2. Comprehension

Can students explain ideas?
The target at this level is to ensure that students can explain ideas.

3. Application

Can students use ideas?
Targets developed at the application level have as their purpose something practical—use.

4. Analysis

Can students see relationships?
Targets written at the analysis level are designed to enable students to see relationships, make comparisons and contrasts, and look for patterns.

5. Synthesis

Can students combine ideas?
Synthesis represents a pulling together or combining of elements.

6. Evaluation

Can students make judgments?
Targets for the evaluation level include those encouraging students to take their own points of view or to express their ideas on issues.

During the 1990s a group of cognitive psychologists revised Bloom's Taxonomy and its use has also become widespread. You probably will come across both versions and, since this is a foundational taxonomy in the field of education, should be familiar with both. Briefly, the later version is:

1. *Remembering:* Can the student recall or remember the information? This level is crucial because students who do not possess basic knowledge cannot carry out meaningful analyses of language issues, or exercise any disciplined creativity. This is the "starting point."
2. *Understanding:* Can the student explain ideas or concepts? It is one thing, for example, to be able to identify different regions of the world (remembering) and another to be able to explain (understand) their various influence in international relations.
3. *Applying:* Can the student use the information in a new way? The issue at this level is whether students can use skills, concepts, and information in new situations. For example, in history, one needs to know how to remember events in time sequence to understand concepts, and to apply these ideas appropriately in an essay or story.
4. *Analyzing:* Can the student distinguish between the different parts? Analyzing, as the term implies, is an attempt to break down whole entities into their component parts. For example, in the study of advertising and other persuasive techniques, students will identify appeals made to status, power, group affiliation, and gender.
5. *Evaluating:* Can the student justify a stand or decision? At the evaluation level, divergent thinking is encouraged and differences of opinion are to be expected. Students make judgments and determine "best options" based on their evaluations of all information and factors. A class debate or papers including students' individual opinions or judgments are examples of evaluating.
6. *Creating:* Can the student create a new product or point of view? As a creating-level target, you might ask students to develop and record the various arguments for and against a controversial issue. Or, having taught your students the mechanics of letter writing, you ask them to create/write a letter using the fundamentals they have learned.

A site from Iowa State University offers an excellent visual to see the revised Bloom's Taxonomy and examples of targets/objectives for each level: http://www.celt.iastate.edu/teaching/RevisedBlooms1.html. These targets include the action students will carry out to facilitate their achievement of particular content/information. Figure 3.3 compares the two taxonomies.

	Evaluation Synthesis Analysis Application Comprehension Knowledge		Creating Evaluating Analyzing Applying Understanding Remembering
	Original Version		Revised Version

Figure 3.3   Updating Bloom's Taxonomy.

Knowledge	Comprehension	Application	Analysis	Synthesis	Evaluation
Cite	Arrange	Adapt	Analyze	Arrange	Appraise
Choose	Associate	Apply	Appraise	Assemble	Approve
Define	Clarify	Catalogue	Audit	Build	Assess
Label	Classify	Chart	Break	Combine	Choose
List	Convert	Compute	Calculate	Compile	Conclude
Locate	Describe	Consolidate	Categorize	Compose	Confirm
Match	Diagram	Demonstrate	Certify	Conceive	Criticize
Name	Draw	Develop	Compare	Construct	Critique
Recall	Discuss	Employ	Contrast	Create	Diagnose
Recognize	Estimate	Extend	Correlate	Design	Evaluate
Record	Explain	Extrapolate	Criticize	Devise	Judge
Repeat	Express	Generalize	Deduce	Discover	Justify
Select	Identify	Illustrate	Defend	Draft	Prioritize
State	Locate	Infer	Detect	Formulate	Prove
Write	Outline	Interpolate	Diagram	Generate	Rank
	Paraphrase	Interpret	Differentiate	Integrate	Rate
	Report	Manipulate	Discriminate	Make	Recommend
	Restate	Modify	Distinguish	Manage	Research
	Review	Order	Examine	Organize	Resolve
	Sort	Predict	Infer	Plan	Revise
	Summarize	Prepare	Inspect	Predict	Rule on
	Transfer	Produce	Investigate	Prepare	Select
	Translate	Relate	Question	Propose	Support
		Sketch	Reason	Reorder	Validate
		Submit	Separate	Reorganize	
		Tabulate	Solve	Set up	
		Transcribe	Survey	Structure	
		Use	Test	Synthesize	
		Utilize	Uncover		
			Verify		

Figure 3.4   Verbs to Help Identify Student Behaviors at Each Level of Bloom's Original Cognitive Taxonomy.

Adapted from work by Kathy V. Waller, PhD, CLS(NCA), National Accrediting Agency for Clinical Laboratory Sciences (NAACLS) Board of Directors. http://www.naacls.org/docs/announcement/writing-targets.pdf (accessed November 2004).

Affective Domain

The *affective domain* refers to learning that is tied to feelings or emotions. Learning in this domain does not require students to develop particular feelings or emotions, but it helps students use their emotions and feelings to learn. Whereas Bloom is usually associated with the cognitive domain, Krathwohl is most often associated with the affective domain (Krathwohl, Bloom, & Masia, 1964). Krathwohl suggests that attitudes, beliefs, and value systems should be identified so that children can learn about them and with them in a cohesive manner. Below is a summary of the affective domain, and examples of activities students may undertake in a classroom.

Receiving

Targets written at the receiving level are aimed at helping students become aware of or sensitive to the existence of certain ideas, material, or phenomena. Students engage in such actions as looking, asking, accepting, listening, and noticing.

Responding

Responding involves some degree of interaction or involvement with the ideas, materials, or phenomena being learned in class. The interactions promote greater awareness and appreciation than simply "being aware" or receiving the content. Examples include complying, discussing, and supporting.

Valuing

At this level students show a commitment to certain ideas, materials, or phenomena. In short, they are able to find value in them. For example, they may participate freely, share, volunteer, withhold judgment, and support.

Organizing

Targets written at the organizing level encourage students to defend their values, and to consider how consistent they hold these values when confronted with new ideas, materials, or phenomena. Examples of student activities include theorizing, questioning, comparing/contrasting, and examining.

Characterizing by Value

For this target students act consistently with the values they have already organized. They are now able to "put into practice" their values. For example, students will adhere to a belief, influence others, verify a feeling, defend a belief, and solve problems.

Figure 3.5 provides ideas for writing learning targets about affect. Each level includes words that will allow you to assess students' actions or behaviors.

Receiving	Responding	Valuing	Organization	Characterizing by Value
Accept	Agree	Adopt	Anticipate	Act
Acknowledge	Allow	Aid	Collaborate	Administer
Attend (to)	Answer	Care (for)	Confer	Advance
Follow	Ask	Complete	Consider	Advocate
Listen	Assist	Compliment	Consult	Aid
Meet	Attempt	Contribute	Coordinate	Challenge
Observe	Choose	Delay	Design	Change
Receive	Communicate	Encourage	Direct	Commit
	Conform	Enforce	Establish	Counsel
	Cooperate	Foster	Facilitate	Criticize
	Demonstrate	Guide	Follow through	Debate
	Describe	Initiate	Investigate	Defend
	Discuss	Interact	Judge	Disagree
	Display	Join	Lead	Dispute
	Exhibit	Justify	Manage	Empathize
	Follow	Maintain	Modify	Enhance
	Give	Monitor	Organize	Excuse
	Help	Praise	Oversee	Forgive
	Identify	Preserve	Plan	Influence
	Locate	Propose	Qualify	Motivate
	Notify	Query	Recommend	Negotiate
	Obey	React	Revise	Object
	Offer	Respect	Simplify	Persevere
	Participate	Seek	Specify	Persist
	Practice	Share	Submit	Praise
	Present	Study	Synthesize	Promote
	Read	Subscribe	Test	Question
	Relay	Suggest	Vary	Reject
	Reply	Support	Weigh	Resolve
	Report	Thank		Seek
	Respond	Uphold		Serve
	Select			Solve
	Try			Tolerate

Figure 3.5 Verbs to Help Identify Student Behaviors at Each Level of Krathwohl's Affective Taxonomy.

Adapted from work by Kathy V. Waller, PhD, CLS(NCA), National Accrediting Agency for Clinical Laboratory Sciences (NAACLS) Board of Directors. http://www.naacls.org/docs/announcement/writing-targets.pdf (accessed November 2004).

MAKING IT WORK IN YOUR CLASSROOM

Consider a favorite topic of yours within the social studies—something that you look forward to helping students learn. For example, *e pluribus unum* (Latin for "out of many, one"), or *Federalist Paper #10* are two favorites of mine. What would be a cognitive target for a lesson on that topic? Some content benefits from the affective domain, and some does not. If your topic would so benefit, write a target that would explore this area. Refer to the categories for each of the domains, and try to write targets that are as high on the hierarchy as possible.

CONTENT, SKILLS, AND SOCIAL INTERACTIONS (CSS): A DIFFERENT APPROACH FOR THINKING ABOUT LEARNING TARGETS

Another way to think about these domains is in terms of content, skills, and social interactions (CSS). By thinking of student learning in terms of these three domains, you consider the academic content your students will need and use, the skills that are required for them to perform effectively, and the social skills you will ask them to have if they will be interacting with classmates.

Although schools often adhere to the domains of learning advanced by Bloom and his colleagues, the CSS alternative approach for thinking about what students will learn in your classroom will enhance your learning targets. This approach does not overturn the domains just reviewed, but simply attempts to make student learning more specific. In class, your future students will learn academic course content, develop intellectual thinking skills, and be asked to develop ability working with others in groups. It is therefore helpful to think of the classroom as a place where students attain content, skill, and social targets. When you want to be sure students will learn facts, concepts, ideas, or other content-based information, you plan with a *content target*. When your students need to learn processes or thinking skills such as supporting an opinion with facts, searching the Internet, or developing a hypothesis, you plan with a *skill target*. If your students need to develop specific skills that have to do with interacting with classmates, cooperating with one another, or supporting each other's learning, then you will develop *social targets*.

Consider the following activity to demonstrate how targets in these three areas might help your planning, and allow you to back up into the lesson activities and assessments after you have identified the targets: Identify a current event that is slightly controversial. Here are a few ideas to get you thinking: a current case of banning books; a recent Supreme Court ruling; a foreign policy decision; or a news item about immigration. Next, consider these questions: "If a civically minded adult were to develop an informed opinion about this issue, what content and skills would he need to have?" and "What social abilities would be needed to interact with others in a civil discussion?

Often it is helpful to think of this in terms of a four-column chart delineating *issue/event*, *content*, *skills*, and *social interactions*. By completing this chart for several different issues/events, you will find that the skills and social interactions remain fairly consistent, but the information changes depending on the issue. For example, if you decided to complete a chart for global warming, it might look like Figure 3.6.

Issue/Event	Content	Skills	Social Interactions
Global Warming	Causes Effects Current U.S. policies Case studies opposing viewpoints	Critiquing ideas Discussing controversy Researching a topic Supporting opinions Listening to others	Openness to opposing ideas Interest in the topic Desire to identify truth Respect for other opinions Belief that sharing ideas is helpful

Figure 3.6   CSS Chart for Global Warming.

If this is what an adult needs when developing an informed decision, then what should you do with your students in your classroom to prepare them for adulthood? More than likely the contents of the "content" column will change as you teach your course. The skills and interactions, however, can be addressed throughout a course. You may be able to write more specific and appropriate targets by thinking of the cognitive and affective domains in terms of content, skills, and interactions.

The CSS approach allows for diagnostic target writing: You determine the learning needs of your students, then write out daily learning targets to target specific content, skills, or social interactions.

FOUR ELEMENTS OF A TARGET: THE ABCDs OF TARGET WRITING

Targets, when written correctly, will help you design a lesson; they serve as a tool to help you think through what students will learn and what types of activities will help them learn best. Think back to the target diagram earlier in the chapter. A target is written as a concise statement, and writing targets takes some skill and practice. One approach for writing a target is to think in terms of the letters *ABCD*. Each of these letters represents a part of the target. Consider the following modified approach for using this technique.

A/B: Audience and Behavior. Who Will Be Learning, and What Activities Will They Engage in?

The students are almost always the audience, but the students' performance and what they will produce by their actions varies. By writing them in first person, the students are able to personalize the learning. More and more schools are asking teachers to use first person, because it helps students identify the learning target. For example:

- I can list reasons for . . .
- I will write a 300-word essay on . . .
- I can use U.S. Census 2010 data . . .

C: Condition. When Will Students Be Undertaking the Activities?

In this second step you will describe the conditions under which students will produce/perform. These conditions might be on a test, after being given a ruler and calculator, after a Socratic seminar, using class notes, etc. Thought of another way, although your students will be with you during the entire class session, you will not necessarily assess their learning at all times. By including the condition in your target, you are better prepared to determine when your students will demonstrate that they have learned the desired content.

D: Degree. How Well Do You Want Students to Perform?

This final step simply states the criteria for the students. Again, think back to the target in Figure 3.1, and to where on the target students' performance might be. Although this may be based on predetermined criteria (e.g., your school expects all ninth graders to be able to write out all ten amendments of the Bill of Rights), you will often need to determine your own criteria for student learning. When the students meet your criteria at this level or degree, then you have confidence that the students have learned the content. Examples of criteria might be:

- nine out of ten times
- whenever asked to do so
- according to guidelines provided on the rubric.

These elements do not need to appear in the order presented above, but any learning target should have all four of the elements. Consider the following examples:

- I will demonstrate my understanding (A, B) of the items on a map's legend/key (C) with 100% accuracy (D).
- After a classroom discussion about the reasons for and against the electoral college (C), I can write a one-paragraph opinion statement (A, B), that is supported with at least two reasons (D).
- With four out of five primary documents (D), I will correctly identify the source (A, B), and write it down in a reference list (C).

THE ROLE OF TARGETS IN DAILY SOCIAL STUDIES LESSON PLANS

Targets help to focus on the critical content or processes that you will teach during an activity, day, unit, or academic year; they therefore need to be thought about each day. Targets also help to identify the learning you expect of your students and the specifics for how you will determine if they have learned the content adequately. Learning targets also help your students: Telling them your expectations for their learning, and identifying how the day's activities will help them learn, prepares them for the expectations of your lesson. The previous section explained why targets use a concise formulaic language. When telling students these targets, you should adjust the wording so that the targets are easily understood. The "I can" or "I will" helps with this. The point is that targets should be explained and accessible for your students; students should know *what* they will learn, *why* they will learn it, and *how* they will be assessed. This will help them master the content, especially if they know how they will be assessed. Telling students ahead of time how they will demonstrate what they have learned helps them concentrate on what they are learning during the activities. Rather than causing angst or worry in the students, this approach can relieve pressure to perform because the assessment technique is no longer a mystery. Again, in the previous section you read this target: *With four out of five primary documents, I can correctly identify the source, and write it down in a reference list.* Students know from this target that they will be expected to identify source information from primary documents (such as a letter, journal entry, or publication). By being aware of this, they will be prepared to focus their learning on this skill. This not only helps you focus your instruction, but it helps the students focus their attention and learning.

As you teach, you will want to consider the relevancy of social studies content to your students' lives outside school. Not everything needs to be readily applicable to the outside world; sometimes students need to learn facts and concepts simply to help their thinking skills and to help them understand more complex content. However, your students will appreciate opportunities to understand how information learned in your class might help them outside the classroom. If, as you read in Chapter 1, the social studies are to help promote civic competence, then these ties to everyday life should be readily available.

MAKING IT WORK IN YOUR CLASSROOM

Identify a social studies standard from your state that you have not worked with before, and compose three targets according to the following criteria:

*   Write one target for learning course content (e.g., a key concept, fact, or perspective).
*   Write one target for a skill students will need in your class (e.g., skill in researching a topic, skill in discussing issues with others).
*   Write one target that will help students learn to interact with one another (e.g., work cooperatively to accomplish a task, respect for other opinions).
*   Make sure each target has the ABCD elements.

You might want to follow up on this task by asking a middle/high school social studies teacher to critique your targets, and to tell you when, during the school year, this content is conventionally learned.

AN INTRODUCTION TO ASSESSMENT

Assessment is a key component of teaching. By assessing student learning you can determine how effectively you are teaching, whether you need to reteach a particular area, and how engaged the students are in their learning. Assessment is not merely the assignment of grades; it is a plan that allows you and your students to monitor their progress toward meeting specified goals and targets. Assessments certainly provide information that can be graded, but— more importantly—assessment provides a systematic approach for guiding student learning. In this part of the chapter you will be introduced to the basic elements of assessment. Specific assessment ideas are addressed in each chapter about instructional strategies in Part II of this book. Each strategy requires specific assessment approaches. By contextualizing the assessment principles for each of the strategies, you will be in a strong position to appropriately determine your students' progress and learning of social studies content and skills.

Wiggins and McTighe's Idea of "Understanding by Design"

The work of Grant Wiggins and Jay McTighe is helpful when thinking about assessment, learning, and planning. Understanding by design is an approach that highlights the important role of assessment when planning learning activities; the teacher and students promote student understanding by intentionally designing what happens in the classroom. The following points describe the key elements of understanding by design, and reveal the importance of assessment (Authentic Education, 2011):

- A primary goal of education should be the development and deepening of student understanding.
- Students reveal their understanding most effectively when they are provided with complex, authentic opportunities to explain, interpret, apply, shift perspective, empathize, and self-assess. When applied to complex tasks, these "six facets" provide a conceptual lens through which teachers can better assess student understanding.
- Effective curriculum development reflects a three-stage design process called "backward design" that delays the planning of classroom activities until goals have been clarified and assessments designed. This process helps to avoid the twin problems of "textbook coverage" and "activity-oriented" teaching, in which no clear priorities and purposes are apparent.
- Student and school performance gains are achieved through regular reviews of results (achievement data and student work) followed by targeted adjustments to curriculum and instruction.
- Teachers become most effective when they seek feedback from students and their peers and use that feedback to adjust approaches to design and teaching.
- Teachers, schools, and districts benefit by "working smarter" through the collaborative design, sharing, and peer review of units of study.[4]

Validity, Reliability, and Usability

Students commonly complain that they have studied information that was not on the test. They also wonder why exams sometimes include "trick" questions: those where the obvious answer is not the correct one. These complaints are challenges of validity. *Validity* means that the assessment is an accurate and appropriate measurement of student learning. An implication of this is that assessments have to be tied to instructional strategies. If you are lecturing to your students about water rights in the American west, and ask them to prepare for a quiz the next day by studying their notes, then the assessment needs to be closely tied to the content in the notes. If they engage in a debate about a topic that is only remotely related to water rights, or if they write an essay about a topic loosely related to the notes, the validity of the assessment is questioned.

Targets help to ensure that an assessment is valid. An infamous phrase in education is "teaching to the test." It is often used as a way to express frustration that some outside authority is determining the content of the tests, and teachers are in the unfavorable position of merely teaching students the content of the impending tests. Testing is certainly a significant part of the education scene these days, and many stories circulate about how teachers have needed to abandon their conventional curriculum to prepare students to know the content upon which they will be tested. However, as the teacher, you will have many opportunities to develop assessments for your students. When you develop the assessments/tests based on what you want your students to learn, "teaching to the test" becomes a tool used to help students learn. The ABCD approach to developing targets is one example of how you might teach to the test/assessment. By being very aware of the condition under which and degree to which you will assess student learning, you help to ensure that the assessments are valid. If an assessment is not valid, it should not be used.

Along with validity, assessments need to have a high degree of *reliability*. Reliability refers to the degree of confidence that an assessment tool will produce the same results over time. Scholastic Aptitude Tests (SATs) are designed to be highly reliable so that colleges have confidence that all students taking the SAT have been assessed on similar information. Reliability is a concern when teachers grade an essay. If the teacher does not have a rating scale (also known as a rubric, or a series of components she is looking for in the essay), then grading will be less reliable. This is sometimes referred to as "subjective" grading. If you have 75 essays to grade, how assured are you that you will grade the 75th essay the same way as the first? The more assured you are, the greater the reliability.

Usability is simply how difficult an assessment tool is to administer. One of the reasons that the traditional true/false test or multiple-choice test is popular among teachers is because of its ease of use and grading. Imagine that a teacher has four classes of 30 students (120 students total). If students can complete a true/false test in 15 minutes, and the teacher can grade each test in one minute, the teacher uses only 15 minutes of class time and needs two hours (120 minutes) of grading time. However, if the students each make five-minute presentations, and the teacher needs five minutes to compose a written evaluation for each presentation, the teacher uses 600 minutes of class time and uses 600 minutes of grading time! The true/false test is a more usable assessment than the presentations. Chances are, however, that the presentations will provide a more valid assessment of student learning than the true/false test.

All three of these components need to be considered when determining how to assess your students. Assessments must be valid, first and foremost. They must also provide information about your students' learning that is reliable. Finally, assessments need to be usable.

To make the assessment of student learning more valid and reliable, educators are utilizing different techniques for determining how well students have learned. The quiz or test is not the only tool that you have for determining learning, and it is often not the most valid assessment tool. Tests or quizzes tend to emphasize competition among students, and emphasize a student's ability to recall information and/or create a particular product. Instead of using an exam, the trend is to look at the whole picture of student performance in class and during all assignments, and to assess students' understanding of the process they have engaged in to create product. For example, document-based questions (or DBQs) are used in high school history courses to engage students in the process of analysis. Rather than assessing if students have the correct answer, teachers using DBQs assess students' ability to answer a question by analyzing and describing primary sources/documents.

Students are engaging in more self-assessments, in which they are taught the tools needed to examine and evaluate their own performances. Earlier we mentioned that telling students your learning targets will help them learn. Similarly, the trend now is to make students aware of the assessments ahead of time, so they can master the relevant content. Assessment is seen not as an end in itself but as a critically important feedback loop for instruction. A test at the end of a unit on Mesopotamia may not be as valid an assessment as a presentation three days earlier. If the presentation reveals that a student's understanding is incorrect, then the teacher is in a position to help that student relearn the content. Assessment is now seen as a tool for learning and not just for grading. Hammond (2004) has done considerable work on this subject. Figure 3.7 summarizes some of his findings on recent trends in classroom assessment.

From. . .	. . . Toward
Written examinations	Coursework
Teacher-led assessment	Student-led assessment
Implicit criteria	Explicit criteria
Competition with classmates	Cooperation with classmates
Product assessment	Process assessment
Content (facts/concepts only)	Competencies (facts and skills)
Assessment for grading	Assessment for learning

Figure 3.7   Criteria for Student Presentation: Recent Trends in Classroom Assessment. Adapted from Hammond (2004).

Assessments are used to look closely at students' formation of knowledge, skills, concepts, etc. This type of measurement, known as "formative assessment," is useful for the student, because he or she can use the assessments to see what still needs to be learned, and for the teacher, because he or she can use the assessments to direct future learning experiences.

Authentic Assessment and Performance Assessment

What is it that a historian does? What skills does a cartographer need to design a map? How does an economist develop a supply/demand chart? *Authentic assessments* resemble tasks that might occur outside of the school as well as in the classroom (Hiebert, Valencia, & Afflerbach, 1994; Wiggins, 1993). For example, authentic assessments ask students to read real texts such as primary source documents, or to write on meaningful topics for authentic purposes such as providing a public opinion to a newspaper editorial page. In addition, authentic assessment values the thinking behind the work—the process—as much as the finished product (Wiggins, 1998). *Performance assessment* is a term that is often synonymous with authentic assessment. Performance assessments require students to demonstrate what they have learned and emphasize problem solving, thinking, and reasoning. Even the U.S. Congress determined that performance assessments are valid measures of student learning, and composed the following definition for educators over 20 years ago:

> Performance assessment . . . require[s] students to construct responses, rather than select from a set of answers, . . . are criterion-referenced . . . [and] in general, they focus on the process of problem solving rather than just on the end result.
>
> (Congress of the United States, 1992)

Authentic or performance assessments are usually longer and more complex than traditional pen-and-paper tests. On authentic assessment, Wiggins comments about many content areas and not only the social studies, but his words are helpful:

> Do we want to evaluate student problem-posing and problem-solving in mathematics? Experimental research in science? Speaking, listening, and facilitating a discussion? Doing

document-based historical inquiry? Thoroughly revising a piece of imaginative writing until it "works" for the reader? Then let our assessment be built out of such exemplary intellectual challenges . . . Comparisons with traditional standardized tests will help to clarify what "authenticity" means when considering assessment design and use:

- Authentic assessments require students to be effective performers with acquired knowledge. Traditional tests tend to reveal only whether the student can recognize, recall or "plug in" what was learned out of context.

- Authentic assessments present the student with the full array of tasks that mirror the priorities and challenges found in the best instructional activities: conducting research; writing, revising and discussing papers; providing an engaging oral analysis of a recent political event; collaborating with others on a debate, etc. Conventional tests are usually limited to paper-and-pencil, one-answer questions.

- Authentic assessments attend to whether the student can craft polished, thorough and justifiable answers, performances or products. Conventional tests typically only ask the student to select or write correct responses—irrespective of reasons.

- Authentic tasks involve "ill-structured" challenges and roles that help students rehearse for the complex ambiguities of the "game" of adult and professional life. Traditional tests are more like drills, assessing static and too-often arbitrarily discrete or simplistic elements of those activities.

(Wiggins, 1990, p. 1)

Wiggins's mention of "ill-structured" challenges allows for the students to determine the structure and organization of their approach. The notion of a "clearly defined" but "ill-structured" task might help you think through authentic assessments in your content area. For example, your student teaching (also known as your internship or "clinical practice") is a powerful authentic assessment that is both clearly defined and ill structured: Student teachers are asked to promote student learning on par with the cooperating teacher (a clearly defined task), but the planning, organizing, implementing, managing, and assessing of myriad classroom elements is left to the student teacher (an ill-structured task). We considered "backward design" earlier, but if you revisit it again here you can more clearly see how it impacts learning (Wiggins & McTighe, 2000). Consider how a conductor assesses the performances of the musicians in an orchestra, or how a coach assesses the performance of the players on a basketball team. Both might be based on the performance during the very *authentic tasks* of playing a musical score and competing during a game, and the performances are clearly understood before the very first practice session. This assessment is much more valid than a paper-and-pencil test. (Imagine how strange it would seem to not have a concert, but to have orchestra members complete a true/false test about the musical composition.) When each of the instructional strategies is described in Part II of this book, appropriate authentic assessments are contextualized and examined in depth. Each instructional strategy lends itself to particular assessments, and a thorough examination of valid, reliable, and usable assessments is addressed for them in the respective chapters. However, some examples of authentic, performance assessments are:

- writing to real audiences such as a newspaper or magazine
- short investigations about a local community issue
- translating hieroglyphics into text
- developing a museum display

- engaging in a service-learning activity
- portfolios of work showing progress over time and examples of self-selected "best" work
- self-assessment by students of their performance.

Further, Wiggins and McTighe (2005) set up a continuum of assessment tasks. A slightly modified version of that continuum is as follows:

Informal checks for understanding (e.g., Q&A, observations during class, exit cards) →
Tests and quizzes (e.g., simple, content-focused questions, assess facts, concepts, skills) →
Academic prompts (e.g., open-ended questions, high-order thinking) →
Performance tasks (authentic, complex challenges; require high-order thinking).
(Wiggins & McTighe, 2005, p. 152)

Each of these provides opportunities for you to collect evidence of student learning. Informal checks for understanding are simpler, shorter, and less authentic than the others. Likewise, performance tasks are more complex, require more time, and are contextualized and more authentic than other assessments. The three remaining assessments fall in between.

Figure 3.8 compares five different assessment techniques. By looking over the chart, you can see that deciding how to assess your students needs to be a thoughtful process that is as important as any other part of the curriculum.

Assessment Method	Advantages of the Method	Disadvantages of the Method
Traditional pen-and-paper test (e.g., multiple choice, true/false)	Students are familiar with format High in reliability and usability	Often not a valid test of real-world actions Time-consuming to develop
Essay	Highly valid in that it allows students to demonstrate understanding of concepts, opinions, and attitudes Possibility for student to express a unique understanding is greater	Reliability: less control, therefore harder to quantify Usability: time-consuming to write questions and grade responses
Interview and oral exam	More relaxed and personal feeling may enhance validity Confusion can be clarified and jargon defined	Teacher may not want to be critical on a face-to-face level Hard to transcribe and quantify
Performance assessment (e.g., presentation, recital, game)	Student demonstrates skill Close to real-world experience Rubrics (rating scales) help focus student performance	Reliability: can be difficult to grade Usability: time-consuming because it depends on direct observation
Product assessment (e.g., homework, research paper, photo portfolio)	Useful to determine accomplishments Able to provide a standard to measure by	Validity: does not show the process, but emphasizes the end result Reliability: can be difficult to grade

Figure 3.8   Criteria for Student Presentation: Five Assessment Techniques Compared.

MAKING IT WORK IN YOUR CLASSROOM

What is the equivalent of a concert or a game in a history or geography classroom? How about a class focusing on current world issues? In other words, how might students in a social studies class engage in assessment tasks that are authentic measurements of what they have learned, and that are tasks they might engage in outside school? Refer to the list of examples in the previous section to get you started, and brainstorm at least three different activities that are authentic and/or performance assessments.

RUBRICS

Like any evaluation process, authentic assessments must provide fair and reliable measurements of student learning. A *rubric* is a tool that lists the criteria for student performance, and describes levels of quality for each of the criteria. For example, a rubric in Figure 3.9 might be used to assess students' presentations. It clearly lists the criteria and levels of quality in four categories: demonstrated knowledge; use of visuals; explanation of main points; and presentation skills/mechanics. Students receive a score from 0 to 3 in each category.

This might also be a good time to turn back to the target figure (Figure 3.1) that we explored at the start of this chapter, and the different student performances represented by

Categories	3	2	1	0	Points
Demonstrated knowledge	Shows complete understanding of the content s/he researched, and answers questions accurately	Shows substantial understanding of the content s/he researched, answers some questions accurately	Shows limited understanding of the content s/he researched, and has difficulty with questions	Shows a lack of understanding of the content s/he researched, and is unable to answer questions	_____/3
Use of visuals	Clear diagram, PowerPoint slide or poster, highlighting main ideas	Clear diagram, PowerPoint slide or poster, but missing some main ideas	Inappropriate or unclear diagram, PowerPoint slide or poster	No visuals	_____/3
Explanation	A complete response to the main question, with a detailed explanation	Good solid response to the main question, with clear explanation	Response and explanation to the main question is unclear	Misses key points	_____/3
Mechanics	Presentation is well rehearsed, fits in the time allocation, and easy to understand	Presentation is practiced, and/or is close to the time allocation	Presentation needs more rehearsal, and/or is not close to the time allocation. Difficult to understand main points	Lack of preparation is apparent. Main points are unclear	_____/3
				Total:	_____/12

Figure 3.9   Criteria for Student Presentations.

the different rings on the target. Rubrics help students and teachers define "quality." They increase reliability, and reduce subjective or biased grading. Rubrics also help teachers clearly explain to students why they received a particular score. If students receive a rubric at the beginning of a project they can accept more responsibility for their learning, because they know the expectations of the assessment from the start. If a student needs extra assistance with one area of the rubric, for example with mechanics, then you will be able to focus on the criteria listed on the rubric for that area. Additionally, when you create a rubric at the beginning of a unit, you are able to plan your lessons in ways that allow your students to meet the criteria stated in the rubric. As we mentioned earlier, this is a form of backward design. I suggest first identifying the categories that you will assess students on by thinking through your expectations. Once the categories are established, you should consider the criteria for two extremes of student work for each category: excellent performances and unsatisfactory performances. The remaining criteria can then be modified for the number of levels you are willing to let students attain. The example above has four levels, so you would need to identify different criteria for each. With more levels you will be able to differentiate the quality of student work more, but it will be a more difficult task to create unique criteria for each level. RubiStar (http://www. rubistar4teachers.org) is an Internet link page that connects teachers to different websites for helping teachers design, develop, and use rubrics. Visit this site, because it will aid your thinking about the categories and criteria you could have for an assignment. The downside of a website or program that helps you develop a rubric is that it is usually very generic, and does not provide specific expectations for each criteria level. Ideally you will have criteria, and even examples of work, for each of the levels of the rubric. You want the expectations to be clearly understood by students. This is not always possible with ready-made rubrics. Consider using generic rubrics as a starting point, then adding your own detail, specific to your expectations of an assignment. In Part II of this book you will read about additional examples of rubrics designed specifically for an instructional strategy.

DIAGNOSTIC, FORMATIVE, AND SUMMATIVE ASSESSMENT

Diagnostic Assessment

Although some authors describe diagnostic assessment as a component of formative assessment, most consider it a distinct form of measurement (Kellough & Kellough, 1999; McMillan, 2004). Just as a medical doctor looks at a patient before coming up with a diagnosis for treatment, diagnostic assessments usually occur prior to instruction, and attempt to determine students' strengths, weaknesses, knowledge, and skills. Identifying these helps teachers differentiate the curriculum to meet each student's unique needs. For example, a history teacher might give a pretest on the first day of class to see how much information students remember about feudal Europe or Japan. Depending on the results, the teacher is able to determine the course content that needs to be learned. At one high school, the social studies department gives a diagnostic assessment to all freshmen about their knowledge of the countries around the world, and about their knowledge of the U.S. Constitution. Teachers then use the scores to determine the curriculum in a social studies class that combines world history and world geography (called "world connections"). The teachers also use the scores to help monitor the progress of each student during their first year of high school.

Formative Assessment

Formative assessment occurs continually during each school day so the teacher is able to monitor student learning. Formative assessment provides information on how students are "forming" their understanding. An excellent definition of this type of assessment is from Black and Wiliam (2009):

> Practice in a classroom is formative to the extent that evidence about student achievement is elicited, interpreted, and used by teachers, learners, or their peers, to make decisions about the next steps in instruction that are likely to be better, or better founded, than the decisions they would have taken in the absence of the evidence that was elicited.
>
> (p. 9)

Another helpful definition of formative assessment is "an active and intentional learning process that partners the teacher and the students to continuously and systematically gather evidence of learning with the express goal of improving student achievement" (Moss & Brookhart, 2009, p. 6). Assessment then is to help students learn. Is that a different way of thinking about the purpose of assessment? Moss and Brookhart (2012) describe a formative learning cycle where content is modeled and explained, students engage in guided practice, students demonstrate their understanding, students and teacher provide formative feedback and assessment, students' understanding is improved.

Formative assessment also provides information to the teacher about how to appropriately "form" targets for future lessons, and promote student learning. For example, if several students misunderstand the concept of scarcity, formative assessments will identify this learning problem and allow the teacher to take strides toward remediation. Formative assessments often are not graded, and allow for the teacher and students to develop a deeper understanding of the curriculum. They provide information for adapting teaching and learning to meet student needs (Boston, 2002). Sometimes formative assessment is labeled *progress monitoring*. When teachers monitor students' progress, and are able to identify where students are having trouble, they can make necessary instructional adjustments, such as reteaching, trying alternative instructional approaches, or offering more opportunities for practice. These activities can lead to improved student success (Black & Wiliam, 1998a). Teachers can formatively assess students' understanding in the following ways (Black & Wiliam, 1998a, 1998b; Boston, 2002):

- Have students write their understanding of concepts before and after instruction.
- Ask students to summarize the main ideas they've taken away from a lecture, discussion, or assigned reading.
- Have students complete a few problems or questions at the end of instruction and check answers.
- Interview students individually or in groups about their thinking as they solve problems.
- Assign brief, in-class writing assignments (e.g., "Why is this person or event representative of this time period in history?"). A similar strategy is often referred to as an "exit card." Exit cards can be used to determine what students have learned. Students write down one or two main ideas that they learned during class, or they respond to a question from the teacher. As they leave the class they hand this in (it serves as a pass that allows them to exit the classroom).

Most assessment you will use in class will be some form of formative assessment, and will provide opportunities to meet your students at their current level of understanding. With diagnostic and formative assessments working together, you will be better able to differentiate your instruction so that all of your students can learn. In Part II of this book, I provide extensive examples of assessments that are specific for each instructional strategy. Most of the assessments are formative.

Summative Assessment

Summative assessment is the attempt to determine the total, or summation, of student learning. This is the assessment that students, parents, and the public tend to value most because it is so closely tied to grades. Whereas diagnostic and formative assessments provide direction for future instruction, summative assessments typically do not. Consider this analogy for understanding the difference between formative and summative assessments: When the cook tastes the soup, that is formative assessment; when the customer tastes the soup, then that is summative assessment (Stevens, Lawrenz, & Sharp, 1996). Summative assessment occurs at or near the end of a unit, chapter, term, or course. The purpose is to evaluate student learning. The Scholastic Aptitude Test (SAT), the Miller Analogies Test (MAT), and most standardized exams are also examples of summative assessments. Most statewide assessments are summative (including testing to address the Common Core State Standards with the *Smarter Balanced* assessments). They are not designed to provide the immediate, contextualized feedback useful for helping teacher and student during the learning process. High-quality summative information can, of course, shape how teachers organize their courses or what schools offer their students. However, it is not often useful for helping teachers work to improve the learning of individual students.

TWO MORE IMPORTANT ASSESSMENT TERMS

When thinking and reading about assessment, two other terms will often be used: *norm-referenced assessment* and *criterion-referenced assessment*.

Norm referencing allows for people to be ranked, put in an order based on their scores. It is competitive. For example, in a class of 25 students, a teacher might use norm referencing to assign grades to students by determining that the top 20% receive As, the next Bs, and so on. Such a scale looks like this:

A: the five students with the highest grades
B: the next five students
C: the next five students
D: the next five students
F: the five students with the lowest grades.

Although this is a traditional grading scale, these figures are arbitrary. If the results of any assessment allow you to rank students from high score to low score, then the test is norm referenced. Many standardized tests are norm referenced, as is an IQ (intelligence quotient) test. This approach is rarely is ever used by teachers. Rather than having students compete against each other for a grade, teachers would rather have them focus on meeting and mastering specific criteria.

Criterion referencing is the term used for assessment against fixed criteria. Potentially, everyone can pass a criterion-referenced assessment—or everyone can fail. Whereas norm referencing also has criteria (e.g., the criterion for an A grade is to have one of the top five point totals in the class), criteria-referenced assessments determine whether a student has adequately met a minimum level or standard. Criteria are usually determined in advance to ensure that they are valid and appropriate. One high school in Washington state requires students to list on a world map the location of 100 countries. It does not matter if you know more, just that you are able to complete the specified number of tasks or questions correctly. A pass/fail grade might serve as another example. If you earn a specific number of points (e.g., 70% of the total), you pass the course. It does not matter how many points you earn, as long as you meet the criterion. The concern with this assessment is that it identifies only a minimum level of achievement. This is often justified by the advantage of not basing success on comparing scores with others.

Many teachers determine the criteria needed for different grades. For example, a percentage of the total points is needed for an A grade. A grade scale that uses multiple criteria could look like this:

A: 90–100% of the possible points
B: 80–89%of the possible points
C: 70–79% of the possible points
D: 60–69% of the possible points
F: 59% or less of the possible points.

MAKING IT WORK IN YOUR CLASSROOM

Return to the targets you wrote earlier in the chapter. For each target, develop appropriate diagnostic and/or formative assessment activities that will help students meet your target. For example, if you are teaching a world geography class, you might have the learning target for students read: *I will be able to distinguish between "renewable" and "nonrenewable" resources.* You could diagnostically assess students' understanding by handing out a list of resources in each of these two categories on the first day of class and have each student sort the list. This information will help you know the content knowledge students have prior to the unit. You could formatively assess students during the unit by having them write down the resources on a particular continent, and then asking them to identify the renewable resources, and explain why they are not likely to run out. This will allow you to assess how accurately students are acquiring knowledge, and allow students to identify areas where they need to improve their understanding of the information about resources. An additional formative assessment could be a PowerPoint presentation through which the student provides slides and descriptions of each of the two types of resources, and details about where supplies of several resources are located throughout the world. This serves as a cohesive plan for helping meet the target.

Using this as an example, develop assessments for your targets, and what the purpose of each assessment might be.

CHAPTER REVIEW

- Long- and short-term learning targets
  - Targets specify how and when you can help students develop skills and understand important course content
  - Using the sentence stem "I can . . ." or "I will . . ." helps phrase the targets in student-friendly language that also helps students better understand what they need to learn
  - Long-term targets will be accomplished after a longer unit, semester, or even an entire course
  - Short-term targets are met during an activity or after a few class sessions
  - The ABCD approach helps keep targets focused:
    - **AB**: **A**udience and **B**ehavior
    - **C**: **C**ondition
    - **D**: **D**egree
- Different domains of learning
  - Cognitive domain
  - Affective domain
  - Content, Information, and Skill (CIS) provides another approach for considering domains of learning
- Assessing student learning, and the specific importance of formative assessment
  - Assessments must be:
    - valid
    - reliable
    - usable
  - Authentic assessments resemble tasks that might occur outside of the school as well as in the classroom; performance assessment is synonymous with authentic assessment
  - Assessments should be developed at the beginning of a unit so you can "design backward" by developing lessons that prepare students to meet the assessment expectations
  - Rubrics help students and teachers define "quality"
  - Assessments occur at different points in the learning process:
    - Diagnostic assessments are used near the start
    - Formative assessment occurs continually during each school day to monitor student learning. The results are helpful for students and the teacher
    - Summative assessment provides a summary of what students have learned

NOTES

1. The term *learning targets* is widely used, but not the only one educators will use. Similar terms that you might hear are *instructional targets, student learning targets, learning objectives, and learning outcomes.*
2. Steven Zemelman, Harvey Daniels, and Arthur Hyde from their research, *Best Practice: Bringing Standards to Life in America's Classrooms* (4th ed.), 2014.
3. See Figure 3.3 for a list of activities/verbs that can be used when writing cognitive targets at each of the six levels.
4. These bullet points are from the website Authentic Education, a company of which Grant Wiggins is president. We added emphasis to these points. The website for this overview is located at: http://www. authenticeducation.org/ubd/ubd.lasso.

REFERENCES

Authentic Education (2011). Authentic Education. Retrieved October 18, 2011, from http://www.authenticeducation.org/ubd/ubd.lasso.

Biehler, R. F. (1971). *Psychology Applied to Teaching*. Boston, MA: Houghton Mifflin.

Black, P. & Wiliam, D. (1998a). Assessment and classroom learning. *Assessment in Education*, 5(1), 7–74.

Black, P. & Wiliam, D. (1998b). Inside the black box: Raising standards through classroom assessment. *Phi Delta Kappan, 80*(2), 139–148.

Black, P. J. & Wiliam, D. (2009). Developing the theory of formative assessment. *Educational Assessment, Evaluation and Accountability, 21*(1), 5–31.

Bloom, B. S. (Ed.) (1956). *Taxonomy of Educational Targets: Handbook I, Cognitive Domain*. New York: David McKay Co., Inc.

Boston, C. (2002). The concept of formative assessment. *Practical Assessment, Research & Evaluation, 8*(9). Retrieved November 9, 2004, from http://PAREonline.net/getvn.asp?v=8&n=9.

Congress of the United States, Office of Technology Assessment (February, 1992). *Testing in American Schools: Asking the Right Questions*. Washington, DC: U.S. Government Printing Office.

Hammond, G. (2004). Testing and evaluation. Retrieved March, 2006, from http://xnet.rrc.mb.ca/glenh/outline.htm.

Hiebert, E. H., Valencia, S. W., & Afflerbach, P. P. (1994). Understand authentic reading assessment: Definitions and perspectives. In S. W. Valencia, E. H. Hiebert, & P. P. Afflerbach (Eds.), *Authentic Reading Assessment: Practices and Possibilities* (pp. 6–21). Newark, DE: International Reading Association.

Kellough, R. D. & Kellough, N. G. (1999). *Secondary School Teaching: A Guide To Methods And Resources; Planning For Competence*. Upper Saddle River, NJ: Prentice-Hall.

Krathwohl, D. R., Bloom, B. S., & Masia B. B. (1964). *Taxonomy of Educational Targets, Book 2: Affective Domain*. New York: Longman.

McMillan, J. H. (2004). *Classroom Assessment: Principles and Practice for Effective Instruction*, 3rd ed. Upper Saddle River, NJ: Allyn & Bacon.

Moss, C. M. & Brookhart, S. M. (2012). *Learning Targets: Helping Students Aim for Understanding in Today's Lesson*. Alexandria, VA: ASCD.

Moss, C. M. & Brookhart, S. M. (2009). *Advancing Formative Assessment in Every Classroom: A Guide for the Instructional Leader*. Alexandria, VA: ASCD.

Stevens, F., Lawrenz, F., & Sharp, L. (1996). *User-Friendly Handbook for Project Evaluation: Science, Mathematics, Engineering, and Technology Education*. Arlington, VA: National Science Foundation.

Wiggins, G. (1998). *Educative Assessment: Designing Assessments to Inform and Improve Student Performance*. San Francisco, CA: Jossey-Bass.

Wiggins, G. (1993). Assessment: Authenticity, context, and validity. *Phi Delta Kappan, 75*(3), 200–214.

Wiggins, G. (1990). The case for authentic assessment. *Practical Assessment, Research & Evaluation, 2*(2). Retrieved December 6, 2004, from http://PAREonline.net/getvn.asp?v=2&n=2.

Wiggins, G. P. & McTighe, J. (2005). *Understanding by Design*. Alexandria, VA: ASCD.

Wiggins, G. P. & McTighe, J. (2000). *Understanding by Design*. Alexandria, VA: ASCD.

Zemelman, S., Daniels, H., & Hyde, A. A. (2012). *Best Practice: Bringing Standards to Life in America's Classrooms*, 4th ed. Portsmouth, NH: Heinemann.

CHAPTER 4

Long- and Short-Range Planning

CHAPTER GOALS

In this chapter, you will learn about:

- Four common classroom elements to consider while planning
- Writing unit plans that contain eight frequently used components
- Understanding by Design's six facets of learning
- Lesson planning.

Planning helps teachers organize what they hope their students will learn during the school year, the semester, the unit, and the daily lesson. Planning also helps teachers organize and structure the school day so that student learning is maximized. Many classroom management and discipline problems can be avoided if the teacher is organized and a strong planner. If you have a clear idea of what you intend for students to learn, not only during that day's lesson but for the coming weeks, then you will be in a good position to address student concerns about the content, and have a better understanding of your expectations for student learning.

YEARLONG SCOPE AND SEQUENCE

According to the National Center for Education Statistics,[1] American schools are open an average of 180 days per year. These days are divided by districts and schools into smaller segments such as two 90-day semesters, three 60-day trimesters, or four 45-day quarters. *Scope* and *sequence* are two terms that many educators use; they refer to the breadth of content and skills students should learn (scope), and the order in which students will learn this content (sequence) during these 180 days. *Yearlong planning* is simply the scope and sequence for a course during the school year. Each state usually determines the scope and sequence for courses in each of the grades K–12. In the social studies, the scope and sequence across middle school and high school grades has conventionally been:

Grade 6: ancient civilizations
Grade 7: world geography
Grade 8: U.S. history
Grade 9: civics/state history
Grade 10: world cultures/world history
Grade 11: U. S. history II
Grade 12: social studies electives (such as U.S. government/sociology/anthropology/ economic/current world problems and issues).

States will modify this scope and sequence, and it will be interesting for you to examine what your state suggests for the social studies in each grade level. For example, in Washington state, the scope and sequence for grades 6–12 is:

Grade 6: world history I (8000 BCE–600 CE)
Grade 7: world history II (600–1600) and Washington state history
Grade 8: U.S. history (1776–1870)
Grade 9: world geography
Grade 10: world history III (1600–present)
Grade 11: U.S. history (1776–1791 and 1877–present)
Grade 12: contemporary world problems.

In Massachusetts, the scope and sequence is similar, but world geography is taken in sixth grade. What is the social studies scope and sequence for grades 6–12 in your state?

Within each of the 6–12 grade levels, scope and sequence is considered for each course. Consider these two examples of scope and sequence for sixth grade world geography and eleventh grade U.S. history.

The State of Massachusetts' Scope and Sequence for Sixth Grade Geography[2]

Sixth graders systematically study the world outside of the United States and North America by addressing standards that emphasize political and physical geography and embed five major concepts: location, place, human interaction with the environment, movement, and regions. Students systematically learn geography around the world continent by continent, similar to the way in which atlases are organized. They also learn about each continent in an order that reflects, first, the early development of the river valley civilizations and then the later development of maritime civilizations in the Mediterranean area and in Northern and Western Europe. In so doing, students are better prepared for the study of early civilizations around the Mediterranean area in grade 7.

The State of Washington's Scope and Sequence
for High School U.S. History

- Our Foundations (1776–1791)
- Industrialization and the Emergence of the U.S. as a World Power (1877–1919)
- Reform, Prosperity, and Depression (1918–1938)
- World War II, the Cold War, and International Relations (1939–Present)
- Post–World War II Domestic, Political, Social, and Economic Issues (1945–Present)
          (Washington State Office of the Superintendent of Public Instruction, 2003)

As you can see, Massachusetts provides a narrative description about geography, whereas Washington provides bulleted points. Although the format will differ, the focus and intention of state-level scope and sequence documents attempts to provide structure to the social studies curriculum. Many states and districts have developed or are developing expectations for the content that should be taught at each grade level to ensure that as students move through the grades, they learn content in a predetermined sequence. Many of these are available online, and are usually based on the national standards for the social studies, history, economics, civics, and geography. Scope and sequence documents are a great help for you as beginning teachers because they provide insights into the content students should have learned prior to your class, suggest the content that students need to learn in your course, and identify the content that students will need to know for the years after your course.

School districts and individual schools also develop a yearlong scope and sequence for each grade level. These are tied to the state expectations, but may include additional content that districts or schools believe are important. In our work with schools we have found that some districts provide teachers incredible freedom to develop their own scope and sequence, whereas other districts require teachers to adhere to a specific program. For example, a common set of topics and concepts for a high school American government course is as follows:

- theories of democracy
- federalism
- formation of the Constitution
- adoption of the Constitution
- political beliefs
- political behaviors
- separation of powers
  - legislature—congress
  - executive—presidency
  - judiciary system
- elections
- special interest groups
- the budgetary process
- taxing and spending.

You might work in a district where you are expected to teach just these topics, and to teach them in this order. If that is the case, your yearlong scope and sequence is predetermined. You still have opportunities to determine how to promote student learning as you select instructional strategies, but the overall content of the course must meet these expectations. Just as likely, however, you might work in a district that allows you to add to these topics, and does not specify the sequence in which students learn them. In this latter situation you will need to determine the instructional strategies and the overall topics for the school year.

As the planning moves closer to the daily lesson, the level of specificity increases. As can be seen with the Massachusetts and Washington examples on pages 94 and 95, the yearlong scope and sequence are often not very specific. They usually do not specify the number of days to be spent on a topic, subtopics students should learn, assessment tools, or learning targets. They simply provide an overarching idea of the content students should learn during the school year, and the order in which topics and concepts should be learned.

Textbooks present content in an order that attempts to match the yearlong scope and sequence of a course. For example, world history textbooks usually present content in the chronological order that most teachers use. Students, then, are able to read through the textbook as they learn the course content. Often, textbooks provide superficial coverage of too much information; I suggest that you determine how the textbook might supplement your planning and curriculum, and not depend on the textbook to determine the scope and sequence of your course. Textbook publishers are one of many powerful influences on a teacher making curricular decisions. Scope and sequence are also important when planning a series of lessons that will constitute a unit plan, and even when planning for a single day's activities. The scope of the content and the sequential ordering of events need to be thoughtfully considered when planning. Teachers develop lesson plans for each day they teach, and these plans are placed in a sequence, or order, that the teacher thinks will help students understand the content. Often a series of lesson plans are placed together to form a unit plan. Unit plans are sequenced together to form a course plan, and the courses are sequenced to form a yearlong plan. We will explore this more as we examine unit planning and lesson planning.

You might be wondering at this point where and how the national standards you read about in Chapter 1 fit in with a state or school's scope and sequence. Common Core State Standards for English language arts/history, the National Council for the Social Studies ten themes, or the College, Career, and Civic Life frameworks provide general ideas for skills and broad concepts in the social studies. For example, the Common Core provides these two reading standards for high school history:

> Cite specific textual evidence to support analysis of primary and secondary sources, connecting insights gained from specific details to an understanding of the text as a whole.
>
> (CCSS.ELA-Literacy.RH.11-12.1)

> Determine the central ideas or information of a primary or secondary source; provide an accurate summary that makes clear the relationships among the key details and ideas.
>
> (CCSS.ELA-Literacy.RH.11-12.2)

You will notice that these standards do not specific particular primary or secondary courses. The ones you explore in your classroom may be determined by what you believe fits best with the lesson, or by your school, district, or state. The CCSS sets the general standards (in the above example, reading history in grades 11 and 12), but allows states and schools to determine specifics. The ten NCSS themes suggest that any topic can be used to explore the themes in more depth. For example, learning about the first Chinese empire might allow for explorations into theme number six: Power, Authority, and Governance. And the NCSS College, Career, and Civic Life Framework (C3) focuses on inquiry-based instruction in the social studies (and this is explored more in Chapter 11). The content or focus of the inquiry can be flexible and developed based on the state or school expectations. It could be an inquiry about the cost/benefit of building the Erie Canal if that fits with the content students are learning about in your classroom. All of this to say that the national standards help inform the year-long scope and sequence in your classroom. They work together to promote students' learning of content, skills, and dispositions in the curriculum.

MAKING IT WORK IN YOUR CLASSROOM

Using your state's standards and the national standards for world history (refer to the links to these standards in Chapter 1), write down the yearlong scope and sequence for that course. Talk with a world history teacher, and compare what you have come up with and what the teacher has developed for the 180-day school year. Consider the following questions: What is the difference between what you came up with and the teacher's plan? What is similar? How do the two plans reflect the state standards? How do they reflect national history standards? How did the two of you go about the process of making your selections? World history often uses a chronological scope and sequence. Geography, on the other hand, tends to be more thematic. You might find it interesting to repeat this "Making It Work in Your Classroom" activity and examine the scope and sequence for geography.

FOUR COMMONPLACES IN SCHOOL

Awareness of the standards, goals, and suggested scope and sequence for your course is the first step in planning. As we mentioned earlier in this chapter, these will be available to you at the national, state, district, school, and even department levels. The scope and sequence plans provide topics for more focused unit plans, which in turn provide direction for the specific lesson plans. Before thinking about these unit and lesson plans, however, it is important to consider all that is involved when planning. Schwab (1973) developed the idea that all classrooms have four elements in common: They all have a *teacher*, *students*, a subject matter or *content* that is to be learned, and an environment or *milieu* in which teaching and learning take place. If any one of these four commonplaces is hindered, then learning is thwarted. Any planning or thinking about curriculum—of what should be taught and learned—must consider how these four aspects of every classroom interact.

These four commonplaces should not be thought of as a hierarchy. Though it is tempting in an age of testing and accountability to think of content as the most important aspect of the classroom, Schwab's ideas remind us that all four commonplaces must work together if learning is to occur. As illustrated in Figure 4.1, if any of the four sides is removed, the entire structure collapses. Consider how the following examples show teacher, students, content, and milieu codependence affecting teaching and learning:

- If your students already understand the key concepts you want them to learn, then the content will effect what you have planned for the day. Similarly, if the content is too difficult for students to understand (for example, the reading level of a text is too high, the premise of your main point is not accepted by the students, or students do not have adequate prior knowledge), then the learning will be affected by the *content* commonplace.

• If the students are not prepared, not engaged, or distracted, they will not be ready to think about the content you planned for them to learn. This might happen if they did not complete a reading assignment, if your class meets immediately following a school assembly, or even if a noisy lawnmower is cutting grass outside your classroom. In each of these instances the *students* will affect you (the *teacher*), the *content*, and the *milieu*.

• If you are discussing a controversial subject in your classroom, students may perceive the milieu as unsafe, and feel uncomfortable sharing their ideas. In turn, this will affect the depth in which a topic can be examined, and your selection of an instructional strategy.

• If students are making presentations to the class and the desks are positioned in groups of four (so the students are facing each other and not the front of the room), the physical setup of the room, the *milieu*, may distract students from listening to the presentations. This will affect the students' opportunities to learn from the presentations, or to present to classmates who are listening; and you, the teacher, might even get frustrated that students are talking too much.

When working with student teachers, I encourage them to reflect on a lesson after the students left the room and went home. The four commonplaces provide focus for that reflection. By asking questions such as "How prepared was I (the teacher) for the lesson?", "Were the students engaged in the learning process?," "Was the content age/ability appropriate?", and "Did the classroom environment promote learning?" teachers are able to critique the class session. For example, consider a case in which students in your history class are distracted by a physical education class playing soccer outside the classroom (affecting the *student*), causing the student teacher to became annoyed and frustrated (affecting the *teacher*); this put a damper on the positive tone that had been established (affecting the *milieu*), thus causing the role-play exercise that was occurring to fizzle out (affecting the *content*). While reflecting on this lesson, a student teacher might mistakenly think that students don't learn much during the role-play exercise and become wary of trying the strategy with another class. Realizing the interdependence of the commonplaces will help a teacher more clearly reflect upon the events of the classroom. This reflective approach could lead to the

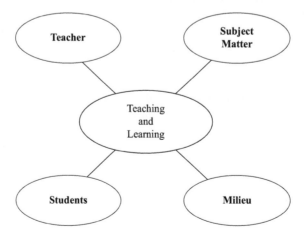

Figure 4.1 Schwab's Four Commonplaces.

conclusion that to simply shut the shades quietly without responding emotionally could positively affect the other commonplaces.

The point of thinking about Schwab's work is simply to remind you that part of planning is taking into consideration all the aspects of the *student* (maturity, diversity, ability, motivation, etc.), the *content* (standards, goals, targets, etc.), the *milieu* (a perception of safety within a community of learners, the sense of respect amongst classmates, etc.), and the *teacher* (a knowledge of the content, an understanding of the students, skill at managing the classroom, a choice of instructional strategies, etc.). These four commonplaces direct your planning, and determine how effective the instruction has been in promoting student learning.

MAKING IT WORK IN YOUR CLASSROOM

Imagine that you wanted to help your students understand the concept of compromise, and this concept's role in developing treaties. Envision that you will be able to spend about 45 minutes on this concept with your students. Now, consider each of the following situations that could occur in your classroom, and the commonplaces that are most affected (remember that, if one commonplace is affected, all four will be).

- *Situation 1:* Of the 30 students in your class, 20 are in the gifted program at your school. Which commonplace is affected? How does it impact your classroom and all students' learning?
- *Situation 2:* A fire drill occurs for the first 10 minutes of class. By the time you have students back in class, you have 10 minutes left. Which commonplace is affected? How does it impact your classroom and student learning?

Brainstorm other situations where different commonplaces might interact to affect student learning.

THE UNIT PLAN

The *unit plan* is the compilation of lesson plans during a specific amount of time—for example, two weeks—and provides specific focus on course content. By placing daily lessons in a unit, the content students learn is connected. Students are able to recognize relationships in each daily lesson, because of a conceptual or thematic link that the unit plan provides. A few examples help explain this:

- During a unit on China, a geography teacher is able to examine five common geographic themes (location, place, human/environment interactions, movement, and region). Since the unit is on China, students know that the different geographic concepts will all be applied to content about that country.
- During a unit on the economy, a current events teacher equips students with the knowledge and skills necessary to make sound personal economic decisions.
- A U.S. history teacher connects two weeks of lesson activities that include child labor laws and health restrictions to help students understand reform movements at the turn of the 20th century.

By segmenting the school year into units, you are able to think clearly about needed resources for upcoming units, prerequisite knowledge for each unit, and key concepts and skills that a unit presents. The 180 days of school could be divided into 18 units of 10 days each. We do not mean to imply that units must be about two weeks long. Often they are three or four weeks long, or they can be merely one week long. Rather than thinking of a unit as a specific number of days, think of a unit as helping students learn a specific portion of content and/or develop particular skills.

Revisiting Understanding by Design

When thinking about long-term planning, the work of Grant Wiggins and Jay McTighe provides the metaphor of "backward design" that you read about briefly in Chapter 3. In addition, their work with curriculum development reminds us all that students do not learn and understand automatically as a result of teaching. Student learning is the result of designing effective lessons to match student understanding. Wiggins and McTighe rightfully remind us that understanding is the result of appropriately designing learning opportunities:

> Students reveal their understanding most effectively when they are provided with complex tasks that allow for authentic opportunities to:
>
> 1.   explain
> 2.   interpret
> 3.   apply
> 4.   shift perspective
> 5.   empathize
> 6.   self-assess.
>
> When applied to complex tasks, these "six facets" provide a conceptual lens through which teachers can better assess student understanding and determine what to plan next to ensure student success.[3]

These are similar to the hierarchy of thinking that Bloom developed and that was described in Chapter 3. Look at Figure 4.2 and contextualize these facets with the following example adapted from from Wiggins and McTighe (2011):

Step 1 provides the opportunity to state the learning target(s). In Step 2 evidence of learning is considered for each facet of understanding. Step 3 then becomes an opportunity to consider appropriate assessments that will allow you to gather the evidence. In this way, the target is tied to the demonstration(s) of learning and to the assessment(s). As the teacher you would not expect to have students meet each level of understanding. Rather, it is an opportunity for you to consider what students will be able to demonstrate to you if they really understand the content. Perhaps really understanding the horrors of the Holocaust means that students are empathetic. Really understanding the Columbian Exchange, however, might mean that they are able to explain the movement of goods. Try to re-create this chart about a different topic. Select something you are familiar with, and that you know will be learned in schools. Then consider what each facet of understanding would look like if the student were to demonstrate what they learned, and consider the assessments that would help you, and the students, demonstrate their understanding.

Step 1: State the learning target(s):
"Learners/Students will demonstrate their understanding of: _____."

Step 2: State the evidence:
"The teacher needs evidence of student's ability to: _____."

Step 3: Identify valid assessments:
"Assessments that will gather this evidence will be: _____."

Example:

Step 1:
Students will demonstrate their understanding that price is a function of supply and demand.

Step 2:
The teacher needs evidence that students are able to (note the different evidence for each of the six facets):
1. **Explain** why supply and demand cause similar items to be priced differently
2. **Interpret** data on how prices change for the same item over time
3. **Apply** their understanding by suggesting a price for an item for sale
4. **Take on the perspective** of buyers and sellers of the same product
5. **Empathize** with a farmer who is trying to sell a crop that has been overproduced, or with the person trying to determine the market price
6. **Self-assess** the influence of price on what you buy. Consider food prices and technology items, for example.

Step 3:
Valid assessments for gathering evidence for each facet of learning might include:
1. **Explain** in two paragraphs why the price of a specific item will vary (e.g., price of a new smartphone)
2. Create a presentation that **interprets** changes is prices over time (e.g., price of a hotel room in the city hosting the Super Bowl before and after the game)
3. **Apply** ideas about pricing, supply, and demand by interviewing classmates about a school sweatshirt and determining the best price.
4. **Take on the perspective** of a student buying a rare comic and of someone selling this same comic on-line
5. **Empathize** with an apple farmer and a fruit buyer who are setting market price. Consider prices after a "bumper crop" and after a freeze caused a 50% drop in the normal apple harvest.
6. **Self-assess/reflect** how you have a better understanding that prices are not fixed and/or predetermined.

Figure 4.2 Three Steps for Generating Assessments Using the Six Facets of Learning.

© Adapted from Wiggins, G. & McTighe, J. (2011), *The Understanding by Design Guide to Creating High-Quality Units*, Alexandria, VA: ASCD, p. 97.

Essential Questions

Without a unit, daily lessons lack cohesion. Lessons should be developed because they will help students learn the specific knowledge or skills identified for the unit. As you can see, units are an effective tool for designing lessons that meet your targets, goals, and curriculum standards. They allow teachers to map out the activities and strategies that will help ensure that students learn specified course content. Erickson (2002) suggests that unit plans should be developed around "essential questions." Essential questions are about the big ideas or fundamental concepts that we want students to think about and learn during the span of a unit. By posing questions, students and the teacher are able to focus their attention on content that will help answer the questions. Wiggins & McTighe (2005) indicate that essential questions provide a focus for the unit and have five important characteristics. Essential questions

- don't have one obvious answer
  - e.g., *Why are governments created?*
- raise other important question often across disciplines
  - e.g., *What policies can help reduce CO_2 emissions?*
- address philosophical or conceptual foundations of a discipline
  - e.g., *What is power?*
- recur naturally and are important enough to show up periodically
  - e.g., *What evidence of Time, Continuity, and Change is present in the U.S. military?*
- are framed to provoke student interest
  - e.g., *What starts a riot?*

A unit with essential questions is provided at the end of this chapter to provide an example of how to organize curriculum.

Components of a Unit Plan

Unit plans can have many components, but the following eight are frequently used by teachers when planning:

1. overview and rationale
2. goals and essential questions
3. targets
4. outline of content (the scope of the content in the unit)
5. calendar (the sequence in which students will learn the content)
6. daily lesson plans
7. assessments and evaluations
8. materials and resources.

The following descriptions of these components will clarify their purpose in the unit plan.

Overview and Rationale

The *rationale* for the unit provides a general *overview* and justification for teaching a unit on the topic you are selecting. The overview and rationale allow you to consider your reasons for developing the unit, and to determine how the content will build on your students' prior knowledge and skills. The overview also prepares you to consider available materials and resources, and how the unit fits into the overall scope and sequence for the school year. An overview and rationale often include:

- A title for the unit.
- The course in which this will be taught (e.g., world history, civics, current world problems).

- The grade level (e.g., ninth grade).
- A full introduction to the unit that addresses the question: *What is it you will be teaching, and more critically, what is it that students will be learning?* Be specific about the content of the unit and the activities that the students will be engaged in in order to learn the content.
- A description of how the unit fits into the existing curriculum. For example, what topic would precede the unit? What will follow it, and why? What existing skills and abilities should students possess before studying this unit? What skills, abilities, and knowledge will the students gain from this unit?

Your rationale statement considers the idea of what you selected for this unit out of all the possible topics you *could* have selected, and why you selected it. The rationale also prepares you to answer colleagues, parents, students, and others who might wonder why this content is important for students to learn. You might also consider how students will be able to use content and skills learned in the unit outside school.

Goals and Essential Questions

Goals (which were described earlier in Chapter 3) are often explicitly connected to a skill or content standard at the state or national level. Unit goals should include both academic content goals and skill goals. Often, *essential questions* come from these goals. As you read above, these are broad questions that will help the development of the unit. A unit typically has two to four essential questions.

Targets

Targets are concise statements that you want students to achieve during the study of your unit. Before teachers compose targets, they often pre-assess their students to see what content and skills students already have (or what deficits exist). These pre-assessments could occur during an informal question/answer session or discussion, or from a more formal pretest, survey, or series of interviews. Teachers also use their knowledge and previous experiences of what students typically know when they come to class. For example, high school U.S. history teachers are very aware that students do not remember important information related to the American Revolution, even though they study it in middle school. Therefore, high school teachers expect to have learning targets on this content. This allows teachers to activate students' prior knowledge about a given topic or skill. Concise, well-articulated, and focused targets are critical for a well-organized unit, because they focus the unit and will assist in your daily and long-range planning. Many unit targets are not met until partway through, or at the end of, a unit; therefore, they are broad and not tied to specific daily lessons. Targets should be written for academic content/information you want students to learn, skills you want them to gain, and dispositions you want them to develop. Follow the criteria for well-written targets that you utilized in Chapter 3, and include the following:

- What content will students be learning, and what activities will promote student learning?[4]
- How well should students be able to perform to demonstrate they have learned?

Try to list the unit targets under each learning goal you have established. This will establish a link among the goals and targets.

Outline of Content

An *outline of content* provides a concise overview, and answers the question: *What academic content will students learn from this unit?* The content outline is not a list of activities or instructional strategies—those will be determined after you determine the content that needs to be learned by your students. The content outline is often referred to as the scope of the content in the unit. You should not feel that you are creating this outline on your own. National and state standards provide guidance, as do some scope and sequence guides, and textbook teacher guides. Unit content outlines do not list everything that students will learn. Rather, they provide key concepts, categories, and topical areas in the unit. For example, part of a content outline for a unit on American democracy might include the following:

- ❖ Branches of Government
  - o Executive Branch
    - ▪ President
      - ✓ Terms
      - ✓ Requirements
    - ▪ Powers
      - ✓ Chief Executive
      - ✓ Chief of Staff
      - ✓ Commander in Chief
    - ▪ Checks and Balances
      - ✓ Veto
      - ✓ Nomination
  - o Legislative Branch
  - o Judicial Branch
- ❖ Elections

Calendar

The unit calendar gives an overview of the sequence of lessons. It provides the teacher with a "unit-at-a-glance" in regard to content, instructional strategies, and classroom activities. This aids in developing daily targets and lesson plans. Each day of the unit calendar identifies the topic to be taught, possible instructional activities, and assessments of student learning. The calendar becomes a device for considering the order in which the content will be taught/learned. It also helps you think about how much time you need to spend on each topic. By putting the unit targets into the calendar, you will be able to ensure your targets are fully addressed during the unit. Similarly, by listing the instructional strategies you might use, you can check that you are using a variety of activities, both within and across days. In this way, the calendar serves as a learning progression for your students. Notice that a calendar is *not* a lesson plan. Teacher interns new to a classroom sometimes misunderstand the cooperating teachers' depth of knowledge and experience and think they too can teach from brief descriptions on a calendar. Often this turns into lack of focused "winging it" and unhappy cooperating teachers. Also, a calendar is *not* set in stone, in that you must complete the tasks in the time specified. You will find that you need to decide what to do each day based on what students learned. That is why formative assessment is so important. In other words, you will make decisions about tomorrow's class after you determine students' understanding today. You may need to repeat or rethink several activities because students did not meet their learning targets. You might also need to teach tomorrow's plan, because students learned the content for today more quickly than you planned. In either case, the calendar gives the initial structure for the unit, but almost always changes so you can differentiate the learning for your students based on their progress.

The unit calendar could look like the example in Table 4.1.

Daily Lesson Plans

Daily lesson plans provide the structure and instructional strategies for each day. While the lesson plan is used each day, practically speaking, the daily lesson plan itself might address several days. For example, a teacher might have one lesson plan that takes three days as students are researching in the computer lab and meeting in groups to share their findings. Functionally, the lesson plans are expansions of the unit calendar, providing much more detail about each of the activities, content, assessment, and other particulars needed. The lesson plan is a document that takes many forms. It ranges from fully scripted comments by the teacher to a brief outline for the day. The lessons in a unit need to show in detail how each of the unit goals, essential questions, and targets are met.

Assessments and Evaluations

What could you do to determine that your students learned what you planned for them? Unit plans should address the range of diagnostic, formative, and summative *assessments and evaluations* you will use during the unit. Assessment principles were described in Chapter 3, and assessment will be considered throughout Part II of this book when each instructional strategy is examined. For purposes of planning a unit, assessments should be taken directly from the unit goals and targets. Assessments should also be sketched onto the unit calendar to match them with the content students are learning. When working with pre-service teachers, I have them describe each assessment tool they will use, and explain why that tool is valid in determining whether or not their students have learned. Assessment is a recursive process, whereby the teacher and students are continually examining what they are learning and using this insight to help determine future instruction and learning. Assessments are not merely the "final unit test." Rather, they occur throughout the unit, and planning for them ahead of time is crucial.[5] Again, the six facets of understanding can be a helpful guide for determining appropriate, valid, and authentic assessments. Note also that assessments and evaluations are listed near the end of the unit components. In actuality, you will want to develop the assessments at the start of your unit-planning time. It gives focus, and helps develop mastery learning by your students.

Materials and Resources

Materials and resources include both the sources used in writing your unit and the sources you will need as you write lesson plans, develop assessments, and prepare to help students

Table 4.1 Unit Calendar for a High School World History Class.

Unit Title: The Age of Discovery and America

Day 1	Day 2	Day 3	Day 4	Day 5
Topic: Introduction	*Topic:* Columbian Exchange	*Topic:* Discuss Columbus	*Topic:* Discuss Columbus, cont.	*Topic:* Discuss Columbus, cont.
Targets: 1.1, 1.2	*Target:* 2.1	*Target:* 3.2	*Target:* 2.2	*Target:* 2.2
Event: Questioning session to diagnose prior knowledge, perceptions, and misperceptions about Columbus and the discovery of America. Complete a K–W–L chart (where students identify what they Know, and what they Wonder about in regard to Columbus and his travels. This will be reviewed on Day 10 to examine what students learned). Short lecture highlighting key description of the discovery of America in students' textbook.	*Event:* Students will engage in a concept formation lesson about the broad idea of "exchange," and then tie that to examine examples of exchanges between the "Old World" and the "New World" during the age of discovery.	*Event:* Understanding the basics of debating. The format, pattern, rules, and formalities of debate will be explored and practiced with three different controversial topics. The purpose is more to learn about debate than to actually engage in a lengthy debate.	*Event:* Using a structured academic controversy, students will examine labels given to Columbus and consider why he should be remembered as a hero, villain, or somewhere in between these two extremes. Three primary source documents and two editorials will be reviewed.	*Event:* Engage in small group discussions about the legacy of Columbus. Start in groups of four, then combine these groups to make groups of eight that will come to an agreement about Columbus and how history should remember him.
Assessment: Diagnostic and formative recording of prior knowledge.	*Assessment:* Observation of working independently, completion of an "exit card" that asks students to differentiate between examples and non-examples of the concept.	*Assessment:* Observation of students engaging in civil conversations.	*Assessment:* Student writing: Opinions are supported with facts, and arguments are logical. Observation during the discussion.	*Assessment:* Student writing: Opinions are supported with facts, and arguments are logical. Observation during the discussion.

Day 6	Day 7	Day 8	Day 9	Day 10
Topic: Analyzing documents	*Topic:* Simulation about Native American death from disease	*Topic::* Simulation finish and debrief	*Topic:* Columbian Exchange revisited	*Topic:* Conclusion of unit
Targets: 1.1, 2.1	*Targets:* 1.1, 1.2	*Target:* 2.2	*Targets:* 2.1, 2.2	*Targets:* 1.1, 1.2
Event: Using primary source documents, develop a hypothesis about Columbus's travels to America.	*Event:* Students will engage in a simulation of how new germs might spread within a community, and then extend their understanding to the spread of smallpox and other diseases within the Native American groups after contact with Europeans.	*Event:* Complete the simulation from Day 7 and debrief of the connections of it to historical events about disease amongst native groups in America in the 1500s.	*Event:* Compare and contrast native plants taken from the Americas to Europe and European plants taken to the Americas. Students will investigate trade routes and understand the movements of plants and other goods between Europe, America, and Africa.	*Event:* Small group discussion of what the "age of discovery" is as an historical era. Discussion about the geographic concepts of "movement," and "human–environment interaction." Introduce the next unit on "colonization."
Assessment: Written assessment of an essay in which students present their ideas with evidence from primary sources.	*Assessment:* Observation of participation.	*Assessment:* Exit card of three connections between the simulation and historical details.	*Assessment:* Short essay exam.	*Assessment:* Participation during discussion, and short essay. Return to the K–W–L chart completed on Day 1.

learn the unit content. Some resources will provide materials only you will access, and some will be materials your students will need. Examples of materials and resources include:

- a resource list/references
  - print resources (books, articles)
  - media resources (videos, recordings, software, podcasts, blogs, other Internet sources)
  - community organizations, field trip ideas, businesses, guest speakers or other potential resources
- a materials list for each day of the unit (e.g., 15 globes; 30 computers reserved in the lab; 30 copies of *The New York Times*; 30 copies of the United States Constitution)
- graphic materials, such as transparencies/overhead projections, charts, graphs, diagrams, and photos; many of these will be developed with each lesson plan.

If you have not written a unit plan before, these eight components may seem daunting. Unit plans do require a significant amount of time and energy but, if they are written thoughtfully, individual lessons are then taught in a well-sequenced order that promotes student learning. It is important to develop the skills necessary to write a thoughtful unit. Pre-service teachers who have this ability are more likely to be successful during student teaching than those who do not (Harwood, Collins, & Sudzina, 2001).

As you read above, the calendar is important, but is often the most revised section of a student teacher's unit plan. It is not uncommon for the calendar to be two days off after you finish teaching the first week of a unit! For example, compare the revised calendar in Table 4.2 with the calendar in Table 4.1.

Additionally, schools are using block schedules, resulting in extended class sessions. Conventionally, students meet in class for about one hour, five days per week. In a block schedule, students may meet in class for two hours every other day, for 90 minutes every day, or for some other combination of hours and days. By the end of the school year, any given course will have met for 180 hours, but you will not necessarily have met every day. Block schedules are varied, and provide excellent opportunities to reduce the number of students you teach, integrate the curriculum, and meet for longer sessions to explore topics together and in more depth. Most social studies teachers we know use block days for simulations or learning activities that benefit from longer, more extensive meeting times. For these reasons, we suggest that the lesson plans be outlined in the calendar (so you know the order in which the content will be learned, and so you can prepare materials and resources in advance), but the actual lesson plans be finalized about a week in advance.

A portion of a unit plan on the Hundred Years' War that could be taught in a high school world history class is below. Note how each component is applied to this particular content area.

Overview and Rationale

This unit will help students examine how the Hundred Years' War, the Black Plague, and Joan of Arc all affected European society at the time and in the future. First, students will examine the role that feudalism played in society to bring about conflict between England and France that came to be known as the Hundred Years' War. After discussing the Hundred Years' War for three full days, students will be introduced to the Black Plague (day four). The plague interrupted fighting between the years 1348 and 1356. This will focus on helping

Table 4.2 Revised Calendar for a High School World History Class.

Unit Title: The Age of Discovery

Day 1	Day 2	Day 3	Day 4	Day 5
Topic: Introduction	*Topic:* Columbian Exchange	*Topic:* Discuss Columbus	*Topic:* Discuss Columbus, cont.	*Topic:* Discuss Columbus, cont.
Targets: 1.1, 1.2	*Target:* 2.1	*Target:* 3.2	*Target:* 2.2	*Target:* 2.2
Event: Questioning session to diagnose prior knowledge, perceptions, and misperceptions about Columbus and the discovery of America. Complete a K–W–L chart (where students identify what they Know, and what they Wonder about in regard to Columbus and his travels. This will be reviewed on Day 10 to examine what the students Learned). Short lecture highlighting the key description of the discovery of America in students' textbook.	*Event:* Students will engage in a concept formation lesson about the broad idea of "exchange," and then tie that to examine examples of exchanges between the "Old World" and the "New World" during the age of discovery.	*Event:* Understanding the basics of debating. The format, pattern, rules, and formalities of debate will be explored and practiced with three different controversial topics. The purpose is more to learn about debate than to actually engage in a lengthy debate. *Teacher's note:* JV football game and JV soccer game—half of class gone. Had those present understand debate and prepare a skit to present to the class.	*Event:* Using a structured academic controversy, students will examine labels given to Columbus and consider why he should be remembered as a hero, villain, or somewhere in between these two extremes. Three primary source documents and two editorials will be reviewed. *Teacher's note:* Skit presentation demonstrating effective discussion skills for controversial topics.	*Event:* Engage in small group discussions about the legacy of Columbus. Start in groups of four, then combine these groups to make groups of eight that will come to an agreement about Columbus and how history should remember him.
Assessment: Diagnostic and formative recording of prior knowledge.	*Assessment:* Observation of working independently, completion of an "exit card" that asks students to differentiate between examples and non-examples of the concept.	*Assessment:* Observation of students engaging in civil conversations.	*Assessment:* Student writing: Opinions are supported with facts, and arguments are logical. Observation during the discussion.	*Assessment:* Student writing: Opinions are supported with facts, and arguments are logical. Observation during the discussion.

(Continued)

Table 4.2 (Continued)

	Day 6	Day 7	Day 8	Day 9	Day 10
Topic	*Topic:* Analyzing documents *Targets:* 1.1, 2.1	*Topic:* Simulation about Native American death from disease *Targets:* 1.1, 1.2	*Topic:* Simulation finish and debrief *Target:* 2.2	*Topic:* Columbian Exchange revisited *Targets:* 2.1, 2.2	*Topic:* Conclusion of unit *Targets:* 1.1, 1.2
Event	*Event:* Using primary source documents, develop a hypothesis about Columbus's travels to America. *Teacher's note:* Inquiries took longer than planned. Had to bump this activity into the next day, and move all days forward.	*Event:* Students will engage in a simulation of how new germs might spread within a community, and then extend their understanding to the spread of smallpox and other diseases within the Native American groups after contact with Europeans.	*Event:* Complete the simulation from Day 7 and debrief of the connections of it to historical events about disease amongst native groups in America in the 1500s. *Teacher's note:* Ended early, and began Columbian Exchange Route conversation at the end of the class.	*Event:* Compare and contrast native plants taken from the Americas to Europe and European plants taken to the Americas. Students will investigate trade routes and understand the movements of plants and other goods between Europe, America, and Africa.	*Event:* Small-group discussion of what the "age of discovery" is as an historical era. Discussion about the geographic concepts of "movement," and "human–environment interaction." Introduce the next unit on "colonization."
Assessment	*Assessment:* Written assessment of an essay in which students present their ideas with evidence from primary sources.	*Assessment:* Observation of participation.	*Assessment:* Exit card of three connections between the simulation and historical details.	*Assessment:* Short essay exam.	*Assessment:* Participation during discussion, and short essay. Return to the K–W–L chart completed on Day 1.

students understand how the outbreak of the Black Plague is similar in scope and severity to many other plagues that have happened throughout our world's history, including modem pandemics. Students will learn about the plague primarily through an inquiry project.

After examining the Black Plague, students will be introduced to Joan of Arc. After examining and learning about the set of events surrounding her rise to power and eventual capture, students will engage in a mock trial of Joan. Students will learn why Joan was accused of heresy, and ultimately sentenced to death. The hope is that students will be able to explain why she was found guilty, and how her martyrdom affected both Christianity and European society in the many years after her death.

This is an important unit for students to learn. Even though the material deals with events that took place many hundreds of years ago, the concepts and ideas of the unit are still relevant today. For example, the Hundred Years' War is important to study because the events that preceded and then fueled the conflict are very representative of the type of conflict and problems that came to symbolize the "dark ages" in early European society. The Hundred Years' War is a perfect case study of how feudalism, specifically familial loyalties, led to conflicts and disagreement over inheritance, ascendancy, and possession of land and resources. Finally, studying Joan of Arc's rise to power, capture, and eventual trial and death is important because it clearly shows the type and amount of power that the Church held in society during this time.

Goals and Essential Questions

Upon completion of this unit students will be able to:

1. Analyze the change and continuity in Western European society as a result of the Hundred Years' War and bubonic plague. (State history standard 4.1.1)
2. Analyze how Joan of Arc shaped world history. (State history standard 4.2.1)
3. Evaluate the viewpoints and arguments of both themselves and others within the context of a discussion. (State social studies skill 5.3.1)

Essential Questions:

*   How does change affect society?
*   What legacy do acts of bravery leave?
*   How should canonized figures be remembered?

Sample Targets (each is tied to one of the above three goals, and written as an "I can" statement)

1. Analyze the change and continuity in Western European society as a result of the Hundred Years' War and bubonic plague.

    a) I can write a short paragraph explaining why the Gascon Fief, coming out of feudalistic loyalties, led to the French ascendancy crisis and thus the Hundred Years' War.
    b) I can describe what key people did during the Hundred Days' War, and why it was important to the outcome of the war and European society during and after when I see their name on a list.

c) I can examine primary sources and other documents relating to the Hundred Years' War, the bubonic plague, and Joan of Arc and then explain why they are significant, what we can learn from them, and how they reflect the given time period in which they are located.

2.   Analyze how Joan of Arc shaped world history.

a) I can explain why and how Joan of Arc rose to significance in a paragraph as an exit slip.
b) I can show I understand how Joan of Arc was captured, imprisoned, and killed, by writing a descriptive paragraph detailing these conditions.

3.   Evaluate the viewpoints and arguments of both themselves and others within the context of a discussion.

a) I can decide if I strongly agree, agree, have no opinion, disagree, or strongly disagree with issues related to the Hundred Days' War and Joan of Arc.

Portion of the Outline of Content (the scope of the content in the unit)

1 Hundred Years' War

A: Causes
   I   1066: Norman Conquest
   II   French Ascendancy Crisis
         i   Armagnacs vs. Burgundians
         ii   1314: Philip IV's death leads to Charles IV
         iii Edward II and III claim French throne
   III Feudalism's Role
         i   Gascon Fief
               a   Philip reclaims fief, saying Edward has broken his oath by not attending to demands of his lord
               b   Edward responds by saying he is rightful heir to French throne

B: Engagement
   I   First Peace: 1360–1369
         i   Treaty of Bretigny
   II   Second Peace: 1389–1415
         ii   Armagnac vs. Burgundian Civil War
   III French Ascendancy under Henry V
         i   Battle of Agincourt and Crecy
               a   English victory: longbow
   IV French Victory: 1429–1453
         i   Joan of Arc
         ii   Battle of Orleans
         iii Treaty of Arras

C: Significance
   I   War of Roses

  II Military Weapon Advancement

  III Questions about English Monarchy

   i Wat Tyler rebellion

  IV Estates General and Great Ordinance

2 The Black Plague

A: Causes

  I Rats

  II Malnutrition/Disease/Hunger

  III War

B: Scope and Severity

  I 75 million people worldwide 1348–1351

  II 25–50 million people died in Europe

  III 30–60 percent of Europe's population dies

C: Symptoms/Experiences

  I Symptoms

  II Prognosis

D: Effects

Select Days from a Calendar (the sequence in which students will learn the content)

Day 1	Day 4	Day 8	Day 9	Day 14
Topic: Introduction to unit, background to High Middle Ages, feudalism—Gascon Fief	*Topic:* The Black Plague: introduction of plague, causes, scope and severity, symptoms/experiences, effects	*Topic:* Joan of Arc: Rise to power, leader of French Army	*Topic:* Joan of Arc mock trial introduction	*Topic:* Debrief Joan of Arc mock trial
Targets: 1.a; 1.b	*Targets:* 1.d,1.b	*Targets:* 1.b, 1.d, 2.a	*Target:* 3.a	*Targets:* 2.b, 2.c
Activity: Lecture/Think–Pair–Share; ID Gascon Fief	*Activity:* 75 Million Simulation, Lecture/Think–Pair–Share, Primary Source Analysis: ID The Black Plague	*Activity:* Primary Source Analysis: ID Battle of Agincourt (1415), Siege of Orleans	*Activity:* Choose characters; pretrial multiple choice test; Joan of Arc legal issues: take-a-stand activity	*Activity:* Class discussion and reflection; write descriptive paragraph about or draw a picture of her detention
Assessment: Exit-slip paragraph: Explain why the Gascon Fief led to the French ascendancy crisis and thus the Hundred Years' War by writing a short paragraph as an exit slip.	*Assessment:* Assess student success at beginning and end with response questions. Homework: Visit Spanish Flu of 1918 website, and AIDS website.	*Assessment:* Exit slip: Write a quick paragraph explaining how and why Joan of Arc rose to significance. Check identification sheet. Summative: Data Collection Charts.	*Assessment:* Pretrial multiple choice test. Homework: Joan of Arc historical essays 1, 2, 3, 4.	*Assessment:* Collect and give participation points for descriptive paragraph or creative drawing relating to Joan's detention conditions.

Daily Lesson Plans

These are described in the lesson plan section of this chapter and examined extensively in Part II of this book.

Assessments and Evaluations

For this unit example, assessments are included in the calendar.

Materials and Resources

Morice, L. (1991). *Joan of Arc*. Lakeside, CA: Interaction Publishers.
Curriculum Guides and Journal Articles (2002). Duplin County Schools. Retrieved June 10, 2008, from World History Curriculum. http://duplinschools.l1et/BOE/Instruct.
Bingham, M. (1994). Joan of Arc and women's medieval military tradition: A lesson plan. *Social Education*. 58, 71–73.
Renton School District No. 403. (1997). Social Studies Curriculum Guide World History Grade Ten. [Brochure]. Renton, WA.

Sample of Materials

Day 1:
- Vocabulary Identification Worksheet (30 copies)

Day 4:
- Toggenburg Bible Sheet Introduction Question (30 copies)
- Mathematical Unit Cubes: (1, 10, 100, 1000)
- Envelopes—stuffed with rats or running shoes
- Gabriele de' Mussi's Account of the Plague sheet (30 copies)

INTERDISCIPLINARY UNIT PLANS

Interdisciplinary unit plans integrate topics from more than one course around a common theme or idea. These are increasingly being used in middle schools and high schools because they allow students to identify connections across several content areas. Teachers develop interdisciplinary units to provide learners with opportunities to think about course content in relation to other courses (or disciplines). The eight components listed on page 102 are the same for an interdisciplinary unit. The unit is more complex because it takes into account more information, and because it needs to describe how the content areas will be integrated. The most common approach for developing interdisciplinary unit plans is to focus the plan around a common theme. Interdisciplinary units are built around a theme that multiple content areas could address. For example, "conflict" might be addressed in a history course (studying causes of a war), in an English course (studying the use of conflict in plot development), in a mathematics course (learning to graph data related to population growth and conflict with natural resources), and in a biology course (examining the conflict of people and natural resources). These topics would be taught anyway, but the teachers agree to teach them at the same time to help students make connections across disciplines. Some schools promote "team teaching" whereby students share the same teachers during the course of a day. These teams often represent the core subject areas of mathematics, science, language arts/English, and social studies. This allows teachers to know what was learned in other classes that was related to the theme. Other subject areas (e.g., music, physical education, foreign languages) are often electives for students. Although these subject areas can join the thematic approach, it is more difficult to have a structure in place that ensures interdisciplinary units.

MAKING IT WORK IN YOUR CLASSROOM

Think about how you could develop each of the components of a unit plan for a social studies course you might teach at a middle school or high school. Think of a topic that would require at least two weeks of curriculum, and has connections to state and national standards. Consider how you would answer these questions:

*   What would you write for a unit introduction and rationale?
*   What goals and essential questions would students meet/answer?
*   What information/content targets would students meet?
*   What skills would they develop?
*   What dispositions would students form?
*   What would a content outline for the unit include?
*   How could you assess student learning during the unit?

Some teachers teach interdisciplinary units—for example, language arts—and social studies teachers' content might be combined for a "core" class at the middle school level. Discuss the questions above with a teacher or colleague from another content area.

THE LESSON PLAN

A *lesson plan* is most commonly thought of as the daily plan. Though a lesson may span more than one day (for example, a mock trial could take three days from start to finish), the plan specifies the "look and feel" of a day in your classroom. In this section you can see the components of a lesson plan, but in Part II of this book we will return to lesson planning with each of the instructional strategies described.

Components of a Lesson Plan

Many formats for lesson plans are available, and you will develop your own preference for a lesson plan as you prepare to teach. The following nine parts of a lesson are commonplace in schools, and will provide structure to your class sessions:

1. lesson targets
2. language targets
3. assessments
4. initiation or start of lesson
5. teacher activities
6. student activities
7. closure
8. materials and resources
9. reflections.

Each is briefly described below:

Lesson Targets

These are the specific learning targets that you have for the lesson or day. They should meet the criteria described in Chapter 3, so not much more detail will be included here. Include content, skill, and social interaction (CSS) targets. Your students should be able to accomplish these targets by the end of the lesson. Consider having two to four targets for each day. You should plan to tell students the daily targets, because they need to know what they will be learning. Write the targets on the board so everyone can see them, and use "I can . . ." or "I will . . ." to help students personalize them.

Language Targets

As we discussed in Chapter 1, all students need to be focused on improvement of academic language, not only the ELL students. These are specific targets related to the academic language focus you have for the lesson. These daily targets can be directed by the teacher or created democratically with the class. What language do *they* think they should be accountable for at the end of the day? This language can be added to a board or butcher paper at the front of the room each day to help create a unit language list. In each chapter of Part II, you will read specific examples and ideas for addressing language targets for ELLs, and these can be easily modified to use for all students as they develop academic language.

Assessments

These are closely tied to the targets. The assessments may be diagnostic, formative, or summative, depending on when the lesson will be taught in the unit. Formative and summative assessments occur near the end of a lesson, but planning a lesson with a "backward design" (Wiggins & McTighe, 2005) means that you think of the assessment before you plan the lesson's activities. This will ensure that the activities are authentic tasks that prepare students to demonstrate their learning on the assessments. Refer to the descriptions of assessment in Chapter 3.

Initiation or Start of the Lesson

Starting the lesson has also been called the "anticipatory set," or the manner by which you will help the students anticipate what will be happening for the day (some refer to this metaphorically as the "hook" by which you catch the students' attention). This could be a question, a poster, music, or even a short activity. The initiation of the lesson is important to consider because it helps the students focus on the lesson. The initiation should have some connection to the content of the lesson. For example, a lesson about the great influenza outbreak in 1918 might start with a map of the U.S. showing locations of the deaths from the epidemic, or a video clip about epidemics, or simply the number "1918" written on the whiteboard. Another way to think about the initiation is this: Students will be coming to your classroom with many things in their minds; what can you do at the start of your lesson to gain their attention and help them start thinking about your course?

Teacher Activities

These are the activities you will undertake during the course of the lesson. By specifying your activities during the lesson, you can think about how you will present information, where you will stand, or the order in which you provide information to your students. These will be described in detail when the logistics for each instructional strategy are outlined in Part II of this book. When planning what you will do to lead the class, consider student diversity, individualized educational plans (IEPs), student motivation, and classroom management. Many beginning teachers choose to write a script for difficult portions of their lessons. If they are concerned about placing students in groups, or about their key points they want to be sure students consider, then scripts help teachers think through what they might say. Oftentimes, teachers do not use these scripts during the lesson, but the process of writing the script helps them think through the ideas and content. Scripts can easily be placed in the "teacher activities" section of the lesson. This section of your lesson plan is also a good place to estimate the amount of time each activity will take. At the end of the lesson your estimation can be compared with the actual time needed. For example: How long will it take for the initiation? How long for a quiz? How long for introducing a concept?

Student Activities

The emphasis of any teaching activity is whether students have learned. By specifying student activities, you can plan for direct connections between the activities you are engaged in and the activities of your students. It allows you to be clear about your expectations for student behavior that will help maximize learning. For example, if the teacher activity is to present information in a PowerPoint presentation, then what should students be doing—taking notes? listening? If you are facilitating a simulation, then what are the students to do during the simulation? Your estimation of minutes for student activities should also be included. Taken together, the minutes for teacher activities and the minutes for student activities must equal the amount of time allocated for your class session. Additionally, if you have many more activities than your students, then you are probably having too much of a teacher-centered lesson. Consider shifting the classroom dynamic so students are more engaged in learning activities.

Closure

Just as the initiation started the lesson, closure brings an end to the day. When planning the closure, consider how the lesson should be concluded, how the content and skills can be reviewed to be sure students have learned them, or even a comment that will set the stage for the next class session. Sometimes teachers close a lesson with a short quiz or other assessment activity. If you recall from Chapter 3, **exit cards** can be used to determine what students have learned. If a lesson has good closure, the students feel confident about the teacher's management of the classroom. The clock should not signal the end of class; the end of the closing activity should. Some lessons need to continue into the next day. If that is the case, then the closure activity should help students see how the day's activities will be revisited the next day.

Materials and Resources

A materials and resources list provides a quick overview of what is needed for the day. It should be safe to assume that your classroom will have paper, pencils, chalkboard/whiteboard, and an overhead projector. More and more classrooms are having projection units and document cameras. Materials and resources are those beyond the standard items, and could include handouts for your students, copies of parts of a speech, or other materials that you will use during the lesson. Additionally, materials and resources may include lecture notes, primary source artifacts, a blog, a video, or anything that you will need to successfully conduct the lesson. The materials and resources will be specific to each lesson and should be similar to the list you created for the unit plan.

Reflections

It is important to reflect on a lesson after you have taught it. In Chapter 2 you read about differences among *planned, taught, hidden, null,* and *learned* curricula. By including a space at the end of a lesson plan to reflect on your assessments and targets, you can determine what your students have learned. If you planned something different from what they learned (for example, if the content was too difficult and your students did not meet a learning target), then you can modify the lesson plan for the next day. Your reflections can also be directed by the four commonplaces of Schwab that were described earlier: Consider the role of the *teacher,* the *students,* the *content,* and the *milieu* in student learning. It is important to reflect and comment on the lesson plan as well, so that you can improve your lesson the next time you teach from it. These reflections could help you make improvements for the next period, or they could be used a year later when you teach from a unit plan again. Every time you teach a lesson it should improve because of the reflections. We will explore reflections more later on in this chapter.

The following lesson-plan template is a sample that teachers might use, and identifies each of the components in the plan. In addition, this template includes a title, and names the unit from which the lesson comes.

Sample Lesson Plan Template

TOPIC FOR THE LESSON: Date:
Grade Level/Course:
Unit:
Lesson Targets (information, disposition, and skill targets):
   1)
   2)
   3)

Assessments:

Activities:

Initiation/Opening		Time
Teacher's Activities	Students' Activities	Time
Closure		Time

Pre-planning:

Materials/Resources:

__Video recorder	__DVD	__Worksheets	__Computer Lab
__Handouts	__Notes	__Other (list items needed):	

Instructional Strategies to Be Used:

__Discovery Learning	__Cooperative Learning	__Simulations	__Debate
__Discussion	__Concept Formation	__Questioning	__Lecture
__Inquiry	__Other		

Reflections/Notes:

_____

The following lesson plan shows how the template might be filled in by a teacher prior to class:

Sample Lesson Plan[6]

TOPIC FOR THE LESSON: Veterans Day Project Introduction   Date:
Grade Level/Course: 11th Grade/U.S. History
Unit: "The Hot and Cold War, 1939–1960"
Lesson Targets:

1) I can research about one U.S. veteran's duty by creating a presentation board and short speech of him/her. (Note: This is the introductory lesson for an activity that will require several days to complete.)

Assessments:
Outline of plan of action for locating and interviewing a veteran for this project

Activities:

Initiation/Opening "Have any of your relatives served in the United States Armed Forces? Do you have any friends who have served in Iraq, Afghanistan, or the Middle East?		Time 5 min
Teacher's Activities Tell the students the target of this project. Students are to actively seek out a veteran and interview them about their thoughts, feelings, and experiences during their time on duty. Use the rubric to help them understand what is expected of them. (Paper length and content, as well as the presentation board and short speech.) The rubric will break these down. Give an outline and rubric to the students. Give students plenty of time to ask questions regarding the project. Explain that a veteran doesn't necessarily have to mean that the person has to have fought in a war. A veteran is anyone who has served in any of the armed forces. An example is that of a nurse in the army. The veteran doesn't have to be a United States veteran either, as long as they are a veteran of some country's armed forces.	Students' Activities Gain an understanding of the outline and the grading rubric. Be prepared to go out into the community and actively find a veteran if you do not know one (out-of-class). Students are welcome to start researching during class time at a computer or the library, as long as they do not have any further questions regarding the assignment. A student may wish to research different conflicts and try to interview a veteran from a particular conflict. Begin research if all questions have been answered. If students go to the library, make sure they are back before the class is over.	Time 30 min
Closure Bring students back together, whether they are researching or finalizing their questions. Give the students the last 10 minutes of class to talk openly about their thoughts on what it means to be a veteran.		Time 10 min

Pre-planning:

Materials/Resources:

__Video recorder   __DVD   __Worksheets   __Computer Lab
_X_ Handouts   __Notes   __Other (list items needed):

Instructional Strategies to Be Used:
_X_ Discovery Learning __Cooperative Learning   __Simulations   __Debate
_X_ Discussion   __Concept Formation   __Questioning   __Lecture
_X_ Inquiry   __Other

Reflections/Notes:

_____

Pre-service teachers often notice that some experienced teachers do not have a lesson plan with them when they teach. It seems as though the teacher simply guides the students without referring to the written document that is required of most student teachers. When you observe teachers you may find this to be true. However, we encourage you to consider that the teachers you observe may not have a written lesson plan, but they do use a lesson plan— that is, their plans may not be written out, but they have thought through the components of such a plan. If asked to, these teachers could usually produce a written plan. The Interstate New Teacher Assessment and Support Consortium (InTASC) and the Educational Testing Service Praxis II and III assessments and most states' Teacher Performance Assessments (TPA) require that beginning teachers thoughtfully consider and document lesson planning.[7]

Lesson plans provide documentation of what students should have learned in your classroom, and they document how your class is helping students learn content that is tied to district, state, and national content standards. During your student teaching, and when you are observed as an in-service teacher, you will be expected to write lesson plans. By having a written document, you will be able to ensure that you deliver all you have planned, that you pace your lesson to maximize class time, that your lesson efficiently moves through the learning activities, and that you are able to assess student learning and determine when your targets have been met.

THE IMPORTANCE OF REFLECTION WHEN PLANNING

In the previous section on lesson planning we noted that reflection is an important part of the plan. Reflection is a progressive process through which you consider what happened—good and bad—so that your future actions are improved. In this section we suggest that reflection and planning should take place during the lesson, after the students have left the classroom, and when planning future lessons. Killion and Todnem (1991) describe these three types of reflection as "reflection-in-action," "reflection-on-action," and "refection-for-action" (p. 15).

Reflection-in-Action

Reflection-in-action is the process of monitoring students' work and progress during the class meeting. This involves noting whether time spent on an activity needs to be extended or shortened based on your students' understanding and engagement. The lesson plan is what you take into the classroom, but reflection-in-action is a continual process of determining whether the plan optimizes student learning. The opposite of this type of reflection is being oblivious to the various phenomena occurring in the classroom. Consider how a history teacher might reflect in action; if you are teaching about a historical event and a student brings up a current event that is related and similar, you need to make a quick decision: Is the time needed to talk about the current event an appropriate step to take? You might quickly assess if you have enough time in class, and if the current event will make the historical event more relevant and understandable. You might gauge students to determine if they are interested in the current event. Finally, you might decide to spend the rest of class time exploring the current event, and revisit the historical event the following day. All of these thoughts are reflections while you are teaching. They impact the lesson at the moment, and will modify and adjust what your students are learning.

Reflection-on-Action

Reflection-on-action is defined by Killion and Todnem as "reflection on practice and on one's actions after the practice is completed" (1991, p. 15). This is the most well-known reflection. You ask yourself: *What went well? What needs improvement before the next period starts? What need to be changed before teaching this lesson again?* This reflection is a powerful way to benefit from your successes and failures. For example, if you allocated 15 minutes to read a four-page article, and your students needed 30 minutes to read it, then you can plan for longer reading times in the future. As we mentioned earlier, Schwab's four commonplaces (1973) are a helpful heuristic tool for reflecting on your practice. These questions could guide you to consider each of these commonplaces:

- How did the teacher impact student learning in today's lesson?
- How did the student(s) impact learning in today's lesson?
- Was the content learned? If not, was the content appropriate? Inappropriate? Too difficult? Too simple?
- How did the classroom environment help or hinder student learning in today's lesson?

Reflection-for-Action

The third type of reflection that is important for teachers is *reflection-for-action*. Reflection-for-action is assumed in the previous two types of reflections, but singling it out helps teachers focus on how to make future teaching promote student learning. We assume that when you reflect while teaching you will also determine what actions to take during class so learning is enhanced. When you reflect at the end of a class, the intent is to improve the lesson. Reflection-for-action simply puts a label to this type of thinking. You reflect with an eye toward improving future actions. Teachers reflect on what they did and on what their students learned, and gain insights from these reflections that will inform future actions. Figure 4.3 outlines this process.

Often, reflections simply identify problems that occurred. Reflection, for example, might help you realize that shy students are not talking during discussions, or that better Internet sites need to be located, or that students lack note-taking strategies. The point of reflection, however, is to create meaning from your observations and reflections, and to develop

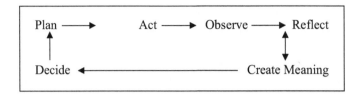

Figure 4.3   Planning for Improving Future Lessons.

Adapted from Killion and Todnem, 1991, p. 15

strategies for your future teaching. Shy students may need more opportunities to share in small groups; search strategies may need to be reviewed prior to embarking on research in the computer lab; and students may need modeling from you about taking notes.

Many schools have adopted a *peer coach* model, whereby teachers observe one another and help reflect on lessons; another term for this is the *critical friend* model. The observations are not an evaluation of the teacher, but an opportunity to identify outcomes of your teaching and strategies to improve your teaching—and to ultimately improve your students' learning. It is an effective approach for pinpointing areas of your teaching. For example, Mr. Green and Ms. Lamb, two social studies teachers, have decided to adopt the peer-coaching model. Ms. Lamb observes a world geography lesson in which students listen to Mr. Green's lecture on sweatshops in third world countries. The students are then asked to create posters that display examples of sweatshops in various countries around the world.

Ms. Lamb has reflective prompts for Mr. Green that include:

- What did you do that effectively impacted student learning?
- How did the students positively or negatively impact learning in this lesson?
- Were your targets met in the lesson? How do you know? Did you ask too much from them? Too little?
- Was the environment of the classroom conducive to learning today? What could you have done about it?

Mr. Green and Ms. Lamb discuss the prompts on a teacher workday. Mr. Green indicates that the students seemed to "go along" with the lesson but were not overly enthused. He is looking for a way to generate more enthusiasm and also to help students "do something more" with the information. From this discussion Mr. Green decides that a change in instructional strategy will improve the lesson. Next time he will try an inquiry approach (see Chapter 11) in which the students, in teams, are asked to create "webquests" (Internet inquiry lessons) on child labor. He decides they could create their own specific questions to pursue, such as "Should you buy tennis shoes made through sweatshop labor?" After completing the webquests, students will have a classroom discussion to help them create a list of possible socially responsible actions related to what they have learned. At the end of their meeting, Mr. Green and Ms. Lamb agree upon a time that he will observe Ms. Green's U.S. history class the following week.

ACTION RESEARCH

Action research is another form of reflection that teachers use; it is often defined as a structured approach with which to examine and learn from one's experience. For teachers, action research is a purposeful way to identify a phenomenon in the classroom, determine an approach for gaining insight into this phenomenon, and assess if the approach was effective. When teachers engage in action research they intend to improve upon their practice. Teachers may do so to evaluate their use of particular instructional strategies, or to find a solution to a problem they are facing. Action research is usually carried out by the teacher, and not outside "researchers," and the results/findings of the research are usually limited to the classroom or school in which the teacher works. For example, if a group of students have difficulty comprehending a section of an Advanced Placement government textbook, then a teacher may devise a strategy for improving comprehension, and develop an assessment tool for measuring the effectiveness of the strategy. This strategy should be based on research findings from other studies, but the teacher often will modify it to fit the needs of particular students in his classroom. After using the comprehension improvement strategy, the teacher then uses the assessment tool to determine the effectiveness of the strategy. In this manner, teachers are engaging in a type of research that relies on their reflections about a problem and systematically analyzes strategies for solving the problem. This gives teachers greater confidence that their planning is going to have a positive impact on student learning. Action research is much more in-depth than this; however, this brief introduction may be helpful as you consider the importance of reflective teaching.

CHAPTER REVIEW

- Four common classroom elements to consider while planning
  - Students
  - Milieu
  - Teacher
  - Content
- Writing unit plans that contain eight frequently used components
  - Overview and rationale
  - Goals and essential questions
  - Targets
  - Outline of content (the scope of the content in the unit)
  - Calendar (the sequence that students will learn the content)
  - Daily lesson plans
  - Assessments and evaluations
  - Materials and resources
- Understanding by Design provides a framework to consider six facets of understanding
  - Explain
  - Interpret
  - Apply
  - Shift perspective
  - Empathize
  - Self-assess
- Lesson planning
  1. Lesson targets
  2. Language targets
  3. Assessments
  4. Initiation or start of lesson
  5. Teacher activities

6. Student activities
7. Closure
8. Materials and resources
9. Reflections.

NOTES

1. To access these data and other statistics related to education, visit the Center's website at http:// nces. ed.gov/surveys.
2. The Massachusetts Department of Elementary and Secondary Education provides this information on its website: http://www.doe.mass.edu/frameworks/hss/final.doc.
3. This is from the Authentic Education website that provides professional development about Wiggins and McTighe's work. http://www.authenticeducation.org/ubd/ubd.lasso
4. As you read about each instructional strategy in Part II, you will be much more knowledgeable about how selecting appropriate and effective activities will help you meet these targets.
5. I encourage teachers not to have a test or exam on the last day of the unit. The traditional unit test is often used by teachers as the closing activity of the unit. Too often students will "cram for the test," and then move on to the next unit. If you want your students to take a test, I suggest having them take it a few days before the end of the unit. End the unit with a simulation, presentation, or some other activity that will allow students to think about the unit content at a high level. Not only will their studying for the test help them for that task, but it will help them as they access the information during a more authentic activity at the end of the unit.
6. Appreciation to Derek Olson and Nevada Black for their ideas contributing to this lesson.
7. The Praxis II exam is reviewed at this URL: http://www.ets.org/praxis.

REFERENCES

Erickson, H. L. (2002). *Concept-Based Curriculum and Instruction: Teaching Beyond the Facts*. Thousand Oaks, CA: Corwin Press.

Harwood, A. M., Collins, L., & Sudzina, M. (2001). An examination of student teacher failure: Implications for teacher education programs. In J. Rainer and E. Guyton (Eds.), *Teacher Education Yearbook*. Dubuque, IA: Association of Teacher Educators/Kendall Hunt Publishing.

Killion, J. & Todnem, G. (1991). A process for personal theory-building. *Educational Leadership*, *48*(6), 14–16.

Schwab, J. J. (1973). The practical 3: Translation into curriculum. *School Review*, *81*, 501–522.

Washington State Office of the Superintendent of Public Instruction (2003). *Social Studies Frameworks: Grades 9–12*. Olympia, WA: Author.

Wiggins, G. & McTighe, J. (2011). *The Understanding by Design Guide to Creating High-Quality Units*. Alexandria, VA: ASCD.

Wiggins, G. & McTighe, J. (2005). *Understanding by Design*, 2nd ed. Alexandria, VA: ASCD.

PART II

Instructional Strategies for Social Studies

CHAPTER 5

Lecture and Interactive Presentations

CHAPTER GOALS

In this chapter, you will learn about:

- Research support for using lectures and other interactive presentation techniques
- Step-by-step procedures for selecting, planning, and using lectures
- Managing the classroom/learning environment during lectures and presentations
- Assessing student learning appropriately during and after lectures
- Using technology to enhance learning
- Considerations for English language learners during lectures and interactive strategies.

Teacher-centered   Student-centered

Lecture

Questioning

Concept Formation

Simulation/Role-Play/Drama

Cooperative Learning

Discussion

SDI

In 1944, March 19, the Nazis occupied German. They put us in the ghetto. From the ghetto they took us to the factory. From there, in the cattle car they took us to Auschwitz. First of all, it took me a long time before I was even able to tell my story . . . After I got liberated I didn't want to talk about it. I lost my grandma, my mom, my little sister and brother. They had taken all five of us, and I came home alone . . . they ask me if I still hate and I say a big "no." If I would have hate now in my heart, I would not be free. I would be the prisoner of my own hate. And Hitler is dead and he would be still winning. I don't want to be a prisoner any more. I want to be free, and I am a free woman . . . I know that maybe this is the last generation that could say, "I heard a Survivor. She told me what happened."

Ms. Noemi Ban is a well-known speaker in the city of Bellingham, WA, because she brings a stirring first-hand account of the atrocities of the Nazi concentration camps. She is a regular at school assemblies as well as in history classrooms. Teachers and students welcome her, because she is able to present her story in a compelling and concise manner. Teachers will often build on her lecture, and the ensuing question and answer session with students and Ms. Ban, to introduce the topic of the Holocaust. Teachers often prepare students to come to class with one or two questions, and to write down questions while she is speaking.

OVERVIEW

We have all experienced lectures at which the teacher was a gifted speaker and the students were enthralled by the stories, anecdotes, and details being delivered. Most of us have watched a teacher use pictures, artifacts, video, and/or other visual aids to highlight key points and help us understand the topic. Most of us have also been a student in a class where a guest speaker comes and tells about firsthand or real-life experiences. However, just as likely, we have all had teachers who talk and talk without much regard for their students. Lectures from those teachers and guest speakers become something to endure because they contain an excessive amount of facts, do not actively engage students or require much thinking, or are simply boring. To be blunt, lecturing to students is overused because it is easy for the teacher to control the students and the content being presented. Very quickly, lecture can turn into a class session where the teacher merely tells students what s/he knows. Certainly information is being distributed, but most of the research on lecturing suggests that students remember very little from a lecture, and the information they do remember is not retained very well after a few days or weeks. However, if done well, a lecture or presentation from the teacher or a guest speaker has the potential to be a powerful strategy that you need to consider using as part of your repertoire of instructional strategies.

The following definitions of a few terms will help describe those instructional strategies that fit in this chapter. *Lecture* is an instructional strategy with which the teacher presents a specified set of information to students. These presentations take a variety of forms that will be examined in this chapter. For lecture to be most effective, it should provide opportunities for interactions amongst students and with the teacher. That is why the title of this chapter includes *"interactive presentations."* Another category of teacher-centered and teacher-directed instructional strategies is often called direct instruction. The teacher directs students purposely to ensure that specific content or skills are learned. This is not the focus of this chapter, but a concise description later in the chapter will help you understand its usefulness in the classroom.

A DESCRIPTION OF LECTURE, PRESENTATIONS, AND RESEARCH FINDINGS

Lecture and Presentations

Lecturing offers several advantages and reasons for using it in the classroom (Barbetta & Scaruppa, 1995; Heward, 2005). Lecturing allows the teacher to present a specific amount of information quickly and efficiently. It can be used with large or small groups and can be used in each of the social studies content areas. When lecturing, the teacher has a tremendous amount of control over how much emphasis will be placed on certain concepts, facts, and course content. Lecturing enables you to present important content that your students may not be able to learn on their own (for example, a complex economic theory such as an embargo could initially be presented at the appropriate level of understanding during a lecture). During a lecture you control the content and information and use class time to focus students' attention on topics that are particularly important or difficult to learn. Lectures allow you to highlight the keys points that students may overlook or not understand during independent reading, working on the Internet, or participating in project-based activities. If you are passionate and enthusiastic about the topic of the lecture, then this excitement for the content is often passed on to the students. I watched a teacher excite students about the U.S. Supreme Court through a simple 35-minute lecture. She talked about the personal lives of the justices, the role of the court in deciding issues that impact our daily lives, and how the court serves as a check and balance to the President and the Congress. More important, however, was her excitement about the topic. She was animated and enthusiastic, brought in personal stories about her interest in the Supreme Court, and generally exuded a passion about the topic. The students' engagement with the talk stemmed partly from the content of the lecture, and partly from the affective impact of the teacher's enthusiasm. Lecture is not always thought of as a strategy for exciting students about content, but it has tremendous potential for this.

As mentioned earlier, students are often passive observers during lectures, because most lectures do not require students to participate beyond listening, note-taking, and asking periodic questions. This passive role is one that many students will enjoy, because it is non-threatening and easy. One of the most long-standing and important educational research findings is that students who make frequent, relevant responses during a lesson learn more than students who are passive observers (Brophy & Good, 1986; Fisher & Berliner, 1985). The challenge for you when using lecture is to determine how to promote students to respond in some way to the lecture or presentation. For example, during a lecture on the economic causes of the Great Depression, the teacher might ask students to turn to a partner and for one minute discuss whether they agree or disagree with the idea of govenment bailouts of corporations that are so large that if they went bankrupt the economy might suffer drastically; in essence, bailing out corporations that are deemed to be "too big to fail." This allows for engagement and responding to the content, and moves the students from "passive listeners" to more engaged thinkers. Frequent responses by students needs to be an expectation of your lectures. Donald Bligh (2000) suggests that teachers who only rely on lectures may encourage a superficial understanding of concepts and facts. As he states, lecture may "encourage a surface approach and discourage the very intellectual skills that . . . education claims to foster" (p. 61). Bligh suggests that teachers can help promote more active and "deeper" thinking by providing students with graphic organizers, being aware of students' ability to sit attentively in class, interjecting discussion questions into the lecture, and teaching note-taking skills. Thought of this way, lecture moves from being an instructional strategy of its own to more of a starting point for helping students interact with content through more active strategies. Descriptions of how to engage students during lectures are provided later in this chapter.

If not thought of in conjunction with other strategies, the lecture method presents other challenges for students and teachers. The teacher organizes the lecture as she believes is best, but this may not be the order that promotes understanding for every student. For example, a U.S. history teacher may decide to lecture on the historical background of Steinbeck's novel *The Grapes of Wrath* before distributing the book to the class, but some students may not see the relevancy of the lecture until they are confronted by characters in the story. Even more prevalent is the teacher who "moves away from the topic" or "gets off track" from the main topic of the lecture. This may occur from a student question or simply because the teacher believes she has an interesting story to tell. While these are opportunities to make the lecture more engaging, students are often confused by these stories because they distract what is important with something that is tangential. Similar to this, students often have difficulty keeping track of lecture content in their notes. Strategies for effective note-taking exist (Saski, Swicegood, & Carter, 1983), and teachers need to teach them to students. In Part I of this book we read about learning targets that focused on developing skills as well as learning content. A learning target about note-taking is important. Without it, students are put in the difficult position of receiving a large amount of information without the skill of knowing how to record and review it (Ormrod, 2006). Students who have challenges in listening and attending, who have difficulty writing, or who speak English as their second or third langauge face additional difficulties when trying to learn from lectures or presentations (Sandock, 2000). It is a difficult task for all students to identify important lecture content and record it accurately and efficiently in their notes. Consider the challenge of your future student who does not speak English as his primary language. He could easily write one idea in his notes and miss the next two key ideas in the process. These concerns emphasize that relying too heavily on students to learn from a lecture or presentation is not going to benefit all students in your classroom.

Direct Instruction

Direct instruction is a term that is often synonymous with "explicit teaching": The teacher explicitly/directly provides information or guides students in learning step-by-step skills. Therefore, the instruction is controlled by you, and the students will look to you for guidance about what to do during the class. Direct instruction is a scripted and sequential approach for helping students learn by anticipating students' responses and questions. It allows students, often in special education programs, to master specific knowledge and skills that have been determined to be important (Engelmann & Carnine, 1991; Kame'enui, Carnine, & Dixon, 1998). The learning theory of direct instruction contends that learning can be greatly accelerated if instruction is clear, removes opportunities for misinterpretations, and facilitates generalizations. As a result, students are placed in appropriate instructional groups based on their performance, and as they progress are re-grouped to stay with those similar to them. To a certain degree, direct instruction is based on behaviorism (you may want to refer to Chapter 1 to recall this idea). Teachers clearly define the tasks they expect of their students, they explicitly teach concepts and skills by telling and demonstrating them to students, students respond with hand signals, choral responses, and other ways to demonstrate their understanding, and the teacher adjusts the lesson to accommodate student learning (Kame'enui, Carnine, & Dixon, 1998).Engelmann and Carmine (1991) have developed lessons for reading, writing, mathematics, social studies, and most other content areas, that provide the specific scripts and learning objectives needed for a direct instruction lesson.

Direct instruction is in a chapter about lecturing, because we can learn from its research about leading students. Rosenshine has suggested that ten general principles should be adhered to when writing an explicit or direct instruction lesson plans (Burden & Byrd, 2007, p. 168; Rosenshine, 1987, p. 76):

1. Provide students with a concise statement of goals.
2. Review prior knowledge that is necessary for the day's lesson.
3. Present new information in small chunks, and allow students opportunities to practice frequently with the new information.
4. Clearly explain and describe new skills and information.
5. Provide opportunities for student practice with the skill or knowledge.
6. Check students' understanding by posing frequent questions.
7. Guide students during initial practice.
8. Provide feedback that includes praise and correction on their skill and/or understanding.
9. Provide independent practice through specific activities and seatwork exercises.
10. Continue practice until the skill or content is mastered.

Much of the research and ideas about direct instruction apply to lecture and several other instructional strategies. Chapter 6 on Questioning and Chapter 7 on Concept Formation both tap into some of the Rosenshine principles outlined above. Rather than providing step-by-step procedures for a direct instruction model, I chose to introduce it here, and then integrate particular principles of direct instruction into several instructional strategies to improve their effectiveness in promoting student learning.

If you would like to know more about direct instruction, and how it might assist students, you may want to examine some examples online at the National Institute for Direct Instruction (http://www.nifdi.org) or the Association for Direct Instruction (http://www.adihome.org) once you have identified specific needs of individual students in your class.

STEP-BY-STEP PROCEDURES FOR PLANNING AND IMPLEMENTING LECTURES

The remaining sections of this chapter focus on helping you consider how to plan and deliver effective lectures and facilitate interactive presentations.

Teachers use different types of lectures to meet different purposes in the classroom. They can be to the whole class, or to small groups of students. Lectures may be short—a brief overview of the 1890 Wounded Knee Massacre, or they may be lengthy, as when describing Native and U.S. government relations in the second half of the 19th century. When planning to lecture, teachers are very aware that they need to be prepared for being in front of their students. If you plan to lecture all period, and you teach five one-hour periods, you need to be ready for five hours of talking. This has implications for your content knowledge as well as for your physical stamina and the attention span of your students. In this chapter we examine five key steps for lecturing:

1. planning the topic outline
2. planning the lecture
3. student note-taking skills and preparing the audiovisuals
4. delivering the lecture
5. concluding the lecture.

Step 1: Planning the Topic Outline

A topic outline allows you to think about the sequence in which content should be presented, as well as the level of detail that the students need. If you are lecturing on the history of immigration in the United States, then your topic might be organized in this way:

I.   Settlers of the New World (approximately 1600–1820)
II.   Mass Migration (1820–1890)
III. A Wave Becomes a Flood (1890–1918)
IV.   Legislating Immigration (1918–1965)
V.   The Hart-Celler Act (1965–present)

A topic outline, such as this does, can pull from your textbook, state or national standards, suggestions from experts, or your own knowledge base. For example, the five-point topic outline above comes from an article by Timothy Keiper and Jesus Garcia in the journal *Social Studies and the Young Learner* titled "Crossing Borders: Contemporary Immigrant Stories in Historical Context" (Keiper & Garcia, 2009, pp. 4–7). Each of the above five key points should then have definitions, minor points, and other details and explanations added that will help students understand the facts and concepts. This topic outline also allows you to begin estimating how much time you want to spend talking about each point. Beginning teachers often find that a challenge of lecturing is deciding what to leave out. As you have learned, this becomes part of the *null* curriculum. In the above example, you likely know many examples of "settlers of the new world" from the years you have studied early American history. If you determine that you only have time to describe several of these stories, you will need to omit the many other excellent examples. That is difficult to do. You will often know more information about a topic than you will present in a lecture. The lecture should only include information that is critical for the students to know; this will help keep the lecture focused on important content.

Step 2: Planning the Lecture

After the content of the lecture has been outlined, you will create a lesson plan that has your lecture notes, opportunities for student interactions, and questions you want to ask during the lecture to assess student learning. Learning targets for a lecture will usually fit into one of two categories: *academic content targets* and *skill targets* (these were explained in detail in Chapter 3). Teachers usually highlight the key ideas of the topic outline in their notes, with additional information included to help remind them of the content. These key ideas will comprise the content target(s) for the lesson. The skill targets of lectures will describe how students will develop their skills at synthesizing information or at note-taking. Examples of these two types of targets for a planned lecture on the construction of the North American transcontinental railroad might be as follows:

- In my notebook I can explain two reasons why investors were willing to fund the building of the railroad (content target).
- I can identify key ideas during a lecture by taking accurate notes about the building of the trans-continental railroad (skill target).

Many teachers will write out an entire lecture (much like a speech) and then bring a script to class. These teachers either read this script to their students or refer to it when they talk about a particularly difficult topic. Scripting is a very effective strategy, because it lets you think through the content and the manner in which you will present it to your students. The process of writing the script helps you estimate the amount of time needed for the lecture, and provides you the opportunity to think through the words you will use to help make an idea clear and understandable. Of course, if you simply read your script to the class, you will not be engaging, dynamic, or flexible with the content. Opportunities to interact with the class will be further restricted if you only keep to the written words. A balance of using scripts when planning a lecture, and outlines or topical notes during the lecture often allows for more opportunities to engage students. The scripts can be with your notes, but not the main document you refer to. If you lose track of the topic, or need to present a very technical or difficult concept, then the script is available to read. The rest of the time, the script provides a backup for the detailed outline of the lecture topic.

Step 3: Student Note-Taking Skills and Preparing the Audiovisuals

The third part of the lecture is to consider the audiovisual components that you will use. Students need help with taking notes and focusing on key concepts. You may want to provide copies of your topic outline to your students. This could provide them with a framework/outline on which they can add additional points and details gleaned from the lecture. If these notes are so detailed that you are merely repeating the information on the handout, then your students could be less engaged in your lecture. If you intend to write notes on the whiteboard or project them with the document camera, you should plan out the key ideas you want students to learn from the lecture and ensure that you write them accurately. Visuals often present information in a different and compelling fashion. They must be large enough so that students in the back of the room can read them with ease. If you plan to project a map, picture, or diagram, be sure they are easy to read as well. Projecting a visual that is too complex for easy reading may cause more confusion than help. However, handing out paper copies to the students so that they are able to follow along on their own sheet may help simplify or explain the visual.

Students who have not had much practice taking notes will need explicit directions from you. They will record in their notes whatever you put on the board, overhead, or in notes you hand out, so these notes need to be planned thoughtfully and written logically. Provide students with a format for recording notes, and tell them how to record their ideas.

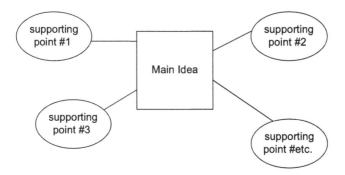

Figure 5.1 Sample "Outline Web" of Main Ideas.

For example, you can tell them, "This is the main idea," or, "This is a supporting point under the main idea that you just put in your notes." An outline format is most common, but teachers might also use a web format, such as Figure 5.1:

When helping students learn to take notes, they are learning a skill. Recall Chapter 3, when we differenitated between learning targets. Some learning targets focus on academic content; for example, the topic of your lecture. Others focus on skills; for example, the skills needed to take notes. For a lecture, you might want to have a skill-learning target for your students such as: "I will be able to record the three main ideas of today's lecture in my composition book."

Of course, this means you will need to spend some time teaching students how to take notes. The outline web above is one approach (see Figure 5.1). Walter Pauk developed another system for note-taking that is popular in schools today, called "Cornell Notes." This approach is a skill that students learn. Note paper is divided into two columns: a narrow column on the left and a wider column on the right. Students record their notes on the right, and put questions, vocabulary words, or new insights in the left column. Pauk and Owens (2011) suggest that students engage in the following process when taking notes:

1. *Record* (during lecture)

    a. write down facts and ideas in phrases
    b. use abbreviations when possible
    (after lecture)
    c. read through your notes
    d. fill in blanks and make scribbles more legible

2. *Reduce or Question* (after lecture)

    a. write key words, phrases or questions that serve as cues for notes taken in class
    b. cue phrases and questions should be in your own words

3. *Recite*

    a. with classroom notes covered, read each key word or question
    b. recite the fact or idea brought to mind by key word or question

4. *Reflect and Review*

    a. review your notes periodically by reciting
    b. think about what you have learned

5. *Recapitulation* (after lecture)

    a. summarize each main idea
    b. use complete sentences

I mention this approach to emphasize that teaching the skill of note-taking will likely require lesson planning and learning targets along with presenting a lecture. Most teachers believe that teaching students how to take notes is best done during the lecture. In other words, you build into your lecture directions about taking notes. Cornell Notes is not the only way to help students learn, but it is a powerful skill for students to learn and it provides a nice structure. You will notice that students reflect on the notes after writing them. This way the content is processed and students do not merely write notes and then forget about them. Many lessons are available online for teaching note-taking, and you might want to pause your reading and search to see what is available.

If you will be using audio or video clips, then put a comment in your lecture notes where you want to present those to the students and your purpose for using them (e.g., if you are going to play audio of a protestor who is afraid of a group of policemen, you could tell students, "Please listen to the fear in the voice of this civil rights protestor").

Step 4: Delivering the Lecture

Effective teachers use an introduction or "hook" to focus students on the content and help them engage with the content. This hook activity is important because it sets the stage for the ensuing content. These activities will vary greatly depending on your personality, the makeup of your classroom, and the content being examined. Teachers may use hooks such as playing a song, reading a poem, showing a video clip, or viewing a webcam. I have watched teachers dress in costume, display an old artifact or primary source document, and have an oddity set up in front of the classroom to promote interest (for example, one teacher placed a skeleton in front of the room). In addition to generating student interest, teachers may also introduce a lecture with a brief overview of the content they will examine, a statement of the learning targets for the day, and the purpose of the day's lesson.

One creative govenment teacher pretended she was upset with the way her students were treating each other during discussion time. She railed against their mistreatment of classmates and how they were generally too disagreeable. The teacher informed the class that they would not be spending so much time discussing their opinions in class because "obviously" it was a waste of class time that could be spent on other things. She went so far as to require them to sign a form she had prepared in advance, stating that they would no longer discuss their views in class unless a proposed discussion was submitted in writting for her approval prior to class. After most of the class had signed the form (not without some grumbling and push back) she informed the class that they had given up their rights to free speech too easily. She then used this as an opportunity to give a lecture on the Supreme Court case of "Tinker vs. Des Moines" and other Court cases that helped define the constitutional rights of students in public schools.

Keep the following things in mind when delivering a lecture. As an instructor, you want to minimize student distraction and maximize student learning. Clearly talk through your notes/scripts. Pace and pause to engage students' interest and to allow them to note important points. Most of the hard work will have been done when preparing the lecture outline and lesson plan. The delivery is now your verbal presentation of these notes. Be sure your voice is clear, that you clearly enunciate your words, and that your mannerisms help your lecture. For example, standing motionless behind the lectern will make you appear separated or nervous. Move and incorporate hand gestures to emphasize particular points and key ideas.

In addition to presenting the information accurately and enthusiastically, the single most important element of lecturing is to be acutely aware of your students. Throughout the lecture, look to see if they are engaged and attentive (this will be evident through body language, eye contact, note-taking, and other behavior). Look to see if they are keeping up with you in their notes. When working with teachers, I will encourage them to pause and look at their students' notes to see how closely they align with the teacher's lecture notes, or to pair up with a classmate next to them to compare notes. This helps students with the skill of note-taking, and allows them to think about the content more actively. If students are not following, then you need to revisit the content, slow down, or remember who is having difficulty and provide more one-on-one attention after the lecture. It will be rare if all of your students will learn the same amount of information from a lecture. Attention deficits, English language skills, awareness of academic language, or even the weather outside influence students' learning during a lecture; especially when you are lecturing to the whole class. You must closely monitor students and assess their learning so you are able to follow up with individuals who do not learn from your lecture. This close monitoring of students also provides you with insight about student note-taking skills. It is very important to tell students that they should "include this in your notes," or "write a synopsis of what I just said in your own words in your notes," or to give other prompts to help student note-taking skills. And just to restate what has been written earlier, while students are learning academic content from your lecture, you will also need to help them learn the skills of synthesizing information, writing notes, asking questions for clarification, and other advanced thinking skills.

Effective teachers do not merely present: They help students understand what they are presenting. This is more important when students have had fewer opportunities to take notes during a lecture. Therefore, middle school students will need more time spent on these thinking skills than most high school students. As a teacher, the more time you spend on these skills, the less time you will have for lecturing on content. However, by contextualizing note-taking skills into your lecture, you will better prepare students to learn how to best receive information from a lecture. Periodic questions or checks of students' understanding should also be used while you deliver the lecture (questioning is addressed further in Chapter 6). These questions should focus on specifics of your topic outline and not be generic. For example, if you've just finished describing different types of native lodging in the 19th century, a question such as "Could you explain the differences between common Lakota homes and Iroquois homes during the 19th century?" is a more effective and focused question than "Do you have any questions about native lodging?"

Step 5: Concluding the Lecture

Typically, the conclusion of a lecture will involve a review of the main points that you want your students to remember; you also should remind them of the overall purpose of the lecture. The conclusion is also an excellent place at which to tell students how the information from the lecture will connect with the next day's class. For example, if a world history teacher just finished a lecture on Roman architecture, she may end the lecture by telling students:

> This lecture provided you with a general understanding of the archeitctural and engineering advances made by Ancient Rome. Look over your notes to be sure you have the following six points listed (teacher lists the six points). You should also have a few details that explain each point in more detail. Does anyone need help with these six points? The information we explored today will prepare us for tomorrow, when we look at these same features found in the United States today.

It is also an excellent idea to collect students' notes at the end of class, or to have students complete **exit cards**, so you can have evidence of what they did: evidence of their notes and of their learning. Exit cards are documents that your students must have ready when they leave the class, and are a quick assessment of student learning. These could be lecture notes from the day, answers on a note card (e.g., "Write the titles of the five themes of geography that I described to you"), verbal responses ("As you leave today, tell me one thing you learned that was new to you"), or any other concise strategy for checking students' understanding at the conclusion of your lecture. Assessments will be addressed later in this chapter.

The following lecture/presentation planning chart provides a helpful format for planning lectures. The right column is useful for you to write your responses to the prompts in the left column. This is adapted from work done by Wingert (2001), and from the University of Minnesota's Center for Teaching and Learning Services. You can access this planning sheet online at: http://www1.umn.edu/ohr/teachlearn/tutorials/lectures/planning.html:

Beginning the Lecture/Presentation	
What would you like your students to do/know by the end of your presentation? (This is your daily learning target. It may be a **content target** and/or a **skill target**.)	
How will you share your learning target(s) (including how and why it is important) with your students?	
Introduction: Think of an overview, anecdote, problem/case study, question, demonstration, quotation, relevant fact/statistic.	
Delivering the Lecture/Presentation	
First segment of information (10–15 minutes): List the main points you will present. List the audiovisual aids you will use (handouts, PowerPoint presentation, video, overhead projections, notes on chalkboard, etc.). Active processing/participation activity: What might students do to help them think about the content? Share with a neighbor? Take a brief quiz? Participate in a question/answer session?	

Second segment of information (10–15 minutes): List the main points you will present. List the audiovisual aids you will use (handouts, PowerPoint presentation, video, overhead projections, notes on chalkboard, etc.). Active processing/participation activity: What might students do to help them think about the content? Share with a neighbor? Take a brief quiz? Participate in a question/answer session?	
Third segment of information (10–15 minutes): List the main points you will present. List the audiovisual aids you will use (handouts, PowerPoint presentation, video, overhead projections, notes on chalkboard, etc.). Active processing/participation activity: What might students do to help them think about the content? Share with a neighbor? Take a brief quiz? Participate in a question/answer session?	
Ending the Lecture/Presentation	
Wrap-up: How will you know students have learned/mastered what you intended? (Refer to the assessment section of this chapter.)	

LOGISTICS FOR LECTURE AND PRESENTATIONS

Many of the courses you have taken in college have utilized lectures. A lecture hall at a university is a very common structure. Rooms designed for lectures usually have rows of desks or tables that face the front, a screen for a projection unit, chalkboards or whiteboards, and a podium or table for the speaker's notes, computer, or other equipment. These rooms usually seat a large number of students. Thinking about the structure of these rooms reveals much about the lecture strategy: The teacher is the focus of attention; students do not interact much with one another; a large number of people can hear the lecture without much opportunity to interact with the teacher; and audiovisual aids help the presentation.

When you lecture to your future high school or middle school students, you will be in a classroom, not a lecture hall. You will also be talking to a smaller number of students who do not necessarily have the needed note-taking skills or discipline to concentrate during a lecture. As a result, several logistical considerations will help your lectures. The setting of the classroom is an important initial consideration. Determine if all your students can see you and can see your visual aids. Students who have auditory or visual impairments should be close enough to see and hear you.

The following eight recommendations can help make your lectures more effective. They have been adapted from assessments of effective teaching conducted by Cashin (1990, pp. 60–61):

1. *Fit the lecture to the audience.*

    Be sure that the words you use, the examples with which you illustrate your ideas, and the content of the lecture will engage your students. Middle school students will need direction from you about what to focus on during the lecture, while high school students may have had more experience with lectures. With any age student, recognize that you will be more active than your students during a lecture, so you must be sensitive to their attention spans. There is not an ideal length for a lecture, but the more concise you can be, the better.

2. *Focus your topic—remember that you cannot cover everything in one lecture.*

Focus on the key ideas, skills, facts, and/or principles that your students will use after the lecture. Do not think of the lecture as an end in itself, but as a lesson that helps students gain information that they will use during other activities.

3. *Organize your points for clarity.*

The topic outline should help you decide the best order for presenting the main points of the lecture. This order should move from less complex to more complex ideas so that students are able to build upon their prior knowledge. Hand out notes or a graphic organizer that will help students follow along during your lecture.

4. *Select appropriate examples or illustrations.*

As mentioned above, these should help the students understand the information. Therefore, the examples and illustrations should be appropriate for your students' age, experience, and interests.

5. *Present more than one side of an issue and be sensitive to other perspectives.*

Since you are leading the class during a lecture, your students are a captive audience. This means that they cannot leave (in general, students will not often question a teacher's authority, and the teacher needs to be aware of this power dynamic). As a result, the teacher must be aware of different opinions, experiences, and ideas that students could bring to the classroom. If an issue is controversial or multifaceted, then you need to consider how to represent multiple perspectives during your lecture.

6. *Be aware of your audience—notice their feedback.*

As mentioned earlier, you need to be acutely aware of your students. Watch them during the lecture for nonverbal feedback that will help you know their interest level, degree of engagement, and their understanding of the topics.

7. *Repeat points when necessary.*

Students will benefit from your overemphasis of key ideas and points and from your willingness to explain a complex topic multiple times.

8. *Be enthusiastic.*

You don't have to be an entertainer, but you should be excited by your topic. If you lack enthusiasm for the topic, students will notice. However, if you model enthusiasm, then students will likely be more interested in the topics examined.

CLASSROOM MANAGEMENT AND STUDENT MOTIVATION

During a lecture, the students' attention will be up front and on you (or on the audiovisual aid you are using). Lectures do not require students to talk unless you ask for their insight, ideas, and questions. As a result, your expectations for them to listen must be very clear. Many beginning teachers try to lecture when their students are talking quietly, looking about the room, or simply not paying attention. When you are lecturing you must require that the classroom is quiet, that the students are not distracting one another, and that the learning environment is conducive to listening and taking notes. This means that if several students are talking, you will request them to stop. If the sunshine is making a glare on the board, then you will close the blinds. If students do not have paper and pencil with which to take notes, then you will either provide that to them or have them get the needed materials.

Your proximity, or location, during the lecture will help with many management issues. For example, if two students are talking to each other during the lecture, then you can move next to them as you talk. Your physical presence will often make the students pay closer attention. If you cannot move next to a student, then stop the lecture and ask the students to please stop and listen (e.g., "I need you two to listen because your talking is distracting me and others who are trying to learn from the lecture"). If students continue to talk, then you may need to rearrange seating assignments. As was mentioned in Chapter 2, however, discipline problems this severe usually reveal a relationship problem, and may require more long-term interactions with the students. The bottom line during a lecture, however, is that the classroom needs to be quiet and focused in order for all students to have opportunities to hear what you have to say.

Lecture is a teacher-centered activity. As such, you, the teacher, will need to be sure you are ready to "lead the class." Students should clearly understand your expectations of them during the lecture. Possible expectations include:

- bringing pencil and paper to class
- having read any assigned texts
- listening to the teacher
- actively taking notes
- raising hands when questions come up.

You should also set high expectations for yourself. If you prepare your notes and are knowledgeable about your lecture topic, move the lesson along at a pace that keeps the students engaged, continually monitor your students' level of engagement (e.g., are they actively taking notes, or gazing out the window?), and show enthusiasm and excitement about the topic, then you will experience fewer management and discipline problems.

Student motivation during a lecture is a significant issue to consider. Many students welcome a lecture because it is an opportunity for the teacher to tell them what they need to know for the test. These students are motivated extrinsically. Thinking about course content is limited to repeating what they heard from a lecture or from assigned readings. However, look for opportunities to communicate to students that a lecture is not merely presenting information for a test. Inform students why you are lecturing to them so that they know the purpose of the lecture. If you are planning to lecture about how to use census data in a current events class, be sure that your students know why this information is important and how it will be used in the future. Similarly, if you are lecturing on volcanoes in a world geography class, the content will seem more relevant if you explain why it will help them understand Pacific Rim culture, which will be learned in a future unit. In each of these cases, you are helping the students see the relevancy of the lecture beyond preparation for a test.

During a lecture, the teacher is active. Students need to also recognize that they should also be actively listening, thinking, and taking notes. Hearing a lecture can be a very passive activity, unless you remind students to engage with the content. For most adolescents, however, "engaging with the content" is too abstract. Instead, the teacher can facilitate this by asking students to engage in higher-order thinking tasks with the lecture content. For example, they can compare and contrast important information, predict outcomes of events, or write a personal reflection paper about new facts they learned during the lecture. Another approach for motivating students to remain engaged during lectures is to consider whether or not their own experiences might add to the lecture. By knowing your students' backgrounds you are in a position to help incorporate their ideas and stories into your lecture. This could occur as you plan the lecture, or if you allow students to interject their ideas while you lecture. Either approach will provide a greater sense of ownership by the students, which often increases their motivation to learn and helps you manage the learning environment.

As we know, the old teachers' adage is to change the instructional mode every 20 minutes. Some teachers tell that the length of a lecture in minutes should not exceed the age of the student. For example, middle schoolers will only be attentive for 11 to 15 minutes. While there is little research to support or refute this claim, most teachers have ample anecdotal evidence that students struggle to sit for an entire period. Students might engage in and learn from your lectures if you limit them to half of a class period, or intersperse other activities. Later, in Chapter 6, we will consider questioning strategies, and in Chapter 10 will describe discussion. In the assessment section that follows, the "Think/Pair/Share" strategy is explained. These all may help you engage students during the lecture.

REALITY CHECK

When you see teachers lecturing, what are their topics?
　　What are students doing during the lecture? Are they taking notes? Using advance organizers?
　　How long are the lectures? What other activities does the teacher intersperse during the lecture? Does this seem to be effective in helping students learn?

APPROPRIATE ASSESSMENT TECHNIQUES TO USE WITH LECTURE

Lectures present students with information, but do not allow students many opportunities to apply the information. As mentioned earlier in the chapter, this is a criticism of lectures. The relatively passive role of the student also has implications on how you assess student learning. Consider the following example.

> Persuasive writing is a technique used by social studies teachers to help their students learn about participation in a democratic society. A middle school social studies teacher has just finished a lecture on techniques that authors use when writing a persuasive essay. Her lecture was full of examples from several essays, detailed notes, and her own demonstrations of these writing techniques. Students listened at their desks, took notes, and asked periodic questions.

When this teacher is going to assess her students' understanding of the information presented in her lecture, she must take into consideration the following ideas:

- What content did the students learn?
- How might they show an understanding of the content that is consistent with how they learned it?

These questions are useful for any teacher to consider when assessing students' learning after a lecture. The general answer to the first question is that students were to have learned the content described in the **topic outline** of the lecture. In the example on page 141, the students learned about a writing technique. The second question, however, is a bit trickier; the teacher will only be able to assess students' understanding of the topic outline by using assessments that are consistent with the lecture technique. A valid assessment technique for this teacher would be for students to write on a piece of paper a description of two techniques that create a more powerful persuasive essay. An inappropriate assessment would be for the students to demonstrate their skill at writing an essay. The lecture presented the facts and skill required, but it did not allow for students to use or apply the facts or skills. Assessments after a lecture, therefore, should be limited to the content presented in the lecture. The following assessments are valid and reliable techniques for determining what students learned from a lecture.

Exit Cards

In brief, an exit card is an assessment of the key points a student learned from the lecture. These are usually short and concise assessments (one to five minutes of writing). If you collect students' notes, then you can identify what they wrote down, but you cannot assess what they learned. Having students separately write out what they learned will be a more accurate assessment. With the example used above, the middle school social studies teacher might ask students to write an exit card using the following prompt: *Today I talked about how writing persuasively is an important skill to learn so you can participate in our democratic society. On your card, write down two of the techniques I told you about that will help you write more persuasively.* The teacher might then stand by the door and collect these cards as students leave/exit the classroom.

Journal of Facts and Feelings

I often encourage teachers to ask their students to keep a "facts and feelings" section in their notes. This can also be a separate journal that the students keep. Students record new *facts* and ideas that they learned during the lecture, and then describe their *feelings* and questions about these new facts. These are easily placed in the left column if you use the Cornell Notes format. This allows the teacher to assess students' thinking and understanding of the information presented during a lecture. The following is an example from a "facts and feelings" section of a student's notes:

> *Fact:* I never knew that Lewis and Clark were leaders of an official army corps sent by Jefferson.
> *Feeling:* This makes the Lewis and Clark expedition seem more official, because they were on government business. I can imagine that many were excited to hear about what they found. I also wonder if this was the beginning of confrontations between the U.S. government and Native Americans.

The "facts and feelings" entry is also useful for having students write what they consider to be the most confusing or complicated part of a lecture; this often allows you to determine if a portion of your lecture was unclear. It is also a useful technique when students complete a reading assignment, or listen to a presentation.

Think/Pair/Share

This assessment technique is an informal strategy. The teacher provides students with a prompt or question from the lecture, then asks students to "*think* about the question, *pair* with a partner, and *share* your answers." These questions should be about the content of the lecture, but they can push students to apply the content to other situations. For example, after an economics teacher has finished a brief lecture on the causes of the stock market crash of 1929, he might ask students, "Is it likely a crash this severe could happen again during our lifetime? Think about your answer to that and when you are ready, turn to your neighbor and share what you think." The students would then pair and share. The teacher can listen to the pairs' comments, ask students to share their comments after they share with their partner, or ask students to write what they shared on a piece of paper.

Recall of Specific Information

Students can be given a writing assignment where they must recall specific facts and details from a lecture. These could take the form of a true/false test, fill-in-the-blank quiz, or essay exams, but they can also be written or verbal explanations of information presented during the lecture. These recalls are not necessarily memorization tasks. Students could be asked to compare and contrast information learned during the lecture with information they learned in previous class session or readings. The key point to remember is that if the students have learned the content, they should be able to use and apply it in a variety of tasks. However, if the assessment requires skill or knowledge that they have not learned from the lecture, then the assessment is an invalid measure of what they have learned. Consider the following assessments following a lecture on five themes of geography (Location, Place, Human–Environment Interaction, Movement, and Region):

- The sinkhole in the picture is an example of which theme?
- A county surveyor would be concerned with which geographic theme?
- What is a recent story you read that refers to one of the five themes of geography?
- With a partner, recall the meaning of the the geographic theme "Place." Search the Internet for the "location" of 44.4605° N, 110.8282° W. How have humans interacted with this (it is the location of Old Faithful in Yellowstone National Park)?

The first three examples are valid assessments, because all the information was presented in the lecture. The fourth, though interesting and engaging, requires skills that need practice and cannot be addressed in a lecture; this should not be used as an assessment of what students have learned. Assessments that follow a lecture determine student learning, and they provide insight into how effectively you have presented the information. If all students are confused about the same information, then you should consider how you might revisit that information to promote their learning.

ENHANCING LECTURE WITH TECHNOLOGY

PowerPoint or Powerpointless?

Technology can be a wonderful enhancement to lecture. YouTube videos of exploding volcanoes, mento propelled rockets, an individual stopping a tank in Tiananmen Square, or other film clips used as hooks can be excellent. Digital models or 3-D imaging for exploring places far way from the classroom, web-based maps for current or historical events, and other imagery have been used to assist with focusing students on lecture topics in an interesting way. With that said, the most commonly used computer technology for organizing lectures has been the presentation software PowerPoint (although others are available, see Google Docs, for example). Most university students have had, or will soon have, a course on creating good "PowerPoints." This software can be a very useful organizer for main points of a lecture along with embedded video, maps, models, graphs and other visuals. If, however, using PowerPoint leads to an endless listing of bulleted points or even worse, full pages of text that the class reads while the teacher is talking about something else, well, what is the point? The question to ask while using software with a lecture is "what value is added?" Below is a listing of ideas to help you with creating PowerPoint presentations that add value to your lecture:

1. *Why are you talking?* Prepare your lecture first then create the PowerPoint to aid your lecture points instead of creating the PowerPoint and adjusting your lecture to fit the visuals you have found.
2. *Stop, Drop, and Roll.* Well, at least pause once in a while, and if you really want to express yourself and add interest, you probably could drop and roll. Just because you have plenty of great visuals does not mean you forget about public speaking skills. Pause to make a point, add emphasis, or for dramatic effect. Remember to use vocal variety (pitch, pace, volume) to avoid the monotone drone. It isn't about the flashy PowerPoint you made; it is about your message.
3. *Techno no-nos.* Don't put too much text on each slide, include too many flying objects that distract, use text color that is similar to the background, have a busy background, or use text size that is smaller than 18pt. A good layout example that includes non-examples can be found at the International Association of Science and Technology Education website: *www.iasted.org/conferences/formatting/presentations-tips.ppt.*
4. *Visualize.* Using visuals is probably the most important reason to use PowerPoint. Every slide could have a visual of some sort, and the best slides add visual meaning to support you the speaker. This could be a photo, graph, chart, symbol, or some other image that informs that portion of your lecture. The best slides will be those that are of little use to someone who misses your narration. It may even be appropriate to print an outline of your notes and use slides that have very little text whatsoever. If you choose to use video, embed the footage in the slide if possible so you are not Internet dependent.
5. *Keep it simple,* keep it simple, keep it simple. If you spent too much time tweaking your PowerPoint, you have not spent enough time on the content of your lecture. PowerPoint glitz is passé and distracting. I recently watched a high school student make a presentation he built through Prezi (prezi.com). "Prezis" feature zooming in and zoming out and can be quite compelling. However, this particular classroom of students became more

interested in where the Prezi would zoom in next, and less interested in the content being presented. Use impact visuals with lots of white space that aren't flying all over the place.

In the following section you will probably notice that some of the conversation around the benefits of using PowerPoint also apply to assisting ELLs in your class.

MAKING A LECTURE MORE MEANINGFUL FOR ELLS[1]

Lecture can be an effective way to assist English language learners. Oftentimes, students who have recently immigrated feel more comfortable with the teacher-centered model. In their culture, many of our student-centered approaches may either be unheard of or counter to cultural norms. In addition, as you read in Chapter 2, most students acquiring a new language go through a period of adjustment in which they prefer to listen rather than create language. When using this strategy, consider ways you can adapt for the ELLs in the class.

- Activate prior schemata: Make connections to students' background knowledge, or provide contextual information to help provide that background.
    - Have you ever . . . What do you remember about . . .
    - I remember when I was in high school classes and the teacher would lecture . . .
    - Look at the pictures on the wall with a partner. Write down what you think the picture is about, or a question you have about the picture.
- Provide the target: Let them know at the start what you want them to be able to do at the end of the lecture that they couldn't do at the beginning.
    - At the end of today's lecture you will be able to list three reasons that apartheid was disbanded in South Africa in 1994.
- Provide a graphic organizer to help them take notes and categorize what they are hearing.
    - A partially filled-in outline (the amount left to be filled in can be modified for different students within the same class—those with the strongest listening skills can have more blanks).
    - An information grid with headings—students fill in the appropriate cells.
    - A flow chart showing cause and effect to fill in.
    - Cornell note-taking technique, using frequent discussion times to identify what "key words" can go in the review column.
- Use visuals to clarify what you are talking about—it helps student who may not be understanding every word follow along and make logical guesses about the vocabulary they are hearing.
    - Visuals don't have to be fancy. Learn to use a document camera effectively, and write important points on the board when you say them.
    - Imagine (or actually try by videoing) listening to a recording of your lecture with the sound off. How much about the topic would the viewer be able to grasp?
- Interrupt your lecture every ten minutes and ask a question (which you've prepared in advance) that pairs can quickly discuss for 30 seconds to two minutes).
    - What are the three reasons for . . . that I just mentioned?
    - How would you feel if you were in the situation I just mentioned?
    - Explain to your partner how . . . and . . . are different.

- Be aware of your speech.
  - Second language learners need to see your face and hear your words.
  - Don't speak slowly or overly loudly—but *do* enunciate.
  - Avoid slang or sayings, unless you "sandwich" them with more spoken language.
  - Use academic language, students need to hear it and learn it. *But* be sure to "sandwich" this academic language with brief spoken language versions. For example, "We will write an autobiography, writing about yourself, autobiography."

In actuality, all of us are learning to speak, understand, and use English more effectively. As a result, we are all learning English. Each student in your classroom will benefit from the adaptations described above. Even though these are proven methods to assist ELLs, they are also highly effective modifications and approaches for helping students who speak English as their primary or only language, and it is beneficial to incorporate them into your teaching.

GUIDELINES FOR DECIDING IF A LECTURE IS APPROPRIATE FOR THE CONTENT OF A LESSON

The lecture is a valuable part of a teacher's instructional repertoire if it is not overused and if it is not used when other methods would be more effective. When lecturing to your students, you must have solid knowledge of the content, speak clearly, highlight main points and key concepts, engage students with periodic questions, and monitor student note-taking and learning. Since lecturing is a teacher-centered strategy, students can easily become passive learners when you lecture to them. The concern here is that students will not stay engaged in the topic and their attention span will be limited. Good and Brophy (2003, p. 371) have summarized suggested criteria that provide an excellent set of guidelines for determining when to use lecture:

- When the objective is to present information that is not readily available from another source, is original, or must be integrated from different sources.
- When the material must be organized and presented in a particular way.
- When it is necessary to arouse interest in the subject.
- When it is necessary to introduce a topic before students read about it on their own or to provide instructions about a task.
- When the information needs to be summarized or synthesized, for example, following a discussion or inquiry project.
- When curriculum materials need updating or elaborating.
- When the teacher wants to present an alternative point of view or to clarify issues in preparation for discussion.
- When the teacher wants to provide supplementary explanations or material that students may have difficulty learning on their own.

Many students may not readily learn content that they hear during a lecture, and it is widely accepted at all levels of education that content presented during a lecture is rapidly forgotten by students (Bligh, 2000; Edwards, Smith, & Webb, 2001). This is often called the "curve of forgetting." Cross found that one week after a lecture, students recalled only 17% of the information (1986). This percentage is higher if students use the information after a lecture (e.g., in ways we considered earlier in this chapter). Still, this forgetfulness is a concern that should steer you away from having lecture be the default approach for teaching. When students' primary language is not the same as the language used for the lecture, and when students have learning difficulties that are exacerbated when listening to someone speak, lecture is not an appropriate strategy. Use lecture when you have confidence that it will enhance student learning more than will other instructional strategies.

PRESENTATIONS FROM GUEST SPEAKERS AND STORYTELLERS

Guest speakers can provide your students with excellent insights and perspectives. Imagine the information that your students might learn from speakers such as a 'sixties civil rights activist, attorney, survivor, eyewitness, writer, POW, historian, or politician. Some community organizations have a speakers' bureau that you can contact in order to line up a speaker for your class. If the speaker has made a presentation to adolescents before, she may have a pre-planned series of activities for your students. Usually, however, a speaker will come to your class and lecture or present information. Herein is the caveat for inviting guest speakers. You will take many courses in preparation for becoming a middle school or high school teacher. These courses, much like this book, are designed to help you facilitate student learning, and to use class time effectively and efficiently for this purpose. A guest speaker usually does not have this experience. Since she will be speaking to your students, you want to be sure that she is able to teach, and that your students will learn from her comments. Guest speakers should help your students learn information and skills that are different from what you can provide. I suggest that teachers ask the following questions when considering whether or not to invite a guest speaker:

- Will she provide information or skills equal to or more effectively than you?
- What experience has she had speaking to students?
- What evidence do you have that the speaker will help your students learn?
- Do you know the specific content to be presented?
- Can you provide guiding questions or topics for the speaker?
- Does the content fit in with your curriculum scope and sequence?
- Do parents need to be notified?
- Why will your students benefit from hearing the speaker?
- What preparation should your students have prior to the speaker? For example, should students read a text or prepare questions ahead of time?

Storytelling is another type of presentation/lecture that is a powerful supplement to your instructional strategies. Stories incite the imagination and provide narratives and descriptions that help information come alive. Most of us have heard someone who is a good storyteller, who can engage listeners in a unique manner that captivates their attention. There are several organizations that promote storytelling and have a list of storytellers who can come to your classroom (for example, the website http://www.storyarts.org/ provides lesson plans and ideas incorporating storytelling into the classroom; www.storynet.org is the home page of the National Storytelling Network, and provides resources and ideas for teachers). These are usually professional speakers, but the above questions should be asked for them as well.

MAKING IT WORK IN YOUR CLASSROOM

Effective lectures are a result of careful planning. Consider the following topic outline for a lecture on the transatlantic slave trade in a history course:

I. Transatlantic Slave Trade

> A. 16th to 19th centuries

II. First System

> A. 1500–1580
> B. With Spain and Portugal temporarily united
> C. Largely by Portuguese to South American colonies
> D. Only 3% of entire slave trade
> E. Ended with break up of union of Spain and Portugal

III. Second System

> A. Dutch, English, French took over
> B. Largely traded to Caribbean colonies
> > a) Plantation demands
> > b) Labor shortage
> C. Slaves kidnapped from Western and Central Africa
> D. 39% of total from Congo/Angola region
> E. Traded to Europeans at coast from interior by African traders

IV. Conditions on the "Middle Passage"

> A. 12 million people transported
> B. 10–20% of captured died on voyage
> > a) may equal 2.5 to 4 million people who died
> C. Passage took about two months
> D. Conditions horrendous, disease rampant

Describe the rationale for choosing the issue:

- What makes this a good topic for a lecture?
- What topics will immediately precede and follow this lecture?

Lesson procedures:

- Write a script for the opening of your lecture. For the next point/topic of the lecture, write detailed notes. Decide whether you are more comfortable with notes or scripts, and complete the lecture using detailed notes or scripts for the rest of the topics you identified above.
- What graphic organizers, overheads/computer slides, or other audio-visual aids will help with your lecture?
- Write out some questions you could pose to your class to assess their understanding of your key points. These should be interspersed throughout the lecture to help your students understand your main ideas.

- Reread the section on assessing student learning from lectures, and determine which ideas you might use. Consider whether you want to assess them through written work or through an oral review.
- Adjustments: What academic language will present barriers to ELLs? How would you modify this outline for a US history vs. world history course? How would you modify this outline to include African perspectives? How might you modify this outline for a middle school vs. high school class?

CHAPTER REVIEW

- Research support for using lectures and other interactive presentation techniques
  - *Lecture* is an instructional strategy where the teacher presents a specified set of information to students
  - It allows the teacher to present a specific amount of information quickly and efficiently. Lectures help the teacher highlight the key points that best meet students' interests and needs
  - Students who make frequent, relevant responses during a lesson learn more than students who are passive observers
- Step-by-step procedures for selecting, planning, and using lectures
  - We examined five key steps for lecturing:
    - planning the topic outline
    - planning the lecture
    - preparing the audio/visuals
    - delivering the lecture
    - concluding the lecture
- Managing the classroom/learning environment during lectures and presentations
  - The following eight recommendations can help make the lecture approach more effective:
    - fit the lecture to the audience
    - focus your topic—remember you cannot cover everything in one lecture
    - organize your points for clarity
    - select appropriate examples or illustrations
    - present more than one side of an issue and be sensitive to other perspectives
    - be aware of your audience—notice their feedback
    - repeat points when necessary
    - be enthusiastic—you don't have to be an entertainer but you should be excited by your topic
- Assessing student learning appropriately during and after lectures
  - What content did the students learn?
  - How might they show their understanding of the content that is consistent with how they learned it?
  - The following assessments are valid and reliable techniques for determining what students learned from a lecture:
    - exit cards
    - facts/feelings journal

- think/pair/share
- recall of specific information
- Using technology to enhance learning
  - Technology provides great tools such as YouTube, computer models, and even authoring and editing software
  - When using PowerPoint or other presentation software, consider:
    - why are you talking?
    - Stop, Drop, and Roll
    - techno no-nos
    - visualize
    - keep it simple
- Considerations for English language learners during lectures and interactive strategies
  - Activate prior schemata: Make connections to students' background knowledge, or providing contextual information to help provide that background
  - Provide the objective: Let them know at the start what you want them to be able to do at the end of the lecture that they couldn't do at the beginning
  - Provide a graphic organizer to help them take notes and categorize what they are hearing.
  - Use visuals to clarify what you are talking about—it helps student who may not be understanding every word follow along and make logical guesses about the vocabulary they are hearing
  - Interrupt your lecture every ten minutes and ask a question that pairs can quickly discuss for 30 seconds to two minutes
  - Be aware of your speech

NOTE

1. This ELL section was created in association with Trish Skillman and Maria Timmons Flores, Western Washington University.

REFERENCES

Barbetta, P. M. & Scaruppa, C. L. (1995). Looking for a way to improve your behavior analysis lectures? Try guided notes. *The Behavior Analyst, 18*, 155–160.

Bligh, D. A. (2000). *What's the Use of Lectures?* San Francisco, CA: Jossey-Bass.

Brophy, J. & Good, T. (1986). Teacher behavior and student achievement. In M. Wittrock (Ed.), *Handbook of Research on Teaching* (pp. 340–370). New York: Macmillan.

Burden, P. R. & Byrd, D. M. (2007). *Methods for Effective Teaching*, 4th ed. Boston, MA: Allyn & Bacon.

Cashin, W. E. (1990). Assessing teaching effectiveness. In P. A. Seldin (Ed.), *How Administrators Can Improve Teaching* (pp. 89–103). San Francisco, CA: Jossey-Bass.

Cross, K. P. (1986). A proposal to improve teaching or what taking teaching seriously should mean. *AAHE Bulletin, 39*, 10–11.

Edwards, H., Smith, B., & Webb, G. (Eds.) (2001). *Lecturing: Case Studies, Experience and Practice*. London: Kogan Page.

Engelmann, S. & Carnine, D. (1991). *Theory of Instruction: Principles and Applications* (rev. ed.). Eugene, OR: ADI Press.

Fisher, C. W. & Berliner, D. C. (Eds.) (1985). *Perspectives on Instructional Time*. New York: Longman.

Good, T. L. & Brophy, J. E. (2003). *Looking in Classrooms*, 9th ed. Boston, MA: Allyn & Bacon.

Heward, W. L. (2005). Fast facts for faculty—Guided Notes: Improving the effectiveness of your lectures. Retrieved November 24, 2005, from The Ohio State University Partnership Grant Improving the Quality of Education for Students with Disabilities website: http://telr.osu.edu/dpg/fastfact/notes.html.

Kame'enui, E. J., Carnine, D. W., & Dixon R. C. (1998). Effective teaching strategies that accommodate diverse learners. In E. J. Kame'enui and D. W. Carnine (Eds.), *Effective Teaching Strategies that Accommodate Diverse Learners* (pp. 1–17). Columbus, OH: Merrill.

Keiper, T. & Garcia, J. (2009). Crossing borders: Contemporary immigrant stories in historical context. *Social Studies and the Young Learner, 22*(2), 4–7.

Ormrod, J. E. (2006). *Educational Psychology: Developing Learners*, 5th ed. Upper Saddle River, NJ: Merrill.

Pauk, W. & Owens, R. J. Q. (2011). *How to Study in College*. Boston, MA: Wadsworth, Cengage Learning.

Rosenshine, B. (1987). Explicit teaching. In D. Berliner and B. Rosenshine (Eds.), *Talks to Teachers* (pp. 75–92). New York: Random House.

Sandock, B. (2000). Enhancing learning of students with LD without compromising standards: Tips for teaching. Retrieved April 17, 2006, from http://www.ldonline.org/ld_indepth/postsecondary/facultytips.html.

Saski, J., Swicegood, P., & Carter, J. (1983). Notetaking formats for learning disabled adolescents. *Learning Disability Quarterly, 6*, 265–272.

Wingert, D. (2001). Basic presentation skills. Teaching Enrichment Series, University of Minnesota, Minneapolis, Minnesota. Retrieved April 19, 2006, from http://www1.umn.edu/ohr/teachlearn/tutorials/lectures/planning.html.

CHAPTER 6

Questioning

CHAPTER GOALS

In this chapter, you will learn about:

- Research support for using questioning
- Step-by-step procedures for selecting, planning, and using questioning
- Managing the classroom/learning environment during questioning
- Assessing student learning appropriately during questioning
- Using technology to enhance learning
- Considerations for English language learners during questioning.

Teacher-centered   Student-centered

Lecture   Simulation/Role-Play/Drama   Discussion

Questioning   Cooperative Learning

Concept Formation   SDI

Priscilla Robinson stared blankly at her government teacher. It was the second day of class of her senior year and she just wasn't in the mood for "playing school." She wanted to go to college and didn't want to waste her time. The teacher again asked, "From the data on the overhead, who did most African-Americans vote for in the last presidential election?" She had stayed up late last night doing the reading and thinking about the guiding questions and this answer was on the document camera right in front of them. "This is so obvious it's embarrassing," she thought. She remained quiet, and finally one of her classmates answered the question. The teacher then asked: "How do Democrats differ from Republicans"? Priscilla perked up a bit but let several other students give responses. Her teacher then asked: "Why did the vast majority of African-Americans vote for the Democratic candidate in the last election? Turn to a partner for one minute and share your thoughts." Priscilla recalled hearing her parents talk about this at the dinner table many times and eagerly turned to her partner. By the time the teacher brought them back together to further prompt them toward a deeper exploration of the issue Priscilla was ready . . .

OVERVIEW

During the years of schooling, the average student has been asked over a million questions. Some researchers have found that a teacher may ask as many as three to four hundred questions in a single day (Wilen, 1991). Others have found that questioning is one of the most dominant teaching strategies used in middle and high school classrooms, second only to lecturing (Gall, 1984). Of course, many believe that both of these strategies are overused, and often misused. This chapter provides a description of questioning as an instructional strategy, proposes procedures for planning and implementation, and discusses appropriate uses of technology, ideas for helping English language learners, classroom management, and valid assessments. Finally, it will propose guidelines to help you decide if questioning is appropriate for the content of a lesson.

DEFINING QUESTIONING

You have heard, answered, or asked innumerable questions at school, but you probably have not considered the significance of using questions for learning. Not all teacher questions used during a lesson are intentionally used to help students learn. The instructional strategy of questioning, as used in this text, is a teacher-centered approach that encourages students to think more deeply. Some might call this strategy a question-and-answer session, or "questioning to learn." The teacher uses a series of questions to lead the class or the student toward the lesson's learning targets. Often, questioning is either blended or confused with discussion. Although questions are certainly a part of a discussion, in this text we will think of these as different strategies with different purposes—the primary distinction between the two being that questioning is teacher centered and discussion is student centered. During a discussion the teacher may choose to move to the background; during questioning, the teacher remains an integral part of the strategy. Discussion is a strategy used to give students opportunities to engage in substantive dialogue while exchanging ideas and examining a variety of perspectives. Questioning is a strategy used by a teacher to help students develop examine a particular line of thinking. Some teachers have designed and used methods to merge the two strategies in order to help achieve lesson targets. The instructional strategy of discussion is presented in detail in Chapter 10. Additionally, some teacher questions are used as an assessment technique and not as part of an instructional strategy; this use of questions will be addressed later in this chapter.

In the same way, there is also a distinction between student questions and the questioning strategy. Student questions are usually either an essential part of inquiry learning, another student-centered strategy (see Chapter 11), or are used simply for clarification purposes. It is possible that some student-generated questions will help a teacher move the class toward lesson targets related to higher-order thinking and, in that case, may be examples of the highest form of questioning. At some point the distinction between all these types of questions blur. Of course, the common denominator for using questions at all is developing thoughtful, verbal participation by students. However, a clear understanding of the meaning of questioning as an instructional strategy is important as we move toward using it effectively.

A DESCRIPTION OF QUESTIONING, AND RESEARCH FINDINGS

Purposes for Teacher Questions

As we have noted, there are many reasons teachers purposefully ask questions. Most of these questions will fall into one or more of three categories: (1) as part of instruction; (2) as part of classroom management; and (3) as part of assessment. Questions are used to help students move between what is commonly referred to as higher- and lower-order thinking, or as an attempt to encourage student participation and investment in learning. Questions can be used for classroom management purposes to create an open and inviting atmosphere, to encourage self-monitoring of behavior, or to manage the pace or direction of the class. Finally, questions can be used during a lesson to formatively check for student understanding, summatively as a test, or to help a teacher reflect upon the effectiveness of a lesson.

Myths about Teacher Questioning

As a new teacher, you may be tempted to go with your intuition when it comes to using questions. After all, you have seen this strategy in practice many times during your years of schooling and may have developed some strong opinions based upon your observations. My purpose in the following paragraphs is to help you glean highly effective uses of the questioning strategy, as noted by research on teachers using questions. Wilen (2001) proposes nine common myths about the questioning of students that still apply today, and offers research-based principles for a pedagogically sound approach to counter the "myths."

Myth 1: Questioning Is a Natural Teaching Behavior that Does Not Require Planning

To effectively lead students beyond recitation of factual information teachers should plan most questions but allow for some spontaneous questions related to student answers. Planning questions provides structure and direction, increased engagement, and increases the likelihood that thinking and understanding will occur. Challenging students to think deeply has been found to increase and enhance participation and interest (Newmann, Wehlage, & Lamborn, 1992; Wilen, 1990). Good planning for questioning might include a list of potential questions to be asked during a class. So for example, a government teacher might have the following learning target: Students will understand the basic structure of the United States government and the process in which bills are passed into law. On her lesson plan she would write down question prompts she could potentially use such as: How do the three branches of government interact? How does the Legislative differ from the Executive? How does the Legislative branch pass a bill? If the President vetoes a bill, why is it a good idea for the House and Senate to have an opportunity to override? Do you think this structure of government is effective?

Myth 2: The More Questions a Teacher Asks, the More Students Will Learn

Research by Good and Brophy (2000) has shown that frequent questioning *does* help students recall factual information. It does not show that frequent questioning helps students think at higher levels. The *quantity* of questions is not as relevant as the *quality* of questions in situations where students would need to analyze an issue or evaluate a response. Unless a teacher wants students to recall factual information, it is better to focus on fewer questions of a higher quality that lead to higher-order thinking. Notice in the example of the government class above, the teacher plans to move the class quickly into more thoughtful questions beyond basic recall of factual information.

Myth 3: There Are No Bad Questions

This myth generally applies to student questions. In an attempt to encourage students to think and clarify their understanding, teachers will often tell students that "any question is OK to ask," or "there are no bad questions." As far as teacher questions, however, there is a difference between good and bad questions. Good questions are easily understood and stimulate student thinking. These questions are usually brief, naturally phrased, adapted to students in the class, and sequenced to help students reach objectives. Bad questions are those that frustrate or intimidate students. These questions call for yes/no responses or guessing, give little direction, or intimidate a student into agreeing with the teacher (Gamoron & Nystrand, 1992; Groisser, 1964). For example, our government teacher above planned to ask the opening recall question: *How do the three branches of government interact* instead of *What are the three branches of government?* or *Are there three branches of government?* Simply asking students to recite the three branches, or to answer a yes/no question, might be useful for a simple check for understanding, but probably not for helping students learn. It reduces questions to assessment. Bad questions may be "trick" questions (e.g., which is correct: The yolk of an egg is white, or the yolk of an egg are white?), or questions where the answer is so obvious that students are hesitant to answer (e.g., In what "house" does the President live in Washington, DC?).

Myth 4: Higher-Level Cognitive Questions Are More Critical than Lower-Level Questions

A person might think that with the emphasis on moving students toward higher-order thinking this might be true; but it is not so. Lower-level questions—those questions that prompt students to recall facts, or apply basic understanding—can be more important at times because they can help a teacher diagnose a student's readiness to move into higher-order thinking. In addition, recall of factual information might be the objective for a particular lesson, and thus lower-level questioning might be appropriate. Ultimately, the goal for adolescent students is to be able to solve problems and make decisions that will assist them in becoming competent citizens.

Myth 5: Higher-Level Cognitive Questions Elicit Higher-Level Answers

Several studies have uncovered this to be untrue (Costa & Lowery, 1989; Hunkins, 1995; Mills, Rice, Berliner, & Rousseau, 1980). It is interesting to note that it has been found that the cognitive level of student responses aligns only 50% of the time with the cognitive level of teacher questions. Students tend to answer at a lower level, while teachers tend to assume student answers are at the same level as their questions. Teachers do not always inform students of their own expectations for student responses or explain why they are questioning them. Teachers should inform students of the types of questions they will be asked, and why they are being asked them. Teachers who use action verbs in their questions that correspond with a particular cognitive level more clearly express their expectation for student responses. For example, it is helpful to use verbs like *identify, compare, predict*, or *judge* in a question to lead the student to a particular cognitive level. Using these approaches will assist a teacher in establishing a stronger relationship between the cognitive level of the question and the response. For example, our government teacher might ask: *Predict what would happen if Congress lost veto power* instead of *Think about if Congress didn't have the veto.*

Myth 6: Teachers Should Ask Lower-Level Cognitive Questions Before Progressing to Higher-Level Questions

Many see the use of Bloom's[1] Taxonomy as hierarchical in that one level cannot be reached until the previous level has been reached. Because of this, many believe that a student should start at the bottom and work his way up, as if climbing rungs on a ladder. It may be necessary to review the basic facts and concepts before proceeding. For example, it would be difficult for students to compare the Russian Revolution with the American Revolution before they understand the basic facts of each. At times, however, starting a lesson with a higher-order question could be appropriate if there is no need for review or a teacher wants to use the question as a lesson "hook" to stimulate interest.

Myth 7: Teachers Give Students Enough Time to Answer Questions

In classrooms where teachers gave students enough time to think through their responses it has been found that the quality of student responses increased dramatically, student participation increased, and responses were more thoughtful. Rowe (1974, 1986) and Tobin (1986) found that waiting as long as three to five seconds for a response to difficult questions will have positive results.

Myth 8: When Questioning Students, Teachers Should Call Only on Volunteering Students

This myth probably stems from classroom experience in which a student is painfully embarrassed or intimidated. On the other hand, students learn more when actively involved in class. Answering questions gives students an important opportunity to practice oral communication skills, and there is a positive relationship between calling on students who do not volunteer and achievement gains. Some argue that students, as all citizens, have an obligation and responsibility to engage in public dialogue and so should practice this process in the classroom. The classroom expectation should be that all students participate, especially in cases of recitation. However, students should be given the option of nonparticipation if questions are of a sensitive nature and they feel their privacy is threatened.

Myth 9: Teachers Encourage Students to Ask Questions

Research findings (Brice & Johnson, 1999; Dillon, 1988; Hunkins, 1995) have shown that adolescent students do not ask many questions in class and that they do not expect to ask questions in class but to answer them. This is primarily because many teachers spend over 75% of class time talking. With so much of the class time centered on teacher talk, there is little time left for student talk. One main reason students do not ask many questions is because they are not encouraged to do so by teachers. Questioning by students increases interactive involvement and student thinking, and can be encouraged by teachers who model how they pursue answers to their own questions and by teachers who value student questions. For example, one social studies teacher I know has Bloom's Taxonomy posted in the room along with associated action verbs. He will direct students to try to ask questions at different levels of the taxonomy during a lesson on the causes of the Great Depression.

STEP-BY-STEP PROCEDURES FOR PLANNING AND IMPLEMENTING QUESTIONING

As we have seen, good questions can serve to engage, motivate, and challenge students. On the other hand, poorly designed questions can frustrate students and turn them off. Have you ever been in a class where no one responds to a teacher's question because the answer is embarrassingly obvious? Other common questioning errors are described later in this chapter. There are a variety of proposed schemas designed to help you create effective questions that help students think critically. We will focus on one that is research based, and build upon what has been described in this text about the way students learn.

Framing Questions and Prompts

Chapter 3 noted that Bloom's Taxonomy has been widely used to help design instructional targets. In the same way, it has been a primary means by which effective questions for learning have been constructed. You will recall that this taxonomy covers six cognitive levels ranging from lower order to higher order—Remembering, Understanding, Applying, Analyzing, Evaluating, and Creating. Questions designed for the lower levels, especially for remembering and understanding, will focus students on recitation (Dillon, 1988). Questions at the other levels will ask students to move increasingly into more complex and difficult thinking (Dantonio & Beisenherz, 2001). The sample questions on page 159 are each of the cognitive levels to help you consider the type of questions you might ask in your class. Notice how any of the action verbs that reflect a particular cognitive level can easily be turned into a question or be used in "command" form to ask a question through the intonation of the teacher's voice. For example, "List the main characters involved with the assassination of Lincoln" can become "Who are the main characters involved with the assassination of Lincoln?"

Remembering

- Overarching question: Can students remember information?
- Sample action verbs that reflect this cognitive level: *list, locate, define, describe*.
- Sample questions: When was the Civil War? How would you describe the leaders of the civil rights movement?

Understanding

- Overarching question: Can students explain ideas?
- Sample action verbs that reflect this cognitive level: *explain, describe, estimate, paraphrase*.
- Sample questions: How would you explain differences between communism and socialism? What is a concise paraphrase of unilateralism?

Applying

- Overarching question: Can students use ideas?
- Sample action verbs that reflect this cognitive level: *chart, predict, expect, compute, classify*.
- Sample questions: How might what has been described as Chamberlain's Appeasement Policy be used to predict the U.S. involvement in Vietnam? Given what you have just learned about the Pacific Rim region, what three cities would you expect are most likely to be devastated by an earthquake?

Analyzing

- Overarching question: Can students see relationships?
- Sample action verbs that reflect this cognitive level: *analyze, compare, contrast, solve*.
- Sample questions: How would you solve the problem that Iraq waited for Carter to leave the White House before releasing hostages? How would you compare and contrast reasons that the Soviets sided with the Nazis and not with England?

Evaluating

- Overarching question: Can students combine ideas and make judgments?
- Sample action verbs that reflect this cognitive level: *arrange, compose, formulate, hypothesize*.
- Sample questions: Who would you hypothesize are the five greatest U.S. presidents of all time, and why? According to Gandhi, "he who clings to wealth cannot be loyal to truth." Why do you agree or disagree with this statement?

Creating

- Overarching question: Can students develop their own ideas or point of view?
- Sample action verbs that reflect this cognitive level: *judge, diagnose, apprise, assess*.
- Sample questions: In your judgment, what changes would you make to our community to help the homeless? In your assessment, how fair is the current immigration policy?

A diagram that may be helpful is the question construction matrix consrtructed by Linda G. Barton (see Figure 6.1). Notice how the matrix offers not only the verbs for question

LEVEL 1—REMEMBERING	LEVEL 2—UNDERSTANDING	LEVEL 3—APPLYING
Exhibit memory of previously learned material by recalling facts, terms, basic concepts, and answers.	Demonstrate understanding of facts and ideas by organizing, comparing, translating, interpreting, giving descriptions, and stating main ideas.	Solve problems to new situations by applying acquired knowledge, facts, techniques, and rules in a different way.

Key Words	Questions	Key Words	Questions	Key Words	Questions
choose	What is . . .?	classify	How would you classify . . .?	apply	How would you use . . .?
define find	Where is . . .?	compare contrast	How would you compare . . .?	build	What examples can you find to . . .?
how label	How did ___ happen?	demonstrate	How would you contrast . . .?	choose	How would you solve ___ using what you've learned . . .?
list match	Why did . . .?	explain extend	State in your own words . . .?	construct	How would you organize ___ to show . . .?
name omit	When did . . .?	illustrate infer	Rephrase the meaning . . .?	develop	How would you show your understanding of . . .?
recall relate	How would you show . . .?	interpret outline	What facts or ideas show . . .?	experiment with	What approach would you use to . . .?
select show	Who were the main . . .?	relate rephrase	What is the main idea of . . .?	identify	How would you apply what you learned to develop . . .?
spell tell	Which one . . .?	show summarize	Which statements support . . .?	interview make	What other way would you plan to . . .?
what when	How is . . .?	translate	Explain what is happening . . .?	use of model	What would result if . . .?
where which	When did ___ happen?		What is meant by . . .?	organize	Can you make use of the facts to . . .?
who why	How would you explain . . .?		What can you say about . . .?	plan	What elements would you choose to change . . .?
	How would you describe . . .?		Which is the best answer . . .?	select	What facts would you select to show . . .?
	Can you recall . . .?		How would you summarize . . .?	solve	What questions would you ask in an interview with . . .?
	Can you select . . .?			utilize	
	Can you list the three . . .?				
	Who was . . .?				

LEVEL 4—ANALYZING		LEVEL 5—EVALUATING		LEVEL 6—CREATING	
Examine and break information into parts by identifying motives or causes. Make inferences and find evidence to support generalizations.		Present and defend opinions by making judgments about information, validity of ideas, or quality of work based on a set of criteria.		Compile information together in a different way by combining elements in a new pattern or proposing alternative solutions.	
Key Words	*Questions*	*Key Words*	*Questions*	*Key Words*	*Questions*
analyze	What are the parts of . . .?	agree appraise	Do you agree with the actions . . .?	adapt build	What changes would you make to solve . . .?
assume	How is ____ related to . . .?	assess award	with the outcome . . .?	change	How would you improve . . .?
categorize	Why do you think . . .?	choose	What is your opinion of . . .?	choose	What would happen if . . .?
classify	What is the theme . . .?	compare	How would you prove/disprove?	combine	Can you elaborate on the reason . . .?
compare	What motive is there . . .?	conclude	Assess the value /importance of?	compile	Can you propose an alternative . . .?
conclusion	Can you list the parts . . .?	criteria	Would it be better if . . .?	compose	Can you invent . . .?
contrast	What inference can you make . . .?	criticize decide	Why did they (the character)	construct	How would you adapt ____ to create a different . . .?
discover	What conclusions can you draw?	deduct defend	choose . . .?	create	How could you change (modify) the plot (plan) . . .?
dissect	How would you classify . . .?	determine	What would you recommend . . .?	design	What could be done to minimize/max . . .?
distinguish	How would you categorize . . .?	disprove	How would you rate the . . .?	develop	What way would you design . . .?
divide	Can you identify . . .?	dispute	What would you cite to defend	discuss	What could be combined to improve (change) . . .?
examine	What evidence can you find . . .?	estimate	the actions . . .?	elaborate	Suppose you could what would you do . . .?
function	What is the relationship . . .?	evaluate	How could you determine . . .?	estimate	How would you test . . .?
inference	Can you distinguish between . . .?	explain	What choices . . .?	formulate	Can you formulate a theory for . . .?
inspect list	What is the function of . . .?	importance	How would you prioritize . . .?	happen	Can you predict the outcome if . . .?
motive	What ideas justify . . .?	influence	What judgment can you make . . .?	imagine	How would you estimate the results for . . .?
relationships		interpret judge	Based on what you know, how	improve	What facts can you compile . . .?
simplify		justify measure	would you explain . . .?	invent	Construct a model that would change . . .?
survey		opinion	What information would you use	make up	Think of an original way for the . . .?
take part in		recommend	to support the view . . .?	maximize	
test for		select support	How would you justify . . .?	y original	
theme		value	What data was used to make the	originate	
			conclusion . . .?	plan	
			What was it better that . . .?	predict	
			How would you compare the	propose	
			ideas . . .? people . . .?	solution	
				solve	

Figure 6.1 Questions Construction Matrix.

Source: Barton, L.G. (2007). *Quick Flip Questions for the Revised Bloom's Taxonomy*, Edupress (www.edupressinc.com).

construction but also sentence stems for posing questions that allow you to assess student undertanding at each of the levels of the revised Bloom Taxonomy:

While you are becoming comfortable using Bloom's Taxonomy to help guide your questioning, it might be helpful for you to become familiar with a simple technique. Many teachers use the idea of convergent and divergent questions to begin planning. **Convergent questions** are those that allow for only one or a few correct responses. These questions tend to be lower-order questions; for example, "Who was president when the stock market crashed at the outset of the Great Depression?" or "Who wrote the Declaration of Independence?" **Divergent questions** are those that require greater deliberation and encourage broader responses. There could be a number of appropriate responses to these types of questions and typically they require higher-order thought processes; for example, "After looking at the presidential election data, why did the vast majority of African-Americans vote for the Democratic candidate?" Keeping these two types of questions in mind when you begin to plan your questioning can be a helpful way to get started—or to think quickly on your feet during class. An even simpler technique that resonates with beginning teachers is to differentiate between "guess what I am thinking" questions and "genuine questions." The guess questions have answers that you are looking for students to give. They can be effective assessments of student learning, but they have the look and feel of a verbal quiz. Genuine questions are ones where you are genuinely interested in what the students have to say. You are not hoping for a "right" answer, but are wanting them to give their thoughts. For example, instead of asking "What is the capital of the United States?" you might ask "If the U.S. were to select a capital city today, where do you think it would be?" The second questions tend to be divergent and higher level. As you ask questions, ask yourself if you hope they guess what you are thinking or if you do not have an answer and want to hear what your students think.

REALITY CHECK

If you are able to observe/participate in a middle school or high school social studies classroom, record some convergent questions and divergent questions that the teacher asks the students. Record student answers to these questions and consider what level of thinking students are engaging in during the class.

If you are able to teach students, make a list of questions you could ask, and predict what answers they might give to the questions. How close were your predictions to actual student responses? You are not trying to guess student answers, but sometimes predicting responses helps a teacher form clearer questions.

LEADING EFFECTIVE QUESTIONING SESSIONS

To help lead you more quickly into effective use of the questioning strategy, the following suggestions are a collection of ideas from the research literature and practicing teachers.

Plan Your Questions Carefully

You may recall that the first myth of using questions relates to planning. Consider your lesson targets. Do they call for recitation? Do they call for higher-order thinking? What is the purpose of the questions? Are you trying to build classroom atmosphere in this way? Thoughtfully write as many questions as you can that will help lead students to the lesson target. Remember as you plan that the purpose of this strategy is not to start a discussion, but to help students share orally their thinking at higher levels or to think about factual information.

Be Willing to Depart from Your Written Questions While Staying with the Plan

If you have planned carefully you will know where you want to go with this strategy. You will be more prepared to come up with questions spontaneously in response to students in a natural way. This can be done while staying with your overall plan as defined by your targets. The strongest implication of this is that you need to know the topic/content very well.

Consider Your Students

What time of day is it? Are the students tired? What about those who are learning English or have other special needs? Think about ways you can encourage shy students without being intimidating. What kind of relationship do you have with your class? How can you use this strategy to improve your classroom atmosphere?

Close the Lesson on a Strong Note

As with any lesson, it is important not to allow a teaching session to fizzle. What can you do to close the lesson? Is there some type of interesting closing activity that uses another learning style, such as pictures or music? Is there a bookend to a "hook" you may have used at the beginning? Can you debrief orally or ask a student to summarize?

THE ROLE AND PURPOSE OF STUDENT QUESTIONS

While the questioning strategy is teacher centered and focuses on teacher-generated questions, we cannot overlook the importance of student-generated questions. These are important for a variety of reasons, the most important being that curious students learn. In this text, Chapter 11 focuses on student-directed investigations; it deals with the development of students' questions and the process of helping them find answers to those questions. Similarly, Chapter 10 examines the use of classroom discussion as a strategy for promoting student thinking, and also uses student questions. However, a good teacher will constantly be encouraging student curiosity, and the environment of that teacher's classroom will promote questioning. We have all noticed how younger children are full of a constant stream of questions—questions that at times seem they will never end. Sadly, for adolescents the desire to ask questions at school has been discouraged by peer pressure or instructional practice. Teachers can help counter this by encouraging students to ask questions in class, by allowing time for written questions, or having students work with a partner to devise questions. One powerful approach to using students' questions is the Socratic seminar (sometimes called Socratic questions, or the Socratic method). The following section describes this approach in detail, and provides links to watching students use it in action.

SOCRATIC SEMINARS

A Socratic seminar is a teaching technique that can blur the line between Questioning and Discussion strategies. These seminars help students develop critical thinking while practicing listening and speaking skills. Essentially, a Socratic seminar is a dialogue, usually about a reading, musical score, or piece of art. The class can be highly directed at times through questions by the teacher or other students but generally the goal of the teacher is to become a participant and not speak more than students. There are several ways a seminar can be run successfully but below is a list of step-by-step guidelines as suggested through conversations with teachers, as well as www.journeytoexcellence.org. Bruce Mansfield, a high school history teacher, leads his students in Socratic seminars frequently. He has put together the following step-by-step guidelines for teachers who want to use questions to promote student thinking and understanding:

1. Choose a text that is interesting to students. Identify the essential idea in this text. Ask yourself questions such as, What do you see? What cries out for analysis? How many different ideas are there in the text? Is there enough here for multiple supported answers to the essential question? If not, then either rewrite the essential question or find a new text. Consider where students are likely to stumble. Is it vocabulary? Sentence construction? Complex ideas? What support is needed for students who struggle with this text?
2. Design possible questions. The success of seminar depends on the deftness of these questions. Pre-write the questions. Try to develop about 15 seminar questions: ~5 low-level, convergent questions to ensure that they know what the text says; ~10 mid- to high-level divergent questions to push them to consider what the text means.
3. Teach background information prior to the seminar.
4. Arrange seats in a circle.
5. Choose a couple of students as outside circle observers and dialogue mappers (see Figure 6.2).
6. Start by explaining the Socratic seminar to the students:
   a. What are the learning targets or goals?
   b. Explain that the conversation is theirs, and that your question is a starting point, which they can move away from as they pose ideas and questions as long as the new ideas and questions can be discussed in terms of the text. You may need to pose follow-up questions to deepen thinking or you may ask other students to take on the role of asking clarifying questions during the seminar. Some teachers will also ask students to take other roles such as being the person who asks: "Can you tie that comment to the text?" or "What evidence from the text do you have to support that comment?"
   c. Tell the students to direct their comments *to other students* and explain to them that you will not comment on what they say, since this will cause them to talk to you rather than to each other. It may help if you look down or avoid eye contact until the discussion takes off on its own.
   d. Encourage the students to think before they talk, try to comment, or add on to what others have said. Listen to others.
7. End the seminar when it feels done and you or others have no more probing questions.
8. Debrief:
   a. Get feedback from the group about your expectations for the seminar (see the description of great Socratic seminars on pages 165–166).
   b. Get feedback from the observers; ask them to share their maps (Figure 6.2 is an example of a student's map).

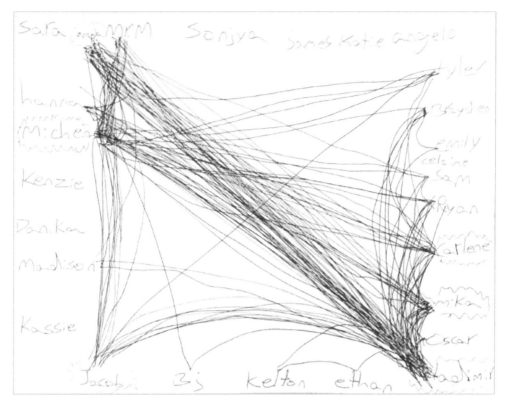

Figure 6.2 Example of a Student Map Created During a Socratic Seminar.

WHAT DOES A REALLY GREAT SOCRATIC SEMINAR LOOK LIKE?

1. *Everyone comes prepared with the assigned text, read and marked up.*
    Have I read and marked up the text? Do I have something to say?
2. *Students do most of the talking and thinking.*
    Are we doing more work than Mr. Mansfield during seminar?
3. *Students speak with each other.*
    Am I responding to what others say or just waiting for my turn to speak?
4. *The seminar stays focused on the assigned text.*
    Are all my comments and questions centered on the text?
5. *Students ask each other questions.*
    Am I asking students for help when stuck? Am I asking questions that can't be looked up or answered right now?
6. *Students avoid speculating and guesses are challenged respectfully.*
    Am I careful to support my ideas with evidence from the text? Am I respectfully asking students to support their comments?
7. *Students help others meet the daily goals.*
    Do I know what today's goals are? Am I helping others meet today's goals?

8. *Students are writing a lot—on the text itself, the white board, on big paper, on word wall slips, and in their own notebooks.*
    Am I writing with purpose to help me make meaning from the text?
9. *The debrief is honest and focused on the day's seminar goals.*
    Are we meeting the seminar goals? What did you see that shows we've met the goals?

Adapted from work by Bruce Mansfield,
Bellingham High School.

WHAT DOES A BAD SOCRATIC SEMINAR LOOK LIKE?

1. Only some of the students have read the text and are prepared to speak.
2. The teacher talks too much and is doing all the work and all the thinking.
3. Students are mostly looking at the teacher and talk to him.
4. The seminar gets off topic easily—students talk about things only a few have experienced.
5. Students don't ask for help—they stay quiet and confused.
6. Lots of speculation and guessing without much evidence offered in support.
7. Students ignore the daily goals and aren't preparing to meet weekly or unit goals.
8. Students stay in their seats and won't use the classroom space to support the seminar—no writing on the white board, no big paper, no word wall words, notebook writing without purpose.
9. The debrief is shallow and doesn't help improve the seminar—lots of "I agree" and "pass" responses.

Adapted from work by Bruce Mansfield,
Bellingham High School.

Stephen Daniels has the following video of his eighth grade students participating in a Socratic seminar about Martin Luther King's speech "I have a dream." In the video you can observe many of the points listed above. You can access the video at this YouTube site: https://www.youtube.com/watch?v=6pGVR6ZF_2M.

LOGISTICS FOR QUESTIONING

Hopefully, you recognize the importance of planning when preparing an effective questioning seminar. At some point, however, it will come down to how you perform in the classroom. Having the skill to ask your good questions is something that will take practice. You can quicken your development if you think through several logistical issues.

One way to improve your questioning technique is through attention to an element researchers have called **wait time**. This refers to the amount of time teachers wait after asking a question (called *wait time 1*) or before responding to a student or asking another student to respond (called *wait time 2*). The concept is simple, but most new teachers struggle with it, thus stifling participation and learning. When it comes to asking questions, teachers tend to be a very impatient group. In fact, Rowe (1974) and Wilen (1991) have found that it is common for teachers to wait less than one second before speaking again to rephrase the question, answer it themselves, ask another question, or fill the quiet in some other way. Perhaps in the many years of your own schooling you can recall instances in which you were about to respond to a question when the teacher began talking.

Waiting for students to respond has been shown to have a number of positive effects. When teachers increased wait time to just three to five seconds, there were positive results according to research done by Rowe (1974) and Tobin (1986), who found that

- the length of the student response increased
- the number of times students failed to respond decreased
- students asked more questions
- students were more confident
- unsolicited responses increased
- students with a broader range of abilities participated.

It is interesting that something as simple as being aware of and applying principles of wait time can have such impact on classroom interaction. Note that these are not new findings. It is not that teachers do not know about this, but it is that waiting can be hard to do. It takes practice. Keeping this in mind will likely help you develop good habits from the start. Some teachers choose to count to themselves for four or five seconds after asking a question and before allowing themselves to speak again. Some choose to do the same before responding to a student. Others will record themselves to help self-assess their technique. You will need to decide what will work for you given all the variables of a classroom. Of course, you should understand that just waiting for a few seconds will not necessarily produce dynamic classroom interaction. In fact, there are times when a "popcorn" approach (having students pop up and respond very quickly) can be effective, such as during recitation lessons or times when exploring affective thinking. Clearly, however, when students are asked to think at a more complex level they need time to respond.

Good questioning seminars depend upon a positive environment in the classroom. You will need to create an atmosphere in the class where students want to participate and interact. If you happen to student teach in a classroom where students are not encouraged to speak (the proverbial lecture class) it will be difficult for you to have a high-quality questioning seminar or discussion. If you haven't established this questioning atmosphere in your first class session it will likewise be difficult. It may take some time for you to establish an atmosphere conducive to verbal interaction in a lesson. You will need to share your expectations with the class, as well as let them know that it is psychologically safe for student talk. This becomes a function of classroom management clearly related to the questioning strategy.

MAKING IT WORK IN YOUR CLASSROOM

Using Tone to Communicate

If you emphasize the underlined word in the sentences on page 168 it will change the meaning of the entire sentence each time. Can you hear all four different meanings?

I like that answer.
I like that answer.
I like that answer.
I like that answer.

Next, try changing the following two sentences from pointed commands into questions or encouraging statements using tone:

Combine those two points of view.
Criticize that argument.

Now, try changing the meaning of the sentence "Someone add to Michael's answer." Start by making the sentence a put-down and change it to an encouraging question just by changing the tone and not the words.

CLASSROOM MANAGEMENT AND STUDENT MOTIVATION

A number of different elements related to classroom management have a profound impact on the effectiveness of this instructional strategy. You will recall that in this text when we think about *classroom management* we are not only speaking of controlling or redirecting a student's behavior, but are also speaking of creating and maintaining a positive climate for learning. The classroom ecology is healthy. There is no formula by which you can create this atmosphere. However, implementation of these elements will help you create an atmosphere more conducive to using questioning strategies with your students.

Responding to Student Responses

The way a teacher responds to students is very important and impacts further student participation specifically and classroom atmosphere in general. Though it seems to be helpful to have a good flow chart for how to respond to students (if they say *this*, you should say *this*), in reality productive responses will depend on careful listening and quick thinking. There is probably no better analysis, synthesis, and evaluation practice for a teacher. With that in mind, there are two basic types of responses to students that enhance learning: prompting and expanding.

Prompting

Students will often need to examine further their responses. Their responses may show that they misunderstand, or that they have not responded at the level of thinking that you require. Do you think that a student gives an incorrect response because she misunderstands your question? Do you think the student needs to work on her analysis? Does she want to apply a principle without careful consideration of implications? Does she evaluate a situation but not show that she has a complete understanding of the facts? Maybe you should rephrase the question, gently redirect it to another student, and ask that student to ask a clarifying question of another student, or quickly paraphrase the pool of information the student would need to respond correctly. Perhaps you need to restate their answers while allowing time for them to clarify.

Expanding

At other times students need to be asked to extend their thinking beyond the original response, or to be challenged. Do you think the student is correct and can go further? You might want to ask the student to analyze or evaluate information. For example, if a student has stated that the Nazis allied themselves with the Soviets, you might ask why they formed the alliance, or what would have happened if they had not formed such an alliance. Do you think a student offers an in-depth evaluation? It might be helpful to challenge the student by asking another student for an opposing evaluation or a differing view from outside of class. For example, "How would you respond to the writer of this article, who disagrees with your evaluation?" Remember, however, that engaging in a direct disagreement with a student in which you "win" the argument rarely enhances a lesson and can shut down others who were thinking of responding. Of course, even this will depend upon the atmosphere that has been established and to what degree the students trust you. Do you think a student's response is off-the-charts amazing? Most of the time praise should be reserved for private conversations.

The environment in your classroom that enhances a questioning session can be destroyed by comments that aren't respectful of students. Obviously, comments that intimidate or embarrass students will not encourage participation. Sometimes a teacher does not realize how his tone or nonverbal responses to students can impact the class. A frown, smirk, roll of the eyes, or blank stare all communicate as much as a smile or an interested look. In much the same way, tone of voice can turn the same statement from an encouraging prompt to a put-down.

Participation Patterns

One reason teachers use questioning sessions is to give students an opportunity to participate orally. However, many times those who participate are the usual volunteers or those "go-to" students the teacher uses when a correct answer is needed. One way to help assess your pattern of questioning is to employ an observer grid, through which an impartial observer uses a seating chart to place a check mark by the name of each student who participates. It is interesting for a teacher to note after a lesson that most of the responses came, for example, from the right front corner or from the boys in the class. Feedback from this type of observation can help the teacher create a more equitable and encouraging classroom.

The eighth myth of questioning claimed that only volunteering students should participate. Research implications show that, within reason, all students should be encouraged and expected to participate. For example, a teacher should expect all students to respond during a review of factual information in a reading assignment. A teacher may opt to allow a student to pass if, for instance, he is asked a question related to his political beliefs regarding a presidential candidate. Some teachers choose to do this through random calling. This could be done through the use of two decks of cards: Each student is given a card from the first deck, and the teacher has another deck from which she randomly draws a card that corresponds with the card of the student who will participate. Other teachers will simply choose students at random, trying to get all students involved. Some will go around the room, having students respond one by one but allowing for a student to pass. As you consider when you will call on volunteers and when you will solicit responses, you will also be deciding whether you want your students to "raise their hands," answer without permission, or be called upon by the teacher. This logistical issue goes hand in hand with your thinking about participation.

One final consideration about student participation is related to culture. White (1990) has found that different ethnic groups communicate orally in different ways. In the classroom, as much as possible, consideration should be given to the student's cultural background when encouraging oral participation. In addition, students who speak English as a second language (ESL) may have considerable difficulty participating at a high level in a questioning session. Alternative strategies should be used to reach this population, or perhaps questions could be provided in written form. Students could follow the text during class or be able to use the text with a helping partner or during an ESL-supported study hall. It may also be helpful to give additional wait time to allow such a student to comprehend the question. Students could also be given several minutes of free-writing time after some questions; this would improve responses from all students without singling out some.

Common Classroom Management Errors

As noted earlier, many different elements should be considered while establishing or main-taining an atmosphere conducive to an effective questioning session. Below are some common errors that are made in this area:

- Questions aren't clear, so students become frustrated.
- The "guess what's in my brain" game, in which the student must try to verbalize what the teacher is thinking. This becomes a "give me what *I'm* looking for" session.
- The teacher calls on favorites or the reliable few with answers, and does not include the whole class.
- Negative uses of questions, thus intentionally or unintentionally embarrassing or intimi-dating students.
- Asking more than one question at a time.
- Not giving enough time for responses.
- The questions are so simple that no one wants to respond because it's embarrassingly obvious.
- The teacher commonly answers his own questions, and students are thus confused about responding.
- Questions leave out a large portion of the class. The teacher fails to frame learning through the use of questions that build to higher-order questions.
- The teacher is not listening well. Perhaps she is thinking about the next question, or a response the students might give or should have given.
- Negative nonverbal cues. The teacher uses cues such as looking at papers, at the clock, raising eyebrows, rolling eyes, and so on to show disinterest or displeasure in a response.
- Rewording an answer into an idea the teacher *wants* to hear.
- The teacher talks too much.

APPROPRIATE ASSESSMENT TECHNIQUES TO USE WITH QUESTIONING

Assessing questioning can be difficult, as can assessing any oral participation strategy. The written objectives for the lesson will again be key in determining how to go about assess-ing students. You may have had a number of purposes in mind when choosing to question the students. The lesson objective may be related to critical thinking skills, participation, or practicing verbal skills. A rubric similar to the one shown in Chapter 10, "Classroom Discussion and Debate," could be used to assess any of these objectives. This would be done with a checklist-style rubric that could quickly be used to rate a response. However, unlike with discussion, this strategy is teacher centered. There likely will be little time to fill out a rubric while fully participating in leading a questioning seminar. Instead, a teacher will commonly use the strategy to support objectives that call for a different type of assessment. Take, for example, this target: *Students will show their ability to evaluate the effects of the Vietnam War on foreign policy decisions during later presidential administrations by writing a two-page editorial according to guidelines on the provided rubric.* Here the target indicates that the point of the lesson is to teach students to evaluate. The teacher may have chosen to use questioning to help students practice their evaluation skills. However, the formal assessment of those skills will be completed during the written assignment. The teacher will formatively, through listening and observation, assess student ability to evaluate during the oral questioning seminar. Most assessment for questioning will be formative and eventually used to modify future lesson objectives or prepare for a summative assessment.

One reminder may be important here: Questions are commonly used as an assessment strategy. For example, a teacher may ask questions as part of a lecture to assess student comprehension. This use of questions *specifically for assessment* is not part of a questioning seminar.

ENHANCING STUDENT LEARNING WITH TECHNOLOGY

You will likely be able to locate some drill-and-practice software or websites that may be useful as part of your questioning strategy, but keep in mind that they rarely function beyond lower-order questioning. It might also be difficult to find software or websites that relate to the exact topic you are addressing with your lesson. Instead, consider the following activity for generating student questions. This is an example activity that could be modified for other social studies topics.

At times history teachers use classroom sets of historical novels to engage the class in a particular historical topic. The class might read a section and then discuss the historical accuracy of the reading or simply use the book to generate interest and questions. During a world history unit on WWI, a teacher might ask the class to read the book *All Quiet on the Western Front.* After reading a chapter students open their devices or go to the computer lab. Ask students to write a question that they would like to explore further or would like to have clarified. Instead of writing a simple question, students should be encouraged to write nonstop about the question until it leads them to a conclusion or perhaps another question. Why did they think of it? Is it related to an event or character? Why is it relevant? Why is it important to them? After several minutes of writing, ask them to switch computers with a partner and continue the writing on that partner's computer. Here the students should write an exploratory response to the other student's initial question and continue the writing until another question emerges. Continue the exchange of computers so that students read, respond to, and add to the comments of other students. This type of writing is helpful for the generation and exploration of ideas, all of which comes from the students themselves.

This idea could be easily modified to use the collaborative sharing function of Google Docs, but as with most effective uses of technology in the classroom, the focus is not on the technology itself but on your lesson target (in this case, exploring this war period of world history).

MAKING QUESTIONING MORE MEANINGFUL FOR ELLS

Research on ESL classroom discourse suggests that effective teachers of ELLs use questions to help their students understand concepts in class, and to understand the texts they read. Over the course of the school year, a student's language proficiency may change. In her review of effective uses of questions in classrooms, Kim (2010) found what is obvious but difficult to accomplish: "Effective teachers reformulate and refocus their questions based upon their understanding of what ESL students know about English language demonstrated in classroom participation and use of English oral language" (p. 114). As a teacher, you can use questions to scaffold students' learning about the course content, and help them better understand their own learning of the English language. Kim's research helps us understand how questions might scaffold learning by thinking of three different types of questions. "Coaching questions" are those where the teacher has the highest level of control and authority. "Collaborating questions" are when the student has the highest degree of authority. Between these two are "facilitating questions." The following examples clarify these roles (Kim, 2010, pp. 130–135):

- Coaching questions occur during activities such as before a teacher begins a new activity (e.g., Does anyone know about quick writing?), to add information (Can I add one more idea to your comment?), to assess students' knowledge or understanding (e.g., Does everyone have an idea of what a raccoon looks like? What do I mean when I say "give you credit"?), and to help students think about the focus of a class activity (What is the format of the equation? What is the outline of this story?).
- Facilitating questions serve purposes such as to invite students' input (Do you have more to add on the list?), to help students deepen their understanding (Can you think of another word that begins with "un"? Can you guess what the author wanted to tell us by using this title for the story?), to help students articulate and elaborate (What do the leaves look like? How can you find out about the names of the leaves? Can anybody say that in their own words?), and to find out students' opinions (Is anyone interested in going to the computer lab to work?).
- Collaborative questions are used to help students reflect on learning and teaching (Which piece shows your best work?), and starting conversations about course content (Did you like the special presentation on Genghis Kahn and Mongolia yesterday?).

It might seem obvious that while these questions help ELLs, they will also be effective for students who speak English as their primary language. If you have the opportunity to observe an ESL teacher, try to identify instances when she "coaches," "facilitates," and "collaborates" with questions, and share what you observed.

Online, a great resource for teachers is the *Internet TESL Journal* (ITESLJ.org). This site has excellent lesson ideas for ESL teachers and students. For example, and specfic to questioning, the journal has a list of over 200 categories of "Conversation Questions for the ESL/EFL Classroom" (http://iteslj.org/questions). Many of these are for specifc content area topics.

GUIDELINES FOR DECIDING IF QUESTIONING IS APPROPRIATE

Questioning for learning is thought to be a useful strategy for the promotion of higher-order thinking skills. If you decide that your students need assistance moving from recitation of memorized fact to being able to analyze or evaluate information, this strategy can be helpful. A skilled questioning seminar leader can have a strong influence on student thought processes. Students often need this guidance to be able to think critically. Simply *asking* a student to evaluate isn't *teaching* a student to evaluate. For example, a student might "evaluate" a character's action as "dumb" by simply depending on his own impressions or emotions. Questioning can help a student go back and look at the factual information and make judgments based on supporting evidence. This interaction between teacher and student can have long-lasting positive results.

The unique student characteristics of a class should also be considered when deciding if this strategy is to be used. If your class has a high percentage of ESL students, it would be problematic to consistently use questioning. In addition, consideration should be given to the types of learning styles that you have in your classroom. Most experienced teachers will tell you that any group of students forms a unique personality. Some seem to be more verbally oriented than others. However, within this class personality there will be students who do not have the same learning style as others. Because this strategy is so verbally oriented, it may or may not be the right choice for habitual use. Using a variety of instructional approaches is key to being able to attend to the needs of the diverse group of learners that will be in your class.

At times, questioning is used to encourage student participation and investment in learning. Studies have shown that when students become more actively involved rather than passive recipients, they learn more. This strategy is one that encourages teacher-led student participation and thus could assist a teacher with purposeful student engagement. Keep in mind, however, that these teacher-centered activities have been commonly overused with adolescents.

CHAPTER REVIEW

- Research support for using questioning
  - Questioning is a teacher-centered approach that encourages students to think more deeply
  - Questions are used to help students move between what is commonly referred to as higher- and lower-order thinking, or as an attempt to encourage student participation and investment in learning
  - Questions can be used for diagnostic, formative, and summative assessment
  - Nine myths about questions help clarify what the strategy is and is not
- Step-by-step procedures for selecting, planning, and using questioning
  - Bloom's Taxonomy provides guidance for questions that promote different levels of thinking
  - Convergent questions are those that allow for only one or a few correct responses
  - Divergent questions are those that require greater deliberation and encourage broader responses
  - Questions need to be planned ahead of time to ensure they match your students' interest, level of understanding, and the content you want learned

- – Socratic seminars are more student centered than conventional questioning, and focus on asking meaningful questions that help students think about the content more so than coming up with the "right answer." These are described in detail in the chapter
- Managing the classroom/learning environment during questioning
  - – Management during questioning is important to keep student focused. Four uses of questions will assist you in managing the classroom:
    - responding to student responses
    - prompting student responses
    - expanding on student answers/comments
    - promoting an open/safe learning environment
- Assessing student learning appropriately during questioning
  - – The written objectives for the lesson will again be key in determining how to go about assessing students
  - – Rubric will be helpful to assess student questions and answers
  - – Teachers will formatively assess, through listening and observation, but may also use written work to assess understanding
- Using technology to enhance learning
  - – Online games are useful for review activities that ask students questions
  - – Questions help keep students focused when researching a topic on the Internet Just like any research, a well-phrased question by the student or teacher is a strong guide.
- Considerations for English language learners during questioning
  - – Effective ELL teachers question to help their students understand concepts in class, and to understand the texts they read
  - – Teachers use questions to scaffold students' learning about the course content, and help them better understand their own learning of the English language These questions can be thought of as:
    - coaching questions
    - collaborative questions

NOTE

1. Bloom, B., Englehart, M., Furst, E., Will, W. & Krathwohl, D. (1956). *Taxonomy of Educational Objectives, Handbook 1: Cognitive Domain.* New York: David McKay.

REFERENCES

Barton, L. G. (2007). *Quick Flip Questions for the Revised Bloom's Taxonomy.* Edupress (www.edupressinc.com).

Bloom, B., Englehart, M., Furst, E., Will, W., & Krathwohl, D. (1956). *Taxonomy of Educational Objectives, Handbook 1: Cognitive Domain.* New York: David McKay.

Brice, L. & Johnson, L. (1999). Discourse as a critical pedagogical form in social studies teaching and learning. Paper presented at the annual meeting of the National Council of Social Studies. Orlando, FL.

Costa, A. &. Lowery, L. (1989). *Techniques for Teaching and Thinking.* Pacific Grove, CA: Midwest Publishers.

Dantonio, M. & Beisenherz, P. (2001). *Learning to Question, Questioning to Learn.* Boston, MA: Allyn & Bacon.

Dillon, J. T. (1988). *Questioning and Teaching: A Manual of Practice*. New York: Teachers College Press.

Gall, M. (1984). Synthesis of research on teacher's questioning. *Educational Leadership, 42*, 40–47.

Gamoron, A. & Nystrand, M. (1992). Taking students seriously. In F. Newmann (Ed.), *Student Engagement and Achievement in American Secondary Schools* (pp. 40–61). New York: Teachers College Press.

Good, T. L. & Brophy, J. E. (2000). *Looking in Classrooms*, 8th ed. New York: Longman.

Groisser, P. (1964). *How to Use the Fine Art of Questioning*. Englewood Cliffs, NJ: Prentice-Hall.

Hunkins, F. P. (1995). *Teaching Thinking through Effective Questioning*, 2nd ed. Norwood, MA: Christopher-Gordon.

Kim, Y. (2010). Scaffolding through questions in upper elementary ELL learning. *Literacy Teaching and Learning, 15*(1 & 2), 109–136.

Mills, S., Rice, C., Berliner, D., & Rousseau, E. (1980). The correspondence between teacher questions and student answers in classroom discourse. *Journal of Experimental Education, 48*, 194–204.

Newmann, F., Wehlage, G., & Lamborn, S. (1992). The significance and sources of student engagement. In F. Newmann (Ed.), *Student Engagement and Achievement in American Secondary Schools* (pp. 11–39). New York: Teachers College Press.

Rowe, M. (1986). Wait time: Slowing down may be a way of speeding up! *Journal of Teacher Education, 37*, 43–50.

Rowe, M. (1974). Wait time and rewards as instructional variables, their influence in language, logic, and fate control: Part one—Wait time. *Journal of Research in Science Teaching, 11*(2), 81–94.

Tobin, K. (1986). Effects of teacher wait time on discourse characteristics in mathematics and language arts classes. *American Educational Research Journal, 23*(2), 191–201.

White, J. J. (1990). Involving different social and cultural groups in discussion. In W.W. Wilen (Ed.), *Teaching and Learning through Discussion* (pp. 147–157). Springfield, IL: Charles C. Thomas.

Wilen, W. (2001). Exploring myths about teacher questioning in the social studies classroom. *The Social Studies, 92*, 26–35.

Wilen, W. W. (1991). *Questioning Skills for Teachers*, 3rd ed. Washington, DC: National Education Association.

Wilen, W. W. (1990). *Teaching and Learning through Discussion*. Springfield, IL: Charles C. Thomas.

Wilen, W. & White, J. (1991). Interaction and discourse in social studies classrooms. In J. P. Shaver (Ed.), *Handbook of Research in Social Studies Teaching and Learning* (pp. 483–495). New York: Macmillan.

CHAPTER 7

Concept Formation

CHAPTER GOALS

In this chapter, you will learn about:

- Research support for using concept formation
- Selecting, planning, and using concept learning activities
- Managing the classroom/learning environment during concept learning
- Assessing student learning appropriately during concept formation
- Using technology to enhance learning
- Considerations for English language learners during concept formation lessons.

Teacher-centered   Student-centered

Lecture

Questioning

Concept Formation

Simulation/Role-Play/Drama

Discussion

Cooperative Learning

SDI

In early August, Steve signed a contract to teach five sections of U.S. history at a local high school. The school district specified that the eleventh grade U.S. history curriculum starts with the Revolution, reviews the events leading up to and following the Civil War, and proceeds with history from the late 1800s to the present day. During the year Steve developed units around the conventional historical eras (e.g., the progressive era, the "roaring twenties," the Depression era, etc.), but he also explored the concept of *authority* during each era. He asked students to think about who had authority during different times in American history, how they had authority, and why they had power. Throughout the year his students examined the relationships among power, authority, and the government,[1] and compared the differences between authoritarian and authoritative governance. The level of interest and insights by his students convinced Steve that anchoring his teaching to a concept helped students learn the course content.

OVERVIEW

A concept is the same as an idea. We create concepts to help categorize or classify the world. As Parker (2009) explains, concepts are

> abstract categories or classes of meaning . . . For instance *island* is the name for a geographic phenomenon whose attributes are (a) land (b) completely surrounded by water. *Kauai* is one specific example of such attributes . . . *Island*, the idea, cannot be observed; but *Kauai*, the example, most definitely can. There are thousands of other specific examples of the concept *island* . . . concept definitions, therefore, tell us only about those qualities or attributes that all examples have in common, and not about the unique features of particular examples.
>
> (pp. 291–292; emphasis in the original)

Many of the words we use refer to an idea, and not to specific or tangible "things." For example, *books, artifacts, cultures, rules, theories*, and *characters* are all concepts. Usually, when we use a word such as *book*, people around us know what we mean: Books all share specific attributes that most people agree make something a book. In your future social studies classroom, however, you will be helping students learn concepts that they have not learned. Then, as they explore specific examples of a concept, they will become better able to categorize and organize this information.

The purpose of the concept formation strategy is to help students form a robust understanding of significant concepts in the social studies. Too often we use concepts and have limited understanding of what we mean. Middle school students may be able to use the concepts of *democracy* and *freedom* in a sentence, but often cannot articulate the meaning of these terms. Consider, for example, the difference between the words *bravery* and *courage*. Most people will acknowledge that they are not synonyms but will find it difficult to specify the differences. Some have referred to this as the "rattle of empty wagons" (Parker & Perez, 1987; Taba, 1967). With this metaphor, wagons are thought of as the word, or label, we use for a particular concept, and the content of the wagon is the understanding of the concept. When we use concept labels without fully understanding their meaning, we rattle along like a wagon would without any contents.

Each of the instructional strategies described in this book promotes student learning of facts, skills, and concepts. In this chapter, however, we examine a specific strategy that helps students form a deep and flexible understanding of a concept that the teacher determines is critical for students to understand. Helping students gain conceptual understandings—literally understanding big ideas—is a critical element of any instructional strategy. Helping middle school and high school students learn concepts is important because it helps them organize information. Concept formation is an approach to learning where students examine examples of a concept and draw conclusions about those examples. In addition to learning about the concept formation strategy, I also hope this chapter challenges you to think about concepts that are important in history, geography, civics, government, economics, and the other social studies courses you will help students learn. As we explore this strategy, continue to consider those ideas that are important for your students to learn during the school year, and consider the instructional strategies that will promote student learning of these important ideas.

A DESCRIPTION OF CONCEPT FORMATION, AND RESEARCH FINDINGS

Imagine that a local high school or middle school teacher asked you to come in and teach for 55 minutes in a world geography class. This teacher wants her students to explore big ideas linked to the national geography standards, so she asked you to help her students learn the concept of "movement" as it related to human geography. You have three days to prepare. Preparing for this will require several hours to determine valid assessments of student learning, preparing learning activities, and writing the lesson plan. Additionally, you will also spend a significant amount of time thinking about the concept of movement, and finding relevant examples of it. It is during those hours of thinking and exploration that you develop a robust understanding of the concept you will be teaching. If you only have 55 minutes of class time, students cannot spend the same amount of time you spent preparing. And you would not want them to. What activities can you have your students do that will help them learn the concept that you learned while preparing? Often, teachers spend time preparing a lesson and learning the content, and then use class time to simply tell students what they learned. This is what you might call **concept telling**; you tell students about a concept. The problem with concept telling is that deep conceptual understanding occurred during the hours of preparation that *you* spent before you taught. By simply coming to class and telling students about a concept, they miss out on the opportunity that you had while preparing—the opportunity to think about, struggle with, and develop an understanding of the concept.

Concept formation is a strategy that takes your students through a process whereby they work to understand a concept. Rather that you telling them, the students form their understanding of a concept. It is a strategy you may have not seen in action, but it is one of the most powerful approaches for helping students understand a complex idea. This approach taps into Vygotsky's theory of learning (1978). You may recall from Chapter 2 that Vygotsky suggested that a "zone of proximal development" exists between our current understanding of something and the next, more robust level of understanding. Usually we need help attaining this new level. According to Vygotsky's theory, people learn when they have proper scaffolds in place to help them reach this next level of understanding. This strategy provides a step-by-step process for helping students learn a new concept. Consider Figure 7.1 as a description of different levels of learning:

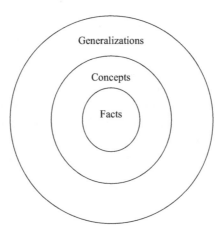

Figure 7.1   Different Levels of Learning.

Facts, concepts, and generalizations rely on each other to help promote deeper understanding. **A fact** is something that can be verified through observing, experiencing, reading, or listening. Facts are necessary for building conceptual knowledge and generalizations. They are the building blocks of concept development. As stated earlier, a **concept** is an idea for organizing and classifying experiences and facts into groups with common qualities. Concepts are timeless and abstract. *Conflict, change,* and *perspective* are three concepts. Examples of the concept *change* are prevalent throughout history, geography, and the other social studies. **Generalizations** are descriptive statements of relationships between two or more concepts. The statement "social change often brings about conflict" is a generalization about two of the concepts stated above. You can only make this statement if you understand the concepts of *change* and *conflict,* and if you have examined many examples and facts about social reform movements. *Generalizations,* as the word implies, are generally true. They can also be called conclusions (Parker, 2005, p. 201).

Before proceeding to the step-by-step procedures for helping your students form their understanding of concepts, we need to define five key terms:

1. *Concept:* A concept is an idea.
2. *Concept label:* Since concepts are ideas, they only exist in our minds. Words are labels that we use to talk about the ideas. A concept label is the word or phrase that people use when referring to a particular concept. Consider the concept of *cooperation.* We all have an idea of what cooperation is, but in order to talk about it we need to use the word/label.
3. *Critical attributes:* These are the traits or characteristics that every example of a particular concept will have. If we return to cooperation, we would conclude that every example of this concept involves at least two people who are working together toward a common purpose. For something to be an example of cooperation it must have these three attributes—therefore, they are critical to the concept.
4. *Examples of a concept:* Every example of a concept has all of the critical attributes. An example of *cooperation* might be a group of four students helping each other complete a task assigned by the teacher. Another example might be a football team successfully executing a play. Both are examples because they have all of the critical attributes.
5. *Non-examples of a concept:* Non-examples simply lack one or more critical attributes. If any of the critical attributes of cooperation do not exist, then it is not an example.

This quotation by Parker (1987) provides an additional example of how these terms work together:

> For instance, the idea *sentence* (or democracy . . . or experiment) does not exist physically, but there are numerous examples of sentence, such as the one you are now reading. What makes it an example is that it has the critical characteristics all sentences must have in order to be called by the label *sentence*: it has a subject, verb, and direct object, either present or implied; it expresses a complete thought; it has a beginning, ending, and, as needed, transition signals.
>
> (p. 57)

It is also important to understand where a concept's critical attributes come from. **Epistemology** is the study of knowledge that seeks to explain how we know—literally how we obtain, use, and think about knowledge of the world around us. Concepts help us think and understand the world, so studying concepts is an epistemological venture. When you help your students learn a concept, you are helping them think and study how they know something to be true. Concepts help us categorize the world. As a result, anyone is able to create a concept that helps him do this. Concepts are proved to be accurate ideas when they are tested. In other words, when we have experiences that require us to make judgments using a concept, we either verify or discredit the concept. Left to our own devices, we might create concepts that appear accurate simply because our individual experiences have not allowed for many judgments using the concept. When others use our concepts, they increase the number of experiences, and prove or call into question our category. Consider, for example, the concept of *democracy*. Two important attributes of this idea are that democracies require a free and fair election process. It is not all that important to know who decided this, as much as it is important to know whether these are defining attributes with which we all agree. As a society, we test the idea of democracy by making judgments about different systems of governance. If examples of this concept all include free elections and a fair election process, then the these critical attributes are confirmed, and the concept is valid. On the other hand, there has been much debate over the concept of *family*. The debate is about the critical attributes of a family, and whether these attributes are accurate when we determine if different scenarios are examples of a family. We all agree that *family* is a good concept label, but may disagree on the critical attributes. In the next section I will refer to *established* and *dynamic* concepts as one approach for determining if the experiences of the greater society have verified the critical attributes. It will be helpful for you to engage in some epistemology and think about how well you know the key concepts in your content area, and how these concepts have emerged.

STEP-BY-STEP PROCEDURES FOR PLANNING AND IMPLEMENTING CONCEPT FORMATION

Concept formation is an inductive approach that helps students learn the critical attributes of a given concept. Telling students the attributes that we, the teachers, have discovered does not promote mastery learning as effectively as helping students engage in a process where they actually think about the concept. In brief, concept formation provides students with the opportunity to inspect several examples of a given concept in light of the critical attributes, and then draw conclusions about the similarities and differences among these examples. Students' conclusions about the similarities are then generalized to be true about other examples of the concept they examined. To promote the type of thinking that will engage students, concept formation follows a sequential eight-step process.[2]

Step 1: Selecting a Concept

The first step in developing a concept-formation lesson is selecting a concept that students need to know. Teachers often tell us that this first step is the most difficult part, because the teacher needs to determine the concept on which the students will focus. Think about a few powerful ideas and issues that you want your students to build on and explore in your class. It might be helpful to follow this process: First, given all the potential topics that could be mentioned during the 180 hours you will have in class with your future students (far too many topics to teach well), identify five or six topics that are critically important for your students to learn. In previous chapters of this book you thought of many topics that you might teach in your future classroom; you might return to one of those. The state and national standards provide excellent ideas for big ideas. When you are teaching you will also have curriculum guides that provide many topics. Next, reflect on these topics and identify concepts that are an integral part of each topic. Think of concepts that you believe students must know well, and upon which other course content can be built. It is from this select list of concepts that you will select the big ideas, the important and powerful concepts for your students to explore. In a course on American government, you might select the topic *constitutional government*. With this topic, the concepts of *democracy*, *checks and balances*, or *e pluribus unum* are all significant concepts. In a geography course you might decide on the topic *sustainability*. Possible concepts could include *natural resources*, *consumption*, or *conservation*. In an ancient cultures course you might decide on the topic *civilization*. Possible concepts could include *government*, *conflict*, *community*, or *scarcity*. Select concepts that are difficult for students to grasp, and that are ideas you can build upon in future lessons. For example, a teacher might decide that the concept of *authority* is critical for understanding U.S. history. This concept will help students compare and contrast authoritarian forms of government with forms of government that gain their authority from the people (an authoritative government).

The concept you select should also have critical attributes upon which your local community has some agreement. While we all could agree on the critical attributes of *transportation* or *civil rights*, we would have more difficulty agreeing on the critical attributes of *love*. Concepts with easily agreed-upon attributes can be thought of as **established concepts**, and concepts with more disagreement as **dynamic concepts**. Concepts are established to help us make sense of the world around us. As a result, previously agreed-upon attributes may change as societal expectations change. Dynamic concepts are often learned best through inquiry projects, lecture, or classroom discussions (please refer to the chapters on these instructional strategies).

REALITY CHECK

Talk with teachers to identify concepts they use in their courses. Ask the teachers how they help students learn these concepts, and how they assess student learning. Look at the standards for your state in history, geography, civics, economics, etc. to indentify at least two key concepts in each area. How well do you understand these ideas?

Step 2: Studying Examples and Gathering Data

Once an established concept has been selected, you will develop a graphic organizer of some form to help students gather and record information about several examples of the concept. This organizer can take any form, but must contain two components: (1) a list of three to five examples for students to study; and (2) a set of three to five focus questions that direct students' attention to the critical attributes of the concept. As such, you will need to come up with examples of the concept, identify the critical attributes of the concept, and develop questions that address each of the critical attributes. Many times teachers feel perplexed as they try to identify examples and attributes of a concept. It is hard work, because you must think in depth about the concept. Usually, you can identify the most critical three to five attributes efficiently by looking up the concept label in dictionaries or web sources (even the oft-criticized wikipedia.org is a good starting point), having conversations with fellow teachers or other experts on the concept, and closely examining examples of the concept. A high school world history teacher developed a concept formation lesson for the big idea of *social caste*. The critical attributes for *social caste* are that it is (1) hierarchical; (2) tied to occupation; (3) based on ideas of purity/cleanliness; and (4) inherited and rigid. A sociologist would likely come up with more than these four attributes. The attributes you select do not have to be an exhaustive list as much as a list of the most relevant and important attributes, given how you will use this concept in the classroom. Below is a chart or matrix that the teacher developed for her students (Table 7.1), and possible student responses. As you look at the chart you will notice four *focus questions* across the top. They are directly connected to the four critical attributes of social caste. Be sure you understand this connection before reading more. Down the left column are three examples of social caste that the teacher found and modified so that her students could understand the descriptions better.

You may have noticed that the words this teacher used in the focus questions and in the descriptive examples might be difficult for younger students, or students who do not speak English as their first language. You need to structure a concept lesson to allow all of your students to learn. A student who is less proficient in English can be partnered with a student who speaks English as a first language. For "social caste" you could add alternative words to the examples and the focus questions. For example, the first focus question reads:

Is this country's social organization hierarchical?

To assist ELLs, you might pose this question as follows:

Is this country's social organization hierarchical? In other words, in this country do some groups of people always have more (or less) power than other people?

A teacher may determine that some of the words in the examples or the focus questions are too difficult for students who do not speak English as their first language. Again, modifying word choice to help students understand is an important consideration when developing the lesson.

Providing students with this chart helps them study particular examples of the concept (examples that have relevance to your course content), and helps students consider the examples in light of the critical attributes. This is undertaken as they think to answer the focus questions. These charts will not necessarily use descriptive paragraphs such as in Table 7.1.

Table 7.1 Data-Gathering Chart for Social Caste.

Data-Gathering Chart	Is this country's social organization hierarchical?	Is the social organization tied to occupation?	How does the idea of purity/impurity contribute to a separation of the social groups?	Can people move from the social groups into which they were born?
1) The Burakumin are a social group in Japan whose occupations consist of unwanted jobs. These jobs include executioners, disposing of dead animals, and sweeping and cleaning. Historically, the Emperor was the exact opposite in Japan. The people believed that he was a deity. In between the Emperor and the Burakumin were several social groups. During the Middle Ages, at the height of this social system, individuals were born into their social group and could not leave it.	Yes	Yes	Burakumin perform unwanted jobs	No
2) In India, one social group called the panchamas, or untouchables, are required to perform work that is considered to be "unclean." A higher social group in India, known as the Brahmins, performs religious duties. Members of both groups are born into these roles and an individual cannot change his or her membership within a group. In order to maintain "purity," marriage between members of different groups is not allowed. In addition to these social groups, there are others in India. The origins of this social structure are based on religion.	Yes	Maybe	Untouchables perform work that is considered "unclean"	No
3) The ñeeño social group in Senegal inherit their status from their parents. The ñeeño are characterized by their occupations such as blacksmiths, leatherworkers, and griots (musicians and storytellers). The geer, members of a higher social order, traditionally have discriminated against the ñeeño. Historically, the idea of pollution and impurity prevents intermingling between the ñeeño and other social groups. The ñeeño, and other social groups, are fixed within their social status.	Yes	Yes	Idea of pollution and impurity prevents intermingling between groups	No

They may present students with examples of a concept by providing video clips (e.g., clips of different examples of propaganda in a history class), words or phrases (e.g., examples of racism in the media during a current-events unit), pictures (e.g., examples of boundaries in a geography class), or even skits (e.g., examples of compromise). One teacher gave his students three examples of *appeasement* along with five focus questions, and then had the students spend a day in the library researching each example and answering the questions.

The focus questions can follow each example, or be placed in a chart. The following could be useful for the concept of *transportation*:

Table 7.2 Data-Gathering Chart for Transportation.

Automobile
Can this move?
Can this move people? Products? Services?
What do automobiles move most effectively?

Canoe
Can this move?
Can this move people? Products? Services?
What do canoes move most effectively?

Jumbo Jet
Can this move?
Can this move people? Products? Services?
What jumbo jets move most effectively?

Although I did not describe the critical attributes of transportation, hopefully you can identify them by looking at the focus questions. The attributes are that transportation (1) involves movement; (2) carries something from one place to another; (3) is an effective way to move people, goods, or services.

Step 3: Reporting Information

During this step the students report to a group or to the whole class what they found out from thinking about the examples and answering the focus questions. By reporting on the data they collected, students compare their findings with others. This allows students to clarify any questions they could not answer, and verify their findings with others in class. The goal is to come to an agreement about their answers. As mentioned above, placing students in small groups to do this step allows for peer tutoring and differentiating the instruction. This is also helpful for assisting ELLs in your classroom.

Step 4: Noting Differences

In Step 4 the teacher talks with the whole class about the examples they have examined, and their answers to the focus questions. During this step, the teacher helps the students focus on the differences among the examples. An effective prompt for this is, "Look at the examples, and describe how these are different from each other." This is an important cognitive step because it requires students to consider how examples of a concept can have very different attributes but still be examples. In the above example of transportation (Table 7.2), attributes such as color, mode of movement, or size would not be critical attributes. Or, consider all of the different examples of scarcity, or social castes, which all possess the critical attributes but present themselves very uniquely.

Step 5: Noting Similarities

After contrasting the examples in Step 4, you as the teacher will proceed to have students compare the examples and identify how they are similar. An effective prompt for this is, "In what ways are the examples all alike?" This question directs students' attention to the answers (data) they provided for each focus question. These similarities will be used during Step 6, "Synthesizing," so list them on the board as the students state them. The list of similarities will match the critical attributes that you came up with when preparing the focus questions. You have not told them to your students, but they have come up with them on their own, and in their own words, as a result of thinking about the different examples. You will keep asking them to identify similarities, and the students will identify all of the critical attributes by using their own thoughts and words. Look again at the data-gathering chart for "social caste." You can imagine how sharing similarities identifies the attributes. Later in the chapter, the section on logistics provides helpful approaches for Step 5.

Step 6: Synthesizing

In this step the students combine the similarities—the attributes—into a sentence or statement. At this point the students write their own definition of the concept, being sure to incorporate all of the similarities that are listed on the board. The students then share aloud their sentences, and check each other to ensure that they have mentioned each similarity; the teacher engages with the students to check their definitions. These definitions will be accurate descriptions of the concept, but will be in the students' own words and not be given to them by the teacher. Instead, the students will have developed these through their own thinking about the examples. As long as the statements have all of the attributes, you do not need to require specific words. For example, the second attribute of social caste was that it is tied to your occupation. A student's statement that states it is "part of your job" is accurate and does not need to be corrected.

Step 7: Labeling

Although concepts are abstract, the word or label that we use when referring to a concept is tangible. The concept label *cooperation* makes a lot of sense because the label is closely related to the critical attributes (*co-* means "more than one," and *operate* means "to do something"). The concept label *law* makes less sense because the label does not seem closely related to the critical attributes. At this step in the lesson, students think of labels that they believe capture the essence of the critical attributes. These labels do not need to be the actual words for the concept. In fact, the teacher focuses more on the reasons a student selected a label than the actual label. Labeling is another type of synthesis, and it ensures that the students understand the gist of the concept.

An effective prompt by the teacher for a label might be, "Think of a word or phrase that captures the idea of your definition and the similarities we listed on the board. In a minute I will have you share what you came up with, and why that word is a good choice." Consider for a minute the concept of *compromise*. A student may suggest that a good label is "give and take," and another may suggest the label "negotiation." Both labels are acceptable *if* the student is able to explain why they are related to the critical attributes of the concept. After several students have the opportunity to state and explain their labels, the teacher provides them with the conventional word for the concept. Just as the students did, this is also a good place to add any insight into why this word is used when referring to this concept. In other words, see if you can provide any etymology for the word. This allows students to add to their understanding of the concept by learning the word that "adults use" when referring to the concept they have just explored. "Social caste" is a label of Spanish and Portuguese descent that literally means the interactions of a pure lineage or breed. It is easy to see how caste systems have led to atrocities and inequality through history. One final note on labeling: Students may say the conventional word when they are thinking of a label. That is great; the teacher should follow up with the same request that students explain why they think this is an appropriate label.

Step 8: Assessing with Classifying Tasks

At this point, the concept has been formed and labeled. Now the teacher assesses students' understanding by asking them to engage in a series of classifying tasks. We will highlight three tasks that become increasingly complex, and that give you increased confidence that the students have learned and can use the concept. These tasks are addressed in the assessment section of this chapter. Before moving to assessment, the following diagram is an overview of the eight steps of concept formation:

1. Teacher selects a concept that will promote students understanding.

2. Students study examples and gather data by answering focus questions.

3. Students report what they discovered about each example.

4. The class notes differences amongst the examples.

5. The class notes similarities amongst the examples, and a note of these is recorded on the board.

6. Students synthesize the similarities into a statement.

7. Students come up with their own label for the concept, and learn the conventional word/phrase.

8. Teacher leads assessment with classifying tasks.

LOGISTICS FOR CONCEPT FORMATION

As mentioned before, preparation before the lesson is extensive. First, you need to select an established concept upon which you can explore future course content, and identify the three to five critical attributes common to every example of the concept. Next, you need to compose focus questions that address each critical attribute, and locate three to five examples of the concept. Ideas for developing the examples were described earlier in the chapter, but some general thoughts bear repeating here, under logistics. Often the concept and examples will determine how students will gather data. For example, if students are exploring the concept of *propaganda*, then the examples will likely be statements, phrases, and/or images, because these are usually the forms propaganda takes. These may best be viewed online or as a handout. If the concept is *theme*, then the examples will be fully developed themes of stories that the students need time to read. The examples need to provide enough information so that the students can answer the focus questions. As a result, you need to consider your students' prior knowledge as you prepare the examples. If you are teaching the concept *civilization* to sixth graders, you should not have as an example the term *Mesopotamia*. While this is a fine example of the concept, your students will not know enough about Mesopotamia to answer the focus questions. Instead, a concise description of Mesopotamia that emphasizes the key characteristics of all civilizations will facilitate students' forming of the concept. Therefore, you need to allow student opportunities to find and use information about the example. At times this can occur simply from the examples given on a data-gathering chart. At other times this may require more in-depth examinations of the examples.

Listing the similarities (Step 5) requires patience on your part as the teacher. Remember, you have already thought about the concept, but this is the first time your students will do so. The temptation is to turn this step into a question-and-answer session in which the students feel they are trying to guess what you want. If you are patient, the students will come up with a list of similarities that very closely resembles the list of critical attributes you identified during your preparation. If students find this step difficult, prompt them with, "Look closely at the focus questions across the top and see if any of your answers reveal how the examples are alike." You might also need to model this for the students. For example, if the concept is *civil rights*, then you might model for your students how to identify similarities in this manner: "When I look at my answers to the focus question about protection I have guaranteed by the law, I see that I have the same answer for all the examples. So, one way these examples are alike is that they all are legal protections. How else are they alike?" Again, since you know the similarities, you need to exercise patience and allow your students the thinking time required to form the concept. The similarities must be listed on the whiteboard/document camera for use in Step 6 (synthesizing).

The synthesis step may require more time than you originally think. During this step, students write their definition of the concept from the list of similarities. Students will originally do this independently, and revise their definitions to ensure that they incorporate all of the critical attributes. You should have many students share their definitions. As they do, encourage the class to cross-check the definition with the similarities listed on the board, noting any gaps. After a student shares, initial definitions may need revisions. Allow time for this, so that all students eventually have a definition that incorporates all of the similarities. This step allows for you to assess student progress and understanding. It is a step where comments from each student are considered together. Students who have a strong grasp of the attributes are able to explain their thinking (which helps them understand the concept even more). Students who are having difficulty understanding are able to hear from peers about the critical attributes of the concept, and compare that with their current understanding. Students who are learning English as an additional language will benefit by hearing others in class share their ideas. If they have an English-speaking partner, then this is a great time for them to pair up and discuss what the class is developing as a definition.

CLASSROOM MANAGEMENT AND STUDENT MOTIVATION

Each of the eight steps in the concept-formation strategy guides the students in their understanding of the critical attributes. The principal classroom-management issues involve ensuring that you are monitoring the students, guiding them through the steps, and providing ample opportunities for them to share their ideas. It is during the sharing that you can assess their learning, and that they can learn from each other's ideas. Therefore, concept formation requires the teacher to facilitate students' independent work and whole-class interactions. The independent work will occur when students gather data, write their synthesized definitions, develop labels, and engage in the classifying tasks (steps 2, 6, 7, and 8, respectively). The whole-class interactions occur when students report their findings, consider differences and similarities, share their labels, and explain their classifying decisions (steps 3, 4, 5, 7, and 8, respectively).

When students work independently, you may want them to work individually or with a partner (*independent* work is not always the same thing as *individual* work). It is often recommended to limit the size of these work teams to two or three, because the steps of the lesson require students to think on their own about the examples and focus questions. The use of partners is to assist this thinking and help with understanding the critical attributes; it is a great opportunity to pair an English-speaking student with an ELL, or to pair a highly capable learner with a student needing extra assistance. If students are in large groups, they may rely on others for answers, and not think as deeply about the examples and attributes of the concept. During the independent work period the students must have time to answer the focus questions and think about the topic. By watching students closely you will be able to decide when they have had adequate time to think. Some teachers do not allow enough time (the result is that students do not gather adequate information to accurately form the concept), and some provide too much time (the result is that the lesson loses momentum, and the students disengage). Because the data gathering precedes a classwide reporting session, you do not need to wait until all students have fully completed the data-gathering phase. However, you should be aware of who is not finished, and watch them closely so you are able to ensure that they complete their data gathering as the class reports on its findings.

The whole-class interactions need to allow as many students as possible the chance to share their ideas. To manage this, it is often helpful to ask for volunteers and to call on students. The only times you need to be up front writing on the chalkboard or on an overhead projection is when students report similarities and when they suggest labels for the concept. The rest of the time, you can walk around the room to encourage student participation. Since students may work with partners and share their ideas with the entire class, consider how the desks might be arranged to facilitate both. The conventional rows of desks/tables facing the front will work well (students then lean across the rows to interact with a partner), but so will any seating configuration in which students are facing the front of the room: They must be able to easily see the board/screen during the synthesis step.

During the entire lesson, you will want students to listen to and critique their classmates' thinking. When students gather data, be sure you are interested in what they are finding. You will need to work at this, because you have already thought about the concept and its critical attributes in preparation for the lesson. You do not want to give the impression that your students are trying to guess what you want; rather, you need to impress upon them that you want them to think about the examples and come up with their own answers to the focus questions. It is a subtle difference, but one that helps motivate students to think for themselves, and not think for the teacher. For example, if you present students with a data-gathering chart, be careful that they do not think it is merely a worksheet that they need to mindlessly complete. Instead, promote the idea that they need to think about the examples and questions. Show enthusiasm and curiosity for their answers as they report their findings, note differences, and suggest similarities.

APPROPRIATE ASSESSMENT TECHNIQUES TO USE WITH CONCEPT FORMATION

The most efficient and valid assessment of your students' conceptual understanding is to engage them in the following three types of classifying tasks: (1) distinguishing examples from non-examples; (2) producing examples; and (3), correcting non-examples (Parker, 2005, p. 198). The great advantage of these three types of concept practice is that they get students thinking about the critical characteristics of the concept. We describe each type below:[3]

Type 1: Distinguishing Examples from Non-examples

In this classifying task you present the students with a list of examples and non-examples all at once. For the concept *scarcity*, the following mixed list might be used: *farm land*, *potable water*, *strawberries*, and *ocean water*. The instructions are, "Study these items and decide which ones are examples of *scarcity*, and which items are non-examples. Also, note the items that you cannot determine. In a minute, I will ask several of you to support your decisions." Or, you might have them write their support as part of the assignment. Whichever way you prefer, be sure to give lots of students, if not all of them, the opportunity to support their decision.

Type 2: Producing Examples

This task is different from Type 1 because you do not provide any examples or non-examples. Rather, you give students only the concept label and ask them to come up with an example of the concept. This time, the instructions are, "Now that we have studied the concept called (state the concept label, for example, 'immigration'), I want you to find (or make/write/produce/construct/look for) an example of it. Remember, in order to be an example, it must have all the critical attributes we identified in our definition. After you have produced your example, be ready to support it by telling us why it is an example and not a non-example." You might recognize that this task assesses students' thinking at the highest level of the revised Bloom's Taxonomy (creating). The students' support for the concept they produced is what you use to accurately assess their conceptual understanding. In other words, can they identify each of the attributes in their example?

Type 3: Correcting Non-examples

Most teachers consider this the most difficult type of assessing conceptual understanding, which is why it is the final classification task (the first type is considered the least difficult). Unlike in Type 1, where you give students the label and several items, and Type 2, where you only give them the label, in Type 3 you give them the label and a non-example. Now the instructions are, "Here is a non-example of the concept we call (state the concept label—for example "democracy"). Your task is to make the necessary changes in this non-example in order to make it into an example. Then, I'll ask several of you to support the changes you made." Cognitively, your students will be comparing the critical attributes of the concept with the critical attributes of the non-example, *and then* they will identify which attributes are missing and make the needed changes. Earlier in the chapter we commented that *courage* and *bravery* are related but different concepts. If the concept the students learned was *courage*, then having them change an example of *bravery* to be an example of courage would be a Type 3 task. Or, if the concept was *interdependence*, then being able to correct a non-example of interdependence would require them to understand the concept well enough to identify the missing critical attributes of the example and make the needed changes.

Of course, other assessments could be used in which the students engage in tasks that require them to use their conceptual understanding. The emphasis of all these assessments is to have students work with examples of the concept, and to demonstrate their understanding of the critical attributes that are part of each example (and that are missing in non-examples).

ENHANCING CONCEPT FORMATION WITH TECHNOLOGY

Having students access a variety of examples of concepts online, after they have formed an understanding of a concept, helps accentuate their understanding. In addition, locating examples beyond the walls of the classroom becomes a powerful approach to enhancing learning. Students who learned about "political revolution" can access news accounts online about current revolutions. Students who learned about "climate change" are able to see this concept by visiting webcams, first-hand accounts, or even university lectures on the topic. Students who learned about civil rights can explore actual examples throughout time of groups seeking civil rights. The world, full of concepts, comes into the classroom to help students examine a wide range of examples, and notice missing attributes of non-examples. You might, for example, provide your students with case studies of different phenomenon (e.g., different types of war, different cultural traits) and ask them to search for examples online, and then identify the crticial attributes in the examples.

Online sources are useful for you, the teacher, in developing your own understanding of a concept. Searches for examples, definitions, and critical attributes will provide you with many learning opportunities. Years ago, a teacher might have hesitated to help students learn a concept because he lacked background kowledge about the idea. Today, learning about any concept is literally at our fingertips.

MAKING CONCEPT FORMATION MORE MEANINGFUL FOR ELLS

Throughout this chapter I have interjected several ideas for assisting ELLs during the concept-formation lesson. More advanced ELLs will benefit from word-formation excerises. In fact, advanced-level English exams such as the TOEFL use word formation as a portion of their assessment. Charting concepts nouns, personal nouns, adjectives, and verbs helps students see the relationship between these categories and improves fluency. Students can use the word-formation chart for language development in many ways, such as by creating additions to the chart or creating sentences using words from the different columns. An example chart with hundreds of words listed from A to Z can be found at this website: http://esl. about.com/od/vocabularyadvanced/a/a_wordforms1.htm. Table 7.3 is a brief example of words from this site:

Table 7.3 Concept Word Formation Chart.

Concept Noun	Personal Noun	Adjective	Verb
accusation	accuser/accused	accusing	accuse
censorship	censor	censored	censure
civilization	civilian	civil	civilize
law	lawyer	lawful/lawless	enforce the law
migration	migrant	migratory	migrate
theory	theorist	theoretical	theorize
volunteering	volunteer	volunteered	volunteer

In Chapter 11 the idea of "word walls" will be examined in the section on helping ELLs. That strategy is also useful for helping students see, recall, and use basic concepts and strategies. Word walls are lists of words written on butcher paper and plastered on walls around the classroom to assist with vocabulary development. Often teachers ask students to help create the lists and add to the lists as appropriate. Additionally, the "labeling" step of the concept-formation lesson allows students to think of their own word/phrase for the concept. Concepts are often specific to subject areas (e.g., theory, culture, fiction, scarcity, and metamorphosis), and as a result the English words we use to label a concept can be very academic and confusing. Allowing students to label the concept allows them to attach a label that makes sense from a conceptual perspective and an English language perspective.

GUIDELINES FOR DECIDING IF CONCEPT FORMATION IS APPROPRIATE FOR THE CONTENT OF A LESSON

The concept-formation strategy is an effective tool for helping your students think through the critical characteristics of a concept. It should not be used to teach vocabulary words to your students, but should be used to explore a few important concepts that will provide a foundation for future learning. One teacher I know uses the concept of *tradition* when teaching a unit on Japanese culture because she believes that exploring this concept in depth will help students understand the nuance of Japan's history and culture. A teacher mentioned earlier begins a U.S. history course by engaging students in a concept-formation lesson about *authority*. If understanding a complex idea is important for learning additional content in your course, then consider introducing the idea with the concept-formation strategy.

Earlier I mentioned the difference between *established* concepts and *dynamic* concepts. The critical attributes of established concepts are agreed upon by most people, but this is not the case with dynamic concepts. If you cannot identify three to five critical attributes that are clearly established, then this strategy will not be effective. Consider the important concept *culture*. Would you consider it dynamic or established? Your answer will help determine the appropriateness of the concept-formation strategy. Similarly, reserve the concept-formation strategy for those significant and/or more complex ideas that students have difficulty understanding, or for those ideas that students often misunderstand. For example, *institutional racism* is more complex than *prejudice* and may be the better concept of the two to explore with this strategy.

Because concept-formation lessons take time to develop and teach, be sure you have the time to develop the lesson fully. If the focus questions are not complete, or if they do not focus students on the critical attributes, then the students might miss an important attribute. Use this strategy after you have double checked that the critical attributes are clearly identified, the examples are descriptive and appropriate, the focus questions are clear, and you have enough class time to develop the lesson. Usually, a concept-formation lesson requires 40 to 50 minutes. If students are engaging in extra research on the examples, then the lesson could take two days.

MAKING IT WORK IN YOUR CLASSROOM

In Step 1 of the step-by-step lesson procedures, you considered a process for selecting a concept you might teach in your content area. In this section you will build on that a bit more. The intention is for you to identify how to use the concept-formation strategy to help students learn at least one "big idea" in your content area. Below is a restatement of that section, so you can build on that activity. Work through the following 12 steps on your own or with a partner.

1. Given all the potential topics that students need to learn in your future classroom, identify five or six topics that you believe are critically important for your students to learn. Next, reflect on these topics and identify ideas/concepts that are an integral part of each topic. From this select list of concepts, select one that is complex and powerful enough for your students to explore.
2. State the concept that your students will learn (actually list the concept label).
3. Find the origin of this label; often the origin, or etymology, provides insight into the label's critical attributes.
4. Describe your rationale for asking students to build on this idea. Why is it significant in your content area? What will precede this lesson? What will follow it?
5. Identify the critical attributes, and list them.
6. List three or four examples, and briefly describe how students will learn about these examples—for example, will they read about the example, or view a video clip?
7. List three or four non-examples for the classifying tasks.
8. Decide which format will be best for the data-gathering chart. Will it be a matrix? Paragraphs and questions? A webpage?

9. Develop a data-gathering graphic organizer that lists examples and focus questions.
10. Develop a list of at least two examples and two non-examples of your concept that students can explore during the first classifying task.
11. Come up with a non-example of your concept that students can change into an example during the third classifying task.
12. Write lesson targets for a concept formation. Since concept formation has the single purpose of helping students learn an important idea, you are writing the target after you have thought through and applied each step of the concept lesson. In future concept lessons, however, you should write the target(s) at the beginning.

CHAPTER REVIEW

- Research support for using concept formation
  - Too often we use concepts and have limited understanding of what we mean
  - Students often learn information superficially
  - The purpose of the concept-formation strategy is to help students form a robust understanding of significant concepts in your content area
- Step-by-step procedures for selecting, planning, and using concept-learning activities
  - Facts, concepts, and generalizations rely on each other to help promote a deeper understanding
    - a *concept* is an idea for organizing and classifying experiences and facts into groups with common qualities
    - a *fact* is something that can be verified through observing, experiencing, reading, or listening
    - *generalizations* are descriptive statements of relationships between two or more concepts
  - Concept formation is an inductive approach that follows a sequential eight-step process

    1. selecting a concept
    2. study examples and gathering data
    3. reporting
    4. noting differences
    5. noting similarities
    6. synthesizing
    7. labeling
    8. assessing with classifying tasks

- Managing the classroom/learning environment during concept learning
  - Monitor students
  - Guide them through the steps
  - Provide ample opportunity for them to share their ideas
- Assessing student learning appropriately during concept formation relied on classifying tasks
  - Distinguish examples from non-examples
  - Produce examples
  - Correct non-examples

- Using technology to enhance learning
  - Accessing examples of concepts from around the world
  - Using the Internet to identify critical attributes of a concept
- Considerations for English language learners during concept-formation lessons
  - Partnering with an English-speaking classmate or in groups will assist the process
  - Word walls of key concepts
  - Charting concept nouns

NOTES

1. Power, Authority, and Governance is one of the ten National Standards developed by the National Council for the Social Studies (National Council for Social Studies, 2010).
2. This procedure was developed by Walter C. Parker (1987, 2012), based on the work of Hilda Taba (1967) and Sydelle Ehrenberg (1981).
3. Adapted from the work of Ehrenberg, 1981; Parker, 2012; Weikel, B., personal communication, December, 2005.

REFERENCES

Ehrenberg, S. D. (1981). Concept learning: How to make it happen in the classroom. *Educational Leadership, 39*(1), 36–43.

National Council for Social Studies (2010). *Curriculum Standards for Social Studies: Expectations of Excellence.* Washington, DC: NCSS.

Parker, W. C. (2012). *Social Studies in Elementary Education,* 14th ed. Boston, MA: Allyn & Bacon.

Parker, W. C. (2009). *Social Studies in Elementary Education,* 13th ed. Boston, MA: Allyn & Bacon.

Parker, W. C. (2005). *Social Studies in Elementary Education,* 12th ed. New York: Prentice Hall.

Parker, W. C. (1987). Teaching thinking: The pervasive approach. *Journal of Teacher Education, 38*(3), 50–56.

Parker, W. C. & Perez, S. (1987). Beyond the rattle of empty wagons. *Social Education, 52*(3), 164–166.

Taba, H. (1967). *Teacher's Handbook.* Palo Alto, CA: Addison-Wesley Publishing Company.

Vygotsky, L. S. (1978). *Mind in Society: The Development of Higher Psychological Processes.* Cambridge, MA: MIT Press.

CHAPTER 8

Cooperative Learning

CHAPTER GOALS

In this chapter, you will learn about:

- Research support for using cooperative learning in the classroom
- Step-by-step procedures for selecting, planning, and using cooperative learning strategies
- Managing the classroom/learning environment during cooperative learning
- Assessing student learning when working in cooperative groups
- Using technology to enhance learning
- Considerations for English language learners during cooperative learning activities.

Teacher-centered   Student-centered

Lecture   Simulation/Role-Play/Drama   Discussion

Questioning

Cooperative Learning

Concept Formation   SDI

Mr. Williams had students in his world geography class read an article about a current issue in sub-Saharan Africa. He broke the class into three groups of seven or eight students, each group to read different articles. The first group read an article related to the impact of AIDS on children; the second group had an article on working conditions in a mine; the third read an article on post–apartheid race relations. He had asked each group to be prepared to give a report to the large group so the rest of the class could learn about the topics they didn't read. It didn't work. Some students complained that they had to do all the work, other students complained that they weren't given a chance to do anything because of the "know it all" student, and others just let it all pass as they looked out the window. After thinking about it overnight, Mr. Williams decided to tweak his idea for the other geography class that met the next day. He had read about a jigsaw strategy and wanted to give it a try. This time he would add a fourth article and group, so the teams were smaller. The class would have four groups of about five or six. When the groups met in different locations around the room, he would explain how the jigsaw worked and that they would be depending upon each other to learn aboout the different topics. They would start with their home group then split up to form new groups. He was hopeful as the bell rang . . .

OVERVIEW

During lessons that use cooperative learning, students work together in groups to help each other learn content and skills. Cooperation requires students to accomplish shared goals. During cooperative learning activities, students work to complete tasks that help them learn individually, and that help group members learn as well. In short, cooperative learning places students in groups to maximize their learning. In the process, students learn to use critical social skills. Teachers across the subjects use cooperative learning, but the social studies are uniquely positioned to use cooperative learning to help students with social skills that will translate into democratic citizenship skills. Cooperative learning groups typically range from three to seven students, with the ideal number being four or five. Keeping the size of the groups small encourages students to work together and to more actively participate. This chapter will help you understand the difference between cooperative group learning and conventional group projects. Many of the instructional strategies mentioned in Part II of this book could employ cooperative learning groups. Cooperative learning, therefore, is an instructional strategy that involves placing students into groups, and helping them work together to complete a given task.

A DESCRIPTION OF COOPERATIVE LEARNING AND RESEARCH FINDINGS

Educational researchers have examined cooperative learning extensively for several decades. Research studies consistently find that cooperative learning has positive effects on student achievement because the process of interacting with others promotes learning. Students often learn more and learn more quickly when compared to students working alone, or not working in cooperative groups (Johnson, Johnson, & Holubec, 1994). Student achievement is highest when the cooperative learning activity requires group members to work together "to earn recognition, grades, rewards, and other indicators of group success" (Slavin, 1989–90, p. 52). Said another way, group goals and tasks requiring students to depend on each other and work together to attain group goals lead to higher levels of achievement. What causes this increase in achievement has been the focus of many years of research. Most research studies conclude that group goals and individual accountability decreases competition among students, and motivates them to help each other learn and enhance their own learning. Cooperative learning has at its core the idea that students must both "pull their own weight" and work together to accomplish a task. The cooperative tasks are designed so that one person is not able to complete the group's assignment alone. By holding members individually accountable, the group is positioned so that members help each other, work interdependently (and not independently), and learn more. Individual students often complain about "working in groups" because they feel as though they have to do all the work, because they have had previous experiences in groups where partners "slack off" or "do nothing." This takes place because a teacher does not have a method in place for holding all the group members accountable. Often teachers assign a group grade. This is in conflict with cooperative learning research, because group grades will not promote individual achievement the way group goals and individual accountability will.

Consider the following example of one approach for holding students individually accountable. A civics teacher places students in groups of three and assigns them the task of analyzing current city policies about urban growth and sprawl. The teacher then specifies that each student needs to analyze one of three different proposed policies, and that each student needs to compose a report comparing her analysis with the other group members' analyses. The group must produce a PowerPoint presentation on the "state of the urban growth plan in our community," and the students each receive a grade for analysis and comparisons. The PowerPoint presentation is recorded as either satisfactory or unsatisfactory. The teacher grades in this fashion so that the students will analyze their policy and hold each other accountable for completing the analyses. The group is interdependent, but each member is assessed on her individual work.

Findings from 164 research studies on cooperative learning specify that placing students in groups (as opposed to having students select their own groups), assigning a task where they must work together, and teaching specific social skills has a positive effect on student achievement (Johnson, Johnson, & Stanne, 2000). Research in these areas reveals that when students cooperate, and the emphasis on competition and individual achievement is decreased, student learning increases. For example, placing students in heterogeneous cooperative learning groups at least one time a week has a significantly positive effect on learning (Marzano, Pickering, & Pollock, 2001). Similarly, students spend more time "on task," are more motivated to complete assignments, and are more capable at transferring their learning to other contexts during cooperative group activities (Johnson & Johnson, 1999; Kohn, 1993). By contrast, when students with lower abilities are grouped together, their academic performance decreases (Kulik & Kulik, 1987, 1991), and when students are placed in groups *without* support structures that reduce competition and increase interdependence, they do not attain higher academic levels of achievement (Anderson, Reder, & Simon, 1997).

Cooperative learning has a positive impact on social interactions among students, because students learn how to interact with one another. When you teach, you will model for your students how to work with others. One of the most consistent findings is that "when students of different racial or ethnic backgrounds work together toward a common goal, they gain in liking and respect for one another" (Slavin, 1989–90, p. 53). When this is thought of in the context of a democratic society that holds as one of its ideals the free and civil discussion of public issues, it becomes apparent that cooperative learning is an instructional strategy that holds potential for developing participatory citizens in a democratic society.

Cooperative learning has also been shown to increase classmates' acceptance of students who are traditionally marginalized because of low academic ability (Cohen, 1994; Cohen & Lotan, 1997; Johnson & Johnson, 1989–90). Students are marginalized, or placed outside of the mainstream of the classroom, for reasons such as ability, ethnicity, wealth/poverty, or appearance. Cohen (1994; Cohen & Lotan, 2014) has examined how student "status" leads to different behaviors in groups, and leads to different treatment by peers; she notes,

> A status characteristic is an agreed upon social ranking where everyone feels it is better to have a high rank than a low rank. Examples of status characteristics are race, social class, sex, reading ability, and attractiveness . . . high status individuals are expected to be more competent than low status individuals across a wide range of tasks that are viewed as important. When a teacher assigns a task to a group of students, some of whom are higher and some lower on any of the status characteristics described above, these general expectations come into play . . . those who are higher status come to hold a high rank in the status order that emerges in the group interaction. Those who hold lower status come to hold a low rank on that status order.
>
> (1994, p. 33)

No one formally assigns status to students, just as no one formally assigns status to people in society at large. It is one aspect of a diverse society that perpetuates the status quo and the current power structure in that society. High-status students are expected to be better (and they come to expect it of themselves), and low-status students are not expected to make important contributions to the group (and they begin to believe they have little to offer). Members of a group often promote some members to be active (high-status students), and some members to be subordinate (low-status students). If left to their own devices, most student groups will reiterate the existing status of students. Even when groups are changed, a student's status often follows him to the next setting (Cohen & Lotan, 1997). However, cooperative learning has been found to increase the status of marginalized students. By assigning students to groups, structuring tasks to require interdependence, reducing competition, and proactively teaching students how to divide the workload, understand group goals, listen, paraphrase ideas, and encourage each other, teachers can help students overcome the barriers of status and marginalization. Additionally, students increase friendships with group mates after working together in cooperative learning groups or teams, and over time students increase their abilities to listen to others, consider ideas from all members of a group, assign tasks equally, and have a greater sense of concern for the success of all members in the group. I often hear from people in a wide range of occupations (e.g., teachers, doctors, lawyers, contractors, retailers, small business owners, community service workers) that the ability to work with others cooperatively is a critical "job skill." Add to this idea that it is also a critical skill for citizens of a democracy. The research clearly suggests that cooperative learning promotes learning of skills and content. The idea that cooperative learning promotes prosocial behavior among students is an added value of using cooperative learning strategies.

The question that arises in the midst of this research support is, *What are these strategies?* Cooperative learning is much more than simply placing students in groups and assigning them a task. This simplistic approach fosters behavior where one or two capable students "take over" and complete the task. Students who are marginalized by peers and even by the larger community because of reputation, ethnicity, gender, lower ability, or other social factors are often further separated from the assignment. At its worst, group work becomes an activity in which students merely go through the motions of interacting with one another. Resentment is stirred up in the student who ends up completing the task on his own, and students who do not participate in class might even be pressured to contribute to a lesser degree. Groups, thus, can create resentment, reinforce stereotypes, and benefit some students to the detriment of others. The teacher must structure group work. Merely asking students to work in groups (even if you assigned them to the groups) can at times do more academic and social harm than good. Very specific attributes are needed to promote positive interdependence (which is another name for cooperation). Johnson, Johnson, and Holubec (1994, p. 26) have developed the following five "essential elements" of cooperative learning that will help you structure your future use of student groups:

1. positive interdependence
2. face-to-face interactions
3. group goals and individual accountability
4. interpersonal and small-group skills
5. group processing.

The following overview of these elements is intended to help you clarify the importance of each when you plan to use cooperative learning.

Positive Interdependence

When people cooperate, they have positive interdependence on each other. Students must see that they need each other to accomplish a task and to learn. Many techniques are available for teachers to use in promoting this. Teachers might request that students share resources, materials, and information so that the students genuinely need each other's ideas and information. For example, in a geography class, each group member might be responsible for learning about the natural resources available in different regions of Africa, but the group needs to use all the examples together. Each member informs group mates about the information she has gathered. The teacher could also have the group establish mutual goals about how members might help each other learn the content or skills. A group might have the goal that each member will complete her research about African regions in the next two days. Or, the group might set the goal that everyone will provide a paragraph description and a representative photo of the region. Goals could also specify the role of each member during a class presentation.

Positive interdependence can also be fostered when the teacher provides group awards. This could be in the form of praise (e.g., applause and commendations after an effective presentation to the class), extra-credit points (e.g., points awarded if all members' test scores are above a certain percentile), or other incentives that the whole group receives other than a grade. Finally, interdependence is fostered by assigning roles within the group that are necessary for the group to progress. For example, students in a group might take on the following roles: (1) the *coordinator* (someone who allocates responsibilities and keeps the group on task); (2) the *checker* (someone who makes sure all members of the group are participating and understanding the content); (3) the *recorder* (someone who takes general notes for the group and organizes the final group solution); and (4) the *skeptic* (someone who keeps the group from leaping to premature conclusions). These are simply suggested roles, and you will develop your own based on the needs of your students. These roles are assessed and monitored by the group and by the teacher. Students hold themselves accountable, and exhort or encourage each other to fully complete their roles. As the teacher you must remember that you are helping students learn content (e.g., Regions in Africa) *and* that you are helping students learn interdependence. You must monitor student interactions with both in mind. We will discuss this in more detail in the assessment section of this chapter.

Face-to-Face Interactions

Many of the cognitive and social benefits of cooperative learning occur during face-to-face group interactions and discussions. Requiring students to meet and work as a group is essential. These meetings may occur during class so that you can monitor student interactions, or they may occur outside of the classroom if the group needs to complete tasks as homework. Students cannot work toward many of the interdependent elements listed above without meeting face to face. Likewise, these interactions require students to engage in higher-order thinking such as summarizing, explaining, elaborating ideas, and seeking clarification. The interactions promote content and skill learning. It is also during these interactions that students cooperate in earnest with others who may be "different" from themselves. As the teacher, you need to assess the degree of cooperation that occurred. We will explore this more in the assessment section of this chapter.

Your students will not have developed much skill at working interdependently with others. Face-to-face interactions are a critical element for developing positive interracial relations in multi-cutural/heterogeneous classrooms that the research on cooperative learning suggests (Cohen & Lotan, 2014). At times you may need to stop a group project and work solely on interaction skills. The following experience of one student teacher serves as an example.

> Jill placed students in heterogeneous groups so they were a mix of ability level, ethnic background, and peer groups. She assigned each group a hypothesized reason that the Civil War in the United States occurred in the mid-1800s and asked the groups to understand their reason in anticipation of a jigsaw task. After the first day, she noticed that most of the groups were not working together. The assigned task required interdependence, but the students were not willing to work together. Jill recognized that they were in groups with classmates they did not "hang out with" outside of class. She decided to work on the relationships of the students, and spent two days engaging in trust-building and team-building activities (e.g., leading a blindfolded partner around an obstacle course, identifying positive character traits of group members). She plainly told students that she placed them in groups with classmates they did not know well, and that she would be watching to see how well the groups worked together. She told them that she wanted little competition in the groups, and that each student would assess his own performance and his group members' performance in helping the group work together. After the two days, she resumed the Civil War assignment, and closely monitored student interactions. As least twice a week she had students turn in group and individual assessments of their progress. Jill used these assessments to teach specific social skills to the class. After working in the groups, every student received at least 85% of the total points possible for the project!

Group Goals and Individual Accountability

Cooperative learning groups all will have goals, such as completing a task/assignment, working to accomplish a project by cooperating, and the mutual goals described above (in the "Positive Interdependence" section). In addition, each student must be held individually accountable for her own learning. Cooperative groups have not met their goals until every member of the group has learned. Group members need to work hard at their own learning, and work to support each other. You may think of creative ideas for holding students accountable, but a few common ideas include:

• dividing a large group project into smaller tasks that group members assign among themselves; that way the group is responsible for the larger project, and each member is responsible and held accountable for completing one or more critical tasks
• quizzing/testing each member individually on material the group was learning together; this will keep students accountable for learning content and for teaching it to each other
• having one member answer for the entire group; this way the students will prepare together so all members can provide answers effectively.

Interpersonal and Small-Group Skills

As with working interdependently, most students (and adults!) do not have adequate preparation to work cooperatively in a group. Cooperative learning is dependent upon you helping your students learn effective interpersonal/social skills. These are taught in the context of the group project. Students need to develop trust, decision-making abilities, conflict management skills, and motivation techniques. For example, the ability to criticize an idea and not the person presenting the idea is difficult to learn. Learning this while working on a group project will allow students to develop this skill in an authentic setting. Similarly, confronting students who are not sharing the workload is difficult, but necessary, and a cooperative group becomes a powerful setting in which to learn how to do this. Many times the interpersonal and group skills are identified because a group is struggling to work together. Rather than fearing this, you need to take full advantage of "uncooperative" group work by identifying and helping students learn the social skills that will help the groups work together more effectively. More on how to do this follows later in this chapter in the section addressing logistics.

Group Processing

You will eventually want your students to learn how to work cooperatively, assign roles, hold each other accountable, and promote group mates' learning. Therefore, you must allow students the time to analyze how well their groups are working, how well classmates are learning, and how well they are using social skills. Not only does it help you and your future students determine if they are learning, but it promotes effective relationships among the group members. The structure for facilitating group processing will vary, but generally it involves students reflecting on how well they are meeting goals, identifying any obstacles/problems that might prevent them from cooperating, and developing action plans for overcoming the problems. Some teachers observe their students during group tasks and provide written feedback about how well the groups have worked together, and areas that need to be improved (some teachers may even have the students undertake these observations). It might be helpful to think of this as a debriefing period. It demonstrates to your students that you value group work, and that you are not only interested in the product, but that the process is important enough to discuss and improve on so that the next group project will be even better.

Implicit in all five of these elements is the point that the teacher helps students learn the process of working together. Students are assigned to groups—on purpose—by the teacher in order to maximize their learning of content and social skills. Cooperative learning usually requires that students are placed in heterogeneous groups. In other words, the students do not form or select their own groups, but the teacher forms groups with mixed ability, mixed ethnicity, and mixed gender. Students will tend to choose to work with classmates who are similar to themselves in terms of culture and ability. This type of homogeneous grouping does not necessarily help strudents learn content more effectivley, and it does not promote the social benefits of cooperative learning. High-ability students do not have opportunities to deepen their understanding by helping group members learn key concepts, and lower-ability students do not have peers who can help them attain a deeper level of understanding (Slavin, 1993). Homogeneous groups have no positive effect on increasing students' understanding of culture or viewpoints different from their own (Mitchell, Rosemary, Bramwell, Solnosky, & Lilly, 2004); therefore teachers need to place students in groups purposefully (as opposed to randomly). When grouping students, deliberately place them as heterogeneously as possible. Consider the ethnicities, genders, and ability levels of your students, and try to group students in a way that cuts across these categories. Personalities of students, previous experiences working together, knowledge of the topic they are exploring, and the amount of time you are able to spend working on social skills will also impact your placement of students. Placing students in groups is a very difficult task, because so many variables interact. However, your thoughtful work in placing students will help promote the type of student achievement reported in the cooperative learning research, and is well worth the effort. As you get to know your students better, you become more insightful at grouping them, and you begin to see how the group projects benefit your students.

The idea of cooperation is not new; nor is the goal of having students work cooperatively in groups. What this chapter focuses on is the intentional grouping of students so they are able to work effectively together to accomplish tasks. Literally any activity that involves groups of students can be improved by implementing the findings from cooperative learning (e.g., writing, reading, presenting, etc.). Cooperative learning is not easy to accomplish, because time and effort are needed to place students in groups, assess their progress, and determine both their social and academic needs. In Chapter 3 we explored three categories of learning targets: *content*, *skills*, and *social*. Cooperative learning will help students learn academic content, intellectual thinking skills as they research and complete assigned tasks, and social interaction skills as they learn to work interdependently with group members.

STEP-BY-STEP PROCEDURES FOR PLANNING AND IMPLEMENTING COOPERATIVE LEARNING

To take full advantage of the content learning and the social benefits of cooperative learning, you will need to make preparations before your students begin working.

Step 1: Forming Groups

You should usually plan on forming groups with three to five students. Groups of this size allow for the benefits of heterogeneity while still being small enough to promote interdependence and individual accountability. Often teachers will place students in groups randomly, or they will allow students to select their own groups. Again, cooperative learning research clearly suggests that the teacher places students in groups to serve a purpose. Usually, this means that each group is made up of students who are different from one another in several categories: ethnicity, ability, gender, and so on. Consider the task you will have students complete, and place students in groups accordingly. I provide the following examples to help guide your thinking about this. Ideally, you will talk with a classmate or teacher about your responses:

> A civics teacher wants his students to create a policy recommendation to the local city government about developing a vacant lot. The space could become a park, shopping center, or community center. How might he place students in groups? He might be sure each group has a student who has some artistic skills so the group can provide a sketch of their recommended land use. He might decide that the perspective of boys and girls need to be considered, so the groups will be of mixed gender. He might also decide that groups with mixed ability will promote better learning of the issue for all the groups' members.
>
> A U.S. history teacher wants her students to write a team biography on the courage of Rosa Parks. Each team member is responsible for learning and writing about a different event in Parks's life that demonstrates her courage. The group will turn their individually written events into chapters, cite primary source documents, and work to ensure that all the chapters flow together. The group will also develop a timeline of Parks's life, a cover page, and an introduction to the biography.[1] The teacher might decide to place students so that each group has a member with strong research skills, and a member who needs help with research skills. She might also create groups of mixed ethnicity.
>
> A current events teacher is exploring recent news reports about China's one-child law. She might decide to have the students explore this topic in groups with the same gender, and then compare possible different perspectives that could result from that grouping. Thus, she creates groups that are of mixed ability but of the same gender. The groups comprise all girls or all boys, but within each group the students' ability is diverse.

The point of these examples is to consider how the content will best be learned with groups, and how placing students purposefully in groups may best promote student learning. Remember, the research on cooperative learning clearly states that mixed groups promote student learning. Research studies consistently find that high- and low-ability students learn and benefit from working in mixed-ability groups. How you mix them will depend on how well you know your students, and on the task you are assigning.

Step 2: Conducting the Cooperative Learning

Any classroom activity using cooperative learning will follow the same general sequence: an introduction to the task; an invitation or request to work interdependently on the task; and a final product or performance by the group that is assessed. During the introduction, you will place students in groups and provide an overview of what you want the groups to accomplish by the end of their time working together. Following this you will assign the task(s) the groups will accomplish, help the groups get started with materials and resources, and assist them as they begin working together. The final part of the sequence involves the groups showing what they have accomplished, and while it is a group product, individual work in developing the final product should be clear.

In my work with pre-service teachers, I have found that it is often useful to consider cooperative learning activities as being informal or formal. Informal cooperative learning involves quickly formed groups that may work together for a few minutes or a whole class period. You might have these groups focus their attention on the content they are learning, talk through a problem, or clarify student understanding (InTime, 2004). If you use informal cooperative learning, you will likely place students in groups spontaneously without a lot of planning. The task may be quickly stated ("Please look at your answer to problem number 4 with the person sitting next to you," or, "I would like you to quickly form groups of three and recall two reasons in favor and two reasons against drilling for oil in wildlife preserves"). And though the task may require students to work together (cooperate), it does not necessarily possess all of the critical cooperative learning elements that researchers have identified.

An example of an informal cooperative learning strategy can be found in "Numbered Heads Together" (in Kagan, 1992). With this approach the teacher asks a question of the group. Each member of the group has a number (one through five, depending on the size of the group). The group members consult to make sure everyone knows the answer. The teacher then calls out one number and the students in each group who were assigned that number must produce the answer. This is an effective review strategy. Another example of a review strategy is "Think/Pair/Share" (see Chapter 5 where we first explored this approach as a way to engage students during a lecture). With this approach, the teacher poses a question, students pair with a classmate near them, and they share their ideas and thoughts about the question. We will also look at this approach when examining classroom discussion in Chapter 10. A third example of informal cooperative learning is the use of "buzz groups." This is the equivalent of small-group brainstorming in which the teacher presents a topic or question to students in small groups and they then talk (or "buzz") with each other about the topic. For example, your students might form buzz groups to brainstorm answers to the question, "Where should we haul our community's garbage?" Or, they could examine a primary source photograph or artifact. Buzz groups, like the Think/Pair/Share method, are also useful as a preparation for whole-class brainstorms or discussions. Students are more likely to talk in small groups (especially if they have worked with each other on previous projects), and after they have talked together in groups, students may feel more comfortable sharing with the larger class.

Formal cooperative learning groups work together longer, usually from one class period to several weeks. You can structure most any assignment to fit within formal cooperative learning (InTime, 2004). As Johnson, Johnson, and Holubec note, "Formal cooperative learning groups ensure that students are actively involved in the intellectual work of organizing material, explaining it, summarizing it, and integrating it into existing conceptual structures. They are the heart of using cooperative learning" (1998, p. 7).

Informal cooperative learning is useful for specific tasks that are completed fairly quickly. Not a lot of time is spent helping students learn "how to cooperate," but time is spent completing assigned tasks. If students lack cooperation and social skills, then informal cooperative learning may be difficult to use. Formal cooperative learning helps students learn content *and* social skills. You will likely have learning targets that focus on academics, skills, and social interactions. It requires additional time to teach social skills. Teachers assess students differently during formal cooperative learning, because of the structure and time students spend together. We will address this more in the assessment section of this chapter.

THREE COMMON TYPES OF COOPERATIVE LEARNING

In this section, you will consider the following three, commonly used, formal cooperative learning strategies:

1. student teams/achievement divisions (STAD)
2. the jigsaw approach
3. group investigation.

A fourth formal strategy, structured academic controversy, fits more appropriately as a discussion technique. In this strategy, students interact with one another to form an opinion about a controversial issue. We will examine it in detail when examining classroom discussions in Chapter 10. Obviously, many forms of cooperative learning exist, and you may develop your own forms that have all of the necessary critical elements. These four strategies are ones that many teachers and researchers consider to be the most common and effective to use. Each strategy involves the important elements listed above (teacher-selected groups, positive interdependence, face-to-face interactions, group goals and individual accountability, interpersonal and small-group skills, and group processing).

Student Teams/Achievement Divisions (STAD)

This method (Slavin, 1983, 1988, 1995) involves competition among groups, and is useful when reviewing information and preparing for a quiz or test. Competition *within* groups destroys cooperation because students become independent (and not interdependent), but competition *among* groups may actually draw members within a group closer. To use STAD you will follow three essential steps. First, you will present content to your students through lecture, reading assignments, or other instructional strategies. Second, you will place your students in mixed groups of three to five members and ask them to complete a series of worksheets and activities that review the content and help them master the information they just received. The students help teammates learn the content; those who need help learn from those who understand the content. The students who already understand the content increase their understanding as a result of explaining/teaching it to students needing assistance. The third step is the assessment. Each student takes quizzes on the information as individuals, and the team receives points based on the level of individual improvement over previous scores. The students are graded on their performances on the quiz, and the groups receive bonus points based on members' improvements. You can see how cooperative learning meshes well with other learning strategies.

STAD is appropriate for a variety of subjects that focus on material with specific "correct answers" (Newmann & Thompson, 1987). Consider the following example: A history teacher wants students to review using primary sources to answer document-based questions (DBQs). He could place students in teams, and provide a number of exercises to help them find common themes amongst several related primary sources, identify the significance of the documents, discover background information that will enhance understanding of the documents and can be later used when answering the question, and develop a thesis statement summarizing the main theme of the documents. After a class session of the teams working together, the students take a quiz on using these principles. The teacher sets aside the next class session for the groups to meet and correct wrong answers and help each other clarify their understanding of the strategies needed to answer DBQs. This is followed by a final quiz over the material, and the group is rewarded for improved quiz scores. As you can see, STAD is a long-term cooperative activity where the students work together for several days or possibly several different times during the year. It is not an approach that can be used for a single segment during the day, because the groups need to work together with an eye toward improving every member's level of understanding and achievement.

The Jigsaw Approach

This cooperative learning method goes way back (Aronson, Blaney, Stephen, Sikes, & Snapp, 1978), but is one of the more commonly used techniques in schools today. It effectively uses groups to examine information that the whole group is studying. Where STAD focuses students on specific facts, ideas, skills, the jigsaw approach focuses students more on connections and relationships among the content. For example, each student in a five-member group is given information that comprises only one of five parts of the information. Each student in the group is responsible for a different piece of information. Students leave this original "home" group and join other students who have been given the same information. These are referred to as "expert groups"; all students with the same piece of information get together, study it, and decide how best to teach it to their peers in the original group. When the "experts" are finished, the students return to their home groups (which are now comprised of one expert on each of the five topics), and each teaches his portion of the lesson to the others in the group. Students work cooperatively in two different groups—their home group and the expert group—and are held individually accountable by the performance of their group on an assessment over all five parts. This strategy was later updated as "jigsaw 2" when it added the idea that all students are presented with all of the information first, and then they are separated into expert groups. This updated approach becomes one of clarifying and learning information that everyone has already seen at least one time.

The jigsaw approach is complicated until you have observed it in use, or tried teaching with it, so the following simple example is an attempt to clarify the strategy:

> In a U.S. History course, students have been assigned to read Stephen Ambrose's book *Undaunted Courage* (1997) to acquaint them with an historical account of the Lewis and Clark expedition. It is a challenging book for high school students to read and the teacher wants to be sure all students understand the first five chapters. After students read the first five chapters, he places students in home groups of five and assigns each student one of the five chapters.

Home Group A: Student 1, Student 2, Student 3, Student 4, Student 5
Home Group B: Student 1, 2, 3, 4, 5
Home Group C: 1, 2, 3, 4, 5
Home Group D: 1, 2, 3, 4, 5
Home Group E: 1, 2, 3, 4, 5
Home Group F: 1, 2, 3, 4, 5

All of the students assigned to Chapter 1 then meet together (as do all of the students assigned chapters 2, 3, 4, and 5) to clarify the characters, setting, and plot of their chapter. Their goal is to become experts on their assigned chapter.

Chapter 1 Experts: 1, 1, 1,1, 1, 1
Chapter 2 Experts: 2, 2, 2, 2, 2, 2
Chapter 3 Experts: 3, 3, 3, 3, 3, 3
Chapter 4 Experts: 4, 4, 4, 4, 4, 4
Chapter 5 Experts: 5, 5, 5, 5, 5, 5

Students then return to their home group. Since each of the five chapters is again represented, the students each tell the group about the chapter on which they became experts, and collectively the group members receive an overview of the five chapters.

Home Group A: Student 1, Student 2, Student 3, Student 4, Student 5
Home Group B: Student 1, 2, 3, 4, 5
Home Group C: 1, 2, 3, 4, 5
Home Group D: 1, 2, 3, 4, 5
Home Group E: 1, 2, 3, 4, 5
Home Group F: 1, 2, 3, 4, 5

Maybe the instructor of your course who is using this book will run a jigsaw in class to demonstrate the nuances involved when practicing it.

Group Investigation

This method (Sharan & Sharan, 1989–90) provides students with a significant amount of choice and control. Groups are mixed, but they are additionally formed to match students who share an interest about the same topic. For example, if the teacher wants students to examine stem cell research and then craft a policy recommendation to their state Senator, some students may be interested in cloning, others in controversies surrounding cloning research, and others in stem cell potential. The group members help plan how they will research the topic and how they will present it, and divide the work among themselves. The teacher facilitates this task based on the needs of the group. Each member then carries out her part of the investigation, and the group summarizes the work and presents its findings to the class and then in an email to the Senator (Sharan & Sharan, 1989–90, p. 17). This strategy requires the teacher to act as a resource while providing direction and clarification as needed. The teacher's task is to create a stimulating work environment. Six specific stages comprise group investigation.[2] To contextualize these stages, think through how each might help students in groups of four who are asked to work on the hypothesis that ancient civilizations often emerged along river valleys because it helped support early agriculture.

1. The teacher identifies the general topic and students identify subtopics.
2. Students work together to plan how they will carry out the investigation of their subtopic or set of questions, and they equally assign tasks.
3. Students investigate the topic, and work to complete their tasks.
4. In their groups students analyze and evaluate the information they have collected, and plan how to present this information to the rest of the class.
5. Each group presents a summary of the results of its investigation so that all students gain a broad perspective of the general topic. The students teach the class about their topic.
6. The teacher solicits feedback from the class about the presentations, and feedback from the group members about the topic, the process, and the presentation. The teacher also assesses each student's part of the investigation.

REALITY CHECK

Observe a classroom when students are working in groups. Why does the teacher have them in groups? Did the students select their own group members? What type of cooperation is taking place? Are the students assigned particular roles? What social skills do the students need in order to work well together? What would be a learning target to help them learn one of these social skills? Share your answers with classmates, and with others who will be endorsed to teach a different subject.

LOGISTICS FOR COOPERATIVE LEARNING

Because cooperative learning requires students to work interdependently, you must set up the room in a manner that is conducive to group work. Desks and chairs should be positioned so that students can meet in their groups and interact face to face. The groups need to be far enough apart so that students are not distracted by other groups. If the physical space of your classroom is small, then be sure students talk with soft voices. As the groups start working together to accomplish tasks, individual students may need to leave your classroom for the computer lab, art room, library, and the like. Be sure you know school policies about allowing students out of the room. Similarly, think about the role of homework for projects that require several days of work. If you allow class time for the work, then you are able to closely monitor the groups and students do not need to coordinate their busy schedules. The drawback of this is that you must use class time. Often a combination of class time and homework is effective. At the start of the task, provide time in class until the groups have identified how they will work interdependently. After that, you can offer short 10- to 15-minute "class meetings" for the groups to check progress and/or exhort one another. By providing class time for meetings, students can complete tasks on their own, and then bring their ideas and answers to the group during the next class meeting.

One of the largest concerns of cooperative learning has to do with group assignments. We examined this earlier in the chapter, but it is worthwhile to restate that students benefit from working in groups that are purposefully formed by the teacher, and are not self-selected. Students report having negative experiences working in groups (and so have their parents), so it is important to provide them with a rationale for using cooperative teams. Handing out a list of the group members, and telling each group where to meet and what their task should be, is a great help in getting groups started working together. For example, if a group of students are meeting to explore American child labor practices in the early 1900s, you might hand out a sheet of paper that has each group numbered and that lists the names of each group member. You might say, "On this sheet of paper I have listed the group in which you will each be working. You will notice that each group has a number from 1 to 7. I would like all members of group 1 to meet at the table by the door, all members of group 2 meet by my desk . . ." and so forth. "Move to these locations very quickly, so we do not waste time. When you have arrived, the first order of business is for each member to tell the group at least one idea about child labor in America during the early 1900s that you learned from your reading last night, and all of you should record these ideas in your notes." This type of script will get the groups into place quickly and help them get started. You could also prepare a handout with a series of procedures that you want the students to follow, and a timeline for the completion of each task. Rather than waiting for your direction, the worksheet provides structure for the groups' work.

If you plan to assign specific roles to students in the group (as described earlier), you need to have the roles clearly described prior to the activity. You also need to think about how successful each student will be in an assigned role, and whether you are adequately serving traditionally marginalized students.

Let's revisit jigsaw and consider one logistical problem specific to this approach. Remember that during a jigsaw exercise students are in two groups: an "expert" group where they learn with others about specific information, and a home group where they share their newly formed expertise. If you are able to form groups that have the same number of students, then jigsaws work smoothly. When one or two groups have a different number of students than the others, logistic problems can arise. For example, a class with 30 students can be divided into five expert groups of six students each. When each of the six "experts" rejoin to make their home group, there will be six groups with five members in each group. Consider how you will move students from expert to home groups if you have 29 students. Thinking through this scenario will prepare you ahead of time for using the jigsaw method.

CLASSROOM MANAGEMENT AND STUDENT MOTIVATION

When students work in cooperative learning groups, the classroom needs to be organized in a unique manner. A characteristic of effective teachers is that they monitor the classroom by interacting with students and assisting them (Doda, George, & McEwin, 1987). During cooperative learning activities you will need to actively monitor each group's progress to ensure that they are progressing according to your plan, that they understand the task and have appropriately divided the workload among themselves, that their questions are answered, and that you provide them with guidance for working together to complete their task.

When you monitor the groups, you are assessing both their group progress and each member's individual progress. Every member of a group should be able to explain both the group task and his individual part in accomplishing that task. When monitoring groups, a good question to ask students is, "How are you helping your group right now?" If they are cooperating, all students should be able to tell you their own progress and the group's progress. If a student is not working very hard, then you will refer him to his role as part of the group and request him to work on completing that task. For example, if a group is in the computer lab using an online geographic information system (GIS) to locate different crime rates in a city, students may each be examining a different neighborhood or looking at different times of the day/night. Each student should be able to tell you his progress in locating information about the city's crimes, as well as how this information fits into the group task. If you come across a student who is off task, you can easily determine what this student should be doing, and ask him a question such as, "What does your group expect you to be doing right now?" In this way, the student will need to answer to the group norms and expectations. This is also an excellent opportunity for students who do not speak English as their first language to be paired with a native English speaker and work together to gather the new information.

Remember, placing students into groups does not guarantee cooperation. Even purposefully placing students into groups to create a mix of ability levels, ethnicities, skills, language level, and gender does not necessarily result in interdependence and cooperation. As the teacher, you will need to establish group norms and expectations. Using cooperative learning requires that you are willing to teach cooperative skills to your students. These skills may not be part of your content area, but they are critical if your students are to work interdependently. The first task is to help students recognize the need for a particular social skill. This need emerges when groups cannot get along, fail to complete a task, or come and complain to the teacher about a group mate. A less frustrating approach for students is for the teacher to communicate to the class before problems arise why different skills are important. You may use skits, video clips, examples from real-life experiences, or other strategies to help students recognize the importance of coop-eration. As the teacher, you need to help students understand particular cooperative or social skills. One effective approach for this is to model the skill as the teacher and incorporate the use of a **T-chart**, or a *looks like/sounds like chart*. These charts help students identify behavioral expectations for specific cooperation skills. By the way, they are called *T-charts* because they have two columns and are shaped like the letter *T*. Consider this example:

T-Chart for "Working Together in a Group"

Looks Like	Sounds Like
Eye contact	"Good idea"
Facing group mates	"Have you thought about this?"
Interested/engaged in the talk	"What is your idea?"
Listening	"That is interesting"
One person speaking	"I don't agree, because . . ."

The whole class, or each group, completes the T-chart. When they complete the first col-umn, they consider what they would see when watching a group of peers working together in a group. For the second column, they come up with comments that they might hear (note that these exact phrases are not what is important, but the ideas behind the comments). Teachers can then post these in the classroom as an additional form of accountability. This could be a type of rating scale of sorts that students adhere to during group projects. Some-times teachers develop T-charts for cooperative skills such as "Criticizing Ideas and Not People," "Encouraging Group Members to Pull Their Own Weight," "Disagreeing with Someone's Idea," and "Coming to a Group Consensus." As mentioned earlier, these are all important skills for citizenship, if citizens are to discuss with one another important public issues. And deficits in these skills often become apparent during the class interactions. For example, when groups are struggling to divide the workload evenly, it may be a good time for you to help them develop a T-chart for that skill. It is an effective tool for accountability because the students develop it, and because the expectations are clearly delineated. Other social skills that you should model to your students, and help them learn to use, include: setting goals, brainstorming with others, encouraging all members of the group to participate, dividing the workload equally, and solving problems together.

One of the key management tasks during group projects is to be aware of the progress each group is making. Just as students will finish at different times when they are working individually, groups will complete their tasks at different times. If it is important that all groups finish at approximately the same time, then you may need to modify the task so slower groups are able to finish on time, or add enhancements to the task so faster groups are able to continue learning while the other groups finish. Consider this example: You want your students to think about the themes of seven Native American legends. You decide to place your 28 students into seven groups of four, and assign each group one of seven different legends. You plan to use the jigsaw approach, and ask the expert groups to take 15 minutes to identify the main characters in the legend, the plot, and possible themes. One group is struggling to complete these three tasks in the time you allotted, and two groups are close to finishing five minutes after starting. If you approach the "slower group," you may find they are not on task, not understanding the task, or some other reason for not moving along efficiently. Check with them shortly after they begin working on this assignment (recall that in Chapter 2 we read about the work of Jones, who suggested that teachers visit all groups quickly at the start of an assignment to ensure that all students understand the task given to them). An additional clarification of the task may be all they need to complete the work on time. However, you may identify other reasons for their delay, and you may need to modify the task. You might ask them to not worry about the characters, and focus only on the plot and the theme. This modification might be just enough for the group to finish with the others. As for the "fast group," often groups finish quickly because they do not complete the task completely. A group that has answered too superficially needs to recognize where they could have gone into more depth, and be asked to finish the original task more completely. If the group has completed your task adequately, then you have the opportunity to challenge them to explore new ideas or content. This group might consider how foreshadowing is used, or how their legend compares to myths they have read. These enhancements should be thought of ahead of time, and they should not be construed by students as "busy work." You should reward students for their efficiency, not punish hard work by assigning irrelevant extra work.

Teachers often share a paradox of using student groups: Students do not know how to work in groups, but they can only learn how by working in groups! As a result, you will find each successive group project may work more effectively then the previous ones. Many teachers have groups of students complete classroom tasks as a way to help them learn cooperative skills. For example, a group of four students may be assigned the task of designing a bulletin board for an upcoming unit; another group might serve as a teacher's steering committee that gives advice about upcoming projects or field trips. A third group might help the teacher update the class website. These duties are then rotated monthly so that all the groups are able to work on the different projects. The idea here is to provide opportunities for students to practice working interdependently, plan together, set group goals, and develop mutual trust. When the students are asked to work on a more academic task, they have had the chance to develop an initial cooperative skill set from the classroom tasks.

APPROPRIATE ASSESSMENT TECHNIQUES
TO USE WITH COOPERATIVE LEARNING

Teachers need to assess the content learning that is taking place, and they need to assess the social interactions and relationships of the students in the group. Many times teachers will need to intervene with a group to help re-establish expectations for interactions during group work, to assist in the division of the workload and tasks, and to facilitate students in understanding the content. The T-charts described in the section on classroom management can be used as a rubric for expected student behavior, and students can be held individually accountable for how closely they meet the expectations described in the chart. You could even assign a grade on how well the students met the criteria stated on particular T-charts.

Self-assessment and group assessments are effective tools for determining how effectively the groups worked together, and for having students reflect on their contributions to the group goals. Box 8.1 provides one example for helping students self-assess and reflect on the process of working in groups.

Please award each member of your project/presentation group a score reflecting their effort in the group work. Score each of the six categories on a scale of 0 to 2, and enter the total score in the space next to each name. A "2" means you/they were excellent. A "1" means you/they were adequate. A "0" means you/they did not meet expectations. Under each name/score, please provide a succinct explanation for the score that you gave. Write these in clear phrases/sentences/statements.

Interaction in group meetings (0, 1, 2)

Contributions to group discussions (0, 1, 2)

Attendance at group meetings (0, 1, 2)

Contributions to presentation (0, 1, 2)

Contributions to packet (0, 1, 2)

Preparation of materials (0, 1, 2)

_____/12 _____

(Your name)

_____/12 _____

(Teammate name)

_____/12 _____

(Teammate name)

_____/12 _____

(Teammate name)

Box 8.1   Group- and Self-Assessment.

In addition to a self-assessment tool, you can also provide the groups with a document that outlines all of the components of the group task. For example, Box 8.2 is a tool that could be used if students are working in cooperative groups to produce a group biography. Each member writes her own chapter, and the group works interdependently to complete several additional components of the biography (this example is adapted from Parker, 2012):

Please complete this with your team members and hand in *before* the end of class today. You will be assessed on how well you complete the task(s) you have signed up to complete for the group.

Group Members: _____

_____

Critical Events/Chapters and Illustrations:

Title of Chapter 1: _____ by: _____

Title of Chapter 2: _____ by: _____

Title of Chapter 3: _____ by: _____

Title of Chapter 4: _____ by: _____

Give the name(s) of those who will be responsible for completing the following:

Foreword: _____

Introduction: _____

Map: _____

Timeline: _____

Bibliography: _____

"About the Authors" page: _____

Cover page: _____

Formatting: _____

Box 8.2 Planning Sheet.

This document is helpful at the beginning of the task, because students can use it to identify all of the tasks that need to be completed. This follows the idea (described in Chapter 3) of making expectations clear to students at the start of a project (Wiggins, 1990). This document is also useful as an assessment tool, because you will be able to connect different aspects of the task to particular students. The group needs to promote excellent achievement from all of the members, but sometimes not all students perform up to this expectation. A form that identifies each student's task allows you to hold students accountable.

You will also develop rubrics for grading the overall quality of student work. Again, the group does not receive a grade, but each student does. You will assess students on their contribution to the group goals, and on their individual contributions to the end task/ product. When you have determined a project for your students, you may want to refer to Chapter 3 and reread the section on designing valid assessment tools and developing rubrics.

ENHANCING COOPERATIVE LEARNING WITH TECHNOLOGY

Computer technology can be used in many ways to enhance and support cooperative learning. Most often this will depend upon the group's task. For example, a group that wants to gather census data can be directed to appropriate websites, or a group attempting to interpret a song can download the music and lyrics. While information gathering is a common use of technology by cooperative groups, an increasingly common method is to use that information and an online application to create a collaboratively written article. One example of this type of writing is given by Jon Orech of Downers Grove High School:

> this is an assignment I have recently given to students. While studying *Lord of the Flies*, students are placed in small groups (no more than four students) and read the book through a particular "lens" which guides their study and discussion. As they read, they research sources that analyze and support their particular lens. Since they are the ones becoming "experts" in their lens or theme, it becomes their responsibility to share their findings with classmates. To do so, they create a collaborative article analyzing the specifics on the theme complete with links to authoritative sources. The final step is to create two "foundation questions" (Inquiry Research) related to the theme and make them available. As a final class assessment, students read the analysis of themes done by classmates (total of four) and answer the foundation questions using the novel as well as their peers as sources to support their answer.
>
> (Orech, 2009)

This article could be created for the public on a website or for private viewing on a shared document. A wiki, a collaboratively created website, is a way that many teachers support these publicly viewed articles. One free site that is useful is http://www.wikispaces.com. If you prefer a more private format, it is not difficult to set up shared documents for specific viewers using *http://docs.google.com*. My hunch is that you have co-written a paper using Google Docs. Consider how that might enhance student learning.

As with any use of technology in your classroom, you should consider what value you are adding. In the above example, how is the technology being used to support proven pedagogy for cooperative learning? What could be done to help facilitate this? Oftentimes inquiry learning is used together with collaborative learning. To see other ideas for enhancing these strategies with technology, visit the chapter on student-directed investigations (11).

MAKING COOPERATIVE LEARNING MORE MEANINGFUL FOR ELLS

In many cultures of the recently immigrated, cooperation is valued far more highly than individualism. For these students, cooperative learning may have added benefits. In addition, the informal cooperative learning ideas presented in this chapter, such as Think/Pair/Share or buzz groups, may be especially helpful for ELLs as they learn to negotiate the nuances of

English in smaller focused groups before trying their ideas with a large group. The following are some specific ideas that may help ELL students become more successful.

- *Grouping:* It is often more successful when you plan who will work with whom prior to class.
    - Partner students for different purposes.
        1. Often, pairing students who share a first language provides an opportunity to build background and conceptual knowledge or clarify class content in the L1, and "catch up" before being asked to produce in English.
        2. Working in mixed language and proficiency groupings provides opportunities to practice and use English language to talk about academic topics.
- *Circulate:* It helps to get down at eye level with your students.
    - Student discussion time is not time to catch up on your organization work. This is when a lot of your most productive teaching happens.
    - English language learners, along with other students, will ask you questions much more frequently in the context of a small group.
        1. Take enough time to stop in the small group so that you really hear the discussion. You might not get to all the groups, but you can make a note of it and come to them next time.
- Provide the words and language patterns to carry out those roles. All students need to practice academic vocabulary and academic language patterns orally.
    - Consider providing a list of "formal" language either for the discussion or the report back, or both.
        1. On a poster in the room, or in a student folder, for discussion language:
            a. I see what you mean, but I think . . .
            b. You've got a point, but I've found that . . .
            c. Could you explain that some more?
            d. I believe _____ because _____.
            e. Can you give me an example of that?
            f. I agree with you because . . .
            g. I can see where you are coming from, but have you ever thought about . . .?
        2. You can make a paragraph with blanks, or provide sentence stems, to help guide students during the report back. This makes it easier for the ELL to do the report back if the entire group fills it in together. It also exposes students to the academic language they are asked to understand when they read.
            a. We agreed on _____, but we disagreed on _____.
            b. Some of the group expressed the idea that _____ .
            c. Although _____ thought _____, others believed that _____.
            d. Despite some disagreement, we now all agree that _____.
- Provide participation roles and cooperative guidelines. This step is essential to ensure that group members all participate and have a reason for ensuring that their group mates understand.
    - Provide an outcome project for the group that includes how to report everyone's ideas.
    - For some activities, assign or have students self-assign "roles."
        1. Reporter and recorder demand high language proficiency.
        2. Participation officer makes sure everyone is heard and that no one dominates—language is not an issue here.

3. Artist, chart maker (copies onto poster board from the recorder's draft), actor, timer . . . see cooperative learning techniques for more ideas. Language is not as much of an issue with these roles.

−   Ask for written notes or a poster that has every student write in a different color—makes it easier to see if people are taking over.

−   Instead of assigning group roles in a discussion, use the technique of assigning students report back numbers prior to discussion.

1. Out of a cup, pull numbers written on tongue depressors. The group member with that number needs to be ready to answer the question.

2. Even if an ELL is called, classmates can coach the answer, as long as the ELL repeats it back. A group can always ask for "more group discussion time" so they can coach someone who hasn't been able to answer—takes the pressure off—but remember to come back to them.

3. Give a round of applause or points to the ELL and the group for being supportive.

GUIDELINES FOR DECIDING IF COOPERATIVE LEARNING IS APPROPRIATE FOR THE CONTENT OF A LESSON

Consider the following five factors when determining its usefulness for your classroom: time; group formation; social skill development; clear task expectations; assessment. Each is described in more detail below.

Time

Cooperative learning is a time-demanding instructional strategy. It takes time for students to think about content together, to work together, and to teach/practice using the social skills that are necessary for working together. Cooperative learning promotes content learning and social skill development. If you have enough time to work with students in both of these areas, then cooperative learning will be effective.

Group Formation

Do you have enough information about your students to place them in mixed groups that will promote learning? You may want to wait a week or more into the school year before using cooperative learning so that you are able to get to know your students. You also want to consider if the cooperative learning should be formal or informal. Informal cooperative learning groups are formed with convenience in mind to allow for quick assignments (e.g., four students are grouped because they are sitting near each other, or a group is formed because the teacher has them count off by fours).

Social Skills Development

As mentioned above, cooperative learning is based on you placing students into groups. Often groups have conflicts until they learn to cooperate with one another. This will require you to motivate and facilitate students to work together as a group. Consider if you are willing and able to help students respect differences and interact with peers who are from different cultures, religions, ethnicities, or socioeconomic groups.

Clear Task Expectations

If you have a clearly stated task for students to perform, consider why working in groups will benefit the students more than working independently. How will a group project enhance student learning of this content? How will it enhance student satisfaction with their learning experience? Formal cooperative learning strategies serve specific purposes. STAD is best used when you want students to learn specific answers to questions. It is an effective review task. The jigsaw approach allows you to efficiently examine a complex topic by dividing the information among the group and having the group members teach each other. Group investigations, unlike STAD, allow groups freedom in completing their tasks. It is an effective approach for inquiry and student-led research projects.

Assessment

Can you separate the task so that students are able to be held individually accountable? Could you create a rubric that clearly states the group goal/task (for example, to make a presentation on the formation of the National Park System) and that assesses students' individual work in the group (for example, each student is assessed on her contribution to the research and presentation on the National Park System).

MAKING IT WORK IN YOUR CLASSROOM

Select a topic from a U.S. History course that you believe students will be able to learn about while working in groups for a jigsaw. If you are currently working with a group of students, consider how you might divide them into smaller groups of four or five. Since you must know your students before you are able to effectively place them in groups, you may not be able to consider the formation of the groups at this time; that will come when you begin teaching. Next, consider the following:

- *List the topic students will work on together:*

  Develop a clear question or statement such as, "How does the Columbian Exchange still impact us today?" or "How did the automobile impact American culture in the 20th century?" What article or reading material will you use to focus students on the U.S. History topic?
- *Write learning targets:*

  Academic targets addressing the knowledge base to be explored ("We will provide three examples of foods in North America that arrived because of the Columbian Exchange").

  Social targets addressing what the students are to learn about working together ("I can provide one example where I built my comments off of a group mate's comments").
- *Forming groups:*

  Describe the rationale for choosing the cooperative learning strategy and for placing students in mixed groups.

In addition to ability, gender, and ethnicity, what are other attributes to consider when placing students in groups for this project?

What makes this a good issue to explore in groups?

How does it fit with the curriculum?

- *Lesson procedures for conducting cooperative group work:*

Student preparation and helping the groups work: What needs to take place before the groups work together? Will students learn new material during the group project, or will they work with material already introduced? What social skills do you think need to be learned before the project begins? How will you teach those to students (e.g., with a T-chart? role-play?)? Also, write down what you will do while the groups work. How will you monitor their progress? What will you do with groups that finish early? What might you do with groups that are moving at a slower pace?

If you are using STAD, how will you present the material to your students? What hand-outs or supplements will the groups need when working together to review and learn the information? Have you designed the quiz or quizzes that you will need at the end of the group work? How much time will the groups need to learn the content?

If you are using jigsaw, what preparation will the students need before the group work? How will you divide the task so students can become experts on one part of the material? What information will they use to build their expertise (e.g., handouts, Internet, books, etc.), and how will you facilitate their learning? How much time should you allow for the expert groups to work?

If you are using a group investigation, how will you present the general idea of the project so the students are interested in the topic? Have you posed the task in a clear statement that the students can understand? How can you facilitate the students as they divide the work load amongst the group members? How will they learn the information? Do you need to reserve a computer lab, library, telephone for interviews, etc.? How will the groups present their information?

- *Assessment:*

Reread the section on assessing cooperative learning, and determine how you might assess student learning. Consider how to assess their "social skills" and/or their understanding of the content.

CHAPTER REVIEW

- Research support for using cooperative learning in the classroom
  - When students cooperate together, and the emphasis on competition and individual achievement is decreased, student learning increases
  - Students of different racial or ethnic backgrounds gain in liking and respect for one another after working in cooperative teams
  - Classmates' acceptance of students who are traditionally marginalized because of low academic ability is increased
  - Five "essential elements" of cooperative learning are:
    - positive interdependence

- • face-to-face interactions
  - • group goals and individual accountability
  - • interpersonal and small-group skills
  - • group processing
- • Step-by-step procedures for selecting, planning, and using cooperative learning strategies
  - – *Informal cooperative learning* involves quickly formed groups that may work together for a few minutes or a whole class period
  - – *Formal cooperative learning* groups work together from one class period to several weeks
  - – Three common formal cooperative learning strategies are:
    - • student teams/achievement divisions (STAD)
    - • jigsaw
    - • group investigation
- • Managing the classroom/learning environment during cooperative learning
  - – When you monitor the groups, you are assessing both their group progress and each member's individual progress
  - – As the teacher, you will need to establish group norms and expectations
  - – Using cooperative learning requires that you are willing to teach cooperative skills to your students
- • Assessing student learning when working in cooperative groups
  - – Assess that content learning is occurring and assess the social interactions and relationships of the students in the group
  - – Self-assessment and group assessments are effective tools for determining how effectively the groups worked together, and for having students reflect on their contributions to the group goals
- • Using technology to enhance learning
  - – Computer technology can be used in many ways to enhance and support cooperative learning. Most often this will depend upon the group's task
  - – While information gathering is a common use of technology by cooperative groups, an increasingly common method is to use that information and an online application to create a collaboratively written article
- • Considerations for English language learners during cooperative learning activities
  - – Think/Pair/Share, or buzz groups, may be especially helpful for ELLs as they learn to negotiate the nuances of English in smaller focused groups before trying their ideas with a large group
  - – *Grouping:* It is often more successful when you plan who will work with whom prior to class. Partner students for different purposes
  - – *Circulate:* English language learners, along with other students, will ask questions much more frequently in the context of a small group
  - – Provide the words and language patterns to carry out those roles. All students need to practice academic vocabulary and academic language patterns orally
    - • consider providing a list of "formal" language either for the discussion or the report back, or both
  - – Provide participation roles and cooperative guidelines. Provide an outcome project for the group that has included a way to report everyone's ideas.
    - • for some activities, assign or have students self-assign "roles"

NOTES

1. This idea is adapted from the work of Zarnowski (2003).
2. Adapted from Sharan & Sharan, 1989–90, pp. 17–20.

REFERENCES

Ambrose, S. (1997). *Undaunted Courage.* New York: Simon & Schuster.

Anderson, J. R., Reder, L. M., & Simon, H. A. (1997). Applications and misapplications of cognitive psychology to mathematics education. Unpublished manuscript. Pittsburgh, PA: Carnegie Mellon University, Department of Psychology.

Aronson, E., Blaney, N., Stephen, C., Sikes, J., & Snapp, M. (1978) *The Jigsaw Classroom.* Beverly Hills, CA: Sage Publications.

Cohen, E. G. (1994). *Designing Groupwork: Strategies for the Heterogeneous Classroom.* New York: Teachers College Press.

Cohen, E. G. & Lotan, R. A. (2014). *Designing Groupwork: Strategies for the Heterogeneous Classroom.* New York: Teachers College Press.

Cohen, E. & Lotan R. (1997). *Working for Equity in Heterogeneous Classrooms: Sociological Theory in Practice.* New York: Teachers College Press.

Doda, N., George, P., & McEwin, K. (1987). 10 current truths about effective schools. *Middle School Journal, 18*(3), 3–5.

InTime (2004). Cooperative learning overview. Retrieved February 8, 2006, from Integrating New Technology Into Methods of Education website: http://www.intime.uni.edu/coop_learning/ch1/types.htm.

Johnson, D. W., & Johnson, R. T. (1999). *Learning Together and Alone: Cooperative, Competitive, and Individualistic Learning.* Boston, MA: Allyn & Bacon.

Johnson, D. W. & Johnson, R. T. (1989, December–1990, January). Social skills for successful group work. *Educational Leadership, 47*(4), 29–33.

Johnson, D. W., Johnson, R., & Holubec, E. (1998). *Cooperation in the classroom.* Boston: Allyn & Bacon.

Johnson, D. W., Johnson, R. T., & Holubec, E. J. (1994). *The Nuts and Bolts of Cooperative Learning.* Edina, MN: Interaction Book Company.

Johnson, D. W., Johnson, R. T., & Stanne, M. B. (2000, May). Cooperative learning methods: A meta-analysis (online). Retrieved April 6, 2006, from The Cooperative Learning Center at the University of Minnesota website: http://clcrc.com/pages/cl=methods.html.

Kagan, S. (1992). *Cooperative Learning.* San Juan Capistrano, CA: Resources for Teachers, Inc.

Kohn, A. (1993). *Punished by Rewards: The Trouble with Gold Stars, Incentive Plans, A's, Praise, and Other Bribes.* Boston, MA: Houghton Mifflin.

Kulik, J. A. & Kulik, C. L. C. (1991). *Research on Ability Grouping: Historical and Contemporary Perspectives.* Storrs, CT: University of Connecticut, National Research Center on the Gifted and Talented (ERIC Document Reproduction Service No. ED 350 777).

Kulik, J. A. & Kulik, C. L. C. (1987). Effects of ability grouping on student achievement. *Equity and Excellence, 23*, 22–30.

Marzano, R. J., Pickering, D. J., & Pollock, J. E. (2001). *Classroom Instruction that Works: Research-based Strategies for Increasing Student Achievement.* Alexandria, VA: ASCD.

Mitchell, S. N., Rosemary, R., Bramwell, F. G., Solnosky, A., & Lilly, F. (2004). Friendship and choosing groupmates: Preferences for teacher-selected vs. student-selected groupings in high school science classes. *Journal of Instructional Psychology*, retrieved April 8, 2006, from http://www.findarticles.com/p/articles/mi_m0FCG/is_1_31/ai_n6073185.

Newmann, F. M. & Thompson, J. A. (1987, September). Effects of cooperative learning on achievement in secondary schools: A summary of research. Madison, WI: Wisconsin Center for Education Research. (ERIC Document Reproduction Service No. ED 288 853.)

Orech, J. F. (2009). Turbo-charged wikis: Technology embraces cooperative learning. Retrieved May 21, 2011 from the Academic Commons website: http://www.academiccommons.org/commons/essay/turbo-charged-wikis-technology-embraces-cooperative-learning.

Parker, W. C. (2012). *Social Studies in Elementary Education*, 14th ed. Boston, MA: Allyn & Bacon.

Sharan, Y. & Sharan, S. (1989, December–1990, January). Group investigation expands cooperative learning. *Educational Leadership, 47*(4), 17–21.

Slavin, R. (1993). Ability grouping in the middle grades: Achievement effects and alternatives. *The Elementary School Journal, 93*, 535–552.

Slavin, R. E. (1995). A model of effective instruction. *The Educational Forum, 59*, 166–176.

Slavin, R. E. (1989, December–1990, January). Research on cooperative learning: Consensus and controversy. *Educational Leadership, 47*(4), 52–54.

Slavin, R. E. (1988, June). *Student Team Learning: An Overview and Practical Guide*. Washington, DC: National Education Association.

Slavin, R. E. (1983). *Cooperative Learning*. New York: Longman.

Wiggins, G. (1990). The case for authentic assessment. *Practical Assessment, Research & Evaluation, 2*(2). Retrieved December 6, 2004, from http://PAREonline.net/getvn.asp?v=2&n=2.

Zarnowski, M. (2003). *History Makers: A Questioning Approach to Reading and Writing Biographies*. Portsmouth, NH: Heinemann.

CHAPTER 9

Simulations, Role-Play, and Dramatization

CHAPTER GOALS

In this chapter, you will learn about:

- Definitions and support for using theatric strategies
- Step-by-step procedures for selecting, planning, and using simulations, role-plays, and dramatizations
- Managing the classroom/learning environment during simulations, role-plays, and dramatizations
- Assessing student learning appropriately during theatric strategies
- Using technology to enhance learning
- Considerations for English language learners during simulations, role-plays, and dramatizations.

Teacher-centered   Student-centered

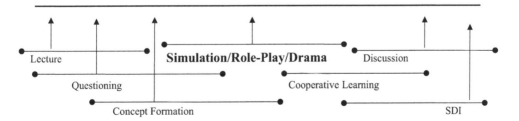

Pierre Cauchon, Bishop of Beauvais, waited anxiously for the jury to return with the verdict. He had been overseeing the trial of Joan of Arc for two days and was sure the verdict would be rendered soon. He wondered if the riveting testimony given by Nicolas Loiseieur would convince the jury that she was guilty of heresy or if they would be convinced by those that testified in her defense. As the jury filed in, the murmur in the courtroom dissolved into silence.

"Have you reached a verdict?" Bishop Cauchon asked the jury foreman.

"We have sir. We find Joan of Arc to be . . ."

About a week prior to "the verdict," Mr. Johnson had assigned each student in his world history class a role in the trial of Joan of Arc. A student jury was to decide if she was freed or burned at the stake. He explained that this was part of the culminating project for their unit on medieval Europe. Some students were assigned key roles because they had shown they were up to the challenge and responsible for the preparation. Others were selected for major roles randomly. Several were selected for the jury because they had a history of poor attendance and the role-play could continue if they were absent. He found detailed role responsibilities in a curriculum guide, but decided to include an essay at the end of role-play to better assess student learning. Now, as he looked at his classroom filled with students dressed in thrift-store medieval wear, he knew they had had fun—but he would wait for the essays before determining if the role-play was effective.

OVERVIEW

Using a simulation, role-play, or dramatization *can* be a fantastic experience. Students have fun and are engaged in learning. Teachers see a learning environment develop, just as they had hoped. Unfortunately, using highly participatory strategies like these can have a downside. Using an instructional strategy that involves a high degree of student interaction, participation, and autonomy can be frustrating. If you ask practicing teachers about using these strategies, you will probably find mixed responses from both the weary and the excited. Some of the risks associated with this strategy include: students who see it as "dumb" and refuse to participate; students who feel uncomfortable performing anything seriously and will play the clown to be disruptive; classes that become out of control; students who fully participate and have fun but are uncertain if they learned anything. Of course, the rewards of enthusiastic, energetic, and effective teaching and learning are possible as well. It is also possible that this might just be *the* unique way to interest several hard-to-reach students in your class. As in many worthwhile endeavors, there is a high degree of risk. Of course, we think the risk of trying is worth it, and so have included these strategies for you to investigate.

Three strategies in this chapter—**simulation**, **role-play**, and **dramatization**—might be thought of as theatric strategies, because they all incorporate some aspect of the stage— a scene change, a particular role, or the use of scripted material. This chapter describes each strategy, provides procedures for planning and implementation, and discusses logistical concerns, classroom management, and assessment issues. Finally, we will consider together guidelines to help you decide if these strategies are appropriate for the content of a lesson.

Definitions and brief descriptions of the strategies will be helpful at this point. Many times it may not be important to precisely determine if an activity is a simulation, role-play, or dramatization; there certainly can be overlap among these methods. However, an understanding of how these strategies are similar and different may help you choose one that best fits your objectives. A simple way to distinguish among the three is to remember that *simulation* focuses on a change in environment, *role-play* focuses on the actor's role, and *dramatization* focuses on scripted dialogue. Simulations allow students to experience simulated phenomena, and then debrief about their reactions. Teachers use them when they are more concerned with students reacting to the environment in which they find themselves than taking on a particular role or personality. A simulation establishes an alternative environment within the classroom and that reflects another scene of life. Part of the classroom may be turned into a spacecraft or a covered wagon, for example. This environment may be reflective of something they could encounter in the real world (the stock market) or it may not (a colony on another planet). Students are asked to engage and interact with the alternative environment or with others situated within that environment. A simulation will ask students to take on a functioning part within the alternative environment (a president, a farmer, an engineer, a waiter) and will give the student enough information (news reports, documents, maps, expert advice) about a specific issue or problem to be able to make appropriate decisions or interact with others. A simulation will not ask a student to change her personality but will ask her to deal with the responsibilities of her job or task within the situation or environment in which she finds herself. A person might become the president of a country but will not be asked to take on the values or attitudes of another person. She may be responsible for a particular part but will always keep her own personality. For example, a student may be asked to take the part of school board member deciding a controversial curricular issue, but will not be asked to play the personality of a particular member of the local school board.

In role-play students learn about and act as someone (or something) different from themselves. This involves taking on the personality of a person in order to empathize, understand, or explore feelings, attitudes, conflicts, or values. Role-play is more concerned with acting a part or imitation than it is with exploring an environment or situation. Role-play, as opposed to simulation, is usually brief and performed in front of an audience of classmates. Typically, the information provided to students would be related to the role to be played rather than the situation in which students find themselves. Simple examples of role-play would include asking students to play various European leaders (such as Neville Chamberlain) during the Sudetenland crisis prior to World War II, or having students explore attitudes or values by choosing roles related to an instance of interpersonal conflict.

At times teachers will combine simulations and role-play so that students experience a phenomenon as they are acting in a particular role or so that roles played by some students will impact the environment of the other students. For example, during a civil rights lesson related to the Harper Lee novel *To Kill a Mockingbird*, several members of the class might be asked to play the role of "enforcer" so that only boys can sharpen their pencils during class time. Another common example is that of a middle school classroom turned into a medieval feudal system: Students are assigned roles (queen, jester, peasant, knight) in the feudal hierarchy.

Dramatization takes students one step closer to the stage. During this strategy, students act in a given role, during a scene, and often with a script. Using this technique can involve professionally written scripts or those written by the students themselves. Dramatization can be as simple as having volunteers do an oral interpretation of a text selection from a magazine, as involved as a culminating research project that scripts a historical event, as innovative as a pantomime, or as elaborate as a full-class play including props, costumes, and purchased scripts. Usually, this technique is used to help students empathize with a particular viewpoint or better understand an event, but it can also be effectively used to help improve student communication skills.

A DESCRIPTION OF SIMULATIONS, ROLE-PLAYS, DRAMATIZATION, AND RESEARCH FINDINGS

Classroom teachers choose to use these strategies for several reasons, but primarily because they require a high degree of student participation in somewhat atypical activity. For many this could lead to increased motivation and engagement. Simulation can be a particularly stimulating strategy since it requires complex thinking that involves difficult moral choices based upon values and beliefs (Bransford, Brown, & Cocking, 2000; Greenblat, 1987). These dramatic strategies can help create an environment in which to examine a variety of perspectives and develop empathy for those from different cultures (Fisher & Vander Laan, 2002). Teachers at times want to have their students become more physically involved in a lesson, and these strategies certainly discourage passivity. Many see the somewhat unusual nature of these activities as helpful in creating an environment to practice communication skills. Partly because of this, these strategies are particularly popular with students speaking English as a second language (ELLs) and in world languages classrooms (a section on ELLs is provided later in the chapter). While many possible reasons for using these strategies exist, the research literature suggests that the strengths of theatric strategies are important to student learning.

One of the strengths of these strategies is student engagement. While many find these strategies *fun*, the real goal is to get well beyond mere enjoyment. An activity that is "just for fun" is not a learning activity; it may be important for establishing a positive environment, but something more is needed to make it a learning activity. Most educators would agree that an important aspect of learning is engagement. An engaging strategy would be part of a lesson that is thought provoking, interesting, and energizing. In feedback from teacher workshops conducted by Wiggins and McTighe (2005, p. 195) it was found that learners are engaged when work

- is hands-on
- involves mysteries or problems
- provides variety
- offers opportunity to adapt, modify, or somehow personalize the challenge
- balances cooperation and competition, self and others
- is built on real-world or meaningful challenge
- uses provocative interactive approaches such as case studies, mock trials, and other types of simulated challenges
- involves real audiences or other forms of "authentic" accountability for the results.

It is easily noted that these strategies encourage most if not all of these findings in one way or another. Each strategy will have its own unique strengths for developing an engaging lesson.

Role-play and simulation, especially, are highly interactive strategies that usually require authentic intellectual work—that is, work that requires application of knowledge and skills that go beyond a routine use of facts and procedures. This type of work moves a student from learning about an ecosystem or watershed, for example, toward learning to apply information to protect the environment while considering the concerns of other interest groups. This involves students using their own ideas to make decisions and solve problems. Researchers have found that interactivity and authentic intellectual work have a positive impact on student achievement. One study examined the link between different forms of instruction and learning. This study of elementary and middle school students and teachers in Chicago showed that interactive teaching methods were factors in increased learning in reading and math (Smith, Lee, & Newmann, 2001). Another study of middle school students examined the relationship between the type of assignment given in class and the quality of student work and achievement on standardized tests. Assignments were rated according to how "authentically" the students were asked to perform work. These researchers concluded that students from a variety of socio-economic backgrounds benefit from assignments calling for more authentic intellectual work, as shown by both classroom assessments and standardized tests (Newmann, Bryk, & Nagaoka, 2001). Other reports on the use of theatric strategies by classroom teachers suggest that students benefit from the unique way in which they focus on analysis in a contextualized learning environment (Houser, 2005; Leonard, Davis, & Sidler, 2005; Steinbrink & Helmer, 2004).

Simulation and role-play in general, but especially dramatization, make use of physical activity during the lesson. As you have seen in Chapter 2, Gardner (1999) has developed a theory of multiple intelligences. This theory suggests that society tends to value those with linguistic or logical abilities while overlooking those with other skills. To the degree that school is a reflection of society at large, this would imply that students with acting, musical, dancing, or other artistic skills may be overlooked in the classroom. These strategies are particularly strong in the areas of bodily kinesthetic, musical, interpersonal, and intrapersonal intelligences. The use of strategies that utilize these intelligences would be beneficial to a diverse group of learners. When Gardner refers to *intelligences*, he is thinking of aptitude, not learning styles (Gardner, 1999). However, even if a learning style or preference isn't an intelligence, it could still be important to consider for the variety of students in your classroom.

Another benefit often associated with simulation, role-play, and dramatization is improved communication skills and confidence building. These strategies not only offer an opportunity for practice, but, as Jones suggests, the "power of a simulation arises from the reality of the communication skills" (1995, p. 7). Learning targets about communication can be achieved through dramatizations. Scenes with scripts have a communication component that is very different from communication in a simulation or role-play. Many times teachers use dramatization in connection with learning about, empathizing with, or understanding a person or event. At other times, the lesson targets primarily focus on communication or preparing students to communicate their learning. In these instances teachers have found dramatization to be useful (Farris & Parke, 1993; Heathcote, 1992; Johnson, 1998).

REALITY CHECK

Simulations take many forms. I find it useful to categorize simulations as being "historical," "process," or "symbolic." Consider the following:

- *Historical simulations:* Re-enacting historical events such as striking grape workers; Boston Massacre trial, colonization, or westward movement.
- *Process simulations:* Simulating meetings or procedures such as the legislative process, the stock market, elections; a budget process, Model United Nations, mock trials.
- *Symbolic simulations:* Enactments of cultures or other events that are telling students what is being represented until the debriefing stage of the simulation. For example, Bafa Bafa, "brown eyes/blue eyes" or others that address complex issues such as apartheid, culture clashes, war, conflicts, or slavery.

Ask teachers to share examples of simulations that they have used/seen in their classroom. Answer this question for each of the three types: "What would be an engaging and effective simulation in my class that will help them learn?" Be prepared to share ideas for simulations with those in endorsement areas other than yours.

STEP-BY-STEP PROCEDURES FOR PLANNING AND IMPLEMENTATION

As indicated above, a simulation would most likely serve a different purpose from that of a drama or role-play. Each has distinct characteristics to consider as you think about the approaches that will help your students meet the learning target. In this section we will consider ways to effectively implement each of these strategies so that you can learn from the experiences of others who have been successful. Lastly, remember that these three "theatric strategies" can be combined. Simulation and role-play can provide opportunities for more in-depth learning as the students connect with a particular role/person, and proceed to act in character during a simulated situation (for example, representing Greece during a European Nation meeting on the future of a common monetary system).

Simulation

The way the facilitator talks about the simulation can lead participants to have expectations and behaviors that do not reflect the simulated environment. One simulation expert suggests "appropriate" and "inappropriate" terminology for use during a simulation. You'll note that, in general, Jones is promoting language that helps communicate that the event is not play or game time, but instead an opportunity to participate as oneself (not play a role) in a unique situation that requires thoughtfulness and problem solving. The suggested language helps others understand that someone views the simulation as a way to interact with others in the way they would in the "real world." A participant wouldn't try to "win" unless the simulation environment caused her to think that was important in some way. She wouldn't act like another person unless the simulated environment required it. For example, if the simulation asks groups of students to give advice to the U.S. president and the Soviet premier during the Cuban missile crisis, they would not be told they were going to play a game where they will role-play political advisors. Nor would they be told that the team that gives the best advice will win.

While use of a specific word may not sabotage your simulation, the words do reflect underlying attitudes about what you are trying to accomplish and can be important. Below is a list of terms (adapted from Jones, 1995, p. 14) for your consideration:

Appropriate Terms	Inappropriate Terms
simulation, activity, event	game, drama, role-play, exercise
participant	player, actor, puzzler, trainee, student
facilitator, organizer	teacher, trainer, instructor
behavior, function, profession	playing, acting, staging
role (functional)	role (acting a part)
real-world responsible behavior	winning (losing) the game
real-world responsible ethics	point scoring, just for fun
professional conduct	performing the game or exercise

When implementing simulation, it is important for you, the future teacher, to recognize that your role has changed. During a simulation the teacher will likely have four facilitating roles (Joyce, Weil, & Calhoun, 2000):

1. *Explainer:* At the outset the class will need to know how to participate in the simulation. Students need to know the general goals, context, and environmental particulars that make up the simulation. Students won't need to know everything about the experience, as much will occur that cannot be predicted. There will be plenty of questions to answer, however.

2. *Referee:* During the simulation, someone will need to help negotiate disputes or make decisions about the simulation that involve the group. This should already be built into the simulation, but nonetheless such intervention may be necessary. This should be done in as limited and nonintrusive way as possible.

3. *Coach:* According to Joyce, Weil, and Calhoun (2000), the teacher should be prepared to intercede as coach to assist participants when necessary. This supportive component would assist the learning during the simulation. However, Jones (1995) argues that a teacher should not intrude into the simulation as coach. There would be no "coach" at a business meeting, or at a United Nations meeting, or at most real-world events. Coaching would disrupt the student "ownership" of the simulation and be counterproductive. We pass this information on to you along with the reminder that a simulation is an *untaught event*, and adolescents may need some prompting.

4. *Discussion leader:* At the completion of the simulation it is important to have a debriefing time. The teacher will need to be prepared to facilitate this discussion.

Most simulations that you find online, or that others have created, come with clear instructions and step-by-step procedures. There are at least four common phases that each simulation should go through (Joyce, Weil, & Calhoun, 2000). The first phase is *orientation*, during which the teacher presents the simulation overview and explains the learning objectives for the simulation. The second phase involves *organizing* the simulation; in this phase the teacher establishes the simulated environment by explaining rules, assigning roles, and explaining the type of decisions that may need to be made. Some teachers will hold an abbreviated practice session if they feel some students may not completely understand. During the third phase the simulation is *operational* and there may be opportunities for feedback or time for metacognitive reflection. The final phase, *debriefing*, is one that is sometimes overlooked but is essential for effective simulation; during this phase students are given the opportunity to summarize and analyze events and offer insights while comparing their perceptions with those of other students. Students are also asked to discuss how the simulation compared to the real world. Finally, students are brought back to the learning targets to discuss how the simulation helped them learn. This would also be a good time to discuss ways the simulation could be improved for future classes. Allow for and expect mistakes or errors of fact made by students. These can be recorded and dealt with during the debriefing if they are not addressed by others within the simulation. Also keep in mind the following:

- A simulation is an untaught event.
- The teacher should let the simulation run its course even if it is heading in an unintended direction (as long as all involved are safe). Again, this can be dealt with at the debriefing.
- Resist the temptation to become involved or to intercede. Sometimes, of course, it is necessary to intercede, but try to stay out of things.
- A debriefing time at the end is vital.
- Simulation is not a game and not about winning or losing. It is possible that winning or losing might be a natural part of the simulated environment (i.e., the stock market or an election), but winning should not be a fixation of students during the simulation.
- A simulation strategy involves the reproduction of a simulated environment not a reproduction of characters as in a role-play.

Role-Play

As we have noted, role-play takes us one step closer to theater. Because this strategy isn't quite as free-flowing as a simulation, it may not be as complicated. It does, however, have its own set of issues and should be considered carefully. Students need time to prepare for a role-play, and it is helpful to think in terms of phasing in the activity over time. Preparation time for different roles can be homework or class time, and could be facilitated with some of the strategies we have explored in earlier chapters. For example, students could work in cooperative groups to understand different roles. I observed a powerful role-play where students took on the persona of current "heads of state" of ten countries. They prepared for these roles by working together in groups of three to research attitudes and opinions about several different international events. Once prepared, the sequence below could serve as a structure for setting up the role-play:

1. *Initiation:* A problem is identified or introduced and questions posed to the class that help focus students on key issues.
2. *Selecting participants:* The roles are analyzed and either the teacher assigns roles or volunteers are selected.
3. *Setting the stage:* The participants show they understand their roles and ask questions.

4. *Preparing the observers:* The peer observers and the teacher decide what to observe and assign focused tasks.
5. *Enacting:* Role-play is executed.
6. *Debrief and assessment:* The class or small group reviews the action of the role-play, discusses major focus areas with observers, and develops modification ideas for the next phase.
7. *Sharing and generalizing the experience:* The class or small group relates the role-play exercise to the real world and explores principles of behavior.

A mock trial is another form of role-play that is widely used in the social studies. In extra curricular programs most often supported by social studies teachers, teams of students assume the roles of lawyers and witnesses in hypothetical cases. These trials help students learn about specific areas of the law, courtroom procedures, the roles of courtroom personnel, and how U.S. courts resolve conflicts peacefully. The procedures of these trials vary from state to state as students compete with teams from other schools while dealing with assigned cases. For example, the Massachusetts Bar Association sponsors a mock trial program. One year, teams were to "try a civil case in which the plaintiff suffers a substantial financial loss after investing her/his daughter's college funds with a financial advisor at a brokerage firm. The case focuses on whether the firm, and/or the advisor are responsible for those losses. This case gives participants an opportunity to learn about the importance of decision-making in the investment of personal funds and provides students with a glimpse of the potential for pitfalls when taking chances with risky investments" (http://mocktrial.massbar.org/).

Other mock trials attempt to revisit historical events. For example, we have observed teachers use mock trials to help students learn about historical events such as the Boston Massacre and the Salem witch trials as well as numerous Supreme Court rulings. While it may be time consuming to create these on your own, they are readily accessible online from numerous sites.

Dramatization

Unless you plan to be endorsed to teach both social studies and theater, you will be less concerned about the quality of the acting and more about what students are learning about your subject. When planning for dramatization, consider the following guidelines.

Targets

The reason you are asking students to perform should be very clear to you and stated in your learning target. Why are you using this strategy?

Class Environment

Creating an environment in class that supports and enhances this strategy is key. This is discussed further in the "Classroom Management" section of this chapter.

Time

It is usually best to think of this strategy in terms of skits rather than plays. Your curricular schedule will probably limit your time, but you will also need to consider the attention and interest level of the students you have in class.

Props

Use limited props as needed, but don't become overwhelmed by this detail, as students can easily use imaginative props. Simple props such as a gavel, hat, or umbrella can add a lot and may be all that is needed.

Scripts

You can find scripts on the Internet, from creatively like-minded teachers, or from published sources; or you can use scripts written by you or your students. Also, remember that oral interpretation, a form of dramatization, makes use of any text such as scenes from novels, magazine or newspaper articles, diaries, or movie scripts.

Casting

It is probably best to ask for volunteers for the various available roles. Assign key parts to those who are motivated and interested and not necessarily to those who are the best actors. More limited roles can go to those who are less interested or less willing. It is usually not in the interest of all involved to require a student to participate in dramatization, but keep in mind that many adolescents will need encouragement to try.

Rehearsal

Make it as serious or as light hearted as you think is warranted for the script and the particular students involved. Be sure that if it is a group project, all the students are interpreting the script and the expectations for the assignment in the same way. Hurt feelings occur when several in a group see this presentation as meaningful and personal and one person wants to make a joke out of it.

Performance

Be sure to give the audience the expectations for the dramatization. Is it a spoof? Is it about a serious personal issue? The classroom audience should know your behavioral expectations in advance based upon your expectations for the dramatization.

Debriefing

Be sure to make time following the drama for a large-group debriefing. It may help to have a guided, written, individual reflection time prior to the debriefing time.

REALITY CHECK

Examining a Theatric Idea

Decide if the following medieval fair—adapted from an idea created by middle school core (English/social studies) teachers is a simulation, a role-play exercise, a dramatization, or a combination of these; explain why. What ideas do you like? What might improve this idea or add your unique twist to the idea? (How would you select the king? How much time would you give students to prepare and participate? Can you describe any other contest ideas?) Talk with teachers about their use of role-plays, simulations, and dramatizations. Can you think of an idea similar to this one for your content area or for high school?

The Medieval Fair

Kingdoms:

Each seventh grade teacher will have her two core classes choose:

A name for their kingdom
A symbol for their kingdom
Royalty for their kingdom: a queen, a king (royalty must also meet qualifications for knighthood)

Knighthood:

Knighthood will be open to both girls and boys. Requirements for knighthood are:

All assignments for a three-week period in core classes must be turned in
A 3.0 grade point average
Demonstration of knightly conduct: respect, courtesy, and promptness

Heraldry:

Each kingdom will have its own symbol for its own coat of arms. Each kingdom will be responsible for making a banner displaying its coat of arms. In addition, each knight and each student will have his own coat of arms, which must include the symbol of the kingdom.

Activities:

1. *Jousting Contest (Outside)*
    One must qualify as a knight to participate in the jousting contest.
    Equipment for jousting:
    Steeds: big wheel tricycles
    Swords: rubber bats
    Armor: football helmets, shields
    Target: egg
    Shield: to be provided by participants, made of cardboard only! It should be 18" x 24" and decorated with the knight's own coat of arms.

Jousters will make two passes on big wheels; then may engage in open combat until one breaks the egg of the opponent. Jousting contest will be an elimination contest until we are down to three people. At this time, the kings and queens may challenge one of the knights to a jousting contest until there is but one unvanquished foe.

2. *Magic Acts*
3. *Juggling: Exhibition*
4. *Riddles and Court Jesters: Exhibition*

5. *Music*
    Gregorian chants, instrumental, vocal (a cappella)
6. *Plays*
    Romeo and Juliet
    Pyramus and Thisbe
7. *Poetry*
Selections to be read by students. Medieval poetry; selections include:

   Shakespearean sonnets
   Beowulf
   Chaucer's *Canterbury Tales*
   The Song of Roland
   Tales of 1001 Arabian Nights
8. *Chess/Checker/Backgammon Tournaments*
To be held in the kingdoms at the teacher's discretion.

9. *Excalibur*

Costumes: knight, lady, jester/minstrel, monk, nun, beggar, wizard (Merlin), squire.
Also consider non-European costumes of the period: Japanese feudal period costumes (daimyo, samurai), Arabian.
The Excalibur event: Split the log and gain royalty. To qualify for a chance to swing the ax and split the log, the royal adzman will require five push-ups. Each qualifying contestant will have just one chance.

Learning Stations:

Each classroom has learning stations that relate to at least one of the following topics:
Castles
Siege weapons
Catapult competitions
The Church
Cathedrals
Monasteries
Stained glass
Village life
Manor life
City life
Knights
Feudalism
Music
The Plague
Dress and food
The Islamic world
The Byzantine world
Crusades
Guilds
Torture
Merchants

Chivalry
Gregorian and Julian calendars
Medieval names
Education
Science
Entertainment
Medieval holidays
Falconry
Heraldry
Architecture
Monk Day
The medieval banquet

LOGISTICS FOR SIMULATIONS, ROLE-PLAYS, AND DRAMATIZATIONS

Probably the most significant logistical need when using these strategies is the ability to acquire appropriate and interesting ideas. However, planning ahead of time, ensuring that resources are available and ready, thinking through how you will place students into groups, and facilitating the step-by-step process that the students will follow can be daunting and will be unique for each strategy. For example, if a current events teacher wants to simulate how cultures clash, she will need to think through how to divide the class into groups, how to assign groups the roles of particular culture groups, when to allow the groups time to research the behavior of their culture, and how to allow the groups/cultures to interact. By the way, a great "symbolic simulation" that simulates culture clashes is called Bafa Bafa (visit this site for a good overview: http://www.civiceducationproject.org/legacy/teachandlearn/other/bafa.html).

CLASSROOM MANAGEMENT AND STUDENT MOTIVATION

The environment of your classroom is key to using these strategies successfully. You do not need to be a drama coach, but you do need to have an environment established in your classroom that encourages creativity, active learning, student responsibility, and experimentation. This section outlines this type of environment in connection with simulation, role-play, and dramatization.

One of the reasons to use these strategies is to promote a lesson-design philosophy that encourages intrinsic rather than extrinsic motivation. Theatric strategies have natural attributes that encourage student-generated enthusiasm and interest. A classroom in which students have been passive and consistently motivated by external factors will have a difficult time instantaneously transforming itself for a simulation. Warning: Student interns may be set up for failure if trying these strategies in this type of a classroom environment. In classes where students are used to passive learning, it is a good idea to bring students along with smaller activities. For example, before using a full role-play try a series of theater games. This site has a pdf that suggests a number of games that might help students develop a sense of trust and confidence in using these interactive strategies (http://www.primaryresources.co.uk/pshe/

pdfs/dramawarmups.pdf). It is time well spent to thoughtfully build an atmosphere conducive to using simulations and role-plays. It will even help you when using other strategies, such as classroom discussion, which we will consider together in the next chapter. A classroom in which these strategies thrive will be one where a climate of trust and support has been established. Students need an environment where they know it is OK to make mistakes and learn from them. Strategies that require a bit of acting and drama will thrive in an environment where creativity has been encouraged and supported—where it would not be seen as unusual or strange to play a quick theater game or do some other unusual activity as a lesson "hook."

Theatric strategies are active strategies. Sometimes students get a bit feisty and noisy. Other teachers may wonder what is going on in your room, and if you are able to "control" your students. You will need to come to peace with that. This will require you to have acquired skill in efficiently redirecting off-track behaviors and helping students understand what is acceptable during a simulation that may not be appropriate in other classroom settings. You will need to clearly and consistently let students know behavioral expectations. They will probably need to be reminded what you want them to accomplish and what type of behavior is appropriate and inappropriate; for example, telling students "during this simulation it is OK for you to wave your poster in the air and shout to get attention, but you need to listen to each other. This will be a challenge that will take practice."

Clearly stated expectations are important to maintaining a positive environment. During an early phase of each of these strategies students should be told the purpose of using the strategy as well as expectations during certain events. For example, hurt feelings or misunderstandings will occur if some students are operating in a simulation mode (not playing another personality) and other students are operating in role-play mode (pretending they are someone else and acting with another's values or beliefs). During dramatization, some students will want to be comedians while others will want to be dramatic. These differences will need to be resolved early to avoid conflict and withdrawal.

When using theatric strategies it will be important for you to consider effective ways to form and work with groups. In Chapter 8, "Cooperative Learning," you read about strategies for holding individuals within a group accountable as well as considerations for group formation.

APPROPRIATE ASSESSMENT TECHNIQUES TO USE WITH SIMULATION, ROLE-PLAY, AND DRAMATIZATION

As with the other strategies, well-thought-out learning targets provide your assessment focus. For example, if the purpose of using a dramatization is to help students learn to *empathize* with different perspectives during a conflict, the assessment should focus on whether students learned to empathize. Can they share the thoughts, feelings, or emotions of several different people after the dramatization? Can they say, "Oh, this is why that was such a terribly difficult decision"? Sometimes, however, when using unique teaching strategies, the process of learning, rather than the intended learning, is evaluated. In other words, should how well a person acts during a dramatization be included in an assessment if acting skill is not the intended learning? It would depend upon where the targets are guiding the lesson. This is not to say these process learnings (performance, participation, responsibility) cannot be included in an assessment in some minor way, but they should not be a focus of the assessment unless they are part of the lesson target. The process could be assessed to the degree that you are assessing participation or responsible behavior in the class as a whole. Most classroom teachers are not as concerned with how a student performs during simulation, role-play, or dramatization. It is likely that content or skills associated with the course are not the only the focus of the lesson. Because of this it would follow that a well-thought-out assessment design would probably include a simple score sheet related to performance, participation, or responsibility as well as another means of collecting assessment data related to the lesson target. For example, a U.S. history teacher has a learning target that states, *After participating in a simulation I will be able to explain three historical perspectives on the dropping of the bomb at the close of World War II according to the score sheet provided.* To assess the "participation in a simulation" phrase in the target, the teacher designs a simple score sheet that is to be completed first by the students and then completed by the teacher. He does this to hold students accountable for their individual work within the groups and because the course syllabus states that participation is expected. Box 9.1 below is an example.

To assess the *content* of the learning target, the teacher requires a persuasive paper, accompanied by the following rubric (Box 9.2).

Simulations, role-plays, and dramas reach students differently than some other strategies. It would follow that the assessment techniques used with these strategies would be unique and address what students are learning from multiple perspectives. Often, teachers will look at products from the experience to help assess student learning. For example, at one high school, as part of a simulation students made tools that Native Americans were using at a given time period. The rubric used by the teacher required students to show an understanding of techniques (drying a deer skin), needs (making a fish hook), and materials of the period (bone or rock), appropriate artistic symbols (what anthropologists have discovered), as well as a certain amount of creativity (making a basket). Another teacher had students choose the type of product from the simulation they would like to create to show their learning as guided by a rubric. This can be a good opportunity for student involvement in choosing how they would like to show what they are learning.

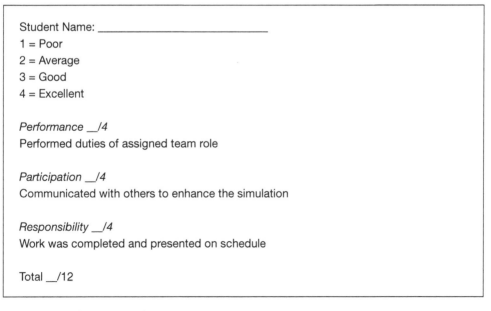

Box 9.1   Simulation Score Sheet.

Criteria	1	2	3	4
Position and perspectives	Position and perspectives unclear	Position stated, poorly maintained, missing viewpoints	Position clearly stated and maintained, missing other viewpoints	Position clearly stated and maintained while showing understanding of two other perspectives
Supporting evidence	Unrelated or unreliable evidence	Limited or questionable sources	Clearly related and reliable but limited	Clearly supportive and sufficient evidence
The six traits of writing	Need for revision outweighs strengths	Strengths and need for revision about equal	Strengths outweigh weaknesses; minor revisions	Shows control and skill

Box 9.2   Persuasive Paper Rubric.

ENHANCING SIMULATION, ROLE-PLAY, AND DRAMATIZATION WITH TECHNOLOGY

Below are resources that have been used by classroom teachers. There are many websites that contain helpful ideas. Several online sources are "link sites," where you are able to search by the name of the theatric strategy and find hundreds of ideas. You could search online for other educational production companies that produce high-quality simulations, role-play exercises, and dramatizations; some are free and some charge. A few sample free sites follow:

Free Online Resources

- *Teaching English as a second language:*
  http://iteslj.org/links/TESL/Lessons/Role_Plays/
- *Reluctant writers:*
  http://www.readwritethink.org/lessons/lesson_view.asp?id=217

Four Free Databases that Provide Examples of the Three Approaches

- The University of North Carolina has a large database of lessons that you might find useful (http://www.learnnc.org/lessons). You can narrow the search to fit your need. For example, this search, for "social studies role-plays" (http://www.learnnc.org/search ?aphrase=social+studies+role+plays&area=lesson+plans), revealed helpful ideas.
- The Library of Congress has an excellent database of lesson materials for teaching U.S. History (http://www.loc.gov/teachers/classroommaterials/lessons). You will need to search for the simulations and role-plays, but in the process you will come across many ideas for helping students learn.
- Teachers.net has numerous lesson ideas, including many simulation and role-play ideas for social studies (http://teachers.net/lessonplans/subjects/social_studies).

- Founded and led by Justice Sandra Day O'Connor, iCivics is a non-profit organization/site that offers interactive lessons: https://www.icivics.org/teachers.

Although thousands of educational simulations exist online, the quality and reliability of these vary greatly. For example, Tech Trekers is a private site that provides links to online simulations for most content areas. You may want to visit it (http://www.techtrekers.com/social.htm) to see what is available for simulations or role-plays. These are meant to serve as initial ideas for what is possible.

MAKING SIMULATIONS, ROLE-PLAY, AND DRAMATIZATIONS MEANINGFUL FOR ELLS

ESL teachers will tell you that role-play and dramatization are especially good fits for English language learners. These strategies are natural ways to encourage listening, speaking, and reading English in fun and interesting ways while giving ample opportunity for support. Of course, each individual will need careful consideration prior to the presentation. This might include an evaluation of levels of English proficiency before assigning roles or tasks in a simulation or role-play exercise. Students having special needs with reading English may need additional time in advance to look through scripts or other directions that are not usually given to other students. This is especially important if it avoids awkward or embarrassing situations for these students in front of the class. For example, after evaluating individual needs, time may need to be provided for small groups to practice reading their parts or the teacher may need to take special time to work with several students to prepare. Some teachers choose to give scripts (or rewritten simplified versions) to their ELLs several weeks in advance and instead of minimizing their role, encourage them to take on roles that stretch their comfort zones without setting them up for failure.

It is important for all students to have a chance to debrief after using one of theses strategies. This is probably even more critical for ELLs. One way this can be done effectively is by using the debrief strategy *Numbered Heads Together*. Students are given review sheets with debriefing questions and put into groups. Group members are given time to reflect on the activity, discuss the questions, and come to a consensus. The teacher will call a number and a student with the corresponding number from each group will stand and give a response for their group. The teacher will facilitate discussion and correct responses as necessary. Students will continue to use listening, speaking, reading, and writing skills with group support until the conclusion of the debriefing.

GUIDELINES FOR DECIDING IF SIMULATIONS, ROLE-PLAYS, OR DRAMATIZATIONS ARE APPROPRIATE

These strategies are considered to be interesting and motivating strategies that require a high degree of student participation in a way that is uncommon. Simulations, in particular, can be intellectually stimulating, as they require complex thinking that involves difficult moral choices based upon values and beliefs.

These strategies can help create an environment in which to examine a variety of perspectives while encouraging active, physical involvement. Many teachers see these as helpful in creating an environment conducive to practicing communication skills. As with all instructional strategies, your choice of a simulation, or a role-play, or a combination of these should reflect the purpose of the lesson—the target(s)—because one strategy will be better suited to certain purposes than another. For example, in general, while simulation may require a high degree of analysis or evaluative skills, dramatization may not.

Simulations, role-play, and dramatization are some of the most effective strategies available to ELL and world language teachers. Based upon the *total physical response* premise that students learn best when they become physically involved in learning a new language, theatric strategies provide an ideal way to accomplish this. They encourage thinking and creativity as they enable students to develop and practice a new language in a fun way. However, many ELL students come from backgrounds where they are used to direct instruction. They may be uncomfortable trying these strategies at first because of this and their perceived English language deficiencies.

Sensitive issues can cause unique difficulties for theatric strategies. Many teachers will avoid a student performance about a sensitive issue for fear that some students will react in immature and insensitive ways. For example, middle school students with the "giggles" may embarrass themselves and others by unthinking, innocent laughing at friends during a performance about the Holocaust. It would be wise to consider the maturity level of your class before using these strategies with sensitive issues. For example, it would probably be better to use dramatization rather than simulation with a group of immature students if the subject was civil rights—or to choose a different strategy altogether.

MAKING IT WORK IN YOUR CLASSROOM

With a partner, create an outline for a role-play or simulations for your future social studies classroom. If possible, work on a lesson that is related to a unit you are developing. The lesson might be symbolic, or an attempt to re-create/simulate an actual event or occurrence. You need to be prepared to do this by fully thinking through the process yourself. (Note: You could do this activity by gathering a specific simulation, role-play, or dramatization exercise from resources available to you, or this can be done in a more general way without a specific simulation/role-play/dramatization in hand.) The following items should be included in your lesson plan:

1. *Learning Target(s)*
   Consider the need for content targets as well as skill targets.
2. *Simulation Preparation*
   Your preparation: Based on the objectives listed above, what needs to be done before the simulation/role-play/dramatization exercise? Consider the roles of students and teacher, the procedures that will be followed, the rules of the activity, background information that you will need, handouts, and "stuff" that will be used during the activity. Some of this is material preparation; some is thinking through the logistics.

   Student preparation: Within what unit of study will this fit? What background do the students need? How will they learn/gain this background information? What will precede this lesson? What will follow? How will students learn their roles, context of the activity, procedures?
3. *Initiation and Direction*
   Describe how you will begin the lesson. Set up the activity for the students, direct them to the proper spots, initiate the day/activity so the students know what is necessary for this to be a successful simulation/role-play/dramatization.

4. *Describing the Scenario*

How will you explain to the students the scenario in which they will be operating? You have already told them what they will be doing (simulation/role-play/dramatization), but now you tell them about the specifics.

5. *Assigning Roles*

Describe, briefly, how students will be assigned to different roles. Consider doing these assignments "on purpose" rather than randomly, and having the purpose be to enhance student learning in some way (e.g., mixing students by gender, or across ability levels, etc.). How will the students know the part(s) to which they are assigned?

6. *Enactment*

Describe what should happen during the simulation/role-play/dramatization. What will the students be doing? What will *your* duties be to ensure that it goes as planned?

7. *Debriefing*

Describe how you plan to examine what happened, examine emotions, draw parallels, and connect the simulation/role-play/dramatization to the content/curriculum and, of course, to life outside of the classroom. Script a good portion of this—at least scripting the questions you could ask after the activity ends.

CHAPTER REVIEW

- Definitions and support for using theatric strategies
  - Strengths of the theatric strategies include student engagement, interactivity, complex thinking, and motivation to learn
  - Simulations allow students to experience a replicated environment
  - Role-play helps students learn about, and act as, someone (or something) different from themselves
  - Dramatization gives students an opportunity to act in a given role, during a scene, and often with a script
- Step-by-step procedures for selecting, planning, and using simulations, role-plays, and dramatizations
  - During a simulation the teacher will likely have four facilitating roles:
    - explainer
    - referee
    - coach
    - discussion leader
  - Role-plays can be thought of as having seven stages that need to be planned:
    - warming up
    - selecting participants
    - setting the stage
    - preparing the observers
    - enacting
    - discussion and evaluation
    - sharing and generalizing the experience
  - When planning for dramatization, consider the following guidelines:
    - targets
    - class environment
    - time

- props
- scripts
- casting
- rehearsal
- performance
- debriefing
- Managing the classroom/learning environment during simulations, role-plays, and dramatizations
  - A classroom climate of trust and support needs to be established and creativity has to be encouraged and supported
  - Theatric strategies are active strategies
  - Clearly stated expectations are important to maintaining a positive environment
- Assessing student learning appropriately during theatric strategies
  - Well-thought-out objectives will focus assessments, just as they do with other strategies
  - Process learnings (performance, participation, responsibility) can be included in an assessment
  - Rubrics will be helpful for assessments.
- Using technology to enhance learning
  - Many websites contain helpful ideas
- Considerations for English language learners during simulations, role-plays, and dramatizations
  - These strategies are natural ways to encourage listening, speaking, and reading English in fun and interesting ways while giving ample opportunity for support
  - Students having special needs with reading English may need additional time in advance to look through scripts, or other directions that are not usually given to other students
  - The debrief strategy *Numbered Heads Together* is a good one for ELLs

REFERENCES

Bransford, J. D., Brown, A. L., & Cocking, R. R. (Eds.) (2000). *How People Learn: Brain, Mind, Experience and School.* Washington, DC: National Academy Press.

Farris, P. J. & Parke, J. (1993). To be or not to be: What students think about drama. *Clearninghouse, 66*(4), 231–234.

Fisher, J. & Vander Laan, S. (2002). Improving approaches to multicultural education: Teaching empathy through role-playing. *Multicultural Education, 9,* 25-27.

Gardner, H. (1999). *Intelligence Reframed: Multiple intelligences for the 21st century.* New York: Basic Books.

Greenblat, C. S. (1987). *Designing Games and Simulations.* Beverly Hills, CA: Sage.

Heathcote, D. (1992). Excellence in teaching: What it takes to do things well. *Teaching Theatre, 4*(1), 3–6.

Houser, N. O. (2005). Inquiry island: Social responsibility and ecological sustainability in the twenty-first century. *Social Studies, 96* (3), 127.

Johnson, A. P. (1998). How to use creative dramatics in the classroom. *Childhood Education, 75*(1), 2–82.

Jones, K. (1995). *Simulations: A Handbook for Teachers and Trainers*, 3rd ed. New Jersey: Nichols Publishing Company.

Joyce, B., Weil, M., & Calhoun, E. (2000). *Models of Teaching*, 6th ed. Boston, MA: Allyn & Bacon.

Leonard, J., Davis, J. E., & Sidler, J. L. (2005). Cultural relevance and computer-assisted instruction. *Journal of Research on Technology in Education*, *37*(3), 263–284.

Newmann, F., Bryk, A., & Nagaoka, J. (2001). Authentic intellectual work and standardized tests: Conflicts or coexistence? Chicago: Consortium on Chicago School Research. Available at: http://www.consortium-chicago.org/publications/p0001.html.

Smith, J., Lee, V., & Newmann, F. (2001). Instruction and achievement in Chicago elementary schools. Chicago: Consortium on Chicago School Research. Available at: http://www.consortium-chicago.org/publications/p0001.html.

Steinbrink, J. E. & Helmer, J. W. (2004). Intervention: Simulating the war on global terrorism. *Journal of Geography*, *103*(6), 239–247.

Wiggins, G. & McTighe, J. (2005). *Understanding by Design*, 2nd ed. Alexandria, VA: ASCD.

CHAPTER 10

Discussion and Debate

CHAPTER GOALS

In this chapter, you will learn about:

- Research support for using classroom discussions and debate
- Step-by-step procedures for selecting, planning, and using classroom discussions
- Managing the classroom/learning environment during discussions
- Assessing student learning appropriately during classroom discussions
- Using technology to enhance learning
- Considerations for English language learners during classroom discussions.

Teacher-centered   Student-centered

Lecture   Simulation/Role-Play/Drama   **Discussion**

Questioning   Cooperative Learning

Concept Formation   SDI

An upside-down black umbrella, littered with playing cards, sat encircled by empty chairs in the middle of Amelia Christie's high school Government classroom. She sat at her desk looking at the scene, wondering if the discussion had worked and, if it had, to what degree? She had hoped that providing each student with three cards to toss into the umbrella when they spoke would encourage the "talkers" to limit themselves and the others to participate. As she reflected on her plans, she thought it seemed to work but it seemed a bit contrived. Some of those who were starting to get excited about the topic ran out of cards and ended up mumbling to those sitting next to them. Other students weren't enthusiastic but made minimal comments so they could toss one of their cards into the umbrella. It wasn't a bad idea, she thought, but how could the idea be improved?

As Amelia reflected upon the discussion, it seemed to her that this discussion could be improved if she simply gave the students in this class more credit. They were mature enough overall to handle the responsibility of the discussion. Maybe she didn't need to be so controlling, so involved. Amelia realized that she really wasn't focusing on their discussion *skills* in this lesson but instead wanted them to discuss the topic to better learn the content. What would happen if she tried to simplify the discussion by breaking the class into small groups of five or six and gave them the discussion prompt? She could walk around the room listening or giving additional prompts if asked or needed. What if she asked for an exit slip listing the major points of three different perspectives on the topic?

OVERVIEW

During discussions students and teacher interact with one another by listening, thinking, and sharing. As the participants discuss a topic, they think about different points of view and new information. Although discussion is a useful instructional strategy to help students learn in any content area, its dependence on social interactions and participation also encourages students to "learn how to talk" with others. This is a powerful skill for citizens in a democracy, where one of the many roles is a willingness and ability to interact with others on matters of common concern (Engle & Ochoa, 1988; Gross & Zeleny, 1958; Hess, 2000; Parker, 1996). Contradicting this positive view of discussion, however, are research findings that suggest it is rarely used in America's classrooms. Recitation persists in classrooms, despite its frequent criticisms (Cazden, 1988; Goodlad, 1984; Hoetker & Ahlbrand, 1969; Stodolsky, Ferguson, & Wimpelberg, 1981), and despite the fact that teachers claim to use discussion frequently. As an example, researchers have observed that a teacher talked for 87.8% of the class period during the portion of the lesson he claimed used discussion (Swift & Gooding, 1983). Recitation and discussion are two methods of instruction with different characteristics. Recitation is characterized as a teacher-dominated classroom activity where the teacher asks a question, the student answers, and then the teacher confirms the accuracy or corrects errors. It is a type of verbal quiz or assessment. In contrast to this, Wilen and White (1991) defined discussion as a "structured conversation in which participants work cooperatively to present, examine, compare, and understand often diverse views about an academic topic or issue" (p. 492). Recitations fit more with a teacher-centered questioning approach (see part of Chapter 6). Strategies that fit the definition of discussion comprise the content of this chapter.

DESCRIPTION OF THE STRATEGY AND RESEARCH FINDINGS

Classroom discussion serves several educational purposes because it is a unique form of class-room talk. Discussion requires students and teacher to talk back-and-forth at a highly cognitive and affective level. James Dillon (1994) has examined classroom discussion, and notes that what students and teachers talk about is "an issue, some topic that is in question for them. Their talk consists of advancing and examining different proposals over the issue" (p. 7).

In a summary of literature about the use of discussion in instruction, Gall (1985) has reported that discussion is an effective way to promote higher-level thinking, develop student attitudes, and advance student capability for moral reasoning. In short, discussion provides opportunities for student thoughtfulness about a chosen topic or issue. Attempts to suggest the necessary and sufficient conditions for discussion have been made (Bridges, 1979, 1987; Haroutunian-Gordon, 1991; Miller, 1992), as have characteristics of different types of discussions (Alvermann, O'Brien, & Dillon, 1990; Gall & Gall, 1990; Larson, 2000; Roby, 1988), and the influence of teacher questions on classroom discussion (Dillon, 1994; Hunkins, 1995; Roby, 1988). These attempts characterize discussion as a structured activity in which the process of discussing encourages students to pool ideas and information, and illuminate alternative perspectives. Students develop skills and abilities in civil discourse, criticism, and argument. These skills are extremely important for two reasons. First, democratic life requires citizens to interact using civil, critical discourse to make policies about important public issues (Barber, 1989; Parker, 1996). The social studies classroom holds the potential for students of different ethnicity, gender, social status, and ability to learn how to engage one another in discussions about issues of common concern. Second, discussion requires students to learn the content so they can talk about it.

If you watch several different social studies teachers use discussion, however, you will see that it is a label for many types of teacher–student interactions (Dillon, 1984; Hess, 2000; Larson, 1997, 2000, 2003; Roby, 1988). Regardless of the type of discussion, certain attributes must be apparent if a discussion is to promote student learning. David Bridges has examined the use of classroom discussion, and established a list of conditions that are necessary if people are to learn from a discussion. Bridges (1987, p. 34) theorized that three defining guidelines or conditions for discussion must be present. Each is presented below with a parenthetical rephrasing to help clarify the suggestion:

1. Discussion involves a general disposition on behalf of members of the group to listen, to consider, and to be responsive to what others are saying. (You cannot have a discussion if the members of the group are unwilling or unable to listen.)
2. Discussion involves members of the group contributing from their different perspectives, opinions or understanding. (You cannot have a discussion if everybody is saying the same thing or nobody is saying anything.)
3. Discussion is guided by the central purpose of developing the group's knowledge, understanding and/or judgment on the matter under discussion. (It is different from group talk, from negotiation of power, from debate aimed at winning votes or defeating one's adversary, from group therapy—none of which has this central purpose.)

From these it becomes apparent that discussion is not merely a time to talk. Rather it is a structured activity that encourages students to collaborate and explore hypotheses, pool ideas and information, and illuminate alternative perspectives. It also develops students' skills in criticism and argument. Thought of in this manner, the three necessary and sufficient conditions for discussion provide a disposition, a set of general rules, and a structure to social studies discussions.[1] Bridges suggests that discussions contribute to discussants' understanding of topics by: expanding each discussant's information on a topic with information from other discussants; fostering different perspectives on a topic; providing opportunities for discussants to present alternative ideas about a topic; providing opportunities for other discussants to criticize, accept, or refute these alternative ideas; and encouraging mutual modifications among discussants' opinions to produce a group decision or consensus. Group interaction is the important component for each of these, as it shapes and directs the exploration of a topic.

Given this use of discussion, students stop trying to "win an argument" or debate a topic. Suddenly, discussions about topics such as U.S. immigration policy, political relationships with China, the North American Free Trade Act, involvement in Sudan and Darfur, or any of the myriad public issues that might be discussed in the social studies classroom are explored and better understood because of students' interactions with classmates.

REALITY CHECK

Before we begin to look at the procedures and different forms of classroom discussion, it will be helpful to see how teachers lead discussions with their students. What types of interactions with students and teacher do you see when discussion is being used? Are discussions similar or different than a "questioning session"? How?

If you can observe a discussion in your endorsement area, keep track of who is talking. With a seating chart, put a check by a student's name to record both who is talking, and how often a student talks. By looking at these patterns, what might you infer about participation during this discussion?

How does the teacher assess students during discussions? Talk with the teacher afterward about assessment of discussions.

STEP-BY-STEP PROCEDURES FOR PLANNING AND IMPLEMENTING DISCUSSION AND DEBATE

Teachers use different forms of discussion to serve different purposes in the classroom (Larson, 2000). Classroom discussions will vary according to the purpose of the discussion, use of questions, and the issue being discussed. This chapter examines six effective types of discussion. While each serves different purposes, each is appropriate for examining current, controversial, and/or perennial issues. Social studies teachers report that simply planning to have a classroom of students sit at their desks and discuss an issue is difficult. Very few students actually talk, and valuable class time is often wasted with irrelevant comments and student behavior problems. The six types of discussion described below are "tried and true" ways to promote student involvement in classroom discussions, and more importantly to engage students in thinking about the topic. These discussion strategies will be effective in middle school and high school classrooms. They provide specific structure for engaging students in small-group and whole-class discussions. The six types are:

1. taking a stand
2. the issues/values continuum

3. the future's wheel discussion
4. the fishbowl discussion
5. the structured academic controversy
6. the electronic threaded discussion.

While debate has completely different learning objectives than discussion, it is also examined at the end of this chapter. It is important for you to know how to use this strategy as well. By identifying seven different strategies for helping students talk with each other about course content (six types of discussion, plus debate), you can better ensure that the strategy is aligned with your learning objectives.

Taking a Stand

This type of discussion is useful with large classes, and is best used when teachers want students to consider opposing viewpoints around a controversial issue. The primary focus is to clearly and systematically discuss public policy issues in the classroom by aiming conversations "at *persuasion*, *problem solving* and *clarification* when discussants take a stand on public issues" (Oliver & Newmann, 1972, p. 6; emphasis in original). Students consider the pros and cons of an issue, devise solutions to problems, and determine a specific policy or action to implement. During policy discussions, the teacher continues to pose questions that encourage students to follow a rational process, consider multiple points of view, and decide on a course of action that the class advocates as a group. Discussants have to think on two levels. First, they must choose a position about an issue and think of reasons to defend it; second, they must reflect on the discussion process itself (the process of verbally interacting with classmates). A "taking a stand" discussion has five steps:

Step 1: Present an Overview of the Issue, and the Opposing Sides

Begin the discussion by presenting an overview of the issue. For example, provide a handout describing the predominant reasons for the controversy, without detailing specifics of the controversy. Phrase the issue as a question requiring a choice or a decision for action so students form an opinion on the issue by responding to the question. Following this, present two opposing sides of the issue in a "point/counter-point" format. After the overview, point, and counter-point encourage the students to ask questions, and clarify their understanding. Imagine students are considering an issue such as U.S. immigration policy along the Mexican border. After providing a concise overview of the key points surrounding the issue, and an overview of opposing viewpoints, students are asked a question such as: "What policy should the U.S. government have about immigration along the Mexican border?"

Step 2: Divide the Class in Half, Assign Each Half One of the Two Sides of the Issue

Divide the class in half randomly. One half moves to one side of the classroom and assumes the "point" side, while the other half moves to the opposite side and considers the "counter-point." Be quick to acknowledge to the students that they were assigned these perspectives. Later, they will have the opportunity to stand on the side they truly support. Once in their groups, students pair with someone standing near them, and share in their own words the most compelling points on their side of the issue. This puts each student in a position to talk face-to-face with someone about the one side of the issue. Select students from each side to tell the class these compelling points. By doing so, the issue is described in students' words, and students' understanding can be informally assessed. In the example about immigration on page 251, students might be placed in a group that articulates reasons for "opening the borders" or in a group that takes the position of "restricting" immigration.

Step 3: Encourage Students to "Go with their Own Belief"

With the two sides of the issue restated in their own words, ask students to take a stand based on their own belief about the issue, and move to one of three locations in the room: One side supports the point, one the counter-point, and a location in the middle represents the "undecided." Once the class is divided, have each student consider why he or she moved, and explain the reasoning behind the move to someone standing in the same location. These three locations are to represent students' current thinking only. Encourage them to move freely among these locations, based on the ensuing discussion. Occasionally, one side of the room may be left empty; no students moved to that position. If this happens, you may ask students why they did not move there, or you may need to represent that side of the issue. Your preparation needs to be such that you know how to articulate the main points of the point and the counter-point positions.

Step 4: Encourage Student Interactions and Descriptions

To begin the large-group discussion, ask three or four students on the "point" side of the room to explain their strongest arguments for deciding to stand on that side. After *each* explanation, ask the students on the opposite side of the room (the counter-point) to respond *only to the comments* they heard from their classmate. The interactions proceed in this manner until both the point and counter-point sides have presented what they believe are the most significant arguments for their side of the issue. The teacher's role during these initial "voicing" of opinions is to keep the responses focused on specific lines of reason and comments. When no additional information or ideas are contributed to the discussion, each group gathers in a circle and begins to develop an answer to the following question: "What is a solution to this issue/problem?" Students must consider the pros and cons they have heard on *both sides* on the issue, and determine an appropriate policy decision. With three policy options/solutions roughed out (one each from the point, counter-point, and the undecided), come back together as a large class, and explore together, via discussion, these options. Ask students to try to combine the three so the class can reach a consensus. Often, students will request more information about the issue, and you should allow time to research at home, in the library, and/or on the Internet.

Step 5: Dialogical Reasoning on Paper

Since the purpose for this activity is to encourage students to deliberate about public issues, focus them away from winning an argument or defending a particular side of an issue. Instead, you want the students to consider competing positions as well as their own, and be able to represent the arguments each might make. After the class discussion about an acceptable policy, students write a four-paragraph essay. The paragraphs address the following topics, respectively:

Paragraph 1 Introduce the issue by providing an overview of the main points and major areas of controversy.
Paragraph 2 Describe the primary arguments presented by the "point" side.
Paragraph 3 Describe the primary arguments presented by the "counter-point" side.
Paragraph 4 Conclude the paper by suggesting a policy that might meet the interests of the two sides.

The Issues/Values Continuum

This technique allows the teacher and students to assess the diversity of opinions in the classroom, while requiring students to think about their own positions on issues. This strategy also allows students to describe perspectives to their peers, and explore their own opinions and ideas. You can use this strategy with historical issues by placing students in a specific time period or use it to let them reflect on current or controversial issues. These discussions can be in-depth if students are able to research and prepare before the class meeting. They will be brief discussions if students rely only on knowledge they bring to class without any chance to prepare. This type of discussion has four steps:

Step 1: Make the Continuum

Draw a line from one side of the board to the other. The end points of the line represent extreme points of view. Label the endpoints to represent dichotomous positions of the issue. Common "points" on the continuum are: "Strongly Agree"; "Agree"; "Disagree"; and "Strongly Disagree."

Step 2: Students Move on the Continuum

Select a public concern/problem that is related to your course content. Pose a potential solution to the problem to the class. This might be a current events issue such as "Gun control laws need to be stricter," or "Casinos should be allowed on American-Indian reservations." The concern can also examine specific opinions about course topics such as: "We will not have another 'Great Depression' in America," "Lack of natural resources led to the downfall of the Anasazi," or "The United Nations should attack maritime pirates." Students indicate their positions by moving to the point on the line that reflects their view.

Step 3: Explain Placements

Allow students from each end and the middle to explain their views; allow students to change placements if they hear persuasive arguments.

Step 4: Follow-Up Activity

For an on-going exploration of an issue, you might tape a paper continuum to a wall. Have students write their names on pieces of paper and tape them onto the continuum. As they gain new knowledge or insights they—literally—change their position by moving their name along the continuum. At the end of your exploration of the issue, debrief with students about when and why they may have changed their opinions.

The Future's Wheel Discussion

This technique focuses classroom discussions in a way that leads to decision making. Students think through the implications of potential outcomes on any issue, and begin to think about the future, and the implications of decisions on future decisions, actions, and policies. This activity can be completed in small- or large-group discussion settings, and comprises the following five steps:

Step 1: Describe the Issue

Draw a circle on the chalkboard with a clearly articulated problem or issue in the middle of the circle. Have students think about this problem, and come up with possible solutions. For example, Washington state faced a problem where lawmakers could not determine how to pay for the maintenance and staffing of its state parks. When students were confronted with this problem, several possible solutions were identified (some solutions were published by lawmakers, and some were developed by students). Solutions to this funding problem included imposing parking fees and/or user fees, closing parks that are infrequently used or in remote locations, levying a tax tied to renewing license plate tabs, and engaging in raising money from private donors.

Step 2: Brainstorm

Have students think about possible solutions, and as they share them with the class, the teacher places their ideas on the board in circles surrounding the main issue/problem and attaches them with arrows (like the spokes from the center of a wheel). The more ideas students can generate, the better. Figure 10.1 shows an initial "future's wheel," and then one completed during a student brainstorm about the problem listed about regarding finding state parks:

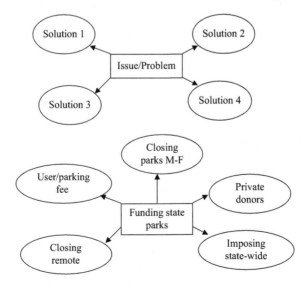

Figure 10.1 Future's Wheel Brainstorm Web.

Step 3: Look to the Future

Extend the wheel one step farther and examine possible results of each solution, and write them on the board. For example, if we decided to solve the problem on page 254 by closing parks in remote settings, then what consequences would result? If Washington imposed a $10 tax on all residents to open a new funding stream for the park system, then what consequences need to be considered? This examination of solutions is best done in small groups, and is where the open discussion takes place. These "second generation" outcomes are attached with arrows as well. These steps can be repeated to the third, fourth, and even fifth generations. They will often require students to go beyond their opinions, especially if the requirement is that all statements must be supported with facts or evidence.

Step 4: Analysis

Students analyze the "future's wheel" to determine desirable outcomes—those can be marked with a "d." Students also identify what they think will be the most probable outcomes with a "p." Have students consider:

*   What outcomes are probable and desirable?
*   What outcomes are probable but not desirable?
*   What can be done to make these less probable or more desirable?
*   What consequences are desirable but not probable?
*   What could be done to make these more probable?

Step 5: Consequences

Students consider how consequences imply relationships between factors they might not always think about—such as technological, economic, political, sociological, or psychological factors.

Extension activity:
Have students make a decision/choose a solution to the initial problem and write about why they chose their solution, considering all the implications of their choice.

The Fishbowl Discussion

This technique is used to help students develop effective group skills of participation and observation (Gorman, 1969; Hoover, 1976; Mail, 1968; Priles, 1993). While fishbowl discussions follow a wide variety of formats, they all are used so that discussants learn about the topic of discussion, *and* develop the requisite skills and attitudes needed to listen and talk during a discussion. It is a technique that helps teachers navigate between using discussion as a method of instruction, and having the skills to engage in a discussion as a curriculum outcome. Fishbowl discussions place one small group of discussants within a larger circle of observers. The smaller group is "in the fishbowl," and as they discuss, they are observed and critiqued by classmates outside of the "bowl." A fishbowl discussion has six basic steps:

Step 1: Grouping the Students

The class is divided into three equal groups. Members of group 1 and group 2 are paired. Group 1 sits in a close circle. Group 2 sits in a circle outside of group 1. Members of group 2 position themselves to see the face of their counterpart in group 1. Members of group 3

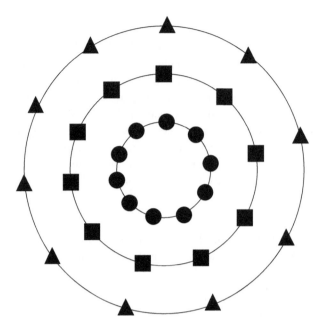

Figure 10.2   Fishbowl Discussion Seating Arrangement.

Source: Larson & Keiper (2013).

form the outer circle, and sit outside of the second group in no particular order. Figure 10.2 provides a visual layout of what this might look like in your classroom:

Step 2: Engaging in a Discussion

Select an issue related to the curriculum that has some degree of controversy. It does not need to be highly controversial, just an issue that will promote some differences of opinion. For example, students might discuss their school's graduation requirements, or their individual responsibility to the homeless, or term limits for senators and representatives. The students in the inner circle (group 1) begin to discuss the different points of views surrounding the controversy. To promote participation by all of the students in group 1, the teacher may limit the speaking of students until all have shared. For example, the teacher may allow each student to share one time until all others in the group have talked, unless the student asks a question of another student. If a student wants to speak a second time, but others in the group have not spoken for the first time, s/he can only speak to ask a question of someone who has not spoken. In that way, all students are limited in their sharing, but all students also serve to encourage each other to share during the discussion. Let the discussion run for 15 minutes, unless the talk drops off before that.

Step 3: Observations

During the fishbowl discussion, members of group 2 observe their partner and take notes on how they interacted with others. The goal of group 2 is to create an accurate recollection of the participation in the discussion. While members of group 2 observe their partners in group 1, members of group 3 observe and take notes on the interaction patterns of group 1.

They do not critique individuals, but observe the whole process to identify how the discussion flows, who the leaders are, what behaviors were observed, and how cooperative/cohesive the group appeared to be.

Step 4: Debrief

After the 15-minute discussion, student pairs in group 1 and 2 meet. The pairs talk about the discussion, and critique the role of the group 1 members in the discussion. Ideas and suggestions are made that might improve the interactions and enhance the discussion. Members in group 3 meet with the teacher and talk about the process they observed. They address the notes that group 3 took during the observation. At this point the teacher may want to share with the large class some observations about the process.

Step 5: Reassemble

The groups reassemble and continue to discuss the original issue. Each class member assumes his/her original role, and the discussion lasts for ten minutes. At the end, students are asked to write their responses to the discussion, what they learned about the issue being discussed, and what they learned about discussion.

Step 6: Switch Roles

Then, next class session, group 1 moves to observe the whole discussion, group 2 moves into the fishbowl, and members in group 3 observe an assigned partner in group 2 (i.e., all the groups rotate through the roles. Steps 1 through 4 are repeated). The roles are rotated a final time, and steps 1 through 4 are repeated.

The Structured Academic Controversy

As mentioned above, using conflicts for instructional purposes is a powerful approach to discussing controversial issues in the classroom. The structured academic controversy (SAC) allows for an organized approach that enhances cognitive and affective learning. This strategy is often considered to be a type of cooperative learning (if you have not read it yet, Chapter 8 examines cooperative learning in more depth), because students work together, cooperatively, to understand a controversial issue. It also requires students to discuss the issue, and provides excellent structure for small-group discussions (Johnson & Johnson, 1988). The purpose for using this approach is similar to a Taking a Stand discussion, with the difference being that the interactions take place in small groups and not with the entire class. The "structure" in a structured academic controversy holds all students to a high level of accountability, because they all must participate. Teachers can also monitor student participation, because students are in groups of four (and not large groups of 15 in Taking a Stand discussions). Students are required to talk in their groups, and to examine different sides of a controversial issue. The format for organizing controversies consists of four steps:

Step 1: Choosing the Discussion Topic

The choice of the topic depends on the interests of the instructor/students and the purposes of the course. Two well-documented positions need to be prepared, and the topic needs to be age appropriate, so select a topic that has information available. For example, students might reflect on the role of America in world politics from a current and historical perspective. Given our history of involvement around the world, students will consider recommendations about U.S. foreign policy by considering questions such as whether involvement in the affairs of other countries is opportunistic or whether involvement can benefit other countries?

Step 2: Preparing Instructional Materials

The following materials are needed for *each* position:

- a clear overview of the controversy
- a definition of the position to be advocated with a summary of the key arguments supporting the position
- resource materials that provide evidence and support for the arguments.

Step 3: Conducting the Controversy

To guide the controversy, the teacher gives students specific instructions in five phases. These phases provide the "structure" to an SAC, and help guide the student thinking:

1. *Learning the positions:*
   Students plan with a partner how to advocate the position effectively. They read the materials supporting their position, and plan a persuasive presentation. They attempt to master the information supporting their assigned position and present it in a way that will ensure the opposing pair will comprehend and learn the information.

2. *Presenting positions:*
   As a pair, students present their position forcefully and persuasively to the opposing pair. Each pair listens to the other and attempts to learn the opposing position. Students take notes and clarify anything that is unclear. In the above example about U.S. involvement in world affairs, one position would support that U.S. involvement in other countries is benevolent and modernizing. The opposing side of this idea might suggest that U.S. involvement in other countries is imperialistic and exploitative.

3. *Discussing the issue:*
   Students argue forcefully and persuasively for their position, presenting as many facts as they can to support their point of view. Students listen critically to the opposing pair's position, asking them for the facts that support their viewpoint. Each pair presents counter-arguments.

4. *Reversing perspectives:*
   Working as a pair, students present the opposing pair's position. The goal is to be as sincere and forceful about this position as possible. This is also a good formative assessment of how well the pairs listened to each other during the previous steps. Any new insights and facts should be added to this presentation. Students elaborate on this perspective by relating it to other information they learned previously.

5. *Reaching a decision:*
   At this phase, the students "leave their allegiance" to a particular point of view, and together the two pairs summarize and synthesize the best arguments for both points

of view. They then attempt to reach a consensus on a position that is supported by the facts. Follow a format, perhaps, similar to that at step 5 of "Taking a Stand."

Step 4: Debrief

Debrief as a class about their decisions, the process, and the dynamics of SAC. Ask questions such as:

- Did you understand all sides of the issue?
- What are the strongest points of your decision?
- What are the weak points of your decision?
- Describe the benefits and difficulties of building a consensus.
- What insights do you now have about committee work?
- What insights do you now have about public policy making?
- What are questions or issues for future discussion?

The Electronic Threaded Discussion

During electronic threaded discussions, students "talk" with one another electronically and asynchronously via a computer. Discussions are typically referred to as "forums," and comments made by students are called "posts." Thus, when students engage in the threaded discussion, they enter a discussion forum and either post a new response to the initial question (known as beginning a new thread), or respond to a classmate's message (known as adding to an existing thread). Merryfield's (2000) description of what such a forum looks like is helpful: "The 'threads' develop as an outline of message headings and grow longer and more complex as people post messages on new topics or respond to messages already posted. Threads can be . . . only one message or quite long with 10–15 messages" (p. 507). By clicking on the thread, the full message is opened for the reader.

A threaded discussion forum is useful for students in interacting about public and controversial issues. Students' responses demonstrate that threaded discussions allow for solid academic interactions with others. Not all quiet students will write to discussion boards, but those students who are quiet thinkers may benefit from sharing their ideas with classmates if they perceive an electronic format to be more conducive to them "talking." Threaded discussion does not replace classroom discussion. The face-to-face talking that occurs provides students with a powerful opportunity to interact about an issue, and practice using the social skills needed by participatory citizens in a democracy. However, threaded discussion supplements face-to-face discussion in the same way that a follow-up writing assignment supplements a face-to-face discussion (Larson, 2003). In addition, the teacher is able to formatively assess students' understanding of the topic under discussion. Complete, accurate records of what was "said" during the discussion are posted at the forum. While it takes a considerable amount of time for students and teachers to read these, it is a very accurate approach for determining who is participating, and to assess the quality of the interactions. Threaded discussions follow four steps:

Step 1: Establish a Discussion Forum

Your school district may also have licenses to use web-based threaded discussion software such as Canvas/Instructure (http://www.canvaslms.com/k-12/), or Blackboard Inc.

(http://www.blackboard.com/k12/index.aspx). Some also use the free open source software found at Moodle (http://moodle.org), or at Google groups (http://groups.google.com/). At these sites, you can manage your classroom activities online, including the free discussion boards.

Step 2: Posting the Initial Thread

Once the site for threaded discussion is established, a topic is posted to the electronic discussion board, and the students are asked to respond. For example, I worked with a group of high school sophomores to engage in an online discussion about the following question:

> Most all communities have people who are poor and/or homeless. What responsibility to the poor or homeless do the "not poor" or "not homeless" have? Does local/state/national government have a responsibility to aid the poor/homeless? Why?

Step 3: Students and Teacher Post Responses

This is where the discussion takes place. Figure 10.3 is a screenshot from a threaded discussion using Blackboard (http://www.blackboard.com). Students respond at least two times:

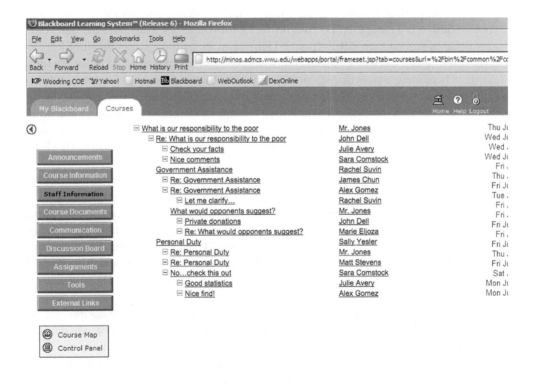

Figure 10.3   Screen Shot of Threaded Discussion.

once to the initial question and once to another classmate's comment. You may decide to reply to your students' postings, or you may decide to let them interact with each other. The time that is needed for these discussions is significant, because students must read classmates' comments, select the appropriate comment(s) to which to respond, and compose a written response. More details about this third step are addressed in the logistics section on page 262. While the other discussion techniques involve skill in listening and speaking, threaded discussions do not. Instead, they require skill in reading and writing.

Step 4: Optional Debriefing

Students respond to the following prompt: "What do you think about your participation in the threaded discussions?"

Structured Debate

By strictly timing a debate and establishing a sequence for who speaks when, you can ensure wide participation in classroom debates. These debates can be planned for 30 students, or fewer, depending on the availability of teacher assistants/parents who will help with the supervision of the process. This strategy works best with issues that have two dominant sides (e.g., a point, counter-point). Debate is more competitive than the six discussion approaches, because it has an emphasis on a "winner" of the debate. Learning about the issue occurs as your students research and prepare for their side of the issue, and prepare responses to arguments from the opposing side. The structure of a debate promotes learning about an issue, and thinking logically, but does not provide students with experience at "everyday conversations" about public issues.

Step 1: Selecting an Issue and Assigning Groups

Choose an issue with clearly opposing views. Place students into groups of six to eight. These groups need to be divided in half. In other words, each group of six will be two groups of three; each group of eight will be two groups of four. These two groups will represent the opposing sides of the debate. You can assign students to these groups randomly, or have students choose the side that reflects their own opinion—the goal is to end up with two groups of equal size. Depending on the number of students in your class, you may have three or four groups of students ready to debate an issue. A class of 32 will have four groups of eight. If this is the case, you might have them all debate the same issue, or each group could investigate a different issue.

Step 2: Preparation and Background

Preparation is important: Provide students with readings (or access to readings and have them do a pre-debate inquiry) that will help them establish the main arguments for each side of the issue.

Step 3: Establishing Rules for Debate

The following rules provide a helpful starting point for structuring a debate:

* flip a coin to see which side starts
* allow a three-minute opening statement from each side
* allow each side to present supporting one- to two-minute speeches

- each student on each side must speak before anyone can speak twice
- no one can talk but the recognized speaker.

Step 4: Regrouping

After everyone on each side has had a chance to speak, give each side five minutes to regroup and discuss their arguments. Continue the debate, this time cutting speaking time to 30 seconds. You can continue to alternate sides, but recognize students at random.

Step 5: Switch Positions (Optional)

After an additional eight to ten minutes of debate, make the groups switch and argue the other side of the issue. This is similar to the "Reversing perspectives" step in a structured academic controversy.

Step 6: Variation Possibilities

Allow some students to start out undecided and join sides as they decide; have groups list the main points they have made when they regroup; have a panel of student judges who record the most persuasive arguments for each side.

LOGISTICS FOR CLASSROOM DISCUSSION AND DEBATE

If you have ever been part of a classroom discussion in a lecture hall, you know the importance of room size and layout. It is difficult to talk with classmates when seated in rows facing the front of the room (and looking at the back of the head of the person in front of you). The layout of the classroom is important. Moving student desks or tables into groups of four or six, or seating students in a semi-circle are easy ways to encourage more face-to-face interactions. Some of the discussion approaches described above specify student location. For example, "Taking a Stand" and "issues/values continuum" discussions have students stand up and move about the room. Chairs and desks might be pushed to the side of the room. Fishbowl discussions require students to sit in a series of concentric circles. Many teachers design seating charts in the shape of a square or semi-circle so they do not have to rearrange the classroom whenever they want to plan a discussion. If you engage all your students in a "whole-class discussion," be sure to monitor all your students' levels of engagement.

Good discussions depend on knowledgeable discussants. You will need to allow your students some time to gather information prior to a classroom discussion. This term is often called "prior knowledge"—knowledge that students have before an activity begins. Not only will student participation increase when they know about the topic, but opportunities to expand on their prior knowledge occur during the interactions with classmates. Before you lead a discussion, you need to determine your students' prior knowledge. If the topic is new to them, then you will plan for a discussion after students learn pertinent information. If you determine that students' prior knowledge is adequate, then the discussion will allow for deeper understandings. For these reasons, classroom discussions are excellent activities immediately following a research project, class reading, or homework. The discussion allows students to talk about what they learned and in the process think about the information anew. They are also useful when examining current events or controversial issues about which students have some prior understanding.

Sometimes discussions will give students the false impression that issues are dichotomous—that only two points of view revolve around a topic. For example, dichotomizing the issue of voting for the President of the United States could result in the following two points of view:

1. the Electoral College is still valid and appropriate
2. the Electoral College is antiquated and inappropriate.

Obviously, the Electoral College is a more complex topic, and it oversimplifies the issues around it to think of it as only being one of these two points. Consider the Taking a Stand discussion approach. It begins by dichotomizing an issue into two sides: point and counter-point. However, at the end, the students are asked to develop a policy statement about the issue, and multiple points of view are incorporated. In other words, structuring the discussion as a point/counter-point initially over-simplifies the issue, but ends by promoting students to think outside these two positions.

How you present the issue to your students is also a very important part of a discussion. Consider this issue:

> A city's drinking water supply is a nearby lake. This lake also is a recreation center for fishing, waterskiing, and other water sports. In addition, the lake is ringed with houses. The drinking water supply is becoming increasingly polluted.

From this issue, you may ask a number of follow-up questions. You might consider the history of the city's water supply, and historical uses of the lake. Or, you could have students develop a policy recommendation for the city council about future use of the lake. You could also have students write an editorial letter for the city paper, where they argue in favor of a particular use of the lake. In each of these cases, the teacher must be careful about posing the question so maximum thinking and talking is encouraged. A poorly formed question will dichotomize the issue. For example, posing the question as "Should this city outlaw the use of outboard motors on the lake?" limits answers to "Yes" or "No." A better question is, "What might the city do about its drinking water problem?" Posed this way, the problem has a wide range of possible solutions, including but not limited to outlawing outboard motors. The point of these examples is that the issues and questions provided to the students need to be carefully designed ahead of time, so maximum thinking is encouraged through the discussions.

CLASSROOM MANAGEMENT AND STUDENT MOTIVATION

Discussion strategies depend on student talking. From the above examples of discussion you notice that students may talk to the whole class, to a small group, and even to a single partner. During whole-class discussions you can easily step in and control the interactions: You can correct errors, challenge student comments, instruct students to respect classmates, and even help them understand that the goal of discussion is not to win but to understand the topic better. However, many students are able to "slip through the cracks" and not participate. They can rely on the more verbal students to carry the conversations. This is problematic for a couple of reasons. First, students who do not engage in a class activity are not able to meet the learning objectives. If a student is able to avoid talking during the whole-class discussion, s/he may not be learning from the talk. Second, students may feel inhibited from talking to the whole class because of their gender, race, or status in the classroom. Walter Parker states this second problem this way: "discussion may appear open and democratic while masking domination" (Parker, 2001, p. 111). Moving students into groups encourages more participation, and usually is more engaging for a larger number of students. However, groups limit the control you have over the discussions. Instead of monitoring one discussion, you will need to oversee several. Discussions, therefore, require management strategies for whole-class discussions and small-group discussions. Both will be examined in this section. However, a set of guidelines for student behavior is helpful to insure the behavior is conducive to learning. For example, the following ideas could be presented on an overhead or classroom poster:

EXPECTED BEHAVIORS

Discussants are to ask themselves:

- Am I listening to what other people are saying or did I miss an important point?
- Am I clearly making claims and supporting claims with facts?
- Am I critiquing ideas and not individuals (keeping a high respect for human dignity)?
- Are we developing together a shared understanding of the problem or issue?[2]

Whole-Class Discussion: As mentioned above, during whole-class discussions you have control over the interactions, but participation by all of the students is often limited. For this reason, I strongly suggest limiting whole-class discussions, and plan discussions for students in groups of seven or less. Some strategies allow for whole-class participation (e.g., Taking a Stand or the issues/values continuum), but the others thrive when the number of discussants is small. For example, if your class has 30 students, and you have one hour for a discussion, each student will be able to talk for two minutes. In all likelihood only about ten students will talk, and the others will listen to them. The "Think/Pair/Share" strategy is a simple yet powerful approach for promoting student engagement and helping move a discussion along. You pose a question and ask the students to *think* about a possible solution, *pair* with a partner (or somebody sitting next to them), and *share* their thoughts about the question. By following this with a whole-class discussion of the same question, students may feel more at ease "going public" with the thoughts they just gave to their partner. Thought of in terms of writing, the "Think/Pair/Share" is their rough draft, and the whole-class discussion is their second draft. Some students may have difficulty "pairing" with someone near them. It is a good idea to place them with partners (for example by simply saying "you two will be a pair," or "you three will talk together"). This is also helpful to ensure that no one is left out, and that the groupings are not too large. If you decide to use whole-class discussions, then it is imperative that all your students are listening to the person talking. Equally important, however, is for you to ensure that one student is not dominating the conversation. In other words, you want to make certain that all students are listening, and that no one is talking too much. This is a difficult task. Many teachers have students raise their hand so they can call on students and help spread out the participation. Others will pull names from a basket and randomly call on students. Still others do not want to play this gatekeeper role, and want students to direct their comments to each other, and not to the teacher. Teachers often move to the back or to one side of the room as a way to encourage more student-to-student interaction. You still must monitor student comments to be sure that they are representing their ideas clearly and factually.

Small-Group Discussion: Elizabeth Cohen, a sociologist who studies student interactions, suggested that the size of a group impacts participation. As mentioned on page 264, groups larger than seven encourage many students to not participate. If students are in a group with seven or fewer classmates, greater participation by all students occurs (Cohen & Lotan, 2014). Most of the discussion approaches discussed previously require having students in smaller groups. As with the "Think/Pair/Share" activity during the whole-class discussions, students often need help forming these groups. Again, the most straightforward approach is to group students who are near each other. If you know of students who do not work well together, then you will want to form the groups to maximize the learning. Students can form their own groups, but you need to monitor closely that all students are included. Recall from Chapter 8 that research on cooperative group work suggests that the teacher should place students in groups for a purpose. You may want to mix the groups so they are heterogeneous in regard to areas such as experience, communication skills, gender, ethnicity, or other categories that will enhance student learning. You may even want to group students in homogeneous groups. For example, middle school students often benefit by talking about controversial issues in same-sex groups. Once in the small groups, you monitor them to be sure they understand the task, know of any time limits, and are engaged in the project. The key at this point is to move continually amongst your students as they interact. Do not engage in lengthy conversations with your students; rather encourage them to talk with their partners/group mates about the topics. If you talk in-depth with students, they will not develop their own understanding of the topics, and you will not be able to observe all of your students. Your primary tasks during group discussions are to be sure students understand the question you have asked them to discuss (e.g., "What are the strongest points on your side of the issue?"), that they are discussing this with their partners, and that these discussions are not taking up too much class time. By reminding them to focus on the question and topic, you can help keep them engaged.

Electronic Threaded Discussions: Electronic threaded discussions posit a management issue slightly different than the other discussion strategies. Often students read the initial question(s) put forth by the teacher, and respond to that prompt with a lengthy statement. Reading and responding to classmates' postings seems to occur less frequently as the discussion continues. Somehow the energy that is present at the beginning of the discussion needs to be perpetuated. Clearly, as students post more messages, the reading task becomes more burdensome. Changing the discussion topic, or attempting to post "refocus questions," periodically helps reduce the backlog of unread messages. As with face-to-face discussion, students need instruction about "how to" discuss electronically. Identifying a structure that allows the teacher's voice to be "heard" is important. While classroom discussions typically take one or two hours, threaded discussions can last an entire semester because the Internet allows the interactions to transcend the time and place restrictions of meeting in a classroom. When the students are together in a computer lab, momentum is not a concern. When students post during their own time, it is. Experienced teachers who use threaded discussions put limits on how long students can post to a given forum. For example, you may limit the threaded discussions to three days. Since students interact over a short period of time, they know their comments will be read, and responses will be posted quickly. Students' interest in visiting the discussion forum is heightened when they know "new comments" will be posted frequently.

APPROPRIATE ASSESSMENT TECHNIQUES TO USE WITH DISCUSSION AND DEBATE

Assessing classroom discussions creates unique challenges. Once you decide the purpose for a discussion, assessment becomes much easier. Consider these two purposes:

1. Discussion is used as an instructional strategy, where the purpose is to have students engage in verbal interactions so they learn more about the topics being discussed.
2. Skill in discussing becomes the desired outcome of using this strategy, where the discussants become more capable in their verbal interactions with others.

If you solely have the first purpose, then you will have an academic learning target, and you may not want to assess students' participation during the discussions. A report, presentation, and/or written response will allow you to adequately assess learning (for example, the "dialogical essay" described after the Taking a Stand discussion). However, if you solely have the second purpose, then you will have a skill-based learning target, and will assess much more of the process during the discussions. For example, during a fishbowl discussion, students are assessed on their skill in explaining their ideas and thoughts, as much as they are on their new understanding of the discussion topic.

Formative assessments of discussions help students listen and respond to each other appropriately. By teaching students how to discuss, the benefits for using discussion in the classroom can be extended to all areas of students' lives. Most teachers believe that discussion skills need to be taught, and students left to their own will not engage in fruitful discussions. Such ideas as supporting opinions with facts and criticizing an idea and not the person suggesting the idea require skill. As such, they need to be practiced, learned, and assessed by students and by the teacher. Usually, you will assess both your students' engagement in the discussion and how well they learned the content. Below are two sample rubrics that will help you assess both.

Use the checklist in Figure 10.4 on a clipboard to keep track of students on a daily basis. You can assess students' discussion skills on a three-point "scale": (1) consistent; (2) emerging; (3) not seen/not observed. Five to eight students can be targeted for observation each day, taking care to vary the days each student is observed. After several weeks, several clipboard checklists can be combined to complete individual rating scales for each student. This allows for more accurate generalizations about students. This rubric has two sections. The first section, labeled "Classroom Observation," assesses students during the discussions. The second section, labeled "Individual Written Work," assesses student learning through a presentation, written paper, or some activity after the discussion ends.

Allowing the students to self-assess their participation allows you to compare your perceptions with theirs. A handout that looks something like Figure 10.5 might be given to students, and then also completed by you.

This scale requires that you and your students decide the gradations between a score of "0" and "6." In other words, you decide before the discussion what a score of "1," "3," or "6" might be. Often this is a helpful rubric when using a fishbowl discussion, threaded discussion, or a debate.

Figures 10.4 and 10.5 are appropriate for formative and summative assessments. Formative assessments are very important to help students learn the skills needed to engage in

Date of Observation: _____

Activity: _____
_____
_____

C = Consistent
E = Emerging
N = Not seen/
Not observed

Student Name	CLASSROOM OBSERVATION	Describes issue clearly	Elaborates with relevant examples	Asks thoughtful questions re: issue	Restates arguments/then counters	Gives relevant support	Notes gaps in logic	INDIVIDUAL WRITTEN WORK	Summarizes others' ideas	Develops on thesis	Gives arguments to support thesis	Examples strengthen argument	Organizes main points to build argument	Strong closing

Figure 10.4 Clipboard Checklist for Classroom Discussions.

Student name:_____   Period:_____

You will see a one number on each line. The numbers represent how you rated in each of the discussion we just had in class. Place your score on the right of each category and the total score at the bottom of the page. I will also provide my perspective of your scores, and we will meet to compare our assessments.

No mention   Integrated into your discussion
(0 pt)   (6 pts)

⬅————————————————————➡
Building on other student ideas   _____ /6

⬅————————————————————➡
Using information from the text   _____ /6

⬅————————————————————➡
Using information from the handout/readings   _____ /6

⬅————————————————————➡
Integrating new ideas/outside information   _____ /6

Total _____ /24

Figure 10.5 Self-Assessment Scale.

discussion. Formative assessments of student understanding also occurs during the pair/share segments of discussions, and as the students talk about the compelling points of the issue. You assess their comments for accuracy. A threaded discussion has the comments in text for review. You and your students can refer to the postings to assess their contributions and/or complete a rubric.

You will have students who are disinclined to talk; in fact, that may describe you. A student who is shy may not feel comfortable speaking, and will require opportunities to talk in smaller groups. Gender has been shown to influence talking in classrooms. Some studies suggest that girls may talk less frequently than boys, especially if the conversations are perceived as combative. Culture is also an influence on student talk. Some cultures promote talking out loud, while others view excessive talking as disrespectful. In any of these cases, it is imperative that you are aware of your learning targets and your students' needs. You can work with your students (and talk with their families) to help negotiate how they might engage in meaningful classroom discussions.

ENHANCING DISCUSSION WITH TECHNOLOGY

Computer technology can support a discussion. To help students prepare, teachers will often lead them to websites or organize their own digital guided inquiry. These might be as simple as hyperlinked questions in a Word document that lead students to rich online information. Aside from helping students prepare for face-to-face discussions, technology can also be used to hold the discussion itself. This leads to a unique take on our spiraling themes of logistics, classroom management, and assessment.

Logistics: In the above text, we considered online threaded discussions. These discussions can be created using a variety of applications. Two good options that provide free web applications are Moodle and Google Groups. Your university may use applications such as Blackboard or Canvas. Both have discussion board components. Your future school could also use online discussion boards, or even wikis. You may want to ask teachers in your practicum or internship about web applications that the district supports for online discussions.

Classroom Management: Electronic threaded discussions posit a management issue slightly different than the other discussion strategies. Many ideas were already described earlier in this chapter. The largest take-away is that students need instruction and practice in "how to" participate in electronic *and* face-to-face discussions. Identifying a structure that allows the teacher's voice to be "heard" is important. While classroom discussions typically take one or two hours, threaded discussions, as we have seen, can last an entire semester. Experienced teachers who use threaded discussions put limits on how long students can post to a given forum. For example, you may limit the threaded discussions to three days. Since students interact over a short period of time, they know their comments will be read, and responses will be posted quickly. Students' interest in visiting the discussion forum is heightened when they know "new comments" will be posted frequently. Of course, some students will need to be reminded that all classroom expectations for respectful face-to-face conversations also apply online even though the medium is different. For example, in face-to-face we don't yell at each other and online we don't use ALL CAPS!

Assessment: As you review the assessment in this chapter you will notice that most of the criteria will also apply here. A threaded discussion has the comments in the text for review. You and your students can refer to the postings to assess their contributions and/or complete a rubric. You may notice that some of your more reserved students begin to come out of their shell as they have a medium to communicate that suits them. For all students, you should consider criteria in your rubric that explain your expectations for number and length of posts.

MAKING A DISCUSSION MORE MEANINGFUL FOR ELLS[3]

Providing discussion time in class between native and English language learners is an outstanding aid to language and content learning. Age-peers are likely to speak in a way that is more comprehensible for the ELL, and the ELL may feel more comfortable with a partner or peers in a small group, because it is less "public" than the whole-class instruction. Pair discussion, small-group discussion and large-group discussion can be successfully used, but they need to be sequenced and well planned in order to provide the scaffolding ELLs need to actively participate.

- Build background.
    - Before jumping into "discussion," provide a reminder of what we have been talking about.
    - Provide a model of what a good discussion might sound like.
    - Introduce (or review) important content vocabulary and concepts and provide visual reminders for students to refer to as they discuss.
- Provide the target of the discussion.
    - Let them know at the start what you want them to be able to do or produce at the end of the discussion.
- Choose the discussion size strategically.
    - Do pair discussion or small-group discussion *before* a teacher/whole-class discussion if you want to increase participation.
    - Frequency of student speaking activity can be increased dramatically.
    - Brief pair discussion allows student to put ideas into English words before having to participate in a small group.
    - Large-group discussion is best to close up a class discussion time.
- Structure the debriefing.
    - Be especially clear during the debriefing about what was accomplished. Consider writing outcomes of the discussion on the board or in some visual format.
- Discussion styles vary significantly from culture to culture.
    - Discussion might be seen as a learning experience in which everyone, prepared or not, can participate. The speed demanded by this kind of discussion is challenging for those who may be searching for words in a second language.
    - Some students may come from cultures in which challenging the intelligence of someone's ideas is not seen at all as a challenge to the individual's intelligence. This can come off as rude and shocking in the American classroom.
    - Some students may come from cultures in which the concept of debating and disagreeing strongly is not acceptable. Some come from cultures where speaking out is viewed as arrogant or challenging the teacher's knowledge. These students may become very quiet in discussions, and seem uncomfortable. Often they excel, however, in discussion where compromise and cooperation is expected and encouraged.

- Some students may come from cultures that place a high value on reflection before speaking.
- Turn taking, with everyone having the opportunity to speak without being interrupted, is comfortable.
- Provide the words and language patterns to carry out those roles. All students need to practice academic vocabulary and academic language patterns orally.
  - Consider providing a list of "formal" language either for the discussion or the report back, or both.
    1. On a poster in the room, or in student folders, for discussion language:
       a. I see what you mean, but I think _____.
       b. You've got a point, but I've found that _____.
       c. Could you explain that some more?
       d. I believe _____ because _____.
       e. Can you give me an example of that?
       f. I agree with you because _____.
       g. I can see where you are coming from, but have you ever thought about _____?
    2. You can make a paragraph with blanks, or provide sentence stems, to help guide students during the report back. This makes it easier for the ELL to do the report back if the entire group fills it in together. It also exposes students to the academic language they are asked to understand when they read.
       a. We agreed on _____, but we disagreed on _____.
       b. Some of the group expressed the idea that _____.
       c. Although _____ thought _____, others believed that _____.
       d. Despite some disagreement, we now all agree that _____.
- Provide a graphic organizer to help them take notes and categorize what they are hearing (many samples are available online).
  - An information grid with headings—students fill in the appropriate cells.
  - A Venn diagram for noting agreement and disagreement while people are talking.
  - Demonstrate this on the overhead or document camera.

GUIDELINES FOR DECIDING IF DISCUSSION/DEBATE IS APPROPRIATE FOR THE CONTENT OF A LESSON

Each discussion strategy listed earlier serves specific purposes. Those purposes were identified as part of the overview for each strategy. This section, however, suggests general guidelines for determining the appropriateness of using discussion to help students learn. While the majority of all classroom talk is synonymous with recitation-style approaches, significant social and cognitive changes have been reported to occur in students when classroom talk shifts more toward adult "conversations" (Cazden, 1988). Cazden explained this move away from recitation and toward discussion:

> One important shift is from recitation to something closer to a "real discussion" . . . talk in which ideas are explored rather than answers to teacher's test questions are provided and evaluated; in which teachers talk less . . . and students talk correspondingly more; in which

students themselves decide when to speak . . .; and in which students address each other directly.

(p. 55)

Discussion is thought to be a useful teaching technique for developing higher-order thinking skills; skills that enable students to interpret, analyze, and manipulate information. Students explain their ideas and thoughts, rather than merely recount, or recite, memorized facts and details. During discussion, learners are not passive recipients of information that is transmitted from a teacher, but are active participants. Their active involvement with each other and the course content helps them construct a deeper and more flexible understanding of the topic (Johnston, Anderman, Milne, & Harris, 1994; Tharp & Gallimore, 1988).

When students interact during discussions and debates, they need to have a deep and flexible understanding of the content, and they need to have skill in discussion itself. The following questions should help you consider whether or not classroom discussion will be an appropriate activity to plan for your students.

Will the discussion help students learn about the issue or topic?

For discussions to educate students, they should be serious interactions where students "support their ideas with evidence, where their opinions are subject to challenge by their peers as well as the teacher, and where the teacher's ideas are equally open to criticism" (Engle & Ochoa, 1988, p. 47). The purpose of probing questions and discrepant viewpoints is to encourage interactions and to encourage students to respond with the most powerful evidence available to them.

Can your students discuss issues?

Teachers think of discussion as a skill that requires practice sessions. As such, they often pre-teach discussion skills to their students in an attempt to front-load behaviors, attitudes, and interactions they consider are critical for classroom discussions. They set time aside to prepare students for discussions; some begin this preparation the first day of school. Teachers tell students about courtesy, respect, and manners for talking, and possibly disagreeing, with classmates. They tell students to view the class as a community, to encourage more interaction. This is something that does not happen without effort by the teacher and willingness by the students. Teachers make efforts to earn students' trust, and students are held accountable to respect their classmates. One teacher reported this was a training process: "I train them from the beginning to become a learning community . . . there is an atmosphere of trust."

What types of interactions do you want during the discussion?

Walter Parker theorizes that discussions can have the "look and feel" of a *seminar* or of a *deliberation* (2001). The purpose of a *seminar* is to improve understanding about a topic, book, and/or idea. He suggests that seminars start with a question such as, "What does (the topic of the discussion) mean?" and proceed in a way that is conducive to improving everyone's understanding. *Deliberations* start with a question such as, "What should we do?" As such, deliberations intend to not only improve the discussant's understanding, but to reach a decision about a shared problem (Parker, 2001, p. 114). Consensus building and compromise are more prevalent in deliberations. With any discussion, however, the emphasis needs to be taken off "winning an argument." Classroom discussions need to value the learning that comes from the process of interacting.

Before ending this chapter, it is important to consider controversial issues and their use in the classroom. Controversial issues hold the potential of distracting students, causing fear of confrontations, or even leading to arguments and conflict. However, they also provide rich potential for authentically engaging students. Controversial political issues are defined as questions of public policy that spark significant disagreement. They usually spark interest and open the door for learning how to discuss as well as learning about the discussion topic. In her explorations of teaching with controversial public issues, Diana Hess suggests that controversial topics are "open," "closed," or "tipping" (2009). Closed topics are those that are settled and are no longer controversial. An example of a closed topic today would be women's suffrage. Reasonable people in democratic societies do not think that women's right to vote is controversial. Open topics are those that contemporary society, and perhaps certain parts of the world, regions of a country, or local communities have not settled. For example, a mandatory military draft may be a closed topic in parts of the Middle East, but an open topic in the United States. Note that closed does not mean that *everyone* agrees. Topics that are thought of to be tipping are moving over time from either closed to open or vice versa. Health care as a basic human right that should be funded by the government tips in the current public conversation. When selecting a controversial issue for a discussion, consider topics that are open or tipping. If the topic is so controversial that it will prevent students from engaging—they feel psychologically unsafe—then avoid it. Likewise, if you are too emotionally attached to a particular perspective of an issue, do not bring it into the classroom. However, many potential controversial political issues abound that are perfect for use in any social studies classroom.

MAKING IT WORK IN YOUR CLASSROOM

Consider one of the social studies courses you will teach at the middle school or high school level. Select a topic that you believe will engage students in a discussion. For example, you might select a high school world history class with the topic as: the dropping of the Atomic bomb in 1945. Productive discussions are a result of careful planning. After choosing a topic, consider the following:

1. Identify the topic students will discuss.
2. Write lesson targets:
   • Targets addressing what students are to learn about discussion skills
   • Targets addressing what students are to learn about course content or knowledge.
3. Describe the rationale for choosing the issue:
   • What makes this a good issue to discuss?
   • How does it fit with the curriculum?
4. Decide what type of discussion will best help student learn the issue. What is your rationale for using one discussion approach over another? How will that be the best approach for helping students learn?

5. Lesson procedures:
   - Student preparation: How will you prepare students to engage in a discussion on this topic?
   - What experiences, readings, and information will they need ahead of time?
6. Discussion questions:
   - Write out actual questions you would pose to your class. Come up with some opening questions (to help students recall information and establish facts), interpretive questions (to help students draw relationships and compare/contrast information), and opinion questions (to encourage your students to draw their own conclusions and articulate them).
7. Assessment:
   - Reread the section on assessing classroom discussion, and determine how you might assess student learning. Tie it to your learning targets, and consider whether you want to assess their "discussion skill" and/or their understanding of the discussion topic. What type of rubric or rating scale could you use?

CHAPTER REVIEW

- Research support for using classroom discussions and debate
  - Teachers value classroom discussions, but struggle to use it frequently
  - Discussion helps students learn content deeply, and helps develop key interaction skills needed for citizens in a democracy
- Step-by-step procedures for selecting, planning, and using classroom discussions
  - "Discussion" is a label for a wide range of classroom activities. We identified six in the chapter, and each has unique procedures:
    - Taking a Stand
    - the issues/values continuum
    - the future's wheel discussion
    - the fishbowl discussion
    - structured academic controversy (SAC)
    - the electronic threaded discussion

Structured debate is more competitive than the six discussions, and serves a different purpose

- Managing the classroom/learning environment during discussions
  - Be aware of logistics such as moving chairs, placing students in groups, student preparation, and establishing a classroom environment that is conducive to talking
  - Students need to be clear about the goals of the discussion, and they must know that their ideas are an important part of the learning
  - Develop a set of guidelines for the students to follow and hold students accountable to them
- Assessing student learning appropriately during classroom discussions
  - You may assess student participation, or you may decide only to assess what students have learned from the discussion itself
  - Rubrics help you focus on the pertinent parts of the discussion in order to better assess students
  - Formative assessments help students listen and respond to each other appropriately

- Certain notions—such as supporting opinions with facts, and criticizing an idea and not the person suggesting the idea—require skill; they need to be learned by students and assessed by the teacher
- Using technology to enhance learning
  - The Internet is useful for researching discussion topics
  - Online discussions provide unique challenges and opportunities that were explored in the chapter
- Considerations for English language learners during classroom discussions
  - Pair discussions, small-group discussions and large-group discussions can be successfully used, but they need to be sequenced and well planned in order to provide the scaffolding ELLs need to actively participate. The following were presented:
    - build background
    - provide the objective of the discussion
    - choose the discussion size strategically
    - structure the debriefing
    - discussion styles vary significantly from culture to culture
    - provide the words and language patterns to carry out those roles. All students need to practice academic vocabulary and academic language patterns orally
    - provide a graphic organizer to help them take notes and categorize what they are hearing (many samples available online)

NOTES

1. These align well with Common Core State Standards such as CCSS.ELA-LITERACY.WHST.6–8.1.B: "Support claim(s) with logical reasoning and relevant, accurate data and evidence that demonstrate an understanding of the topic or text, using credible sources."
2. These guidelines are developed from work done by Barber, 1989; Larson, 1997; and Parker, 1996.
3. This section was created in association with Trish Skillman and Maria Timmons-Flores at Western Washington University.

REFERENCES

Alvermann, D. E., O'Brien, D. G., & Dillon, D. R. (1990). What teachers do when they say they are having discussions of content area reading assignments: A qualitative analysis. *Reading Research Quarterly, 25*(4), 296–322.

Barber, B. (1989). Public talk and civic action: Education for participation in a strong democracy. *Social Education, 53*(6), 355–356, 370.

Bridges, D. (1987). Discussion and questioning. *Questioning Exchange, 1*, 34–37.

Bridges, D. (1979). *Education, Democracy and Discussion.* Windsor, England: NFER.

Cazden, C. (1988). *Classroom Discourse.* Portsmouth, NH: Heinemann.

Cohen, E. G. & Lotan, R. A. (2014). *Designing Groupwork: Strategies for the Heterogeneous Classroom,* 3rd ed. New York: Teachers College Press.

Dillon, J. T. (1994). *Using Discussion in the Classroom.* Philadelphia, PA: Open University Press.

Dillon, J. T. (1984). Research on questioning and discussion. *Educational Leadership, 41*(3), 51–56.

Engle, S. & Ochoa, A. (1988). *Education for Democratic Citizenship: Decision Making in the Social Studies.* New York: Teachers College Press.

Gall, M. D. (1985). Discussion methods of teaching. In T. Husen & T. N. Postlethwaite (Eds.), *International Encyclopedia of Education* (Vol. 3, pp. 1423–1427) Oxford: Pergamon Press.

Gall, M. D., & Gall, J. P. (1990). Outcomes of the discussion method. In W. W. Wilen (Ed.), *Teaching and Learning through Discussion: The Theory, Research and Practice of the Discussion Method*, (pp. 25–44). Springfield, IL: Charles C. Thomas.

Goodlad, J. I. (1984). *A Place Called School*. New York: McGraw-Hill.

Gorman, A. H. (1969). *Teachers and Learners: The Interactive Process*. Boston, MA: Allyn & Bacon.

Gross, R. E. & Zeleny, L. D. (1958). *Educating Citizens for Democracy: Curriculum and Instruction in Secondary Social Studies*. New York: Oxford University Press.

Haroutunian-Gordon, S. (1991). *Turning the Soul: Teaching through Conversation in the High School*. Chicago, IL: The University of Chicago Press.

Hess, D. E. (2009). Controversy in the classroom: The democratic power of discussion. New York: Routledge.

Hess, D. E. (2000). Developing strong voters through democratic deliberation. *Social Education*, *64*(5), 193–196.

Hoetker, J., & Ahlbrand, W. P., Jr. (1969). The persistence of recitation. *American Educational Research Journal*, *6*, 145–167.

Hoover, K. H. (1976). *The Professional Teacher's Handbook: A Guide for Improving Instruction in Today's Middle and Secondary Schools*, 2nd ed. Boston, MA: Allyn & Bacon.

Hunkins, F. P. (1995). *Teaching Thinking through Effective Questioning*, 2nd ed. Boston, MA: Christopher-Gordon.

Johnson, D. W. & Johnson, R. T. (1988). Critical thinking through structured controversy. *Educational Leadership, 45*(8), 58–64.

Johnston, J., Anderman, L., Milne, L., & Harris, D. (1994). *Improving Civic Discourse in the Classroom: Taking the Measure of Channel One*. Research Report 4. Ann Arbor, MI: Institute for Social Research, University of Michigan.

Larson, B. E. (2003). Comparing face-to-face discussion and electronic discussion: A case study from high school social studies. *Theory and Research in Social Education, 31*(3), 348–366.

Larson, B. E. (2000). Thinking about classroom discussion as a method of instruction and a curriculum outcome. *Teaching and Teacher Education, 16*(2000), 661–677.

Larson, B. E. (1997). Social studies teachers' conceptions of discussion: A grounded theory study. *Theory and Research in Social Education, 25*(2), 113–136.

Larson, B. & Keiper, T. (2013). *Instructional Strategies for Middle and High School*, 2nd ed. New York: Routledge.

Mail, D. J. (1968). The fishbowl: Design for discussion. *Today's Education, 57*, 27–29.

Merryfield, M. M. (2000). How can electronic technologies promote equity and cultural diversity? Using threaded discussion in graduate courses in social studies and global education. *Theory and Research in Social Education, 28*(4), 502–526.

Miller, S. (1992). *Creating Change: Towards a Dialogic Pedagogy*. Report Series 2.18. Albany, NY: National Research Center on Literature Teaching and Learning. (ERIC Document Reproduction Service No. ED 349 582.)

Oliver, D. W. & Newmann, F. M. (1972). *Taking a Stand: A Guide to Clear Discussion of Public Issues_*(revised ed.). Middletown, CT: Xerox Corporation/American Education Publications.

Parker, W. C. (2001). Classroom discussion: Models for leading seminars and deliberations. *Social Education, 65*(2), 111–115.

Parker, W. C. (1996). Curriculum for democracy. In R. Soder (Ed.), *Democracy, Education and Schooling* (pp. 182–210). San Francisco, CA: Jossey-Bass.

Priles, M. A. (1993). The fishbowl discussion: A strategy for large honors classes. *English Journal, 82*(6), 49–50.

Roby, T. W. (1988). Models of discussion. In J. T. Dillon (Ed.), *Questioning and Discussion: A Multidisciplinary Study* (pp. 163–191). Norwood, NJ: Ablex.

Stodolsky, S., Ferguson, T., & Wimpelberg, K. (1981). The recitation persists, but what does it look like? *Journal of Curriculum Studies*, *13*(2), 121–130.

Swift, J. N. & Gooding, C. T. (1983). Interaction of wait time feedback and questioning instruction on middle school science teaching. *Journal of Research in Science Teaching*, *20*(8), 721–730.

Tharp, R. G. & Gallimore, R. (1988). *Rousing Minds to Life: Teaching, Learning, and Schooling in Social Context*. Cambridge: Cambridge University Press.

Wilen, W. W. & White, J. J. (1991). Interaction and discourse in social studies classrooms. In J. P. Shaver (Ed.), *Handbook of Research on Social Studies Teaching and Learning* (pp. 483–495). New York: Macmillan.

CHAPTER 11

Inquiry and Student-Directed Investigations

CHAPTER GOALS

In this chapter, you will learn about:

- Research support for using student-directed investigations
- Step-by-step procedures for selecting, planning, and using student-directed investigations
- Managing the classroom/learning environment during student-directed investigations
- Assessing student learning appropriately during student-directed investigations
- Using technology to enhance learning
- Considerations for English language learners during student-directed investigations.

Teacher-centered   Student-centered

Lecture

Questioning

Concept Formation

Simulation/Role-Play/Drama

Discussion

Cooperative Learning

SDI

If an outsider walked into Ellie Abeyta's world geography classroom when the students were engaged in a student-directed investigation, it might appear somewhat chaotic. Some of her students, sitting in the back corner of this classroom, would be taking notes while viewing a documentary about the stories of recent immigrants. Other students would be asking for permission to go to the library computer lab to analyze data and research statistics on ELLs and state test scores. One student might be reviewing recent census data about the countries from which recent immigrants to the U.S. came in the last two decades. Another student would be composing interview questions that will query community members about their traditional customs.

At first glance the class looks chaotic, but it is actually a highly planned student-centered strategy allowing for differentiation during an inquiry lesson. Ms. Abeyta had been considering how she could get her students to understand human movement around the world. She hoped that by creating an inquiry project, her students could generate questions that interested them, and then pursue them in a variety of ways with her and community partners' support. She planned for these questions to move students out into the community. Since they were working in teams, some of the native English speakers could assist classmates who were ELLs. She gave them the topic "Learning about recent immigration patterns around the world." So far the cooperative teams have come up with these questions:

- What interesting stories can we find of recent immigrants trying to earn a living?
- What was the town they came from like?
- How difficult is it for a recent immigrant to learn English and go to school?
- What are jobs like for the recently immigrated?
- Who left the U.S. and what countries did they go to?

The students were working hard at refining their data gathering ideas so they could get interviews and not just information from text as required in their guidelines. Ms. Abeyta was looking forward to inviting some local community members into her class so they could hear the results during student presentations.

OVERVIEW

The students in the above scenario are like students elsewhere in that they want learning about social studies to be personally relevant and engaging. According to Tomlinson (2003), three trends strike at the core of effective teaching and learning in today's schools: (1) classrooms are more diverse than at any time in our past and this trend will continue; (2) due to this trend in diverse classrooms, teachers are looking to teach in more flexible, personalized ways; and (3) there is an escalating demand that students acquire high-level knowledge and skills. Increasingly, teachers must differentiate instruction when they design plans that address these trends. One of the ways to meet the educational needs of all the students in the classroom is to focus on curriculum that both *promotes understanding* and *engages* students. Inquiry and student-directed investigation are important strategies for the social studies teacher who hopes to differentiate instruction to help his/her students learn. As is the case with many of the previous chapters, this chapter describes a series of approaches that are categorized as inquiry.

DEFINING INQUIRY AND STUDENT-DIRECTED INVESTIGATION

You may have heard Benjamin Franklin's proverb, "Tell me and I forget, teach me and I may remember, involve me and I learn." The strategies that you have been exploring through this text have varying degrees of student involvement. The research is very clear that the more engaged in the learning process the student is, the more learning and remembering will occur. Some call this "hands on, minds on," but the premise is the same: Teacher-centered strategies have a purpose, but lasting learning occurs most with student-centered strategies. The teaching approach in this chapter has great potential for student involvement and engagement. Student-directed investigations include several varieties of investigations that share certain critical attributes. While I am labeling them as investigations, you may come across different labels that fit in this category of strategies, such as: inquiry learning, discovery learning, problem-based learning, project-based learning, experiential learning. These all provide opportunities to learn through experiences that include the following attributes:

- offers meaningful, personally interesting challenges
- requires active learning
- provides opportunities to solve problems, answer questions, or address real needs
- allows for student ownership, responsibility, and choices
- offers students an opportunity to perform as experts or professionals.

The title of this chapter includes inquiry because that title is a commonly used term in schools. Inquiry has the attributes listed above. It borrows from science an approach where students identify an issue or problem, develop hypotheses to solve or address it, gather and analyze data to test the hypothesis, and then revise their original thinking. Precise definitions of all the various types of investigations are difficult and somewhat nebulous. However, when you hear of inquiry or of student-directed learning, you can assume that they include the characteristics referred to above in addition to the following variations:

- *Inquiry learning:* A focus on asking and investigating personally relevant questions. The conclusion is not as important as learning the thinking process. These questions might be controversial or have conclusions that are difficult to ascertain.
- *Discovery learning:* A focus on discovering the solution to a particular problem through a process respected by professionals in the field. Specific solutions or conclusions are as important as learning the thinking process and will deal with settled rather than controversial issues.
- *Project-based learning:* A focus on the process used to develop a product or other creation. This may or may not be problem based.
- *Experiential learning:* A focus on learning through an experience usually not associated with a traditional classroom environment.
- *Service learning:* A focus on learning through an experience of service to the community usually outside of the classroom or school.

A DESCRIPTION OF STUDENT-DIRECTED INVESTIGATION, AND RESEARCH FINDINGS

As you may have noted, student-directed investigation is grounded in constructivist learning theory. With this in mind, now is a good time to quickly review the basics of two predominant approaches to learning as described in Chapter 2—*behaviorism* and *constructivism*. Much of the experimental data that serves as the basis for the behaviorist view was first generated by Skinner (1968). This view suggests that knowledge is universal, objective, and independent of the student. The behaviorist teaching approach is primarily focused on direct instruction because knowledge is transmitted to the student and received through the senses. The primary role of the teacher would be to break information and skills into meaningful packages, build them back together through a series of presentations or activities and, when finished, test to see if students have learned. Behaviorist classrooms tend to focus on teaching skill sequences, stress individualized rather than group work, and emphasize methods such as lecture, teacher-directed questioning, skill worksheets, teacher-led activities, and objective tests.

Constructivist theory has a different view of knowledge and therefore holds a different view of approaches to learning. While proponents of this theory hold a variety of opinions about knowledge and learning, they would agree with the underlying belief that people construct knowledge as a result of their personal set of experiences. Constructivists believe that what a person knows is not a function of detached observation but created through interaction with the world and that knowledge and reality are subjective (Fosnot, 1989). Those holding this view give attention to the social context in which learning occurs. Learning environments similar to those in the "real world" are best suited to enhance learning. Constructivists support learning that focuses on the use of authentic tasks—that is, the everyday practices of a particular group such as scientists, historians, or filmmakers. These tasks would be similar to on-the-job experiences or apprenticeships. Proponents of this view would have classrooms focus on problem solving, independent investigation, the pursuit of personal interests, and the utilization of higher-order thinking skills.

A brief overview makes these two perspectives appear to be mutually exclusive, and to some they are just that. In practice, however, perspectives fall on a wide continuum somewhere between two poles (Duffy & Johnson, 1992; Scheurman, 1998). For example, some teachers may not agree with the idea that the individual creates reality but are still proponents of student-centered approaches to learning. However, through this discussion you can see how what you believe about the way students learn has a profound impact on the instructional choices you make in the classroom. This can be reviewed further by revisiting Chapter 2.

Many high school and middle school teachers notice that the naturally inquisitive nature of children seems to slowly fade as they become older. Sadly, our traditional system of education has not always encouraged the pursuit of independent inquiry and curiosity. Too often, students use almost all of their time in a required pursuit of the test answers. The facts, of course, are important, but so also are understanding and the use of information. Research in cognition, authentic learning, and student engagement supports claims that providing students with opportunities to direct their own learning is a beneficial strategy for developing engaging students and promoting learning (Brooks & Brooks, 1993; Brown, Collins, & Duguid, 1989; Scheurman & Newmann, 1998). Others have found that independent inquiry and self-regulation are advantageous approaches for developing understanding and application of knowledge. According to a summary of research on learning conducted by Bransford, Brown, and Cocking (2000), student-directed learning is effective when three components are present. First, students should be placed in settings that prepare them for flexible adaptation to new problems and settings; second, students should organize information into the main ideas that structure a discipline—its most important theories or concepts and their interrelationships; third, students show understanding when they know how and when to put knowledge to use. This is quite different from the more teacher-centered strategies in chapters 5 and 6. A different level of learning occurs when students are more engaged in the learning process.

STEP-BY-STEP PROCEDURES FOR PLANNING AND IMPLEMENTING STUDENT-DIRECTED INVESTIGATIONS

The various types of student-directed investigation will serve different purposes, and because of this, one type may be a better match for a learning objective than another. These strategies are equally effective at both the high school and middle school levels even though students' maturity levels vary drastically. Teachers will consider other variables such as topic, time constraints, community resources and contacts, transportation, and the course schedule when determining which type of investigation to pursue. I provide details for inquiry-based learning and for writing a snapshot biography in the following sections as examples of how student-directed learning/investigation might be used in the class.

Inquiry-Based Learning

Inquiry is an approach that encourages students to respect information/data, and use it to base thoughtful conclusions. You should recall from Chapter 1 that the NCSS C3 Framework *(College, Career, and Civic Life)* suggests that teachers have students engage in inquiry that follows an "inquiry arc." The inquiry arc described by the NCSS has students engage in four dimensions: (1) developing questions and planning inquiries; (2) applying disciplinary concepts and tools; (3) evaluating sources and using evidence; and (4) communicating conclusions and taking informed action. Through inquiry, students do not merely give a personal opinion, or jump to a conclusion. Rather, they engage in a process of formulating and testing hypotheses. In both the formulation and the testing, students engage in research, practice such higher-order thinking as creating, evaluating, analyzing, and suspending judgment until a conclusion can be drawn. The inquiry strategy is also known as the scientific method, or problem solving.

When an inquiry lesson is tied to major learning goals of a social studies course, students engage in an in-depth, critical analysis of that content. Students, rather than the teacher, think and wrestle with the content, and develop a more meaningful understanding of the content. Often the inquiry strategy uses groups. As a result, the students engage in "collaborative inquiry," which often helps students see the value of others' ideas—working together often allows for more insight than working alone. The ideas presented in the chapter on cooperative learning (Chapter 8), as well as the chapter on discussion (Chapter 10), will help with the implementation of inquiry lessons. In addition, students benefit from this process as they negotiate knowledge together, and realize that "experts" often disagree about interpretations of data and information. The accuracy and appropriateness of a hypothesis is not whether or not it sounds good, but whether or not it can be defended and supported.

With inquiry learning, the emphasis is on the pursuit of questions, making hypotheses, investigating, forming theories, and the possibility of taking action based upon evaluative judgments. It is helpful when teachers want students to see things from multiple perspectives or decide for themselves—as opposed to finding a solution that was already pre-determined. From the outset the students are presented with a complex problem or question that has many variables and likely has several solutions (Gallagher, Sher, Stepien, & Workman, 1995). Building on the C3 Framework, I find it helpful to think of inquiry lessons as loosely following a process of inquiry with four sequential steps:

1. Step 1: Doubt, Concern, and Identifying a Problem
2. Step 2: Identifying Possible Hypotheses and Gathering Data
3. Step 3: Interpretation and Evaluating Data/Information
4. Step 4: Reporting and Returning to the Hypothesis

In general, the inquiry process begins with a questioning stage that raises some doubt or concern, and then proceeds to other stages as shown. Opportunities for feedback occur throughout the process. While this four-step process may be of use as an overview of the process of inquiry, it is also misleading in that rarely is a high-quality inquiry lesson so neatly packaged. Many think of inquiry as more of a web. For example, after interpreting information, students may need to form another hypothesis and reinvestigate or ask a different question. Teachers using inquiry techniques would need to have an understanding of the basic process before they could confidently modify plans as circumstances in a fluid classroom would demand. It might be helpful to consider how the inquiry process might "play out" in your future classroom.

Step 1: Doubt, Concern, and Identifying a Problem

Most students will need assistance posing an appropriate question that is both interesting and challenging. Encourage students to consider what really interests them about a topic. Is the question under consideration one that can be answered with little effort or is it challenging and worthwhile? How will pursuing the question give them deeper insight into the overall lesson theme or objective? Students should be encouraged to avoid questions with simple answers, or yes/no questions, unless they need to do in-depth exploration to come to a decision. For example, *Should the Makah be allowed to hunt whales?* could be a poor question choice if students are not asked to provide in-depth supporting information from various perspectives. It is also limited because it is a "yes/no" question. A better question could be, *What is the best response to the Makah's request to hunt the Gray Whale?* This is open ended and allows for students to take it in a number of directions. Care should also be given to guide students away from questions that are too broad—for example, consider the question, *What should be done about immigration?* After speaking with the students about their interest, this could be refocused to read, *What impact does the Mexican economy have on migration patterns?* Students could be asked to form conclusions or take a position after they have answered the question. Another example is found from a government course. One week the teacher had the class look for issues in the paper that interested them, and upon completion of an inquiry lesson, they were to solve the issue by writing a bill for the state or federal legislature. Several students located a news article about a 19-year-old who had had possession of an illegal substance and was arrested. Those in this group decided to explore a question related to the balance between civil liberties and the necessity of legal restrictions. Students could also be posed with a question to get them thinking. For example, why did the U.S. Civil War start in 1861? Why that year and not earlier or later? This "why then?" question is applicable to any number of historical events (consider why 1776 for the Declaration of Independence? Why 1215 for the formal signing of the Magna Carta?). Similarly, why was Jackie Robinson selected to break the color-barrier in major league baseball, why was Rosa Parks the person who became the case urging on the desegregation of buses in Alabama, or why was Nelson Mandela the leader of the anti-apartheid movement? Once an appropriate question has been determined, a *need-to-know* chart can be used to help focus students. On a large visual, the teacher would write headings for three columns:

1.   What do we know?
2.   What do we need to know?
3.   How do we find out?

If the class is pursuing one question together, this could be a large-group brainstorming session; if students are pursuing questions in small groups, this could be done with teacher facilitation. This step is as important as any of the others since, commonly, students who have poor inquiry experiences can trace it back to the question-formulation stage. At this early stage students should be encouraged to formulate an investigation plan in which they meet with the teacher to determine direction and form a work schedule.

Step 2: Investigating Possible Hypotheses, and Gathering Data

Each discipline will have established techniques for investigating a question. For example, obviously using the scientific method is vital in a biology class, while a history class would have its own methods. For example, the scientific method most commonly used would include the following steps:

1.   form the question
2.   make observations
3.   form a hypothesis
4.   do the experiment
5.   draw a conclusion.

Historical methods would include techniques by which historians examine primary sources and other evidence to research and write about history. Guidelines for historical inquiry would require consideration of internal and external criticism prior to forming hypotheses through a process of historical reasoning. Investigating social issues would involve a perspective-gathering component. The steps involved may be similar to the scientific method, but this discipline, like all others, has its own investigative methods.

One source of information common to all fields is text-based resources. The teachers will need to be prepared to give suggestions and guidance for the selection of appropriate resources. This is especially true of the use of Internet resources, as evaluating online information can be confusing and difficult for students. How does a middle school or high school student know if information is reliable? Students should be made aware that consideration of authorship, publisher, currency, perspectives, coverage, and accuracy can help determine the reliability of a source. Many students will be familiar with the online resource Wikipedia; it may be a good starting point for research and be helpful in determining related topics or other guidance to find other resources. However, students should be taught the importance of finding multiple resources and that because there is usually no author to cite in Wiki, it should be seen only as a starting point. For more information about this topic, see the classroom application section entitled Enhancing Student Learning with Technology found later in this chapter. With the example about why Jackie Robinson was selected to break the color barrier, much research can be done with documents and texts from the time period. The movie *41* offers another resource, but always encourage your students to challenge the truth of a movie. In fact, asking students to evaluate the accuracy of a movie that claims to be historical is another form of inquiry. *Selma* is a movie about Martin Luther King's famous march. However, the producer/director could not get approval to use the actual transcripts of King's speeches. She re-created them based on her research (it was her own inquiry project). It would be an interesting investigation for students to evaluate the accuracy of her script by comparing it with King's actual words.

The use of face-to-face or online experts is also a good way to make resource information available. During this investigative stage students could use the teacher for mini-lessons for small groups on an "as needed" basis. In addition, during this stage there may be opportunities to have student experts or community experts available as resources.

Step 3: Interpreting and Analyzing Data/Information

Students are encouraged to analyze information they have collected and draw conclusions. To do this they will need to reflect on *what* information is relevant to the question under consideration and *how* it can help them answer it satisfactorily. Both middle school and high school students will need assistance with the thinking skills needed to draw logical conclusions from the information they have collected. Some computer software—spreadsheets to create graphs, for example—can be helpful to teach students to analyze and interpret information. This example would be especially helpful for those learners with a more visual orientation. At the heart of interpreting and analyzing, however, is a return to the hypotheses. For example, if my hypothesis is that the inauguration of Lincoln in 1861 was the final tipping point in why the Civil War started, then all of my data collection is focused on proving or refuting my hypothesis. Similarly, my analysis of the data and information will be based on how reliable, consistent, and valid the data I collect is, and what new data is needed to inform my thinking.

Students can record both their interpretation notes along with investigative notes in an inquiry journal. A journal like this could be used as an assessment tool by the teacher, as well as a way for students to track their learning. After the interpretation of results is completed, students can record their conclusions and begin preparing for a report of their findings.

Step 4: Reporting and Returning to the Hypothesis

Give students an opportunity to present their findings to an audience. When gathering this audience (small group of classmates, the School Board, PTA), the teacher should reflect upon the amount of time and effort students invested in the inquiry. For example, one middle school classroom used sophisticated computer software on loan from a university to investigate a question posed by the local city council: *Should we have—and if so, where should we place—a city park for our fast-growing town?* The students took several months to investigate information and analyze data until they were prepared to make a recommendation. Their teacher, to her credit, saw this as a wonderful opportunity to have community leaders involved as part of the presentation audience. Naturally, this is not always possible or advisable. Some inquiry projects are small, in-class affairs where informal reports are appropriate. It is important to provide a forum for students to present findings and field questions. This could be an audience of peers, the teacher, or the larger community.

A presentation with a written document is a natural and oft-used form of report for an inquiry-based lesson. However, it is not unusual to find classrooms that take a form of social action as a result of their inquiry. This might involve writing letters to the influential, making video reports that are sent to television stations, creating websites or blogs, or other ways the class desires to draw attention to their findings.

Create times throughout the inquiry that allow for student self-reflection, assessment, and adjustment. For example, take a few minutes along the way to hold a questioning seminar to explore what they are concluding up to that point or what remains to be resolved. Use Think/Pair/Share activities, exit cards ("On a card, write two specific things you learned today"), or one-minute papers ("Write for one minute about a prediction you can make based upon our discussion today"). Students could also use their inquiry journals to record questions about the process or for future pursuit and other reflective internal "talk" that may be helpful.

MAKING IT WORK IN YOUR CLASSROOM

The student-centeredness of inquiry and student investigations means that it is difficult to imagine it in practice without students. If you have access to students, have a conversation with their teacher about possible inquiry topics they could pursue. Guide that conversation away from a research paper, and toward a project where the students are involved in finding and then following-up on a problem or issue. The following steps, and questions, will help you then plan an inquiry lesson.

1. *Lesson targets:*
   a. What course content will they learn?
   b. Will you need a skill target (such as research skills, or analysis skills)?
   c. If students work in groups, how will you help them to cooperate (see Chapter 8)?
2. *Doubt-concern initiation:*
   a. How will you initiate the inquiry process? You might use a current issue, a field trip, a video, or bring in a speaker.
   b. The purpose of the initiation is to get your students thinking about a problem they could explore via inquiry.
3. *Problem identification:*
   a. Clearly state a problem that students could address through an inquiry process. The problem should be relevant and defined broadly enough that students can explore its various angles.

   b.   Your problem statement (this can often take the form of a question!) should be precise and *testable*.
   c.   What is the problem students will explore?
   d.   What are some questions they could seek to answer that will help clarify the problem?
4.   *Hypothesis statements*:
   a.   Write out some potential hypothesis statements students might generate about the problem. You writing them ahead of time will help test your problem statement.
   b.   What might they guess would be potential causes of the problem?
   c.   State some questions that would lead to the generation of hypothesis statements.
5.   *Data collection*:
   a.   Explain how students might collect data to test their hypotheses. How will they gather data?
   b.   What are potential data sources?
   c.   What are some potential methods for gathering data?
   d.   What are some of the viewpoints they should explore?
   e.   In short, in this portion of your plan, explain how the students will actually inquire about the topic.
6.   *Evaluation and analysis of data:*
   a.   Explain how students will analyze the data they have gathered. It is not enough to merely give or make resources available.
   b.   How will you assist with the intellectual skills needed to evaluate and analyze the data?
7.   *Potential results of the inquiry project:*
   a.   Briefly describe what you think/hope the results of your inquiry project would be.

Writing, Inquiry, and Snapshot Biography

Student-written biography is a powerful strategy for teaching writing, reading, history, geography, and cooperation skills while learning about a person and a time period. However, not just any biography writing approach will do. In particular, this is an approach referred to as a **snapshot biography**.[1] This is an approach where students learn about a person, identify "snapshots" of that person's life, and compile them to create a biography. Consider this metaphor: You have a camera that can record 1000 pictures, and you are asked to go to Paris, take pictures, and help those who have not been to Paris learn know about the city. You would likely take pictures of all you saw, come back and present us with an unfiltered "slide show" of your trip. However, if upon your arrival you decided to select five pictures from your collection that really represented the essence of that city, and then went into detail about each of those pictures, we would enjoy your presentation more, and likely learn more about your trip. Literally, the 1000 pictures of Paris represent a traditional biography with lots of details. The five pictures, or snapshots of Paris, represent the snapshot biography approach. The five pictures become five key events, turning points, critical moments, in a person's life. The biography is not a compendium of all that a person accomplished, but is a collection of a few significant moments. Students work in teams of five to write the biography, with each student being responsible for one of the five events (it can also be done in teams of four or six). These "writing teams" work together to research the person, develop a collection of events, identify the five key events, and write about each event. All the while, they are peer editing their work, learning about the writing process, investigating an historical person, and engaged in deep cooperative and interdependent work.

Perhaps a few examples might help describe this in more detail. Students could explore the life of Rosa Parks, Sojourner Truth, Harriet Tubman, or Ruby Bridges. Learning about these women would provide a lot of insights into American history and the struggle against prejudice, oppression, and institutional racism. Each showed tremendous courage, and would be a great topic for a snapshot biography. Outside of the U.S., Mother Teresa, Nelson Mandela, Gandhi, Marie Curie, and Florence Nightingale are all great subjects for students to learn about in detail. Each is identified with a particular historical time period, and learning about these people provides an instant human connection for your students.

In groups of five, students begin their research by finding everything they can about their person (this would be the equivalent of taking 1000 pictures of Paris). They then identify from this large list, the five turning points, and assign each member of the group to one of the event. Research begins anew as each person writes his/her chapter, peer edits team members' chapters, and works with others to create a five chapter biography. This process is described in more detail in these six steps:

Step 1: Teacher Selects the Person (Subject) of the Biography

This person should be of interest to the students, should have multiple perspectives/materials about his/her life available, and should allow for the development of a theme or idea being examined in your social studies classroom. If possible, the teacher will select a person who is under-represented or misrepresented. For example, Rosa Parks is often misrepresented as a tired old woman who did not want to move out of her seat. In reality, she was only 41, and made the decision not to move knowing full well that she would have a price to pay for doing so. As she said, "The only tired I was was tired of giving in." Much has been written about her, and would be an excellent choice during a unit on the civil rights movement in the U.S.

Step 2: Students have Time to Learn about their Person

This is the first chance students have to begin investigating. They may watch a video, read a book, or search the Internet so they can gain information and insights about the person's life. They can practice note-taking skills, reading skills, and research skills as they work to learn about the person. The teacher has placed students in groups of five, and students begin to share notes about what they are learning. For example, Rosa Parks was a co-author of an autobiography *(My Story)* that is an excellent overview of her life. Students could all read that book.

Step 3: The Class Brainstorms a List of Events from the Persons' Life

This will be a large list of over 30 events. Literally, everything they learned can be on the board from the brainstorm.

Step 4: The Students Choose the Five Key Events (e.g., Turning Points, Interesting Events)

Working from the list created in Step 3, the whole class (or each individual team of five) selects the most important events. If you want to guide the students to focus on a particular theme, then you can have them select keys events around this theme. With Rosa Parks, the theme could be to identify key events where she was courageous, or where she used civil disobedience. After selecting the five events, each member of the team selects the one on which they will learn and write.

Step 5: The Teams of Students Write their Chapters

The chapters are simply their telling of what happened. They use descriptive writing, and all of the writing components they use to be persuasive writers. They engage in pre-writing, drafting, self-editing, peer editing, revising, and sharing. Each chapter must fit with all of the others, so the teams are in communication with each other as peer editors as well as co-authors.

Step 6: The Team Compiles the Book

In addition to writing the chapters, the team finds someone outside of the group to write a fore-word. Another author writes the introduction while others find a map of their choice that they think will enhance the book, and a timeline. The map integrates some geography, and the time-line assists with historical/chronological thinking. For the Rosa Parks example, the map could show where Alabama is on a map of the U.S, or it could show the bus route that Rosa Parks was on when she was arrested. The timeline could list several other events in her life, or even a list of key events in the civil rights movement. Eventually, the chapter and other components are com-piled into a book with a title and cover. This book can be distributed, displayed in the library, or even read to elementary children to help them learn about this important person.

I have also seen teachers require students to illustrate their chapter with a picture as a way to push them to higher thinking such as creativity. Some teachers have students write a poem instead, or a short play, or a song. Any of these genres help students in this type of investigation. To provide more autonomy, the teams of five could also find their own person, research on their own, and follow the steps set out on pages 287 and 288. This will allow for more ownership and choice.

Hopefully, inquiry and snapshot biographies provide two tangible examples of student-centered investigations. Strategies of these types put the student in control of how they will use class time to learn. The tasks, be it writing a biography, testing a hypothesis, or develop-ing an recommendation to the city council, are authentic and require students to direct their own investigations.

LOGISTICS FOR USING INQUIRY AND STUDENT-DIRECTED INVESTIGATIONS

Time constraints are viewed by many as the single greatest obstacle to the implementation of this strategy. These constraints involve both the lack of time for the teacher to implement a lesson of this sort and the lack of time in the curricular schedule. Teachers are pressed for time on all sides. Some have found that using collaborative techniques is helpful in the plan-ning and implementation of lessons. Sharing ideas, plans, and resources with a small group of like-minded teachers can be tremendously helpful. Technology can be used to join or create collaborative support systems that will help save time. Additionally, many websites have les-sons and other ideas available so that teachers can save time by modifying investigative ideas rather than trying to create from scratch. (See, for example, http://smithsonianeducation.org.)

Many time pressures present themselves as you schedule lessons for your course calendar. This will create tension between "covering" the material and using additional portions of the schedule to go deeper. Many assume that because of the pressure of state testing, there is no choice but to attempt to cover material in survey-course fashion. However, according to one extensive study that examined middle schools over a three-year period, this may not be the case. The authors concluded, "assignments calling for more authentic intellectual work actually improve student scores on conventional tests" (Newmann, Bryk, & Nagaoka, 2001, p. 29). You will need to be realistic about how you balance "coverage" and "authentic intellectual work," but the question really isn't *Should you do it?* but *How can you* best *do it?*

You should be aware that some challenges will involve student factors. Saye and Brush (1999) identify three of these challenges as student lack of engagement; student failure to consider a variety of competing perspectives; and student lack of content knowledge or the thinking skills necessary to apply the knowledge they possess. So far, this chapter has emphasized the importance of teacher involvement in the process of engagement and perspective gathering. It is also important to prepare students through pre-inquiry activities. These can be thought of as practicing skills in order to get your class ready for true inquiry. By learning these skills independently, students are helped to overcome some of the challenges associated with this type of learning. Two examples provided by Wilke and Straits (2005) include giving students an article with an important section (e.g., the conclusion) missing and ask them to draw conclusions from the information remaining or posing an ethical question and asking students to discuss opinions, solutions, and opposing perspectives.

Students can be confronted with simple (but not immediately obvious) curiosities that arouse interest but also give opportunity for learning thinking skills. For example, one high school teacher wanted her students to learn about creating a hypothesis. At the beginning of class she placed dirty engine oil in a large clear tub with sand and water. The students noticed how the oil spread across the surface of the tub, and that some oil dropped to the sandy bottom. The students were given ten minutes to create a hypothesis about the most effective way to clean the oil (some suggested scooping it out, some suggested containing it with a oil boom, and some suggested vacuuming the water. The geography teacher had students discuss how they might determine which hypothesis was best to test first, and used this as a pre-inquiry technique to teach students about the process of inquiry that they were going to use when considering environmental impacts of humans on the earth (a direct tie to the geographic theme that explores the human/ environment relationship).

Finally, the "future's wheel" technique described in Chapter 10 provides an excellent graphic organizer for some inquiry lessons. The problem or topic in the middle leads to hypotheses (the "spokes" that come out of the problem). These hypotheses each have implications for the future, which can help determine their viability. Please review that discussion technique now in light of what you have considered about inquiry.

CLASSROOM MANAGEMENT AND STUDENT MOTIVATION

Successful student-directed investigations require behind-the-scenes work by the teacher. So, in the case of Ellie Abeyta's classroom described at the beginning of the chapter, what may appear to be "chaos" is actually a well-thought-out, planned system of learning.

A great deal of attention will need to be given to the classroom learning environment. You will need to create and nurture a "community of learners." This is a common concept for classrooms involved with student-centered approaches to learning. The development of a learning community is at the heart of this approach to learning (McGrath, 2003). According to Brown (1997), there are five critical pieces that work together to create a community of learners:

1. *Active, purposeful learning:* The design of a student-directed investigation will give opportunity for active purposeful learning.
2. *A learning setting that pays attention to multiple zones of proximal development:* Brown bases this component on the work of Vygotsky, who promoted the idea that through collaborative work on important topics learners will accomplish what they would not have been able to do alone. For specifics about collaborative and cooperative learning, refer back to Chapter 8.
3. *The legitimization of differences:* Students should be encouraged to develop their individual areas of expertise for the good of the community of learners.
4. *A community of discourse:* A community is developed in which learners value methods for civil and worthwhile discussion.
5. *A community of practice:* Members of the learning community (which includes the teacher) value and respect each other and take responsibility for each other's learning through collaboration.

These five components of a healthy learning community could be explained to the class and perhaps acknowledged on paper and signed by students and the teacher as a way to show commitment to the principles.

You will notice that the roles for the teachers and students in a community of learners are somewhat unique. Teachers are thought of as co-learners, coaches, facilitators, and sometimes experts. Realistically, teachers can immerse themselves in the community only to a certain degree due to their responsibilities with assessing student learning and facilitating the activities. These responsibilities naturally will affect student/teacher relationships even in the most dynamic of learning communities. Student roles will include assuming responsibility for learning, making process decisions, taking the initiative to determine direction, self-initiating, and participation as expert or coach at times.

One of the challenges for facilitating a successful student-directed investigation is to give students the responsibility for their learning while helping them stay on a pathway to success. It is important for teachers to help monitor self-directed work time by helping students consider their work schedule and set deadlines. It would be a mistake to assume that most students could, without assistance, create a work plan and stick to it. Here are a couple of suggestions that may be helpful:

*   *Create a work plan together:* Sit down with each student (or group) and help them create their schedule. Your role is not to give them a schedule but to help them understand what needs to done and when it needs to be completed—to help them learn to take responsibility on their own.
*   *Monitor the students' schedule:* After a schedule is created, a series of deadlines is helpful. These deadlines can be created by the students themselves or provided by the teacher. This again could be thought of as taking the responsibility of learning back from the students; however, this is a way to help students assume responsibility, with the support

needed for them to be successful. This series of deadlines could be part of a scoring guide or a part of a procedure with which students receive feedback. (For example, to help monitor an inquiry project a teacher might say: "You will need to turn in your first reflection for our inquiry learning project on Tuesday so that I can give you feedback before our next meeting." Some use "research accountability receipts," citation forms, or similar forms to keep track of what students accomplish with their time at the library or at home in order to assist them with their schedule. Part of the learning beyond the content is related to making and keeping a schedule to accomplish a task on time. Students will probably need your help.

APPROPRIATE ASSESSMENT TECHNIQUES

Assessment can be difficult during student-directed investigation because the purpose of the strategy deals with thinking skills practice and the use of content. This focus requires techniques that are different from those associated with traditional testing for knowledge acquisition. Performance assessment, or authentic assessment, is a natural fit for this type of strategy because it asks students to demonstrate their thinking. This form of assessment is detailed in Chapter 3.

Planning for assessment follows a logical process. As we discuss the assessment process, I am assuming that you will have aligned your goals and targets and thus have identified desired outcomes for the lesson. We assume these targets will have guided you into deciding that a student-directed investigation is an appropriate strategy to use in helping students learn. The targets will also help you create a scoring guide that reflects your thinking on the valued outcomes. In other words, the criteria you select for your scoring guide should be aligned with the targets you have selected for the lesson. Your students will learn many valuable lessons during their investigation; however, they need to know what in particular you will be assessing at the end of the day. A good way to do this is by sharing the scoring guide with the students "up front." In a performance assessment the scoring guide is often a rubric or a checklist. This gives the teacher the opportunity to reduce (although not eliminate) the subjective aspects of this type of assessment. However, using student-directed investigation allows ample opportunity to use a variety of assessment techniques to collect multiple perspectives of student learning.

The Checklist

A checklist is similar to an analytic rubric, but without the descriptors and with more criteria, it typically is a list of criteria that can be checked off as the teacher sees evidence of students' meeting expectations. Here is an example:

Checklist for Oral Presentations

Student name: _____   Date: _____

Reviewer name: _____

Project: _____

Category	Responsibilities
Content	☐ The information I gave was interesting or important to others.
	☐ I was well informed about my topic.
	☐ I used vocabulary that the audience could understand or defined unfamiliar terms.
	☐ I used an effective and appropriate attention-getting device.
	☐ Logical appeals included reliable, factual information.
	☐ I used emotional or persuasive appeals where appropriate.
	☐ I added supportive detail to the main point(s).
Delivery	☐ I maintained eye contact most of the time.
	☐ I spoke to the entire audience, not just one or two people.
	☐ My pronunciation was clear and easy to understand.
	☐ My rate of speech was not too fast or too slow.
	☐ My voice could be heard easily by the entire audience.
	☐ My voice varied in pitch; it was not monotone.
	☐ I did not use filler words (e.g., "um," "uh," "ah," "mm," "like," etc.).
	☐ My body language was not too tense or too relaxed.
	☐ I didn't fidget, rock back and forth, or pace.
	☐ I used notes sparingly; I did not read from them.
Organization	☐ I organized ideas in a meaningful way.
	☐ The information and arguments/details were easy to follow.
	☐ I stayed focused and did not stray off topic.
	☐ The introduction included a clear statement of the main point(s).
	☐ I included necessary background information about the topic.
	☐ The body of the presentation contained support for, or details about, the main point(s).
	☐ The audience could distinguish the introduction, body, and conclusion.
Presentation Aids	☐ Presentation aids were used during the speech.
	☐ Presentation aids were relevant to the speech.
	☐ Presentation aids improved the presentation or reinforced main points.
Resources	☐ I used resources that addressed the topic thoroughly.
	☐ I used credible print resources.
	☐ I used credible electronic resources.
	☐ I cited my sources using the required format.
	☐ A bibliography was available.

The Conference

By talking with the teacher in conference, the student explains what was learned and provides evidence. The teacher has an opportunity to ask questions or probe for understanding.

The Portfolio

A portfolio is a collection of samples of student work and reflective notes from the student and others, that show progress.

The Rubric

The rubric is a matrix that provides criteria and descriptors for rating students at various levels. *Holistic* rubrics provide criteria that look at the overall quality of the task, while *analytic* rubrics break down the most important aspects of the task.

Box 11.1 is an example of a holistic rubric for writing historical fiction, with a scoring system of 5 down to 1:

5—Historically accurate detail included in narrative. The plot, setting, and characters are developed fully and organized well. The *who*, *what*, *where*, *when*, and *why* are explained using interesting language and sufficient detail.

4—Most parts of the story mentioned in the score of 5 above are developed and organized well. A couple of aspects may need to be more fully or more interestingly developed.

3—Some aspects of the story are developed and organized well, but not as much detail or organization is expressed as in a score of 4.

2—A few parts of the story are developed somewhat. Organization and language usage need improvement.

1—Parts of the story are addressed without attention to detail or organization.

Box 11.1 Holistic Rubric for Writing Historial Fiction.

Adapted from www.teachervision.fen.com

Here is an example of an analytic rubric for making a brochure:

Category	4	3	2	1
Writing and Organization	Each section in the brochure has a clear beginning, middle, and end	Almost all sections of the brochure have a clear beginning, middle and end	Most sections of the brochure have a clear beginning, middle and end	Less than half of the sections of the brochure have a clear beginning, middle and end
Content and Accuracy	All facts in the brochure are accurate	99–90% of the facts in the brochure are accurate	89–80% of the facts in the brochure are accurate	Fewer than 80% of the facts in the brochure are accurate
Spelling and Proofreading	No spelling errors remain after one person other than the typist has read and corrected the brochure	No more than one spelling error remains after one person other than the typist has read and corrected the brochure	No more than three spelling errors remain after one person other than the typist has read and corrected the brochure	Several spelling errors in the brochure
Attractiveness and Organization	The brochure has exceptionally attractive formatting and well-organized information	The brochure has attractive formatting and well-organized information	The brochure has well-organized information	The brochure's formatting and organization of material are confusing to the reader

Box 11.2   Analytic Rubric for Making a Brochure.

Created with the assistance of rubistar.4teachers.org.

The Student Journal

The student journal contains notes kept by the student that can be shown to the teacher or referred to by the student during a conference. The notes are from free writing exercises about learning, or responses to prompts by the teacher intended to help the student think about her learning.

Teacher Notes

Teacher notes are an "on-the-fly" record of notes the teacher makes as observations are made. For example, on an index card a teacher might record, "Observed Zach leading the group through excellent analysis comments during . . ."

ENHANCING STUDENT LEARNING WITH TECHNOLOGY

A popular and long-standing format for online inquiry-oriented lessons is called a *webquest*. The best webquests are not just scavenger hunts, but adhere to principles of inquiry we have discussed in this chapter. Information about the creation of webquests, along with many teacher- and student-created examples, can be found at the San Diego State University web-quest homepage (webquest.org). Webquests have six key elements:

- *Introduction:* Provides background information
- *Task:* Includes either a question or task
- *Resources:* Provide links to helpful resources to give direction
- *Process:* Provides step-by-step guidance for completion
- *Evaluation:* Outlines expectations through a scoring guide
- *Conclusion:* A summary of learning goals

After looking through examples in your discipline at the webquest homepage, you might want to choose one example and decide what type of inquiry (structured, guided, open) is proposed and discuss why you would or would not use it in your class. You could also use the QuestGarden portion of the website to create or modify a webquest for your future class using the principles of student-directed instruction set forth in this chapter. Web inquiry projects (WIPs) are a more recent approach to online inquiries, and provide more freedom to students. An excellent description of WIP, and a list of many social studies lessons that use them, can be found at this site: http://webinquiry.org.

Social studies teachers and their students commonly use primary sources, because they provide opportunities to engage in high-level thinking about important social studies content. The Internet provides access to seemingly unlimited primary sources, which heightens concerns about misleading or inaccurate information posted online and accessed by students. A division of the American Library Association called the Reference and User Services Association (RUSA) has developed a website that facilitates the use of primary resources and attempts to help students become critical users of all that the Internet has to offer. The RUSA site states that

> Users of primary sources have always needed to examine their sources critically, but now with the proliferation of electronic resources from a wide variety of web site producers, evaluation is more important than ever before. Users of web resources must now consider the authenticity of documents, what person or organization is the internet provider, and whether the electronic version serves their needs.

They developed an interactive guide to provide "students and researchers with information to help them evaluate the internet sources and the quality of primary materials that can be found online." This interactive site allows students to learn about and interact online with these four topics:

- What are Primary Sources?
- Finding Primary Sources on the Web
- Evaluating Primary Source Web Sites
- Citing Web Sites.

The following web address will take you to this site, and we encourage you to consider how your students can learn from it: http://www.ala.org/ala/mgrps/divs/rusa/sections/history/resources/pubs/usingprimarysources.

Below are a few sites to practice using these criteria. Our selection of sites is offered as a starting point. Ideally, you will talk with a teacher in your endorsement area about websites that they use for students to gather online information. View each site while you consider the criteria for evaluating online information listed below. You should use the questions below each criteria heading as a guide to consider the major points, as these sub-questions are general aids to thinking critically about the site and may or may not be appropriate for each site listed.

- *The Cuban Missile Crisis:*
  http://www.gwu.edu/~nsarchiv/nsa/cuba_mis_cri/

- *Commemoration of the Holocaust:*
  http://www.ihr.org/other/tehrantimesdec05.html

- *Mankato, Minnesota:*
  http://city-mankato.us

MAKING STUDENT-DIRECTED INVESTIGATIONS MORE MEANINGFUL FOR ELLS

Because the interactions are often with groups of students, and because teachers have more opportunities to differentiate learning opportunities as the students work in their groups, helping ELLs is a plus of student-centered strategies. Below are two ideas: word walls, and using the Internet 2.0.

Word Walls

Word walls are lists of words written on butcher paper and plastered on walls around the classroom to assist with vocabulary development. Often teachers ask students to help create the lists and add to the list as appropriate. During an SDI a teacher might listen to students talking in their groups with an ear toward words that may be confusing, or at some point may take some class time to ask about words "for the wall." Some teachers leave these words for all students to know at the end of a unit (and work on definitions collaboratively, others write definitions on the wall, still others draw pictures or write in native languages. At the end of the investigation the teacher can place the words on 3 x 5 cards or in a three-ring notebook and color code for the unit. This way the students can associate the color (or sometimes pictures are used) with the word and place it in context, which helps with recall. For example, the word *engineer* might be one word written on the wall during an inquiry project dealing with naturally occuring *tessellations*. This was placed in the red notebook, and when referenced by the teacher, the student may recall the inquiry project and the associated word. Of course, this type of coding would be most helpful if the teacher kept a notebook for each unit. Teachers would assist students if they refer to the word wall and notebooks consistently, and model these actions for all students.

Web 2.0 Ideas for English Language Learners

Inquiry is an ideal strategy to incorporate ideas from the latest in Internet technology called Web 2.0, or that many refer to as the read-write web. This new generation Internet is more interactive and has allowed for those with limited technology skills to publish their own blogs, podcasts, photographs, videos, wikis, and much more. It is easy to see that publishing in these ways will involve communication practice that will enable students to utilize developing English skills. Digital storytelling, a method for communicating through video, is one way this technology can be used to encourage ELLs within the inquiry framework. For example, using concepts found in this chapter, students create digital stories on energy conservation by interviewing families in their neighborhoods. This process involves several preproduction techniques such as scripting and storyboarding. You can find many ideas by Googling digital storytelling or you can probably think of several for your own content area.

GUIDELINES FOR DECIDING IF INQUIRY AND STUDENT-DIRECTED INVESTIGATIONS ARE APPROPRIATE

Weighing the advantages and disadvantages of student-directed investigation will be important as you determine if this is an appropriate strategy. Some of the advantages are that it is often motivating to students as they pursue topics that interest them. It can be stimulating to perhaps explore outside of the traditional classroom, especially in a venue that allows you to serve another person or the community. This approach encourages autonomy and initiative, while giving students an opportunity to think deeply about issues. Some of these advantages may be similar to what you have in mind in your objectives.

You should also consider some of the unique challenges in student-directed investigation when deciding if you should use it. It can take considerably more time to complete than other approaches. Remember, you will need to balance a need to "cover" material alongside an opportunity to learn through exploration and experience. You will need to have the appropriate resources, such as community experts, informational media (can you get access to the computer lab or go to the library?), and materials necessary for students to be successful. You should determine if you feel comfortable acting as a facilitator, often being pulled in many directions at one time. How is your energy level? This is not a study hall approach. Are you prepared to engage with students in an environment that at times can look like controlled chaos?

MAKING IT WORK IN YOUR CLASSROOM

Differentiated Learning

Effectively teaching the diverse students in our social studies classrooms is the aim of all quality teachers. Tomlinson (2003) offers criteria for what she calls a *high-quality curriculum* and these are applicable to both middle and high school social studies curricula. This is a curriculum that promotes learning for all students by being engaging and promoting understanding. Obviously, no teacher would be able to achieve all of these in one lesson or probably in one unit. However, these indicators will help you evaluate your instructional direction. After you have created a unit of instruction that includes student-directed investigation, assess your unit using the following checklist. Indicating a check, plus, or minus for each criterion may be helpful before you write self-evaluative comments about your work.

- *Engagement:*
  - Is fresh and surprising to the students
  - Seems "real" and purposeful to the students
  - Connects with the students' lives
  - Allows choice
  - Requires active learning
  - Is pleasurable—or at least satisfying—for the students
  - Is focused on products that matter to the students
  - Taps personal interest
  - Allows students to make a contribution to something greater than themselves
  - Challenges students and provides support for success
- *Promotes understanding:*
  - Is clearly focused on the essential knowledge, understanding, and skills a professional in the field would value
  - Is coherent (organized, unified, sensible) to students
  - Attends to student misconceptions
  - Deals with profound ideas that endure across years of learning
  - Enables students to use what they learn in important ways
  - Requires cognition and metacognition
  - Causes students to grapple with significant problems
  - Causes students to raise useful questions
  - Necessitates that students generate (vs. reproduce) knowledge

CHAPTER REVIEW

- Research support for using inquiry and student-directed investigations
  - Promotes learning through experience in an environment that involves the "real world" and offers meaningful, personally interesting challenges
  - Requires active learning
  - Provides opportunities to solve problems, answer questions, or address real needs
  - Allows for student ownership, responsibility, and choices; and offers students an opportunity to perform as experts or professionals
- Step-by-step procedures for selecting, planning, and using student investigations
  - Different types of student-directed strategies include inquiry learning, discovery learning, problem-based learning, project-based learning, and experiential learning.
  - Inquiry learning involves the steps of:
    - lesson targets
    - doubt-concern initiation
    - problem identification
    - hypothesis statements
    - data collection
    - evaluation and analysis of data
    - return to the problem and begin the process again
  - Snapshot biographies are written following these six steps:
    Step 1. Teacher selects subject of the biography
    Step 2. Students learn about person

Step 3.   Class brainstorms key events

Step 4.   Teams choose key turning points or events

Step 5.   Teams write chapters and other parts of the book

Step 6.   Team compiles book

- Managing the classroom/learning environment during student-directed investigations
  - A great deal of attention will need to be given to the classroom learning environment and to creating and nurturing a "community of learners" with the following components:
    - active, purposeful learning
    - a learning setting that pays attention to multiple zones of proximal development
    - the legitimization of differences
    - a community of discourse
    - a community of practice
- Assessing student learning appropriately during student-directed investigation
  - Be sure to assess student learning of content learning and skill development
  - Align goals and targets with assessments
- Using technology to enhance learning
  - Often will require student to gather online data
  - Students need to be able to become critical consumers of ideas, data, opinions, and other sources of information that will confront them when online
- Considerations for English language learners during student-directed investigations
  - Use of word walls allows for identifying key concepts and vocabulary ahead of time.
  - Web 2.0 allows for opportunities for interactions online and through online networks.

NOTE

1. Myra Zarnowski's book *Learning about Biographies* (1990), and later her book *History Makers* (2003) provide the inspiration for this investigative approach.

REFERENCES

Bransford, J. D., Brown, A. L., & Cocking, R. R. (Eds.) (2000). *How People Learn: Brain, Mind, Experience and School.* Washington, DC: National Academy Press.

Brooks, J. G. & Brooks, M. B. (1993). *The Case for Constructivist Classrooms.* Alexandria, VA: ASCD.

Brown, A. L. (1997). Transforming schools into communities of thinking and learning about serious matters. *American Psychologist, 54*(4), 399–413.

Brown, J. S., Collins, A., & Duguid, P. (1989). Situated cognition and the culture of learning. *Educational Researcher, 18*(1), 32–42.

Duffy, T. & Johnson, D. (Eds.) (1992). *Constructivism and the Technology of Instruction: A Conversation.* Hillsdale, NJ: Erlbaum Associates.

Fosnot, C. T. (1989). *Inquiring Teachers, Enquiring Learners.* New York: Teachers College Press.

Gallagher, S., Sher, B., Stepien, W., & Workman, D. (1995). Implementing problem-based learning in science classrooms. *School Science and Mathematics, 95*(3), 136–146.

McGrath, D. (2003). Developing a community of learners: What will it look like and how will it work? *Learning & Leading with Technology, 30*(7), 42–45.

Newmann, F., Bryk, A., & Nagaoka, J. (2001). *Authentic Intellectual Work and Standardized Tests: Conflicts or Coexistence?* Chicago: Consortium on Chicago School Research. Available at: http://www.consortium-chicago.org/publications/p0001.html.

Saye, J. W. & Brush, T. (1999). Student engagement with social issues in a multimedia-supported learning environment. *Theory and Research in Social Education, 27*(4), 472–504. Retrieved January 16, 2006, from ERIC database.

Scheurman, G. (1998) From behaviorist to constructivist teaching. *Social Education, 62,* 6–9.

Scheurman, G. & Newmann, F. M. (1998). Authentic intellectual work in social studies: Putting performance before pedagogy. *Social Education, 4*(3), 150–153.

Skinner, B. F. (1968). *The Technology of Teaching.* New York: Appelton.

Tomlinson, C. (2003). *Fulfilling the Promise of Differentiated Classrooms: Strategies and Tools for Responsive Teaching.* Alexandria, VA: ASCD.

Wilke, R. & Straits, W. (2005). Practical advice for teaching inquiry-based science process skills in the biological sciences. *The American Biology Teacher, 67*(9), 534–540.

Zarnowski, M. (2003). *History Makers: A Questioning Approach to Reading and Writing Biographies.* Portsmouth, NH: Heinemann.

Zarnowski, M. (1990). *Learning about Biographies: A Reading-and-Writing Approach for Children.* Urbana, IL: National Council of Teachers of English.

Index

findings 179–81; reporting information 185; selecting a concept 182; social caste 183–4; step-by-step procedures 181–8; strategy 178; studying examples 183–5; student motivation 189–90; synthesizing 186; technology enhancement 191; Vygotsky's theory of learning 179–80
concrete operations stage 33
congruent communication 58
Constructivism 33, 280
content 77: academic 104, *see also* Schwab's four commonplaces; target 77, 132–3; outline of 104
content, skills, and social interactions (CSS) 31, 116
controversy 272: closed topics 272; open topics 272; tipping topics 272
convergent questions 162
cooperative learning: appropriateness for lesson content 218–9; assessment and 214–6; *see also* buzz groups; classroom management issues 211–3; conducting 205–7; cooperative skills 212; defined 198; ELLs 217–8; essential elements 201; face-to-face interactions 202; formal 206–7; group assignments 210–1, 265; 205, 238; group goals and individual accountability 199, 203; group heterogeneity *see* heterogeneous group; *see also* group investigations; group processing 203–4; group size 205, 265; informal 206; interpersonal and small group skills 203; *see also* jigsaw approach; monitoring students 211; *see also* positive interdependence; prosocial behavior 200; research findings 198–201; room set up 210; *see* simulations; social skills development 198; step-by-step procedures 204–7; *see also* structured academic controversy discussion; student motivation 211–3; *see also* student status; *see also* student teams/achievement divisions (STAD); *see also* T-chart; technology enhancement 216; *see also* think/pair/share strategy; *see also* cooperative learning types
cooperative learning types 207–10: *see also* group investigation; *see also* jigsaw approach; *see also* student teams/achievement divisions (STAD)
Cornbleth, C. 12
Council for Economics Education 7
course goals 23–4
creating *see* Bloom's Taxonomy, revised
criterion-referenced assessment 89–90
critical attributes *see* concept formation
critical friend model 122
Csikszentmihalyi, M. 52–3
cultural development 31–2

cultural diversity 39
cultural literacy 13
culturally mediated instruction 40
culturally relevant teaching 39
curriculum 9, 21: *see also* backward design; *see also* curriculum, practical suggestions; delivered *see* delivered curriculum; departmental plans 21; district plans 20; formal *see* formal curriculum; hidden *see* hidden curriculum; hierarchy *see* hierarchy of curriculum influence; learned *see* learned curriculum; linking life, education, and school 14; *see also* metaphors of schooling; national standards *see* national standards; null *see* null curriculum; *see also* teacher as curricular gatekeepers
curriculum coordinators 20
curriculum, practical suggestions: advice from experienced teachers 22–3; asking the important questions *see* Tyler rationale; materials 24–5; writing course and unit goals 23–4
curve of forgetting 146

D

debate: *see also* discussion
deliberations 271–2
delivered curriculum 9–10
democracy 4: participative *see* participative democracy; representative *see* representative democracy; thick *see* thick democracy; thin *see* thin democracy
democratic teaching 58
demographic imperative 41–2
departmental plans 21
Dewey, J. 11
diagnostic assessment 87, 89–90, 116
dialogical reasoning 252–3
dialogue 158, 164, 227
differentiated instruction 38, 278: *see also* learner-profile; *see also* student interest; *see also* student readiness
differentiated learning *see* differentiated instruction
digital divide 50
digital immigrants 49
digital natives 49
direct instruction 130–1
disabilities 37, 45–6
discipline 55–6; *see also* classroom management
discovery learning *see* inquiry variations
discussion: appropriateness for lesson content 270–2; assessment and 266–8; classroom layout 262; classroom management 263–5;

Taylor & Francis eBooks

Helping you to choose the right eBooks for your Library

Add Routledge titles to your library's digital collection today. Taylor and Francis ebooks contains over 50,000 titles in the Humanities, Social Sciences, Behavioural Sciences, Built Environment and Law.

Choose from a range of subject packages or create your own!

Benefits for you

» Free MARC records
» COUNTER-compliant usage statistics
» Flexible purchase and pricing options
» All titles DRM-free.

REQUEST YOUR FREE INSTITUTIONAL TRIAL TODAY

Free Trials Available
We offer free trials to qualifying academic, corporate and government customers.

Benefits for your user

» Off-site, anytime access via Athens or referring URL
» Print or copy pages or chapters
» Full content search
» Bookmark, highlight and annotate text
» Access to thousands of pages of quality research at the click of a button.

eCollections – Choose from over 30 subject eCollections, including:

Archaeology	Language Learning
Architecture	Law
Asian Studies	Literature
Business & Management	Media & Communication
Classical Studies	Middle East Studies
Construction	Music
Creative & Media Arts	Philosophy
Criminology & Criminal Justice	Planning
Economics	Politics
Education	Psychology & Mental Health
Energy	Religion
Engineering	Security
English Language & Linguistics	Social Work
Environment & Sustainability	Sociology
Geography	Sport
Health Studies	Theatre & Performance
History	Tourism, Hospitality & Events

For more information, pricing enquiries or to order a free trial, please contact your local sales team: www.tandfebooks.com/page/sales

 Routledge
Taylor & Francis Group

The home of Routledge books

www.tandfebooks.com